Fay Sudweeks

Virtual Collaborative Groups

Fay Sudweeks

Virtual Collaborative Groups

Two Case Studies of Group Development and
Emergent Leadership

VDM Verlag Dr. Müller

Imprint

Bibliographic information by the German National Library: The German National Library lists this publication at the German National Bibliography; detailed bibliographic information is available on the Internet at http://dnb.d-nb.de.

Cover image: www.purestockx.com

Publisher:
VDM Verlag Dr. Müller Aktiengesellschaft & Co. KG , Dudweiler Landstr. 125 a, 66123 Saarbrücken, Germany,
Phone +49 681 9100-698, Fax +49 681 9100-988,
Email: info@vdm-verlag.de

Zugl.: Perth, Murdoch University, Diss., 2005

Produced in USA and UK by:
Lightning Source Inc., La Vergne, Tennessee, USA
Lightning Source UK Ltd., Milton Keynes, UK
BookSurge LLC, 5341 Dorchester Road, Suite 16, North Charleston, SC 29418, USA

ISBN: 978-3-639-03423-3

Dedicated to my father ...

... who wanted to wait longer

ACKNOWLEDGEMENTS

Over the last decade or so, there have been many people who have helped me with this research. First of all, I would like to thank all those who have influenced my understanding that there is a need for studying phenomena from both positivist and interpretivist perspectives: Professor Richard Coyne (University of Edinburgh, Scotland) who tried, unsuccessfully at the time, to persuade me to open my mind to an interpretivist approach; Professor Sheizaf Rafaeli (Haifa University, Israel) who was the inspiration for Case Study 1 and my interest in computer-mediated communication, and reinforced my interest in positivist research; Professor Celia Romm (Wayne State University, USA) who tried and succeeded in persuading me to accept an interpretivist approach; and Dr Andrew Turk (Murdoch University, Australia) who was open to both approaches.

I am indebted to the participants of Case Study 1, who are scattered around the world. Too many to mention all, but I particularly want to thank Carole Marmell, Diane Witmer, Margaret McLaughlin, Ed Mabry and Joe Konstan. And my sincere thanks to the students of Case Study 2, they know who they are.

I thank my parents and my children – Neil, Paul and Caryn – who have given so much moral support. I would like to acknowledge the stimulation provided by many conversations with Dr Ray Webster (Murdoch University, Australia), and I am indebted to my friend and colleague Professor Simeon Simoff (University of Western Sydney, Australia) without whom this research would never have been completed.

TABLE OF CONTENTS

CHAPTER 1

INTRODUCTION

The initial focus of this research was an in-depth analysis of a case study of a computer-mediated collaborative group. The case study was a window on asynchronous collaborative dialogue in the early 1990s (1992-94) at a time when ICTs were at an early stage of development. After identifying the issues that emerged from this early case study, another case study using technologies and virtual environments developed over the past decade, was designed to further understand these issues. The second case study was a window on synchronous collaborative dialogue in the year 2000 when ICTs had developed at a rate which few people envisioned in the early 90s. Not only have dramatic changes been seen in the technologies, the past decade has witnessed the adoption of these technologies into everyday activities. The purpose of exploring these two case studies is to identify and understand differences in group communication rather than identifying similarities. However, the communication trends identified across the decade offer robust support for anticipating future communication directions.

1.1. Background

Less than a decade ago, there were fewer than one million hosts on the Internet.[1] Today there is a web site that calculates the increasing number of hosts and users in real time, and the figures roll over faster than the average car records the kilometres travelled on its speedometer.[2] Clearly, the Internet is changing societal norms. The Internet is changing our concept of how communications can and should work.

During 1992, the number of hosts on the Internet reached the million mark, and the term "surfing the Internet" was coined by Jean Armour Polly (1992). The Internet environment included an array of non-intuitive search tools (e.g. archie, gopher and veronica). It also included a number of cumbersome text-based communication tools on different networks (e.g. Usenet, BITNet, Compuserve[3]) with different protocols and therefore requiring gateways to translate the protocol of one network to another.

---

[1] Source: Internet Software Consortium, http://www.isc.org/.
[2] In February 2001, there were approximately 409.5 million users and 105.8 million hosts (http://www.netsizer.com/).
[3] These communication tools are discussed in detail in Chapter 3.

Following the development of Mosaic, the first graphical web browser, in 1993, the global adoption of the World Wide Web (the "Web") was the catalyst for the widespread acceptance of the Internet as an essential part of the daily lives of a significant portion of the world's population. From a merely passive information system, the Web turned the Internet, at the end of the millenium, into an active "living" environment, populated with a variety of services and events. Through the Internet, we buy goods and services, engage in auctions, take educational courses, win prizes, and find information as diverse as how to treat a rare disease to tracking a commercial flight path in real time.

In terms of information and communications technologies (ICTs) there are three major developments that are primary contributors to the changes we are witnessing in the new millenium – bandwidth, wireless and software.

Bandwidth has been transformed from a carefully hoarded resource to a relatively unlimited one. Ultra-broadband core networks enable the delivery of the next generation's services robustly and powerfully, and in a manner that has been previously been thought of merely as a utopian Internet dream. In July 2000, ADSL[4] was launched in the UK, allowing users to access digital multimedia over a telephone line. By June 2003, there were 516,900 broadband services connected across Australia, which represents an annual increase of more than 100%.

Wireless is another driving force that is fueling the communications revolution. Cell phones have gone from curiosity to commonplace, and perhaps now to annoyance, seemingly overnight. But the real revolution is that they bring high-speed conductivity to places where it is too expensive or too difficult to lay a fibre optic line. Fixed wireless systems can carry information about eight times more quickly than a computer's 56K modem. In the near future, that capacity will be boosted by another 10-20 times,[5] opening up another wide pipeline to carry voice, data, video and all of the pieces that comprise this growing network or networks that surround us. It is estimated that the 4.1 million US consumers using mobile devices to access the Internet in 2000 will increase to 96 million by 2005 (Jupiter, 2001). Beyond wireless is ubiquitous computing. Ubiquitous computing is more than Personal

---

[4] ADSL (Asymmetric Digital Subscriber Line) is a technology for transmitting digital information at a high bandwidth on existing phone lines to homes and businesses. Unlike regular dialup phone service, ADSL provides continuously available, "always on" connection. ADSL is asymmetric in that it uses most of the channel to transmit downstream to the user and only a small part to receive information from the user. ADSL simultaneously accommodates analogue (voice) information on the same line. ADSL supports downstream data rates from 512 Kbps to about 6 Mbps. Several experiments with ADSL to real users began in 1996. In 1998, wide-scale installations began in several parts of the US (searchNetworking.com, 2003).
[5] Bell Labs Report.

Digital Assistants (PDAs) – it is invisible, it does not live on a personal device of any sort. For example, tags on retail products will send radio signals to their manufacturers to collect information about consumer habits (Schmidt, 2001); cell phones signals will monitor the state of the user's health (Jones, 2001).

Software is changing the equation for everything technological, giving us instant Internet access, downloads, universal real-time video conferencing and movies on demand, to name but a few. Wireless technology is possible because of the Wireless Application Protocol (WAP), which allows wireless devices to access information and services on the Internet while WAP Markup Language (WML), the WAP equivalent of HTML allows for quicker download times. Such applications and protocols are the looms that weave extraordinary technical advances into our everyday lives.

Describing the technological scenario of the near future, Weiser (1996) says:

> Previous revolutions in computing were about bigger, better, faster, smarter. In the next revolution, as we learn to make machines that take care of our unconscious details, we might finally have smarter people ... The house of the future will become one giant connection to the world – quietly and unobtrusively, as naturally as we know it is raining, or cold, or that someone is up before us in the kitchen making breakfast.

Concomitant with rapidly expanding ICT landscape in developed and, increasingly, in developing nations, is the ability to engage in dialogue. New technologies encourage collaboration, learning and community by ongoing dialogue among people who are geographically and temporally dispersed. However, despite the global nature of ICTs, the technology must be grounded in locality. The localisation of technology includes sensitivities and adaptation to language, culture, social and organisational norms.

It is crucial therefore to understand more clearly the opportunities and obstacles of *computer-mediated collaboration*, whether it be in an organisational, educational or social environment. Virtual project teams and communities, global research groups and online learning are important features of modern academic, corporate and social life. The impact of technology on communicative and cultural competence in group management is a major area of research (Larson and LaFasto, 1989; Jin and Mason, 1998; Jarvenpaa and Leidner, 1998).

1.2. Definition of Problem

Computer-mediated communication (CMC) is commonly compared unfavourably with face-to-face interpersonal communication because there is little awareness of the presence of others. Non-verbal and paralinguistic cues are minimal—we cannot hear intonation that signals a joke, or see puzzled expressions that convey confusion. Face-to-face communication is generally perceived as the communication standard against which all others are measured and found inferior. The ideal of some face-to-face interactions, though, is merely an ideal rather than a real standard. Schudson (1978) gives examples of the stereotypical conversation that passes between a long-married couple at the breakfast table, and the phatic communication that is typical when two strangers meet. In some situations, social cues such as status, gender and age can inhibit acceptance of ideas. In reality, face-to-face communication is not always a universal ideal nor universally idyllic. If, after thousands of years of dyadic conversations and didactic instruction, ambiguities and misinterpretations occur, one can hardly expect that mediated communication would be perfected in a little more than a decade.

Adding more media layers to mediated communication is usually considered to ameliorate the communication to a closer approximation of face-to-face communication. Adding video, audio and graphics is somehow expected to make the medium more "real". Mabry (1993) challenges the implication that single-channel (text only) communication is less real because "a 'picture is worth a thousand words' only to those with a thousand words to appropriate for construing the pictorial image." More channels do not necessarily mean more effective interaction (Walther, Slovacek and Tidwell, 2001). Mediated text communication remains, and is predicted to remain, the main staple of global Internet communications for both social and corporate needs. It is predicted, for example, that in 2005, advertisers will send 268 billion email messages, 22 times the number of email messages sent in 2000. This figure translates to some 5,600 email messages per year for each email user (Macaluso, 2001).

Another mediated text phenomenon is the use of SMS[6] or "texting". For example, in the United Kingdom, 111 million SMS messages were sent in the 24-hour period between midnight 31 December and midnight 1 January 2004 (BBC, 2004). In Australia, the number of SMS messages sent during the financial year 2002-2003 reached 3.95 billion, which represented an average of 294 messages for each mobile service subscriber (ACA, 2003).

Figure 1.1 illustrates that, in March 2004, non-English speakers dominated the Internet at 64.2% of the online global population (GlobalReach, 2004) and for the

---

[6] Short Message Service.

first time ever, in 2001 there were more email accounts outside the United States than within it (Foley, 2001).

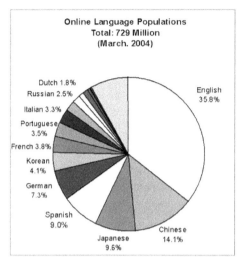

Figure 1.1. Online language populations as at March 2004 (GlobalReach, 2004).

The communication continuum, from written to oral, has optimal points for different communication features. Figure 1.2 highlights some of these communication features and where they are situated on the continuum.

Figure 1.2. The communication continuum.

The rapid changes in communication, learning and organisational collaboration means that the options, and hence the possibilities, for optimisation are much more complex. To be able to model the complexities of communication and facilitate efficient and effective communication requires much more research. Asynchronous and synchronous mediated communication bridges spatial, temporal and societal barriers like no other medium prior to it (Rogers and Rafaeli, 1985; Sproull and Kiesler, 1991; McGrath and Hollingshead, 1994; Pargman, 2000; Preece, 2000). The new technologies and critical mass of Internet hosts and users now makes CMC economically, pedagogically and socially attractive to a significant proportion of the global population. It is necessary to investigate how people communicate, participate and reflectively construct knowledge in an online collaborative environment. It is necessary to investigate the communication strategies and developmental processes that transpire during the acquisition of knowledge.

Research on face-to-face group processes, such as formation, decision making, leadership and dynamics, are well documented, and numerous theoretical models have been developed to describe and predict behaviour. However, the vast majority of group research is on zero-history groups in laboratories, working on short, contrived tasks. During the 1980s, for example, only 13% of group studies were samples from organisational and applied settings. The ability to generalise from laboratory experiments to real-life groups, especially to small groups or teams in organisations, is limited. While it is difficult to use samples from organisations due to legal, ethical and privacy issues, Cragan and Wright (1990: 288) point out that "[t]here is a great need for research that takes existing small group communication theory and demonstrates its utility to small group problems in applied [natural] settings."

Studies on computer-mediated group processes have been similarly reliant on laboratory experiments to explore such phenomena as decision making (Hill, 1982; Poole, Holmes, Watson and De Sanctis, 1993), status (Siegel, Dubrovsky, Kiesler and McGuire, 1986; Dubrovsky, Kiesler and Sethna, 1991) and idea generation (Dennis and Valacich, 1993; Valacich, Dennis and Connolly, 1994), or groups formed for a specific task, usually following preliminary face-to-face meetings (Steele, 1984; McCreary and Brochet, 1992). The focus of much research tends to be on technology rather than communication and collaboration. Precedence is given to the groupware technologies linking communicating humans, rather than to how humans communicate mediated by technologies. We need to understand more about:

1. how communication strategies and processes can be used to transcend temporal and geographic barriers to develop group cohesion, and to improve knowledge creation and acquisition in terms of goal-directed activity.
2. the management of communication to create and sustain group and community identity, and interpersonal relationships.

The difficult choice for communication researchers is to study a group in a laboratory environment in which the entire group development can be observed and analysed, or to study an existing group in a natural or applied environment in which the group's genesis needs to be reconstructed with available oral or patchy historical evidence. It is a distinct advantage when a researcher is privileged to have the opportunity of being a participant observer of a spontaneous or a structured group from creation to closure. It is even more advantageous to have the opportunity of being a participant observer of a *collaborative* group in which all group communication is available as canonical evidence for analysis.

A related advantage for current researchers of online communication is the increased ability to collect and analyse data. New technologies and applications provide researchers with the opportunity of investigating and analysing group processes at a granularity level that was not available a decade ago.

1.3. Research Questions

The overarching question of interest is "How do computer-mediated collaborative communities develop and grow". The definition of *computer-mediated collaborative community* used here is:

> *An computer-mediated collaborative community is a group of people who share, in an iterative process, the creation of norms in the form of rituals and protocols that guide people's interactions, for the specific purpose of constructing knowledge in a shared space that is facilitated and mediated by a computer system.*

The relationship between these concepts is visualised in Figure 1.3.

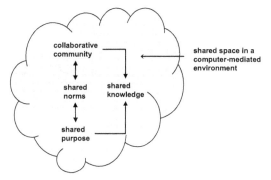

Figure 1.3. The components of online collaborative communities.

According to Pargman (2000), "... virtual communities [are] cultivated or grown; organically, iteratively, incrementally, genetically, over time sprouting several layers of behavioral and computer-coded complexities" (p. 19).

The aim of this book, therefore, is to understand more clearly how computer-mediated group processes change over time. The broad research questions relating to developmental and leadership characteristics, which emerged from the literature and the data, are as follows.

Developmental characteristics

During the lifecycle of computer-mediated groups:
1. are there developmental changes?
2. are there changes in communication content and style?
3. are there changes in the level of personal disclosures?
4. are there changes in the degree of group cohesion?

Leadership characteristics

During the lifecycle of computer-mediated groups:
1. are there changes in management intervention?
2. are there changes in management styles?
3. are there different patterns in communication between leaders and other participants?
4. do leaders emerge as a consequence of the group activity?

In Chapter 6, these research questions are discussed in more detail and hypotheses related to these questions are posed.

1.4. Research Assumptions

The majority of research work connected with gaining knowledge and understanding of societal and communicative phenomena is conducted within the bounds of a narrow set of assumptions, beyond which the researcher rarely deviates. It is useful, therefore, to explore a range of paradigms to understand fully the perspective within which one is located. Social science can be approached in terms of four key paradigms (Figure 1.4) based on different assumptions about the nature of the social world.

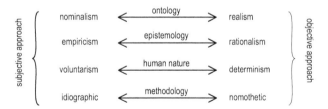

Figure 1.4. The subjective–objective continuum of approaches to social science research (after Burrell and Morgan, 1979).

The sets of assumptions relate to ontology, epistemology, human nature and methodological approach (Burrell and Morgan, 1979; Hopper and Powell, 1985; Doolin, 1995). When the phenomenon being investigated is related to technology-mediated distributed environments, the assumptions become even more complex and abstract notions such as 'reality' takes on an added dimension.

Assumptions of an ontological nature are concerned with the physical and social reality of research questions. Social scientists are faced with a basic dichotomy—is 'reality' imposed on the individual from the external world or is it a product of one's individual cognition? In other words, is reality objective or subjective? When applied to Internet research, on the one hand there is an existing physical medium, which supports information communication; on the other hand, around this medium, there exists a global information ether where social 'reality' takes place in 'virtuality'. What connection is there between the two layers?

Philosophers debate the existence and the extent of our knowledge of material and abstract objects. Nominalism maintains that abstract objects do not exist in any real sense. Occam's arguments for nominalism are based on a principle of simplicity (known as Occam's razor); that is, do not postulate more realms of existence than are necessary. For example, the realist posits three realms of existence: (i) individual objects, (ii) the independent attributes which they have in common and (iii) our concepts of these. For Occham, there are only two: (i) individual objects and (ii) our concepts about those objects. There are a number of theories of realism ranging from direct (or naïve) realism which holds that the physical world is as it is perceived and that it exists independent of us, to representationalism which holds that the external world causes our experiences, and that the object being perceived cannot exist outside of how it is perceived. For Hobbes[7] the external world involves both the external movement of objects and the internal movements within the perceiver. Any change in these movements corresponds to an interaction, thus perception. Locke[8] and Berkeley[9], held that sensations of the external world cannot be selected by the perceiver; only our ideas spawned from those perceptions can be selected and controlled.

Berkeley, for example, argues that we do not perceive material things, but only colours, sounds, etc., and that these are 'mental' (IEP, 1997). In other words, we perceive qualities, not material substances.

---

[7] Hobbes, T.: 1651, Leviathan, or the Matter, Form and Power of a Commonwealth, Ecclesiastical and Civil, cited in (Russell, 1945).
[8] Locke, J.: 1690, *Essay Concerning Human Understanding*, cited in (Russell, 1945).
[9] Berkeley, G.: 1717, *Three Dialogues between Hylas and Philonous*, cited in (Russell, 1945).

> I know that I, one and the same self, perceive both colours and sounds: that a colour cannot perceive a sound, nor a sound a colour: that I am therefore one individual principle, distinct from colour and sound; and, for the same reason, from all other sensible things and inert ideas. But, I am not in like manner conscious either of the existence or essence of Matter. On the contrary, I know that nothing inconsistent can exist, and that the existence of matter implies an inconsistency. Farther, I know what I mean when I affirm that there is a spiritual substance or support of ideas, that is, that a spirit knows and perceives ideas.[10]

Although Berkeley used his argument for the existence of God[11], one can draw an analogy to the distinction between physical and virtual worlds. Although a virtual environment has no matter, just text, colours, sounds, images and 3D models (Schreoder, 2002), our perception renders this representation as reality. Furthermore, the parameters of the physical medium, such as the capacity of links and information storage, affect social behaviour (e.g. slow links lead to the use of different expressive techniques in communication) within the information ether. There is, therefore, a necessity to extend the ontological level to the virtual world by means of rigorous research. An ontological research assumption here, then, is that the universality (or shared meaning) of virtuality represents a perceived reality.

Assumptions of an epistemological nature are concerned with knowledge. The dichotomy for the social scientist here relates to the truth or falsity of knowledge: is knowledge 'soft', something which has to be personally experienced; or is knowledge 'hard', something which can be acquired and transmitted. Empiricists believe that all concepts are derived from experience, or that statements claiming to express knowledge depend for their justification on experience. Apriorists believe that the mind is constitutionally endowed with concepts or ideas which it has not derived from experience. In other words, an apriorist is one who holds the view that new knowledge can be gained by pure reasoning, unassisted by experience.

In Internet research, the issue is the distinction between information and knowledge. Is any experience on the Internet a new knowledge or just a transfer of existing knowledge into a new form? The use of physical metaphors for virtual spaces, for example, provides reinforcement of known information rather than encouraging the experience of new knowledge. In *The Critique of Pure Reason*, Kant maintains that it is possible to imagine nothing in space, but impossible to imagine

---

[10] Excerpt from Berkeley, G.: 1717, *Three Dialogues Between Hylas and Philonous*, cited in the *Internet Encyclopedia on Philosophy*, http://www.utm.edu/research/iep/.

[11] To the famous objection to his theory – that a tree would cease to exist if no one was looking at it – Berkeley claims that "God always perceives everything; if there were no God, what we take to be material objects would have a jerky life, suddenly leaping into being when we look at them; but as it is, owing to God's perceptions, trees and rocks and stones have an existence as continuous as common sense supposes." (Russell, 1972).

no space. Russell (1945) argues that Kant's notion of an absolute space is not possible, that an absolute empty space can not be imagined. There is no reason whatever for regarding our knowledge of space as in any way different from our knowledge of colour and sound and smell.

Yet, rather than being satisfied with subjective experiential knowledge of virtual space, we attempt to fill spaces with known objects. The text-only synchronous environments have been transformed into 3D "worlds". Sites such as the Moove 3D Internet World[12] are carefully crafted to represent our physical world, providing the user with three rooms, each of which can be decorated with furniture, plants and various other interactive objects. As a result, the application of virtual environments, organised as 3D architectural spaces, spans from supporting virtual communities (Kaplan, McIntyre, Numaoka and Tajan, 1998) to information visualisation in collaborative virtual environments (Chen, 1999). Should virtual architectures mimic physical architectures, or develop its own laws and conventions? Our physical personal spaces, comfort zones and territories are defined internally. In cyberspace these spaces exist at the same level – as creations of the mind.

An epistemological research assumption in this book is that the Internet has the potential for the creation and construction of new knowledge; knowledge which has the ability to form a single logically coherent system. This knowledge is not necessarily dependent on transferred knowledge from the physical world.

Assumptions of human nature are concerned with the dichotomy of free will and determinism: are we the master or servant of our destiny; do we control or are we controlled by our environment? In Internet research, the issue is the boundary of the environment. Should we consider the Internet an environment in itself or should we consider it as a complementary part or an extension of our own environment? A human nature research assumption in this case is that the Internet provides an opportunity for behaviour modification but not transformation.

The set of assumptions embraced by the social scientist—ontological, epistemological and human nature—has a direct impact on the *methodological* approach in attempting to investigate social phenomena. A scientist with an objective approach searches for regularities and tangible structures existing in an external world; the researcher who focuses on subjective experiences chooses to understand and interpret the individual in relation to or "being" in the world. The positivist (or objective) epistemological approach is labeled sometimes as "hard" scientific research. The positivists vary in their research design and methodological approach,

---

[12] http://www.moove.com/netscape/

ranging from verifying to falsifying hypotheses, but the intent in both instances is based on a belief that there are immutable structures to be discovered, explored and analysed. The anti-positivist (or interpretivists) methodological approach is to be immersed in situations and allow insights to emerge during the process of investigation.

In general, the research questions of interest guide the choice of methodological tools. If the unit of analysis is the individual, applying a statistical analysis of data obtained from a sample of subjects within a population is generally a more rigorous method of testing predefined hypotheses and determining generalisability of results. Research questions of social and organisational theories, on the other hand, are best suited to inductive analyses.

When conducting Internet research, however, there are even more factors to be taken into account. One consideration is the constant and rapid change in technology. A decade ago, most Internet users were, of necessity, skilled computer programmers or at least had a relatively deep understanding of network applications. With the development of point-and-click graphic interfaces, graphic web browsers, audio and video plug-ins, and wireless connections, the underlying technology is more complex but is a virtually closed system. The effect of this transition is a polarisation of the developers and the users in the Internet population.

A second consideration is the information now available. The average Internet user is often overwhelmed by the variety and vast amount of information and has difficulty processing and selecting the relevant information.

A third consideration is the notion of browsing or "surfing". In contrast to the traditional linear search along shelves of books in a library, the Internet user follows a web-like nonlinear search in which most "pages" emphasise eye-catching designs and attention-grabbing movement rather than a sequential and logical presentation of information.

These considerations complicate classical research methodologies so, increasingly, Internet researchers are turning to methods developed in the fields of information systems and data mining (Jones, 1999). In general, the research questions of interest appear at first to guide the choice of the research design and methodological tools. At the point when the methodology needs to be selected, the qualitative versus quantitative debate begins. Both methods attempt to explain the implicit concepts hidden in the bulk of data about the investigated phenomenon. However, both methods differ in their approach to the problem.

Quantitative methodologies assume that collected data is measurable or, if it is not, then it is necessary to design an experiment or computer simulation in a way that respective measurements can be taken. Once the measurements are done, the problem is to fit (in a broad sense) the data adequately to the quantitative model. Derived dependencies then are interpreted in the context of the initial problem formulation with a possible test of the hypothesis about the nature of the data and the errors in the measurements. In qualitative methods the interest is centered on the qualitative characteristics of the phenomenon. Rather than trying to quantify every detail, these methods try to grasp the form, the content and some constraints of the investigated phenomenon and analyse its qualities (Lindlof, 1995).

This neat qualitative and quantitative dichotomy, though, is under question. Recently, protagonists of both sides have been encroaching cautiously on to rival territory. Thus researchers may quantify qualitative data; for example, coding concepts from interviews and surveys in a manner that is suitable for statistical analysis. Researchers may also qualify quantitative data; for example, using quotes from complementary dialogue to support a statistical pattern derived from data collection. Adding a little of one methodology to the other adds flavor and aesthetic appeal but it is not essential. This is the major drawback in current attempts to develop a research schema that benefits from both methods. Each methodology has its own set of costs and benefits, particularly when applied to Internet research, and it is possible to tease out and match the strengths of each with particular variables of interest. A hybrid approach in which quantitative and qualitative methods of research facilitate each other, outlined in Sudweeks and Simoff (1999) is further developed and applied in this book. This approach is described in Chapter 5.

1.5. Significance of Research

The significance of the research reported in this research is fourfold and concerns: (i) the development of a new methodology (CEDA); (ii) the methodology applied to two case studies; (iii) interpretation of theories emerging from the analyses; and (iv) longitudinal implications.

1.5.1. Complementary Explorative Data Analysis (CEDA) Methodology

Quantitative and qualitative methods are quite distinct in their emphases (Stake, 1995; Silverman, 1997). In quantitative analyses, systematic, statistical or other functional relations between a finite set of variables are sought. In qualitative analyses, argumentation is based on a description of the research objects or observation units, rather than on approximation of a limited number of variables. In both cases, however, the reliability of the analyses relies on the assumption that the results are *replicable*.

Replicability becomes a major concern in CMC research because (i) the underlying networking protocols cannot guarantee the same conditions because the path of information communication varies; (ii) information is subject to time delay and consequences connected with it are different; and (ii) the recursiveness and creativeness of natural language renders every string of words (apart from standard cliches) as a unique utterance.

To overcome these difficulties in Internet research, an integrated methodology for Internet research has been developed. Though at first glance it seems that quantitative and qualitative research are radically different, they share an important common thread. Both methods make interpretations of the phenomenon they want to examine. Both traditions create a framework for their analysis based on those interpretations. In reality, the difference between these two methods is a discursive one.

Numerous attempts over the past two decades to integrate the two methodologies have resulted in labels such as *triangulation*, *micro-macro link* or *mixed methods* (Bryman, 1988; Ragin, 1987; Tschudi, 1989). The idea is to employ a combination of research methods that are typically used to analyse empirical results or interpretations. The rationale is that the weakness of any single method - qualitative or quantitative - is balanced by the strengths of other methods.

CEDA employs quantitative methods to extract reliable patterns, and qualitative methods to ensure the essence of phenomena is captured. The CEDA framework allows the use of different data sets in a common research cycle rather than the traditional approach of applying different analyses to the same data set. It has the potential to conduct parallel and interconnected research. CEDA is described in more detail in Chapter 5.

1.5.2. Case study analyses

Two case studies are explored and analysed. The first case study is a two-year collaborative research project; the second case study is a two-and-half-month series of collaborative workshops. Table 1.1 summarises how the two groups differ.

Case Study 1- ProjectH Research Group
The first case study is the ProjectH Research Group, a spontaneous and heterogeneous computer-mediated group, which was functional for a two-year period

from 1992 to 1994. ProjectH was grounded in common membership of a computer-networked discussion group, a subset of whom proposed a research study to satisfy a common desire to learn more about the nature of communication, culture and community on the network. ProjectH is an example of a multi-year, broad-purpose, multi-person, international collaborative effort – one in which the majority of the participants had never met face-to-face.

The significant aspects of this case study are as follows:

1. The collaborating group was entirely computer mediated.
2. The communication among participants was asynchronous.
3. The collaborating group was a natural group as it emerged from a broader environment and created its own shared aims and purposes.
4. The participants were globally dispersed; most had not met before, and did not meet during or after the collaboration.
5. The data collected from this case study is an accurate corpora of online collaborative research activity.
6. The methodology used to analyse the data is an innovative combination of qualitative and quantitative methods (see Section 1.5.1 and Chapter 5).
7. The analysis perspective is from a coordinator and participant observer.
8. The emerging model of collaborative activity takes into account variables from a wide range of disciplines.

Table 1.1. Feature summary of two case studies.

Feature	Case Study 1	Case Study 2
Medium	Email	Chatroom
Mode	Asynchronous	Synchronous
Duration	2 years	9 one-hour meetings
Leadership	Assigned	Appointed
Formation	Spontaneous	Predefined
Purpose	Research project	Workshop series
Number of participants	143	19
Location of participants	Global	Australia
Age group	20-65	Mostly 20-30
Time	1992-94	2000
Network	BITNet, Usenet, Comserve	Internet
Process	Unstructured	Structured

Case Study 2 – Organisational Informatics Workshop Series
The second case study is a group of students engaged in collaborative learning in a series of nine one-hour workshops over a two-and-a-half month period from July to October 2000. The workshops took place in a chatroom and were part of a unit of

study (Organisational Informatics) in the School of Information Technology, Murdoch University. Although the participants lived within a 100 km range of Perth, Western Australia, and were studying within the same university, the majority of the participants had never met face-to-face.

The significant aspects of this case study are as follows:

1. The collaborating group was entirely computer mediated.
2. The communication among participants was synchronous.
3. The collaborating group, as well as its aims and purposes, was predefined but learning was a shared construction of knowledge.
4. The participants were dispersed within the state of Western Australia; most had not met before and did not meet during the collaboration, but many met after the collaboration.
5. The data collected from this case study is an accurate corpora of an online collaborative learning activity.
6. The methodology used to analyse the data is an innovative combination of qualitative and quantitative methods (see Section 1.5.1 and Chapter 5).
7. The analysis perspective is from a facilitator and participant observer.
8. The emerging model of collaborative activity takes into account variables from a wide range of disciplines.

1.5.3. Interpretation of emerging theories

A deeper understanding of how small groups communicate and interact in virtual environments has direct application to those aspects of society that are, or are likely to be, impacted by information and communication technologies. Any organisation – be it academic, social, government or industry - which engages in information generation and communication in the context of organised human activity will benefit from a more extensive knowledge of the specifics of online collaborative activity.

The collaborative groups in the two case studies are studied in the context of previous research and developing theories. Of particular interest are theories concerning:

- *group development* (e.g. Bennis and Shepherd, 1956; Tuckman, 1965; Kuypers, Davies and Hazewinkel, 1986; Gersick, 1988; Robbins, 1994; McGrath and Hollingshead, 1994; Wheelan, 1994; Wheelan, McKeage, Verdi, Abraham, Krasick and Johnston, 1994; Napier and Gershenfeld, 1999)

- *leadership* (e.g. Marx, 1964; Weber, 1947; Farris and Lim, 1969; Kiesler and Sproull, 1986; McGuire, Kiesler and Siegel, 1987; Lea and Spears, 1991; Fleishman, Mumford, Zaccaro, Levin, Korotkin and Hein, 1991; Lea and Spears, 1992; Spears and Lea, 1992; Chrislip and Larson, 1994; Kostner, 1994; Sosik, Avolio and Kahai, 1997; Hackman and Johnson, 2000; Yoo and Alavi, 2002; Mabry and Sudweeks, 2003).
- *group cohesiveness* (e.g. Farris and Lim, 1969; Sanderson, 1996; Smircich, 1983; Markus and Robey, 1988; Schein, 1992; Gunawardena and Zittle, 1997).
- *communication functionality* (e.g. Daft and Lengel, 1986; Trevino, Lengel and Daft, 1987; Fulk and Steinfield, 1989; Schmitz and Fulk, 1991; Walther, 1992; Fulk, 1993).
- *communication strategies* (e.g. Brown and Levinson, 1978; Ong, 1982; Lakoff, 1982; Black, Levin, Mehan and Quinn, 1983; Baron, 1984; Brown and Levinson, 1987; Finnegan, 1988; Ochs, 1989; Levinson, 1990).

These theories are discussed in more detail in Chapter 2.

The theories emerging from the data analysis of collaborative groups distributed globally and state-wide, working together on different activities and in different modes of mediated communication can build on previous work and can be generalised to similar group activity. Group dynamics can be predicted and modified to ensure efficiency and productivity, as well as meeting and satisfying both task and social needs of its members.

1.5.4. Longitudinal implications

The first case study, in 1992-1994, was developed to explore communication and interaction dynamics in an environment that was novel, using technology that was relatively primitive compared with today's technologies. Communication and interaction issues emerged, some of which were resolved using various types of analyses of the corpora. Other issues raised more questions.

The second case study, in July to October 2000, was developed to revisit some of the earlier resolved issues in a different environment and to address the unresolved issues from the earlier study.

Each case study represents a snapshot of two very different time zones in the development of global communication. The significance of this research is in identifying commonalities that endured the most turbulent decade in the history of information and communication technologies. If these commonalities survived this past decade, then there is strong support to predict communication trends as technologies develop even further.

1.5.5. Summary of significance of research

The significance of the research can be summarised as follows:
1. development of a new methodology, Complementary Explorative Data Analysis (CEDA - Section 1.5.1 and Chapters 5-6), that integrates quantitative and qualitative methods in which one analysis informs and modifies subsequent analyses,
2. analyses of two very different case studies of computer-mediated groups (see Table 1.1),
3. interpretation of theories emerging from the analyses of the two case studies in the context of other developing theories applicable to present-day and future computer-mediated groups and teams, and
4. longitudinal implications in the capture of windows of online collaborative activities over a decade in which technologies and technological diffusion changed at an unprecedented pace.

1.6. Objective of the Research

The objective of this research, therefore, is to observe and analyse two case studies to understand more about communication and dynamics in computer-mediated groups which differed in terms of timeframe, location, space, boundaries and communication modes. This allows the specific research questions to be addressed.

1.7. Outline of the Book

Figure 1.5 is an visual overview of the book. The book initially explores the phenomenon of virtual groups with an overview (Chapter 1) and a literature review (Chapter 2). In Chapter 2, previous research on groups is described. The chapter begins with a discussion of how groups have been defined and classified. The dynamics of interaction that have been studied in both online and traditional groups are described, addressing such issues as developmental processes, leadership and cohesion. Given the interdisciplinary nature of this book, the review of the literature encompasses perspectives from psychology, informatics, communication, cultural studies, anthropology and philosophy.

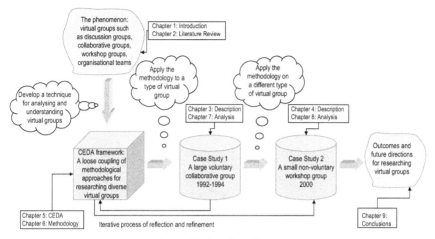

Figure 1.5. Overview of book.

In Chapters 3 and 4, two case studies are presented. Each chapter describes the background, participants, purpose and collaborative activity of the groups. In Chapter 3, the asynchronous collaborative activity of Case Study 1 (ProjectH group) is described. The activity of this case study was the collection of data from electronic discussions and a content analysis of the data. The methodology devised by the case study group for their collaborative research project is described, along with the procedural and ethical issues that this group needed to resolve. In Chapter 4, the synchronous collaborative activities of Case Study 2 (Organisational Informatics group) is described. The activity of this case study group included active collaborative learning through moderation and facilitative discussions on topic issues.

Chapter 5 describes a new methodology for doing Internet research. The CEDA (Complementary Explorative Data Analysis) methodology, developed specifically as an organising methodological framework for the multiple datasets collected for this research. It draws on the strengths of both quantitative and qualitative approaches and loosely couples them in a complementary fashion. CEDA specifies five stages and its uniqueness is in being able to use not only different types of analyses, as in the triangulation procedure, but also different types of datasets.

Chapter 6 describes the application of CEDA to the two case studies explaining in detail the methodologies used to analyse the case studies. The data collection of historical records, surveys and interviews is described, and the variables of interest in studying developmental and leadership characteristics are identified.

Chapters 7 and 8 provide analyses of the two case studies. The analyses focus on two broad group characteristics: development (communication content, awareness, cohesiveness) and leadership (communication style, strategies, structure, emergence).

In Chapter 9, the results are interpreted and generalised with suggestions for application in industry and academic communities. Further directions in research on this topic are also outlined.

CHAPTER 2

LITERATURE REVIEW

2.1. Introduction

Groups are an integral part of society. Everyone, throughout their life cycle, belongs to many groups. Small groups, in particular, are woven into the fabric of our lives:

> We are born with the help of a team of doctors and nurses, raised in a family, and for 13 years or so, the state educates us in relatively small classroom settings ... We work in organisations where decisions are made by task groups and teams. We meet a significant other and marry in the presence of our family and friends. We spend some of our most cherished moments socializing with friends and neighbors, and join support groups ... to share and confront their problems. In the twilight of our years, we may retire to a nursing home and, as a final farewell, our friends gather together at our funeral to pay their respects (Frey, 1994, p.ix).

Unfortunately not all groups are effective. In fact, quite often a heterogeneous collection of individuals is thrown together and expected to form a cohesive and productive team in organisations. The effectiveness of a group depends on how well its members interact and communicate. Communication is not just part of group management, it is the activity and interaction from which a group emerges. Therefore, an analysis of group communication and management will help to predict and identify problem areas, and provide strategies for improving cooperation and productivity.

Early research into groups was primarily laboratory studies in which researchers assigned subjects randomly to different groups to work on a contrived problem over a short period of time. In order to study the variable of interest, the researcher needed to control many features that occur in natural groups, such as culture, gender, age and status. Also, in the limited time of the experiment, these artificial groups did not exhibit characteristics of natural groups, such as cohesion, cooperativeness and consciousness. Now there is an awareness that researchers need to move away from the study of 'zero-history', isolated laboratory groups to groups that occur in natural contexts (Poole, 1990; Putnam and Stohl, 1990). While there is a considerable body of research on groups in context, research on structured and unstructured computer-mediated collaborative groups is less abundant.

In this chapter, the literature on relevant research will be discussed. Every group develops, over a period of time, a structure. The chapter, therefore, includes discussion of how groups are structured. The structure of the group can be explored by analysing the communication of the group. In this book, group development is explored through the communication within the group. Hence, it is important to identify the literature in which the nature of groups and group communication are explicitly stated in order to build theoretical assumptions, specified research questions, and a communication coding scheme. As the two broad areas of interest in this study are developmental and leadership processes, the literature will be presented under these categories. First, though, it is useful to define groups and describe the various types of virtual groups.

2.2. Definition of Groups

In the literature, definitions of groups are varied and they emphasise different aspects, including the structure, type of interaction, and the purpose of the group. A definition offered by Tajfel and Turner (1986) is:

> A collection of individuals who perceive themselves to be members of the same social category, share some emotional involvement in this common definition of themselves, and achieve some degree of social consensus about the evaluation of their group and of their membership in it.

This definition, though, assumes a higher level of homogeneity than is necessary. The definition of a group given by Rothwell (1998, p.55) provides the foundation for the definition adopted in this book:

> A group is a human communication system composed of three or more individuals, interacting for the achievement of some common purpose(s), who influence and are influenced by one another.

Rothwell's definition highlights three features that transform an aggregation of individuals into a group: (i) communication system, (ii) common purpose, and (iii) mutual influence. However, this definition is inadequate as it does not take into account the development of shared processes and the notion of exclusivity; that is, the perception by individuals that a group exists and that they are or are not members of the group. These shared processes are particularly crucial in the development of online groups.

The notion of exclusivity draws on Marx's theory of class consciousness.[1] There are two factors that define class in Marxian terms: the objective economic factor (one's position in the production process) and the subjective conscious factor. A

---

[1] See Lukacs (1967) for a detailed dicussion of class consciousness.

precondition for the existence of a class is that a collection of individuals are aware of their common (shared) interests and are aware that there are other collections of individuals with different interests. Class consciousness does not develop mechanically from economic conditions but is the result of diverse cultural and historical factors. So, too, do groups develop. An essential feature, and perhaps the defining feature, of groups is the development of a *group consciousness*.

The notion of group consciousness is a response to one of the major concerns in research in groups: the 'reality' of a group. According to Hartley (1997), the sum of the characteristics of group members does not equal the characteristic of the group:

> ... being accepted as a member of a group has psychological consequences which in turn can change the nature of the individual.

Harley gives as an example of an independent group process, the development of group norms. Norms are mutually acceptable definitions of behaviours within the group and the norms act as a frame of reference for individual members. Group norms would not emerge if the concept of 'groupness' or group consciousness were not present.

The concept of the virtual or online group is not clearly defined, and it often overlaps with notions such as the virtual or networked organisation, the virtual workplace, virtual communities, electronic commerce and certain forms of teleworking. Virtual teams are seen as essentially project or task focused groups. The team membership may be relatively stable (e.g. in an established sales team) or change on a regular basis (e.g. in project teams). Their members may be drawn from the same organisation (e.g. production planners and production operatives) or from several different organisations (e.g. when projects involve consultants or external assessors). Further distinctions can be made on physical proximity (i.e. whether or not team members are co-located and can interact face-to-face or are geographically separated) and by work-cycle synchronicity (i.e. whether or not members interact in the same or different time periods).

With the inclusion of the development of shared processes, the notion of exclusivity, and the more broad meaning of "shared space" the following definition is derived:

> A group is a collection of individuals, in which communication meaning has been mutually created in a shared space or environment, in which its members interact for the achievement of some shared goal(s) or purpose(s), in which its members influence and are influenced by one another, and in which its members are conscious of belonging to the group and are conscious that there are individuals who do not belong to that group.

2.3. Virtual Groups

Groups have been classified in a number of ways. Tajfel and Fraser (1978), for example, distinguish four types of groups: family groups, friendship groups, work groups and laboratory groups. Robbins (1994) divides groups into two broad categories with subcategories: formal groups, which include command groups and task groups; and informal groups, which include interest groups and friendship groups. In reality, groups do not fit neatly within categories. People may join a work group but still have social and emotional needs to be satisfied within that group; similarly, groups formed specifically for social reasons often develop tasks or programs to fulfil achievement needs.

Virtual groups are even more difficult to categorise, but are commonly referred to as "online communities", a term which is used broadly to describe "any collection of people who communicate online" (Preece, 2000, p.17). A distinction is made here between groups and communities. A group has a clear boundary that defines its membership, even in the fickle world of cyberspace. The boundary of a community, on the other hand, is not so clearly defined. Preece makes a further distinction between networks and communities where the term community "connotes the strength of relationships" (Preece, 2000, p.18).

The Internet offers millions of users the opportunity to communicate. The convergence of computer and communication technologies is a social convergence. In global neighbourhoods, people congregate and meet, conversing on topics from aerodynamics to zoology. However, these congregations are neither mass nor interpersonal, they are a new phenomenon.

Networks are centralised distribution mechanisms that are both democratic and anarchic. The "personality" of a virtual group is shaped, in part, by its mediating technology, most common of which are bulletin boards, listservs, usenet, chats, instant messaging, MUDs/MOOs and immersive virtual environments. *Bulletin boards* are like message boards in public spaces where messages are left for people to read. Messages are posted to the bulletin board and users need to log on to the environment to read them. Often, the technology allows the user to view the messages either in a chronological or threaded order. *Listserv* is a software product that facilitates the subscription, messaging and archiving processes of email discussion groups. There are more than 50,000 public discussion groups[2]. *Usenet* is a set of computers and networks used for creating, forwarding, or displaying

---

[2] According to *CataList,* the official catalog of LISTSERV lists at http://www.lsoft.com/catalist.html (accessed 21 May 2008)

newsgroup conferences. Users access posted messages via a Usenet news community either with a reader software or a web interface.[3] *Chat* (Conversational Hypertext Access Technology) is a technology that allows participants to engage in real-time text communication without storing messages.[4] Messages are instantaneously relayed to all other participants logged into the chat room.[5] *Instant messaging* is like chat, in that it is real-time communication, except that users define their own group (list of addresses). ICQ (I Seek You) is a graphical version of the system. *MUDs* are chat rooms in which participants engage in adventure games. *MOOs* are object-oriented MUDs; that is, text-based virtual environments in which participants create objects (rooms, furniture, dragons, etc.). *Immersive virtual environments* are 3D worlds in which participants are able to see, hear and feel each other with the aid of stereoscopic vision, stereo sound, touch and pressure feedback.

Virtual groups can be viewed as an enigma in traditional, rational and economic terms – they form virtually and "on-the-fly", prompted by common interests. The groups crystallise and disband without deference to time or space differences. Like interpersonal communication, these virtual groups are participatory, their content made up by their audience. Like mass communication, they involve large audiences. Groups overlap with other groups, group members come and go, and tensions are created by contradictory needs. Often, the process is unmanaged in any traditional sense of motivation, profit, control or censorship. Joining and departing participants do so without so much as a required introduction or an agreed upon etiquette. The groups are of an undetermined size or constitution. The communication is neither the classical written nor traditionally spoken form. Virtual groups are neither strictly mass nor interpersonal. In terms of participants and symmetry, a virtual group is either the largest form of conversation, or the smallest form of mass communication.

Why do people make this investment in a virtual group? And why does this phenomenon happen? Is the allure of group CMC in its emulation of face-to-face interaction?

Danet et al. (1998) argue that playfulness is an intrinsic aspect of all computer-mediated communication. Playfulness becomes more prominent as one moves from word processing, to hypertext, to discussion groups (asynchronous communication), and finally to synchronous communication (such as chat, ICQ, and 3D worlds). This

---

[3] See Chapter 3 for a detailed description of asynchronous text-based communication environments such as Usenet, BITNet and listservs.
[4] Although many chat environments have the capacity to log all discussions, individual participants generally do not have access to the archived discussions.
[5] See Chapter 4 for a detailed description of synchronous text-based communication environments, such as chat, MUDs, MOOs, 3D graphic worlds.

transition is from a a purely written genre to one that is experienced as a written conversation (or talking).

Like virtual social groups, collaborative groups are an important phenomenon. They, too, are frequently voluntary, with the participants determining both their duration and focus. In the corporate sector, collaborative groups are increasing as the current organisational restructuring trend is to minimise the vertical differentiation between employees. The informality and interactive features of email, for example, encourage employees to cross social and organisational boundaries to share opinions and ideas (Sproull and Kiesler, 1991). The very boundaries of organisations are being redrawn or called into question. These collaborative relationships represent a distinctive work process, one that appears to be characteristic of many kinds of professional work. Computer-mediated collaborative groups form for specific tasks, such as the CommonLISP development program (Steele, 1984) and NCR's WorldMark computer system project (Lipnack and Stamps, 1997), or just to combine intellectual and material resources to accomplish a project of mutual interest (Sudweeks and Rafaeli, 1996; McCreary and Brochet, 1992). Group work enables scientists, managers and project teams to tackle problems that they are incapable of working on alone because of limitations of resources, skills and time (Kraut, Egido and Galegher, 1990).

2.4. Developmental Characteristics of Groups

Groups, like individuals, experience a cycle of development over time. Theories of group development abound in the literature. There is a preponderance of evidence for the existence of developmental phases in face-to-face groups but less is known about how virtual groups develop. The development of these two types of groups will be described in the following sections.

2.4.1. Development in Face-to-Face Groups

The evidence for developmental phases in face-to-face groups is based, by and large, on either observation or content analyses of verbal communication patterns in groups. In the former case, conceptual categories associated with the stages of group development are determined prior to observation and then the units of analysis (e.g. sentence, utterance, complete thought, conversation turn) are classified as one or more of the predetermined categories (e.g. Bales, 1980; Verdi and Wheelan, 1992). In the latter case, categories or themes emerge as the content of group discussions are examined. Thematic shifts are an indication of turning points in a group's life cycle

(Wheelan, McKeage, Verdi, Abraham, Krasick and Johnston, 1994; Romm and Pliskin, 1995).

Perhaps the most widely known is the sequential model of Tuckman (1965; see also Tuckman and Jensen, 1977), which describes five basic and predictable developmental stages of a task group: (i) *forming* (members feel some discomfort and cautiously test relationships); (ii) *storming* (members feel more comfortable and question authority and task demands); (iii) *norming* (group norms in behaviour are established and tasks defined); (iv) *performing* (members focus on tasks in a supportive environment); and (v) *adjourning* (task closure and a change in relationships).

Other researchers also claim that groups follow a progressive development. The AGIL (*adaptation, goal-setting, latency* and *integration*) model, for example, was developed by Parsons (1961) and revised later as the LAIG model by Hare (1976) and Hare and Naveh (1984). This latter model focuses on the problem solving aspect of group work and includes four stages: (i) *latent pattern maintenance* (members strive for agreement to reduce inevitable tensions); (ii) *adaptation* (members take on roles); (iii) *integration* (members reassess and display flexibility); (iv) *goal attainment* (members reach their goal).

Lacoursiere (1974) developed a four-stage model similar to Tuckman's model. Lacoursiere sees the group as a living organism that responds to stresses in the environment and either matures as a result of the stress or dies. The mature group progresses through orientation, dissatisfaction, production and termination. Lacoursiere (1980) later revised the model to five stages: orientation, dissatisfaction, resolution, production and termination. Similarly, Fisher (1970), focusing on the decision making aspect of group work, found a sequence of orientation, conflict, emergence and reinforcement, and Yalom (1975) identified orientation, conflict, interpersonally close and termination phases.

Other researchers question this concept of a neat linear progression. Schutz (1966), for example, claims that phases recur throughout a group's development. Schutz focuses on interpersonal behaviour that reflects patterns of individual needs within the group as he describes four phases: *inclusion* (issues of involvement – who's in and who's out); *control* (issues of leadership and structure – who's on top and who's on the bottom); *affection* (issues of cohesiveness and harmony – who's near and who's far); *maturity* (commitment to the task and each other). This four-phase process reverses when the group moves towards termination as relationships typically become weaker and group boundaries diffuse.

Gersick (1988; 1989) identified a temporal rhythm throughout a group's lifespan. In her punctuated equilibrium model, she points to two long work periods separated by three short transitional periods. During the three short periods, work is assessed and reassessed, creating some tension. Similarly, in his Interactive Process Analysis (IPA) framework, Bales (1950) suggests an orderly series of phases involving task-oriented activities and a parallel cycle of phases involving socioemotional needs. This framework has been very popular over the past five decades because the theory can be observed by studying a group over a session or over time (Napier and Gershenfeld, 1999).

Cyclical models are also described in the literature. Worchel et al. (1992; see also Worchel, 1994) developed a six-stage model (*discontent, preciptating event, group identification, group productivity, individuation, decay*), claiming that a group's development through the stages can be affected by events which interrupt the linear development of a group, causing the group to regress. Wheelan and Hochberger (1996) describe a five-stage integrative model (*dependency and inclusion, counterdependency and flight, trust and structure, work, termination*) which again recognises that there are factors that can affect the predicted developmental process. Factors that have been identified include changes in the group size, level of member cooperation, increased tension and availability of information resources (Poole and Roth, 1989). More importantly, Wheelan (1994) attempted to close a gap existing in most sequential stage models with the inclusion of a period in which trust among group members and leaders develops.

While many of the models described are mechanistic and reductionist, there is ample evidence that a characteristic lifespan does exist for face-to-face groups. Groups typically experience periods of *joining, conflict, cohesion, goal achievement* and *closure*, regardless of whether the order is sequential, recurring, cyclical or even random. Initially the group has to be formed, which means there is a period in which individuals are *joining*. If the group is not formed for a specific task, it is during this period that the group defines the task, decides how they should tackle it, what information needs to be gathered, and how to obtain the required information. The members exhibit some common behavioural and experiential characteristics. New members, for example, tend to act in a superficial and circumspect manner, observing the group environment to gauge boundaries in terms of dress, language, "pecking order" and so forth. For many, this phase can also be a time of expectation and anticipation. Information is collected by group members and processed through the filter of individual experiences, biases and stereotypes. This phase is also a time for the group to establish rules or standards that define appropriate behaviours or norms. Norms can be categorised as explicit and implicit. Explicit norms are regulated by the group as constitutions and by-laws. Implicit norms are socially acceptable and unacceptable behaviours, developed by observing uniformities in the behaviours and attitudes of members. The main purpose of norms is to achieve the group goals (Shimanoff, 1992), but there are significant psychological benefits and costs as well.

When members feel comfortable and secure in the group environment, there is a natural tendency for assertiveness and for staking out personal "territory", which results in *conflict*. Task performance is a theatre in which the players seek status, power and influence. Issues are polarised as members adopt their particular stance. Conflicts, though, are often not so much about the issues being debated but about individual members estimating and establishing their degree of influence and finding their unique niche within the group. During this phase there is a distinct lack of unity. Members develop an ambivalence towards their leader as being an object of both admiration and criticism.

Collaboration is more readily sought and competition is not as prevalent when the group begins to work together. During this phase, the members who are more willing to compromise for harmony act as intermediaries in (re)establishing communication among the more aggressive members and facilitate the development of cohesion within the group. The group, as a whole, tends to take on an air of confidence. Opinions are discussed about the task and consensus generally achieved. Cohesion, though, brings its own drawbacks. Members are more concerned with harmony than directiveness. Enthusiasm gives way to passive behaviour in the interests of harmony, thus resulting in a lack of productivity and difficulties in decision making. Quite often a group can become dysfunctional if it does not proceed from this developmental stage. Symptoms of dysfunctionality include groupthink (Janis, 1972), social loafing (Forsyth, 1990; Zimbardo, 1992), risky shift (Stoner, 1961; McCauley and Segal, 1987) and polarisation (Moscovici and Zavalloni, 1969; Levine and Moreland, 1990).

As the group becomes more concerned about moving on from conflicts and inefficient structure to finding alternative means of *goal achievement*, solutions begin to emerge. Group members take on roles and restrictions are placed on group members to ensure a more rational approach to decision making. Work procedures are operationalised as the group steers towards greater efficiency. It is during this time that the group matures. As the functions of the group become increasingly complex, there is a need for more resources, greater participation, accountability and personal responsibility.

Although there has been much research on group formation and maintenance, there has been little focus on the *closure* phase of the group. Even Tuckman (1965) initially identified the first four periods, adding an adjournment period some twelve years later (Tuckman and Jensen, 1977). Closure signals an end to both tasks and relationships. However, the way the group has worked does have considerable impact on how members approach later group work. Team leaders should not only understand how to form and maintain groups; according to Shea and Guzzo (1987), they also need to know how to close down groups.

In general, therefore, groups in traditional (face-to-face) environments follow a more or less direct path from inception to termination. In virtual environments, however, where extra coordination efforts are required, communication media are relatively lean and offer fewer behavioural cues, and there are time constraints, one would expect the group developmental path to be more complex.

2.4.2. Development in Virtual Groups

Research in the developmental cycle of virtual groups is much more sparse than for their traditional counterparts. Kat Nagel and David Levine offer anecdotal observations of the life cycle of mailing lists. Nagel (1994) defines six phases: *initial enthusiasm* (introductions and mutual admiration), *evangelism* (recruiting more people to the list), *growth* (people join and post lengthy threads), *community* (people feel more comfortable and activity is high), *discomfort with diversity* (people complain about irrelevant threads), and either *smug complacency and stagnation* (purists criticise inappropriate posts and behaviours, activity and membership drops) or *maturity* (some people leave and list settles down to alternating between community and discomfort). Levine's (1992) theory, on the other hand, is more process oriented than developmental but does shed light on the mailing list cycle. He proposed that "bad postings drive out good". That is, interesting conversations are generally started by interesting people. Less interesting people chime in and as the proportion of (bad) postings from non-busy people rises, it is no longer worth the while of busy people to contribute. They drop out, further lowering the proportion of good postings.

Most of the research on virtual groups has been carried out with virtual teams either in the educational or the organisational setting. Virtual teams have been described as "cross-functional teams that operate across space, time and organizational boundaries with members who communicate mainly through electronic technologies" (McShane and Von Glinow, 2000). A number of instruments have been developed to assess virtual team development and processes, e.g. Lurey's (1998) Virtual Team Survey and Nemiro's (1968) Background Survey of Virtual Team Members.

Whereas groups are, and always have been, an integral part of society, we are now experiencing the most dramatic change in the nature of groups, particularly in the organisational environment. Teams of workers are moving from being primarily "co-located" (team members located in one physical location) to "virtual" (team members are geographically dispersed). The NCR Corporation, for example, built a virtual team of 1000 people to develop a next generation computer system. Working together for more than 11 months in three locations (San Diego, California; Columbia, South Carolina; Naperville, Illinois), their computer system (WorldMark) was largely responsible for turning around a $722 million loss in 1995 to a $29 million profit in 1996. The virtual team was able to communicate at any time by entering the "Worm Hole" – a high-speed open lease videoconferencing line. To enhance the feeling of "being together", even the grain on the conference tables in the three different locations were identical (Lipnack and Stamps, 1997).

Most studies comparing traditional and virtual teams favour the effectiveness of traditional teams, reporting that traditional teams have more interaction and information exchange (McGrath and Hollingshead, 1994), less misunderstanding among members (Warkentin, Sayeed and Hightower, 1997b), and superior internal leadership and coordination (Burke and Chidambaram, 1994; Eveland and Bikon, 1989). Critics of this body of research, though, argue that the findings are limited in that the groups were ad hoc and the time period insufficient to establish effective working relationships. More recent research suggests that if virtual teams have sufficient time to develop strong relationships and adapt to the use of computer-supported collaborative technologies, they may be just as effective as traditional teams (Townsend, DeMarie and Hendrickson, 1998; Chidambaram and Jones, 1993; Andres, 1996; Warkentin, Sayeed and Hightower, 1997a).

All teams take time to develop, and virtual teams tend to take even longer. A team is first and foremost a process: it has a beginning, a middle, and almost always an end. Powerful results accrue when virtual teams consciously work their way through a life-cycle process.

Both Lipnack and Stamps (1997) and Johnson et al. (n.d.), found support for Tuckman's developmental cycle in virtual teams. Lipnack and Stamps identified five phases in organisational virtual teams, consisting of *start-up* (gathering information, exploring ideas), *launch* (establish leadership, obtain commitments, sharpen purpose), *perform* (bulk of the work done), *test* (review of results), and *deliver* (adjournment). In virtual learning teams, Johnson et al. found that virtual learning teams evolve around project timelines, group processes and interpersonal relationships, including activities described in Tuckman's model. The level of team performance appeared to depend on how well teams were able to establish norms and resolve conflicts. Sarker, Lau and Sahay (2001) propose that virtual teams progress through four stages of development: initiation, exploration, integration and closure. The initiation stage is similar to the first stage of traditional group development models. The exploration and integration stages, though, are periods in which team communication becomes an important factor in the successful outcome of the team.

In the higher educational environment, virtual teams are similar to the project or product team of the organisation in that they have a defined but non-routine task, they collaborate over a predetermined length of time, and the team has the authority to make decisions regarding the task (albeit somewhat limited). The educational virtual team differs from the organisational virtual team in that membership is generally fixed rather than fluid.

Studies have shown that cooperative learning environments promote student achievement as well as high productivity, greater social skill development, and increased self-esteem (Johnson and Johnson, 1989). In online degree programs, virtual learning teams are being used to increase collaboration, communication, learning (Bailey and Luetkehans, 1998), interaction (Townsend, DeMarie and Hendrickson, 1996), and knowledge sharing (Horvath and Tobin, 1999).

Of particular interest here, though, is Landrum and Paris's (2000) finding that virtual teams in higher education do, in fact, pass through developmental stages commonly associated with traditional teams, although their effectiveness is questionable. In their virtual team project across two universities, students found communication difficult. Asynchronous communication was counter-productive and a hindrance to the development of ideas, and synchronous communication was difficult to coordinate across different time zones.

Table 2.1 summarises references related to the different theories of group development.

Table 2.1. Summary of literature on group development

Development of Groups	Researchers
Sequential phases	Tuckman (1965), Tuckman and Jensen (1977), Parsons (1961), Hare (1976), Hare and Naveh (1984), Lacoursiere (1974; 1980), Wheelan (1994), Lipnack and Stamps (1997), Johnson et al. (n.d.), Sarker et al. (2001), Landrum and Paris (2000)
Recurring phases	Schutz (1966), Gersick (1988; 1989), (Bales, 1950)
Cyclical phases	Worchel et al. (1992), Worchel (1994), Wheelan and Hochberger (1996)

2.5. Leadership characteristics of groups

Leadership, like group development, has been studied extensively. There is a number of ways to view leadership. An excellent in-depth overview of the different aspects of leadership and the evolution of the notion of leadership is given in Sarros (1999). The literature reports research using both qualitative and quantitative methods, both experimental and naturalistic studies, and both small and large groups. The term "leader", coined about the middle of the nineteenth century, is estimated to have about one hundred definitions (Napier and Gershenfeld, 1999), and there are almost as many different classification systems used to define the dimensions of leadership (Fleishman, Mumford, Zaccaro, Levin, Korotkin and Hein, 1991).

Leadership issues in CMC is vital today because of the increasing prevalence of the virtual organisations, and the corresponding interest in managing virtual groups and teams. Can people be as efficient leaders in a geographically dispersed and mediated environment without meeting group members face-to-face as they would in a traditional co-located environment? How will leadership be reflected in communication patterns and communication style among team members? Are there differences in the trend of these patterns in different scenarios; that is, in the case of leading a group of autonomous and diverse individuals using an asynchronous communication medium over a relatively long period of time versus a group of individuals using a synchronous communication medium and bound by the communication network for a short period of time?

Organisations are increasingly using computers and communication network technology to create "distributed" or "collaborative" team methods of leadership. Managers need to face these new challenges, yet, leadership in such environments is not well understood (Kostner, 1994).

A distinction is made between assigned and emergent leadership. An assigned leader is an individual who is assigned to a position of leadership. An emergent leader, on the other hand, is an individual who is not assigned to a leadership position but emerges as a leader through the support and acceptance of the group over a period of time. This support and acceptance is a result of the individual's actions and their communication behaviours, which include being involved, informed, firm but seeking the opinion of others, and initiating new ideas (Fisher, 1974). Leaders emerge according to the needs of the group (Myers, Slavin and Southern, 1990) and usually exhibit the following characteristics: (i) participate early and often; (ii) focus on communication quality as well as quantity; (iii) demonstrate competence; and (iv) help build a cohesive unit (Hackman and Johnson, 2000).

Researchers have identified characteristics of emergent leaders. McCroskey and Richmond (1998), for example, relate effective leadership to "talkativity". To measure the concept of talkativity, McCroskey and Richmond developed a "willingness to communicate" (WTC) scale, claiming that people with high WTC scores communicate more frequently and for longer periods of time than people with low WTC scores.

Northouse (1997) has defined leadership as "a process whereby an individual influences a group of individuals to achieve a common goal" (p.3). From this definition he identifies four types of leadership in terms of its components: (i) leadership is a *process*, which means that leadership is a transactional event that occurs between the leader and members of the group; (ii) leadership involves *influence* over group members; (iii) leadership occurs in a *group context*, which means the leader influences individuals who share a common purpose; and (iv) leadership involves *goal attainment*, which means that the leader not only influences a group of individuals but also directs them in terms of accomplishing a task or a common end. Each of these components has given rise to a number of theories. It is useful, therefore, to examine the theories from the perspectives of (i) the *leader*, (ii) the *group*, (iii) the *collaboration*, and (iv) the interactive *process* between leader and group.

2.5.1. Leader-centred theories

Leader-centred theories are those that assume there are unique qualities about leaders. One of the mostly widely known leader-centred theories is the *trait theory* (Bryman, 1992; Sorrentino, 1973; Zigon and Cannon, 1974). Initially developed in the early 1900s, it fell from favour in the mid-1990s but the theory is now experiencing a resurgence in interest (Northouse, 1997). Researchers supporting this theory claim that leaders are qualitatively different from nonleaders and possess innate qualities that set them apart; that is, the notion that leaders are born, not just made. Some of the characteristics commonly identified by researchers include intelligence, self-confidence, determination, integrity and sociability (Kirkpatrick and Locke, 1991; Lord, DeVader and Alliger, 1986; Mann, 1959; Stogdill, 1948; Stogdill, 1974). The main problem with the trait theory is that, after nearly a century of research, a universal and definitive list of traits has yet to be found, which brings into question the validity of the construct.

Another popular leader-centred theory is the *style theory* (Stogdill, 1948; Stogdill, 1974; Blake and Mouton, 1964). Whereas the trait theory focuses on the personality characteristics of the leader, the style theory focuses on the behaviour of the leader, particularly in the context of various group activities. Leaders are perceived as engaging in two kinds of behaviours: task behaviour and relationship behaviour. A number of measures have been developed to assess leadership styles, including the Leadership Behavior Description Questionnaire (Stogdill, 1963) and the Leadership Grid (Blake and McCanse, 1991; Blake and Mouton, 1969).

Lewin, Lippitt and White (1939) and White and Lippitt (1968) discuss three styles of leadership: authoritarian, democratic and laissez-faire. Authoritarian leaders create distance between themselves and their team members to emphasise role distinctions. Democratic leaders engage in more supportive communication to facilitate interaction between themselves and team members and encourage involvement and participation. Laissez-faire leaders, sometimes referred to as non-leadership (Bass, 1990), abdicate their responsibility and offer little guidance.

Leadership style has also been categorised in terms of management. McGregor (1960), for example, identifies two basic approaches to leadership – Theory X and Theory Y. Theory X managers believe employees dislike work and must therefore be coerced, controlled and threatened to achieve a goal. Theory Y managers believe employees derive satisfaction from work and therefore work more productively when given responsibility, some autonomy and opportunity for innovation and creativity.

Other leader-centred theories include *leadership as power* (the leader is a central catalyst that moves the group toward action) (French and Raven, 1959; McDavid and Harari, 1968; Fairhurst and Chandler, 1989), and *organisational theory* (power defined in terms of function and position within an organisational hierarchy) (Abraham and Smith, 1970).

There is also considerable literature which discusses the critical role of the leader in the development of the team (see, e.g., Duarte and Snyder, 1999; McShane and Von Glinow, 2000; Sarker et al., 2001). However, an assumption in this literature is that the leader is assigned or appointed. Very little research has involved the study of leadership emergence, particularly in a virtual team environment. One notable exception is the work of Yoo and Alavi (1996).

Leader-centred theories, however, fail to take into account the context of the group and the ability of the leader to adapt to changing situations.

2.5.2. Group-centred theories

Alternative theories to those centred around the leader are the group-centred theories. The most widely used in this category is the *situational theory* (Reddin, 1970; Blake and Mouton, 1969; Hershey and Blanchard, 1969; Hershey and Blanchard, 1975; Blanchard, Zigarmi and Nelson, 1993). This theory emphasises the adaptability of the leader to changes in situations and the needs of group members, assuming that different situations demand different kinds of leadership. According to Blanchard, Zigarmi and Zigarmi (1985), leaders need to diagnose the development level of a team in terms of competence and commitment and adjust their style accordingly. Four types of leadership style were identified – directing, coaching, supporting and delegating – each varying the level of direction and support provided.

Similarly, Vroom and co-workers (Vroom and Jago, 1978; Vroom and Yetton, 1973) claim that no one leadership style is best in all situations, and they identified rules for choosing a particular style for specific circumstance, e.g. when acceptance is important and disagreement is likely, do not use an autocratic style of leadership.

Snow, Snell, Davison and Hambrick (1996) describe a two-year study of international teamwork in thirteen companies. Their leadership model includes a changing role from advocacy in the early stages of team development, to a catalyst as the team evolves and finally to integration as the team matures.

Other group-centred theories include *contingency theory* (matches leaders to appropriate situations to ensure effective leadership) (Fiedler, 1964; Fiedler and Garcia, 1987), and *path-goal theory* (emphasises the relationship between the leader's style and the characteristics of the group and the work setting) (Evans, 1970; House and Mitchell, 1974).

The notion of choosing a leadership style in different group situations meshes well with the research on stages of group development. In the earlier stages of group development, for example, an autocratic style of leadership is warranted, whereas during periods of conflict a consultative or democratic style is more effective. Further support for the effectiveness of leadership adaptability is found in Vecchio's (1987) research. The work of Blake and Mouton (1982), identifying task and relationship styles of leadership is also relevant to group development. However, while these researchers argue that effective leaders pay equal attention to both autocratic and consultative styles throughout the group life cycle, Hershey and Blanchard (1977) argue that this balance should shift at different stages of group development.

It is useful, in the context of group-centred theories, to highlight the distinction between group leadership and facilitation. Group facilitation and leadership, though dedicated to the same outcomes, are not synonymous. Leaders are characteristically viewed as part of the group's membership, whereas group facilitators are often, by design, non-members brought into a group to serve specific functions for the group (e.g. provide feedback, gatekeep, and offer procedural guidance. Frey (1994) characterized group facilitation as practices that assist groups in accomplishing their goals. Barge (1996) made the same point in his characterization of leadership, explaining leadership as facilitating action that helps a group to achieve a goal. Fisher (1986) earlier noted that structuring and guiding group effort toward a goal is a function of leadership. Frey (1994) also noted that facilitation can encompass a variety of perspectives and practices, ranging from specific, leader-like group interventions to group-level instruction in communication processes or decision-making methods. The facilitator as an outside resource person is frequently employed by groups using electronic meeting management systems because this type of facilitation requires an individual who is specially trained both in group facilitation techniques and the system's technological functions (Anson, Bostrom and Wynne, 1995; Niederman, Beise and Beranek, 1996; Scott, 1999).

Most group facilitation activities emanate from one or possibly a couple of parties acting as independent facilitators. Group facilitation initiatives are rare enough to not be covered extensively in the literature. Stohl and Walker (2002) observed that group collaboration is substantially influenced by how effective the collaborators can be at engaging in *knowledge management*, which entails the acquisition and dissemination of reliable and valid information in a way that makes its application to collaborative tasks timely and optimally useful. This type of management is a particularly important aspect of distributed group collaboration. Keyton and Stallworth (2003) claim that the role of leading and facilitating collaborative groups takes on added significance because people who fulfil such roles are typically members of the collaborative group – they have a dual role that affects both their own participation and the overall direction of the collaborative group. This observation is consistent with Pavitt's (1999) conclusion that group leadership should be assessed by taking into account the cumulative impact of a leader's communication on group decision making.

Mabry (2002) noted that participation in mediated group contexts involves a complex interplay between the technological environment and a group's tasks and goals. Turoff's (1991) assessment of computer-mediated collaboration technologies led him to recommend the following set of factors that designers of asynchronous, CMC-based group support systems should include to address *meta-individual* (system-operability functions) and *group processes*:

1. *Regulation*: Managing participation, allocation and ordering of tasks, and process efficacy.

2. *Facilitation*: Organising, extrapolating and summarizing information and resources; filtering out irrelevant information; and integrating group efforts with group goals.

3. *Social-Emotional Activities*: Consensus building, identifying and resolving conflict, and promoting cooperation and cohesiveness.

Turoff's meta-process constructs appear analogous to the action mediational leadership dimensions proposed by Barge (1996). Regulation and facilitation are typically associated with activities that enhance group decision making, whereas social-emotional activities promote relational development and maintenance.

2.5.3. Collaborative Leadership

There is evidence that successful collaboration in computer-mediated groups is influenced by the factors that Turoff (1991) and Barge (1996) identified. Collaborative efforts can succeed if led effectively. Collaborative leaders focus on the process of decision making rather than on any particular outcome. This type of leader believes that diverse groups generate reasonable solutions if group members work together in constructive ways (Johnson, 1998). Collaborative leaders function as "first among equals" as they convene discussions, and facilitate group consensus and solution implementation (Hackman and Johnson, 2000).

Research by Poole and Holmes (1995) on facilitating collaboration in group decision support systems (GDSS) has shown that computer-mediated groups using technologies that assist in decision making are better able to influence group consensus, perceived decision quality, and group members' decision satisfaction than groups not using a GDSS. These results were observed even though computer-supported groups used more than one structurally distinct procedural process path in arriving at a decision. Recent assessments of group collaboration processes in virtual teams and organisations have also identified the development of trust and other attributes of personal relationships as key factors in successful collaborations (Handy, 1995; Jarvenpaa and Leidner, 1998; Kayworth and Leidner, 2000; Shockley-Zalabak, 2002). Walther (1994; 1997), for example, has shown that virtual group members' perceptions of the quality of a group's effort and relational climate (e.g. levels of trust, interpersonal immediacy and member similarity) are influenced by whether members anticipate having continued interaction with their teammates on subsequent group activities.

Barge (1996) and Fisher (1986) argue that leadership is systematic in the sense that it is a group's coherence mechanism for organising collective action and direction. Leadership can be viewed as a shared activity that helps to build cohesiveness in a group (Keyton and Stallworth, 2003).

The main problem with group-centred theories is that they fail to explain how different leadership styles directly affect the motivational levels of group members or the effect of interactive group processes on leadership style. An important conceptualisation, therefore, is to see leadership as a form of activity (Fleishman, 1973). The process-oriented theories were developed to overcome some of these difficulties.

2.5.4. Process-oriented theories

Probably the most widely researched of the process-oriented theories is the *transformational theory* (Burns, 1978; Downton, 1973; Sarros et al., 1999). This theory assumes there is a leadership process that changes and transforms individuals – a process that changes the members of the group and also the leaders themselves. Leadership is concerned with the kinds of values, ethics, standards and morals that an individual or society finds desirable or appropriate (Northouse, 1997). Two types of leadership are associated with this theory – transactional and transformational. The former involves an exchange between leaders and group members, such as offering a promotion to motivate employees or offering a good grade to motivate students. The latter involves a transformation in the level of motivation and morality in both the leader and the group. Sosik, Avolio and Kahai (1997) have shown in a longitudinal study that computer-mediated environments amplify the positive influence of transformational leadership on group outcomes relative to transactional leadership. Variants of the transformational leadership are the *vision theory* (leader focuses on identifying future needs and acting accordingly) (Rouche, Baker and Rose, 1989), and *ethical assessment* (leaders driven by a desire to serve the public) (Burns, 1978).

Another process-oriented theory is the *leader-member exchange theory*, in which leadership is conceptualised as a process that is centred on the interactions between leaders and group members (Dansereau, Graen and Haga, 1975; Graen, 1976). Recent research in this area focuses on the leader promoting partnerships with individual group members – a process that progresses through three phases (stranger, acquaintance and mature partnership) (Graen and Uhl-Bien, 1995).

A substantial body of research shows that leaders can *emerge* from a collaborative process. While there is usually a clear leader-subordinate relationship in a traditional organisational structure, in a team or group environment a leader (or leaders) appear to "emerge" through an interpersonal process in which an individual's contribution to a team is accepted and recognised by other group members (Uhl-Bien and Graen, 1992). A number of researchers have shown that leadership is a reciprocal, dyadic process between a leader(s) and other members (e.g. Farris and Lim, 1969; Graen and Scandura, 1987). However, in computer-mediated environments, Yoo and Alavi (2002) claim that:

> On the one hand, CMC might influence emergent leadership in distributed teams by making the communication processes more task-focused, which will lead to task-focused and vigilant evaluations of individuals' contribution. On the other hand, CMC might influence emergent leadership in distributed teams by depersonalizing the communication processes, which will lead to less salient emergent leadership in distributed teams.

In studying the role of leaders in virtual groups, it is useful to draw from each of the types of leadership theories and attempt to integrate the approaches, in the context of the particular needs of virtual groups. Table 2.2 summarises references related to the different leadership theories.

Table 2.2. Summary of literature on leadership

Leadership Theories	Researchers
Leader-centred theories	Bryman (1992), Sorrentino (1973), Zigon and Cannon (1974), Stogdill (1948; 1974), Blake and Mouton (1964), French and Raven (1959), McDavid and Harari (1968), Fairhurst and Chandler(1989), Abraham and Smith (1970)
Group-centred theories	Reddin (1970), Blake and Mouton (1969), Hershey and Blanchard (1969; 1975), Blanchard et al. (1993)
Collaboration-oriented theories	Gardner (1990), Johnson (1998), Chrislip and Larson (1994), Rost (1991; 1993)
Process-oriented theories	Burns (1978), Downton (1973), Rouche, Baker and Rose (1989), Dansereau et al. (1975), Graen (1976), Graen and Uhl-Bien (1976), Yoo and Alavi (1996; 2002)

2.6. Virtual Group Functionality

Much has been reported about virtual group characteristics, most of it relying on data from organisational case studies (Sproull and Kiesler, 1986; Zuboff, 1988), laboratory experiments (Dennis and Valacich, 1993; Dubrovsky, Kiesler and Sethna, 1991; Hill, 1982; Poole, Holmes, Watson and De Sanctis, 1993; Siegel, Dubrovsky, Kiesler and McGuire, 1986; Valacich, Paranka, George and Nunamaker, 1993; Valacich, Dennis and Connolly, 1994), surveys (Kiesler and Sproull, 1986; Schmitz and Fulk, 1991; Sproull, Kiesler and Zubrow, 1984), and educational settings (McInerney, 1995; Sudweeks, Lambert, Beaumont, Bonney, Lee and Nicholas, 1993; Sudweeks and Simoff, 2000; Landrum and Paris, 2000).

The literature highlights a number of functional and dysfunctional characteristics of virtual groups using a variety of methodologies. Among the attributes studied in laboratory-based experimental work are flaming behaviours (McGuire, Kiesler and Siegel, 1987; Siegel et al., 1986; Sproull and Kiesler, 1991), disinhibition and deindividuation (Hiltz and Johnson, 1989; Matheson and Zanna, 1990) and the ambiguity of the communication (Daft and Lengel, 1986; Trevino, Lengel and Daft, 1987; Walther, 1992). Hiltz, Johnson and Turoff (1986) find CMC in virtual groups to be cold and unsociable when compared to face-to-face contexts. Somewhat more optimistic experimental work produced findings on reflective interaction (Harasim, 1990), status leveling (Dubrovsky et al., 1991), equalising effect of participation (Hartman, Neuwirth, Kiesler, Palmquist and Zubrow, 1995; Olaniran, 1994), consensus formation (Dennis and Valacich, 1993; Valacich et al., 1994), friendships (Baym, 1995; Walther, 1992), brainstorming, creativity and productivity (Valacich et al., 1993; Harasim, 1993). Important as they may be, these concepts neither disprove nor explain the growth of virtual groups. Nor do these concepts explain the "social glue" of these virtual groups; that is, a description of the way in which virtual groups come and hold together.

The picture of virtual groups painted by summing laboratory studies may be somewhat incomplete. The external validity of laboratory studies of groups is problematic for four reasons: (i) subjects are an atypically captive audience; (ii) groups studied in experiments tend to be unrealistically small; (iii) an almost natural inclination of experimental design is to contrast computer mediated communication with a face-to-face standard of comparison; and (iv) experimental groups have a zero history and exist for a very short time period. Hence, results of these studies may be misleading.

Surveys and case study evidence help to complete the picture of virtual groups. Many field studies focus on the narrow bandwidth and cue deficiencies that typify virtual group communication (Short, Williams and Christie, 1976; Rice and Associates, 1984). One of the features that differs between text-based CMC and face-to-face interaction is the degree of dramaturgical expression. The absence of nonverbal behaviour such as as taking the head seat, social distance, tone of voice, touching, gesturing and eye contact, changes group interaction, negotiation and collaboration. Group members have reduced accountability towards others because of the lack of social control that nonverbal cues provide (Rice and Love, 1987). Richer communication environments may assist. However, more bandwidth does not necessarily ensure more effective interaction.

According to various researchers, the fewer channels or codes available within a medium, the less each participant is aware of others using the same medium. The term *social presence* was introduced by Short, Williams and Christie (1976) who defined social presence as "the salience of the other in a mediated communication and the consequent salience of their interpersonal interactions" (p. 65). The origin of the social presence construct, however, can be traced to Mehrabian's (1969) concept of immediacy, which he defines as "those communication behaviors that enhance closeness to and nonverbal interaction with another" (p. 203). According to Mehrabian, nonverbal cues lead to more intense and more immediate interactions.

Communication theorists extended his work investigating the impact of the mediation of a variety of media. Culnan and Markus (1987) also use the term social presence. From a different perspective, Sproull and Keisler (1986; 1991) argue that the critical difference between face-to-face communication and mediated communication is the absence of social context cues. They describe a number of communication behaviours typical in mediated environments such as uninhibited communication (i.e. flaming) and non-deference to higher-status participants (i.e. hierarchical flattening).

The social presence construct has been discussed by various researchers (e.g. Rice and Associates, 1984; Walther, 1992). The fewer channels or codes available within a medium, they claim, the less each participant is aware of others using the same medium, i.e. the lower the social presence. CMC, with its lack of nonverbal cues and paucity of nontextual cues, is low in social presence and preferred for tasks low in interpersonal involvement. Social presence is regarded as a property of the communication medium. The construct, a subjective measure of the presence of others, is both intriguing and weakly defined. Garrison and co-workers (Garrison, Anderson and Archer, 2000; Rourke, Anderson, Garrison and Archer, 1999) have attempted to define the construct more rigorously and derived three categories of social presence: emotional expression, open communication and group cohesion. *Emotion expression* includes the use of emoticons, humour and self-disclosure; *open communication* includes responding and referring explicitly to the content of messages (similar to the interactivity construct described by Rafaeli (1988) and Rafaeli and Sudweeks (1997; 1998)), asking questions and expressing agreement; *group cohesion* includes phatics, greetings, use if inclusive pronouns (e.g. "we", "our", etc.) and addressing other participants by name.

There is evidence that a high proportion of socioemotional communication can be conveyed in CMC (Rice, 1987; Rice and Love, 1987). In fact, a presence, or even an awareness of a presence, may not be a mandatory ingredient of a stimulating and satisfying conversation and in some situations is a disadvantage: "When messages are very simple or unequivocal, a lean medium such as CMC is sufficient for effective communication ... because shadow functions and coordinated interaction efforts are unnecessary." (Daft and Lengel, 1986, p.57)

Rice and Love (1987) identify a significant amount of socioemotional content in messaging with CMC systems (albeit both positive and negative emotions) – an amount that increases with increased usage. Self reports of virtual group members are often in contradiction to the notion of media poverty; experienced members sometimes rate CMC as richer than even face-to-face communication (Steinfield, 1986b). In fact, virtual groups typically exhibit a high degree of group cohesiveness (Sanderson, 1996; Schein, 1992; Smircich, 1983; Markus and Robey, 1988). According to Mudrack (1989) the classical description of a cohesive group is "one that 'sticks together' – one whose members are 'bonded' to one another and the group as a whole" (p. 39). The most common measure of group cohesiveness is the Gross Cohesiveness Scale (GCS) (Cota, Dion and Evans, 1993), which is a subjective appraisal of the attractiveness of the group by its members. Another variation of this measure is equating group cohesiveness to interpersonal attraction (Aiken, 1992)

Trevino, Daft and Lengel (1987) discuss "media richness", noting that CMC is commonly compared unfavourably with face-to-face interpersonal communication. Macaulay (1995) describes text-based CMC in terms of two visual channels only – language content and presentation. Language content includes both manifest (explicit) and latent (implicit) information. Presentation includes additional information that can be conveyed by layout. Face-to-face communication, on the other hand, has access to both visual and audio channels. In addition to the information conveyed by language content (manifest and latent), there are extraneous vocalisations and the visual channel provides information about the interlocutor, such as general appearance, facial expression, body movement and psycho-physiological responses (Figure 2.1).

Other field-based studies, mostly in organisational contexts, search for reasons people join virtual groups, frequently arriving at social influence or cultural construction explanations (Fulk, 1993; Steinfield, 1987; Schmitz and Fulk, 1991). Common to these studies is a focus on constructs such as social influence and critical mass. These are all external qualities, not internal to the communication setting. A focus on content has led some to study creative ways in which members of virtual groups seek to break the bandwidth barrier. For example, the topic of nonverbal behavior on the net – in particular the use of emoticons – has been the subject of much study (Carey, 1980; Hellerstein, 1989; Blackman and Clevenger, 1990; Reid, 1991; Witmer, 1998).

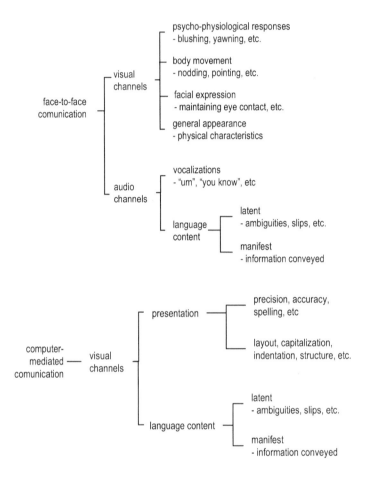

Figure 2.1. Comparing the richness of FTF and CM communication (after McCaulay, 1995).

Case studies of individual virtual groups appear to be more upbeat and optimistic (Danowski and Edison-Swift, 1985). Finholt and Sproull (1990) observed virtual groups within an organisation behaving like "real" social groups, despite the fact that their members shared no physical space, were *invisible*, and their interaction was asynchronous. Hahm and Bikson (1989) report on a field study among retired and employed individuals, in which CMC resulted in increased interaction among members of the group. From the perspective of searching for the "social glue", it seems unlikely that factors such as social presence or the use of emoticons hold the answer. However, because they are case studies of single groups and often intraorganisational, these studies, too, do not offer a convincing driving force that would explain the cohesive "netting" force of virtual groups.

Online group decisions are claimed to be unpredictable, unconventional, democratic, and less constrained by high-status members (Sproull and Kiesler, 1991). In the absence of modifying nonverbal and nonvocal cues, individual influence on group processes is more equitable as there is less emotional and social cost when face-to-face confrontation is remote or non-existent. The consequence of uninhibited behaviour is not necessarily negative. Text-based CMC provides a rich medium that facilitates the formation of a workable group structure featuring both anarchy and democratic leadership in its development (Sudweeks and Rafaeli, 1996; Rafaeli and Sudweeks, 1998; Sanderson, 1996).

Table 2.3 summarises references related to some of the characteristics of virtual groups.

Table 2.3. Summary of literature on virtual group functionality

Characteristics of Virtual Groups	Researchers
Dysfunctional aspects	
Flaming	McGuire, Kiesler and Siegel (1987); Siegel, Dubrovsky, Kiesler and McGuire (1986); Sproull and Kiesler (1991)
Disinhibition/deindividuation	Hiltz and Johnson (1989); Matheson and Zanna (1990)
Decreased social interaction	Hiltz, Johnson and Turoff (1986)
Decreased social presence	Short, Williams and Christie (1976); Rice (1984); Culnan and Markus (1987)
Decreased social context cues	Sproull and Kiesler (1991)
Media poverty	Trevino, Daft and Lengel (1990)
Difficulties with nonverbals	Carey (1980); Hellerstein (1989); Blackman and Clevenger (1990); Reid (1991)
Functional aspects	
Status levelling	Dennis and Valacich (1993)
Consensus formation	Dubrovsky, Kiesler and Sethna (1991)
Coping with nonverbals	Rice and Love (1987); Steinfield (1986a)
Cohesiveness	Finholt and Sproull (1990)
Increased social interaction	Hahm and Bikson (1989)
Increased productivity	Sanderson (1996)

2.7. Research Questions of Interest

The area of interest in this book is computer-mediated collaborative groups; specifically, developmental and leadership characteristics of both structured and unstructured collaborative groups.

2.7.1. Developmental characteristics

The development of groups over time has been researched extensively. The literature primarily addresses two types of groups: the traditional (face-to-face) group and the virtual team. That there are definable stages throughout the group life cycle is well established. Less certain is whether the stages are progressive, recurring or cyclical, and whether the virtual group life cycle is similar to the traditional group life cycle. Very little is known about virtual collaborative groups outside the structured organisational environment.

Similarly, while there is a substantial literature on *how* group members communicate throughout the life cycle of the group, less is known about *what* group members communicate. That groups do attempt to balance task and socioemotional needs throughout their life cycle is fairly well substantiated, but it is not clear how these needs interact with the groups maturity level.

There are various similarities and differences between developmental aspects of face-to-face and virtual groups, and hence many potential areas to investigate and develop theories. However, in the context of this book, it was important to focus on a set of specific aspects capable of being investigated within the constraints of the project. These focus on stages of virtual group development and the balance between directly task related and socioemotional communication.

Perhaps the most widely researched component of virtual groups is their functional/dysfunctional aspects. The literature reports numerous dysfunctional characteristics and equally as many functional characteristics. There is very little research, however, on the "social glue" – the ingredients that contribute to social cohesion. This gap in the literature therefore begs many questions about virtual group characteristics.

The selected research questions of interest relating to computer-mediated group development, therefore, are as follows:

1. Are there definable developmental stages?
2. Does the content of communication change during the lifecycle of the collaborative group and according to the level of task activity?
3. Does the level of personal disclosures change at different times?
4. Does the level of group cohesiveness change at different times?

2.7.2. Leadership characteristics

Much has been written about leadership characteristics but there is a lack of consensus about whether leaders are born with unique traits or whether leaders acquire a specific leadership style through training and experience. There is also some divergence in opinion about the effect of group members on leadership behaviour, and to what degree a leader can adapt his or her style to the needs of the group. This divergent body of research thus gives rise to many interesting questions regarding the role of leaders in virtual groups. Only a specific set of issues are addressed in this book. The selected research questions related to leadership characteristics in computer-mediated groups are as follows:

1. Do leadership management style and strategies change at different times during the collaborative process?
2. Does leadership become more collaborative over the lifecycle of the group?

2.8. Summary

This chapter reviewed the literature related to the research questions of interest. The literature review documented various definitions of groups and described different types of virtual groups.

Virtual groups are an interesting phenomenon to investigate as their communication is neither mass nor interpersonal, and neither written nor spoken (in the traditional sense). Social virtual groups have proliferated on the Internet – groups formed from common interests using media ranging from simple text email to 3D virtual worlds. Less common, though, are collaborative virtual groups – groups formed either voluntarily and spontaneously or formed for a specific collaborative activity.

How do virtual collaborative groups develop? How do leaders manage groups of people who are unknown in the traditional sense?

While there has been an impressive amount of research on developmental and leadership aspects of face-to-face collaborative groups, the literature review has highlighted the need for further work in this area on virtual collaborative groups.

Chapter 3 describes Case Study 1 – a group of volunteer researchers who collaborated on a project over a two year period using asynchronous communication. Chapter 4 describes Case Study 2 – a group of students who collaborated on a learning activity over a two-and-a-half period using synchronous communication.

CHAPTER 3

CASE STUDY 1

The first case study discussed in this book is the ProjectH Research Group, a two-year collaborative research project conducted by an international group of volunteer scientific researchers. The collaborative activity of ProjectH was the collection and analysis of data from elecronic discussion groups.

This chapter describes the research activity of ProjectH participants. It describes the history of the group, how the participants collected the data, and how the participants analysed the data. The data described in this chapter, therefore, is the data collected by the ProjectH participants.

The data analysed for this book, though, is the communication among ProjectH participants as they carried out their research study on computer-mediated groups. The first case study for this book, therefore, could be referred to as a meta-study; that is, it is a study of a computer-mediated group who were researching computer-mediated groups. The analysis of the ProjectH case study is provided in Chapter 7. The data collected for the analysis in Chapter 7 are the archives of interactions among the participants of ProjectH, a survey for demographic information, in-depth interviews with key stakeholders, as well as the author's own observations as a participant in the project.

This chapter is an introduction to, and descriptive overview of, the activities of the ProjectH Research Group, including:

- Aims
- Project coordinators and members
- History
- Structure
- Project integrity
- Data sources
- Project task
- Coders
- Outcomes

3.1. Background

Decades ago, McLuhan (1964) foresaw a global network creating a global village. It turns out that the 'global village' is neither global nor village. The organising principle of the global network is the *virtual neighbourhood*. Virtual neighbourhoods are loosely coupled entities called *discussion groups*, which are defined by common interest rather than geography.

The depth of interactivity varies widely among discussion groups. Some groups are like cocktail parties with many conversations (threads) competing, rather like CB radio. Some focus around specific topics ranging from postcard collecting to yacht design. Some are like noticeboards in the local grocery store where messages are pinned and left for others to read and comment on; and some groups merely function as newspapers, disseminating electronic journals or computer programs, and advertising conferences or job vacancies. Many people are content to just read and listen, even in the most interactive groups, while a relatively few dominate conversations.

The data sources for the ProjectH group were publicly archived messages from discussion groups (or virtual neighbourhoods). Although discussion groups share a similar aim (to provide a forum for the discussion of mutual interests among interested participants), they are dissimilar in various aspects such as creation processes, structure, network, and method of delivery.

The project was conceptualised in May 1992 when an email message about group dynamics was posted to a public discussion group that provides a forum for academic discussion on communication-related topics. The email message caught the imagination and enthusiasm of subscribers to the list and within a few days, some 40 participants of that discussion group agreed to collaborate in a research study to capture the nature of online communication, culture and community formation (Sudweeks and Rafaeli, 1996; Rafaeli, Sudweeks, Konstan and Mabry, 1998).

ProjectH was selected as the first case study for this book because of the pioneering nature of the collaborative process, and because the author was privileged to be a participant from its inception. The research carried out by the ProjectH group, from conception to consummation, was entirely computer mediated, asynchronous, 'on stage', and public. Records of all discussions, decisions, actions, tools and policies were (and are) available. The project as a case study is unique – rarely is one privileged to observe the very beginning of an evolutionary process. In this sense, this case study includes consideration of one of the most poorly recorded aspects of groupwork - the initial concept.

Case Study 1 does not involve an analysis of the results of the ProjectH group's research activities, but an analysis of the ProjectH participants as they communicated and collaborated on their research project.

3.2. ProjectH Aims

The research conducted by the ProjectH Research Group was a quantitative study of the characteristics and content of electronic group discussions. The aims of their research were to:

1. randomly sample a sizable chunk of publicly available, archived computer mediated group discussions;
2. analyse the content of messages contained in the sample;
3. focus on the single message, authors, aggregate thread and the lists as units of analysis;
4. empirically test hypotheses of interest to participants;
5. collect descriptive data to document the state of the medium and the communication using the medium;
6. create a shared database to serve future cross-method, cross-media or historical analyses; and
7. conduct computer-supported collaborative research in a manner unpre-cedented at that time - working with an online group of people diverse in interests, time, age, status and location.

3.3. ProjectH Coordinators and Members

The project was, at the time, a novel approach to groupwork as the participants had never met, either online or offline. It was a collaborative endeavour in that a collective group created specific common goals. Furthermore, the creation of a joint piece of intellectual property, in this case a database of coded discussion lists, is a joint work effort. As group participants went through the process of defining, collecting and utilising the information for the database, group participants built a social and intellectual foundation that strengthened and sustained the collaboration (Sanderson, 1996). Leadership was both assigned and emergent. Two participants who facilitated the collaborative activity were assigned leaders, while committees of emergent leaders recommended policies and processes. However no individual or group controlled the project. Computer-mediated asynchronous communication, both public and private, was used for coordination, participant recruitment, distribution of information, formulation and discussion of policies, decision making, encouragement and technology transfer.

The *coordinators* of ProjectH took on the facilitating role of encouraging the group to work together interdependently in a collaborative manner. The coordinators spent more than 3,000 hours, mostly online, coordinating the project. They fulfilled two facilitative roles within the group: (i) the accomplishment of the project goals, and (ii) the collaborative group process. At the time of the project (1992-94), one of the coordinators, Dr Sheizaf Rafaeli, was an Associate Professor and Head of the Information Systems Division in the School of Business Administration at the Hebrew University of Jerusalem, Israel. He had published on interactivity, computer-administered dialogue, software economics and theft, cable television, electronic bulletin boards, political communication, and decision support systems. He has an eclectic background having been a juvenile delinquent street gang instructor, sailor, prisoner, military officer, journalist, and computer software programmer. The other coordinator is the author of this book. At the time, she was a doctoral student in communication studies at the University of Sydney.

The *ProjectH members* were an international group of scholars. The number of members varied at any one time between 40 and 180 throughout the two-year period but, there were 143 members who were consistently involved in the project. The members represented a wide range of disciplines, ages, positions and nationalities (see Section 6.1.1 for member demographics).

3.4. ProjectH History

Table 3.1 itemises the key events of this project in chronological order. The events are described in this chapter and relevant documents included in Appendix A.

Table 3.1. ProjectH key events.

Date	Event
25 May 1992	Levine's Law posted to CMC-L
29 May 1992	Straw man proposal for a study
May-June 1992	Research questions and hypothesis developed
1 June 1992	Interim mailing list established for interested people
6 June 1992	Poll of CMC-L subscribers posted
10 June 1992	Mailing list moves to ProjectH, a CIOS-sponsored hotline
11 June 1992	Posting of short biographies of ProjectH participants
11-25 June 1992	Ethics dilemma (206 messages)
June-August 1992	Words-L controversy
July-August 1992	Codebook creation
15 January 1993	Solicitation of new participants on lists and news groups
28 January 1993	Posting of copyright policy
7 February 1993	Posting of ethics policy
22 February 1993	Posting of sampling policy
12 March 1993	Posting of reliability policy
15 March 1993	Sampling and downloading of discussion lists begun
April-October 1993	Coding of discussion lists (see codebook)
15 October 1993	Coding completed
15 October 1993	Access to data form and agreement form distributed
19 March 1994	Last post to ProjectH
11-15 July 1994	ICA panel presentation
1998	*Network and Netplay: Virtual Groups on the Internet* published by MIT

On 25 May 1992, David Levine (1992) posted an email message to CMC-L, a Comserve discussion list for people interested in computer-mediated communication, outlining his theory of mediated group dynamics. Briefly, his theory was that people with too much time and uninteresting things to say in an electronic conversation drive out the busy people who have more interesting things to say (see Appendix A.1 for the complete post).

Levine's theory, which he named "Levine's Law", was the catalyst for an intensive two-year project to investigate the nature of communication, culture and community in a networked computer-mediated environment. At the time, interacting with strangers on a daily basis on the Internet was a novel experience. Research on the topic was sparse and little had been documented about the interactivity that develops among people who never physically meet.

Levine's post to the CMC-L discussion list about the nature of electronic conversations initiated a lengthy "thread"[1] as people commented on the theory. It became obvious that electronic discourse was of interest to many academics, which prompted one subscriber of CMC-L to suggest:

> Someone could do a study of all this, comparing lists of subscribers at different time periods, seeing who's still on, how many subscribers there are, etc. (u_1, 25/5/92)[2]

and another subscriber to respond:

> Hmmmmm....., as you think about it, wouldn't this kind of study be relatively simple (albeit time consuming)? It's something a grad assistant could do in a semester or maybe a few of us could do by dividing up a few randomly chosen groups, whipping into SPSS format, and writig[3] something up (as if we don't have enough to do already) (u_4, 26/5/92)

A few days later, interest in a possible collaborative study increased and another subscriber supported the commencement of a research project:

> OK. Here goes. I'm in this for the experience. Put my keyboard where my mouth is. I've been claiming (for ten years) that e-mail holds the potential to form communities out of thin air (thin bits?). Have been, mostly, ridiculed. So lets give it a try (u_{15}, 29/5/92)

---

[1] A series of messages that have been posted as replies to each other. A single forum or conference typically contains many threads covering different subjects. By reading each message in a thread, one after the other, you can see how the discussion has evolved. (Webopedia's definition, http://webopedia.internet.com/TERM/t/thread.html).

[2] The format for referencing participants' posts throughout this book is the utterance number (u_{xx}) followed by the post date.

[3] Excerpts throughout this book are quoted verbatim, including spelling and grammatical errors.

The same subscriber also submitted a 'straw man' proposal of 'things to do' (see Appendix A.2), and suggested the study focus on the nature and longevity of news group threads:

> ... I broke the tasks down to four categories: Generating hypotheses, codebook, identification of lists, and actual coding. I am sure there will be many volunteers for analysis. ... Standing proposal: Let's see if we can sustain discussion of the following points for a few weeks, and aim for crystallized codebook and sample within a month or two? ... (u_{15}, 29/5/92)

By 1 June 1992, twenty CMC-L subscribers had expressed interest in participating in such a study. Those subscribers of the discussion list who were not interested, though, began to object to the 'noise'[4] and requested that discussions be taken 'offline'. As the topic of the proposed study was directly related to the topic of the discussion list, supporters of the study objected to the disgruntled subscribers' objections. The situation was clarified by a survey of CMC-L subscribers.

On 6 June, subscribers of CMC-L were polled on their opinions about the proposed project and their preferred working environment. Respondents were asked to email their responses to one of three subscribers who were facilitating the organisation of the proposed project at that stage. The questions included:

1. Are you willing to take part in the work involved in a quantitative study?
2. How much time do you anticipate you will be able to contribute between now and 30 September?
3. Which of the following do you prefer?
    (a) Stay on CMC: let the discussion be open to more joiners, suggestions, and public scrutiny.
    (b) Break off into a separate group. The congestion on CMC and suggestions from non-participants are counterproductive.
    (c) I have no preference.

Also included in the survey was a list of suggested variables to explore in the study with a request to rank them in importance (see Appendix A.3 for the full survey).

In the interim, an alias address[5] for the embryonic study was created and used while waiting for responses to the survey. Also during this waiting period, one of the facilitators applied for, and was granted, a Comserve/CIOS[6] 'hotline'[7] on which to conduct the study.

---

[4] Excessive messages, particularly messages which are superfluous, do not add anything to the discussion, and do not interest the majority of members.
[5] The alias address was set up at Sydney University, cmclist@archsci.arch.su.oz.au.
[6] In 1986, the Comserve service was established to facilitate a set of online activities for communication researchers. As Comserve services diversified and usership increased it became appropriate to create an organisational structure that would nurture and protect the investments of

The results of the poll were posted to CMC-L on 10 June:

> A majority of respondents have indicated preference for staying on CMC. However, enough CMC regulars have stated that we are clogging up their boxes with unwanted mail, and obstructing traffic that could have otherwise taken place. Not wishing to overstay our welcome, we are moving to a private hotline. We will, for the time being, continue to accomodate lurkers who wish to observe the new hotline. The people who have been in contact with Sarah[8] or me ... will be receiving instructions about joining the new hotline. Others who wish to join, are encouraged to e-mail us. Discussion will pick up in the new location. We will still visit the COMSERVE CMC list with periodic summaries, but these, I promise, will be infrequent. Adios for now, thanks for hosting us this far! (u_{129}, 10/6/92)

Two days later (12 June) the initial number of interested people had doubled to 40, and they all 'moved' to the CIOS-funded hotline[9]. The first task was to "get to know" a little about each other and this was achieved by each participant posting a short biography about themselves – a practice that was requested of every person joining ProjectH. This initial group of 40, plus many others who joined over the following two years, became the ProjectH Research Group.[10]

3.5. Organising Structure of ProjectH

Collaborating in a heterogeneous group, in which the only available contact is an email address, has both negative and positive aspects. Communication among a group of strangers is not easy; communication among a group of strangers with whom continued contact depends on a shared understanding and the whims of temperamental technology can be frustrating. However, the challenge of conducting a large-scale project on the Internet was the initial motivation for forming ProjectH and this challenge sustained the group through the rough patches.

Mediated communication requires a considerable time commitment from all participants. Between May 1992 and March 1994, group participants exchanged

---

time, energy, and resources contributed to the project by so many individuals and institutions. In 1990, the Communication Institute for Online Scholarship (CIOS) was inaugurated, being designed to function as a parent organisation of Comserve. CIOS is a non-profit US organisation, supporting the use of computer technologies in the service of communication scholarship and education. It is supported primarily through individual and institutional memberships, through the publication of its journal (*Electronic Journal of Communication/La Revue Electronique de Communication*, and through sales of software products to assist communication scholarship (e.g. ComIndex). More information about CIOS can be found at http://www.cios.org.

[7] The CIOS electronic conference system is an email-based mass distribution system that is accessible through the CIOS email interface. The CIOS hotline system supports projects relevant to its aim; that is, to link individuals who share interests in the study of human communication processes.

[8] Due to ethical reasons, pseudonyms have been given to participants to protect their identity.

[9] The hotline address was ProjectH@Rpiecs (Bitnet) or ProjectH@Vm.Ecs.Rpi.Edu (Internet).

[10] CIOS numbered their funded hotlines alphabetically. Since the new research group was granted the eighth funded hotline, it was given the eighth letter of the alphabet, i.e. 'H'. Initially there were suggestions for providing an imaginative meaning for 'H' but finally it remained simply 'ProjectH'.

1,130 public messages (messages distributed to all group participants and subsequently archived in the public domain). Throughout this period, there were highly active episodes interspersed with periods of little activity. The monthly list traffic figures are given in Figure 3.1.

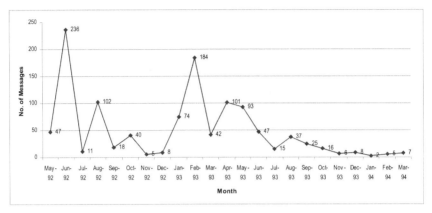

Figure 3.1. ProjectH communication (number of messages x month).

A frequent characteristic of computer-mediated groups is the democratic nature of the mode in which people interact. In the process of collecting a large representative database of CMC, a blend of democracy and restrained 'leadership' evolved as ProjectH's organisational structure. The term *leadership* is qualified because the coordinators were facilitators in their leadership style and assigned from the collaborative process. The only restrictions on people participating equally in generating ideas and developing policies and methodologies were self-imposed restraints such as time limitations, conflicting schedules, and degree of motivation. The coordinators were merely instrumental in facilitating a productive working environment.

The process of group decision making, in particular, highlights the facilitating style of leadership. There were key points during the course of the project at which it was necessary to agree on critical issues. The issues impacting on the integrity of the ProjectH group's research were: (i) *ethics* of downloading and analysing email messages exchanged in a public forum; (ii) *copyright and intellectual property* of the coded database resulting from the analysis of the email messages; and (iii) *access to the database* which was coded by approximately one-third of the participants. The major methodological issues were: (i) *sampling* of email messages to ensure randomisation; (ii) *coding* of the email messages according to variables of interest;

(iii) *reliability* of the coding scheme; and (iv) *'mechanics'* in terms of the technologies for coding and validation.

As each issue was raised, a general discussion usually exposed a wide range of participant opinions. The first issue to be raised in June 1992 was the ethics of downloading and analysing archived list discussions. After a heated debate in which participants exchanged 206 email messages over a period of two weeks without reaching a consensus on an ethics policy for the project, it was obvious that a more efficient structure and management of communication was needed.

When subsequent issues were raised, the coordinators focused and summarised expressed opinions. If it was obvious that all factors relating to an issue had been raised and group consensus unlikely, a committee was formed for further discussion. Such committees comprised 3-10 volunteers who represented the divergent opinions of the group. The task of the committee, in each instance, was to draft a compromise proposal to present to the group, summarising the advantages and disadvantages of options considered and the rationale for choosing one over others. Proposals were posted to the whole group for further discussion or fine-tuning, and a time frame (usually a week) given for further objections. All but one of the committee proposals were adopted without further revision. Figure 3.2 illustrates the evolutionary management process.

(a)   (b)   (c)   (d)   (e)

Figure 3.2. Evolutionary management process of ProjectH.

(a) an amorphous group of individuals; (b) a small group of people, led by the coordinators (dark grey), share ideas; (c) the group expands and small committees (light grey) representing diverse persuasions draft proposals for the group; (d) more committees are formed for different phases and leadership becomes more distributed; (e) individuals and small groups work on different projects using the shared database.

Using this process of committee management, five committees were formed during the project period: Copyright Committee, Sampling Committee, Reliability Committee, Mechanics Committee and the Oracles Committee. Each of these committees will be described in subsequent sections. Each committee exchanged between 20-152 messages (Figure 3.3) to draft a policy so this management strategy reduced list traffic to a minimum, and facilitated a collaborative style of leadership.

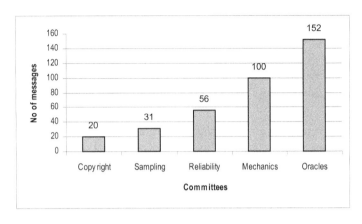

Figure 3.3. Communication within ProjectH Committees (number of messages)

3.6. ProjectH Research Integrity

Before commencing the research, it was necessary for ProjectH participants to address and resolve thorny issues that affected the study globally, such as ethics, copyright and ownership, and access to the collected data and subsequent database. Some questions to be resolved were:

1. Is there an ethical obligation to inform subscribers to a list that their communication is being analysed?
2. Is public discourse on lists really public?
3. Does the principle of 'expectation of privacy' apply?
4. Who holds the copyright of messages that are sent to a list?
5. Who owns the collaboratively-created database from the analysed messages?

In terms of copyright of list messages, the principles of the Berne Convention for the Protection of Literary and Artistic Works (1886)[11] were generally accepted as being applicable to electronic group discussions. Any work created privately was copyright and protected whether it had a copyright notice or not; therefore the copyright of a message to a public discussion group belonged to the author, but ownership belonged to the list owner or moderator. An exemption to restriction on use of copyright material is *fair use*, which was created to facilitate academic use of copyright works without the permission of the author. Fair use was the right to use a 'short excerpt' (informally accepted as a short paragraph) that does not harm the commercial value of the work.

---

[11] See http://www.wipo.org/eng/general/copyrght/bern.htm for more detailed information about the principles.

3.6.1. Ethics

A quantitative analysis of the aggregate of publicly available, archived content of large group discussions that occurred voluntarily may be considered to be subject to fewer ethical concerns than other types of analyses. The object of analysis in the project was not a human subject but human communication; that is, the words written by humans, not humans themselves.

Nevertheless, some ethical issues were raised and hotly debated in June 1992. The debate revolved around three major issues:

1. *Is public discourse on CMC public?*
   Some firmly believed that public posts should be treated like private letters. Regardless of widespread distribution and public access of the posts, there is an expectation of privacy. A post is sent to a list in the expectation that the audience is limited, definable and identifiable, and that the content is not redistributed and quantified. However, other participants regarded public discourse as public domain, and supported the proposed guidelines.

2. *Do authors of posts have any legal, ethical or moral rights?*
   Again, opinions were divergent. Some considered author permissions and citations should not even be optional - authors must be acknowledged and permission obtained if quotations are used. Some questioned the right to intrude in the lives and activities of others, regarding such intrusion as exploitation, particularly if listowners and/or subscribers are not consulted prior to browsing. Some expected that if copyright of public posts is surrendered on joining a list then this should be made clear to subscribers at the time of joining. Some considered use of posts should be governed by professional and academic guidelines, i.e. short excerpts can be quoted without author permission.

3. *To what extent do the issues of informed consent, privacy and intellectual property apply to a quantitative study?*
   The need for different guidelines for qualitative and quantitative research became obvious. In the quantitative study proposed, the object of analysis is the communication that is openly posted and distributed, not the personalities involved. The purpose in using quotes is to illustrate a representative example from a randomly chosen sample of discourse, so it is not necessary to include attribution nor seek author permission. One participant expressed grave concern about the implications of restrictive use and censorship on scientific enquiry:

> If we reify ethical rules/principles (rather than adhere to the spirit and intent of those principles), we risk empirical catatonia" (u_{188}, 13/6/92).

The debate had its humorous as well as hostile moments. Two participants who knew each other in 'real life' engaged in a light-hearted exchange:

> As stupid as Andrew is (and he knows it), I think he is right in this case (u_{157}, 11/6/92)

> As usual, Jeff's right (I know it), so shortly after this post, I fire-bombed his Porsche (u_{187}, 13/6/92)

Some participants were confused about the nature and process of the proposed quantitative research. Concerned that some of her discussions on another discussion list (Words-L) would be sampled and scrutinised, one ProjectH member attacked the integrity of the project by the following post to Words-L:

> Unless these academo-dweebs get down and dirty with us ..., the study is bound to be bogus from the start ... I'm highly unimpressed. They remind me of Masters and Johnson. All observation, no participation. (anonymous, cross-posted to ProjectH, u_{140}, 10/6/92).

Following a spate of flames in response to this message, participants' credentials were questioned and some responded by posting vitas and listing degrees. The flames were extinguished effectively with a well-timed post from one of the coordinators:

> Hi (or as they say around here: shalom - which also means peace): I think it's back to business time ... Am a bit offended that my credentials were not disputed. So, just in case anyone is interested: I have the longest, reddest, and prettiest beard in cyberspace ... Any challenges? (u_{447}, 26/6/92)

Much effort was devoted to compromising on a policy that all could accept as a framework for ethical and scholarly research. When consensus was unlikely after 206 posts to the group, discussion of this topic was put aside temporarily while other issues were discussed.

In February 1993, the ethics issues were confronted again, causing another burst of activity (see Figure 3.1 for a comparison of activity in June 1992 and February 1993 with other months). An Ethics Committee was formed to draft a policy. When it was submitted to the group for approval, objections were raised. A second draft of the policy was submitted. And a third, and a fourth. The repeated iterations were straining the groups' patience. Some, earlier on, had suggested a voting mechanism. The coordinators were intransigent about trying for a consensus. When it appeared likely that the group would vote on holding a vote, the coordinators acquiesced. In lieu of consensus a vote on the fourth draft was called for. In summary, the policy states that the issue of informed consent of authors, moderators and/or archiving institutions does not apply to a quantitative content analysis in which only publicly available text is analysed. Further, as public discussions have no commercial value, are publically archived, and are freely available, quoted material is governed by professional and academic guidelines. If possible, author permission would be sought to quote material and/or to be identified; otherwise short excerpts could be quoted without author permission with author identification kept confidential.

The policy (Appendix A.7) was ratified with a vote of 38:3 in favour. Not all participants voted. Some abstained, and asked that the abstention vote be recorded.

3.6.2. Copyright

Questions were also raised by participants about intellectual ownership and copyright: Who owns the messages that are sent to a discussion list? Who holds the copyright? As the project group was using public data, it was committed to conducting the study publicly and making the data available to all. A Copyright Committee drafted a policy (Appendix A.6) which was accepted unanimously by participants. It stated, in brief, that the processed data would be the intellectual property of those who participated in the work, with ProjectH Research Group holding copyright. Access to and use of the data set was on a hierarchical basis according to contribution rates (see Section 3.6.3 and Appendix A.11). After a two-year exclusive access period by ProjectH participants, the data set was available to the public at FTP and web sites.

3.6.3. Access

On completion of coding, the project participants agreed that the database should be available, in the first instance, to those who coded at least 100 messages, completed a form agreeing to comply with ethics and copyright policies, and specified the precautions that would be taken to protect author identification and the database (see Appendix A.11 for access conditions and Appendix A.12 for a copy of the Agreement Form). The following information was compiled, archived and made available immediately to eligible participants:

- databases
- data index (explanation of column/row numbers)
- list of listids, coderids, listnames and network
- corpora
- list of authorids and author names
- coder questionnaires
- technical report

In 1996, all the above data was made available publicly, with the proviso that ProjectH be appropriately cited in any publications resulting from the use of the database.

3.7. ProjectH Data Sources

The data sources for the ProjectH group were samples of publicly archived messages from discussion groups on BITNet, Usenet, and Compuserve. Each of these sources varied in history, structure, mode of delivery, ownership, and network accessibility. In the following sections, each of these sources will be described.

3.7.1. BITNet Data Source

BITNet[12] (Because It's Time Network) was an inter-university network which operated between 1981 and 1996. It began in the US in 1981 when Ira H. Fuchs and Greydon Freeman, of the City University of New York and Yale University respectively, decided that IBM's Network Job Entry (NJE) communications protocol[13] made computer-based communication practical between their universities. These two universities began using a leased telephone circuit for communications between accounts on their mainframe computers. BITNet reached across the US to California and was joined by its European counterpart EARN (European Academic and Research Network) in 1982. Other cooperating international networks joined, in the ensuing years, to make BITNet a worldwide network.

At its peak in 1991-92, BITNet connected some 1,400 organisations in 49 countries, for the electronic non-commercial exchange of information in support of research and education. In this cooperative network, each participating organisation contributed communications lines, intermediate storage, and the computer processing necessary to make its part of the network function. The network had a long and

---

[12] BITNet's development in the US was facilitated by an IBM grant in July 1984, which provided initial funding for the establishment of centralised network support services. The BITNet Network Information Center, BITNIC, received its initial funding from this IBM grant but, following the grant's conclusion in 1987, was funded entirely by membership dues from participating organisations. In 1987 the BITNet Executive Committee formed a nonprofit corporation whose members were the organisations participating in the BITNet network. In 1989, BITNet merged with the Computer+Science Network (CSNET), and adopted the new corporate name, the Corporation for Research and Educational Networking (CREN). The growth of the Internet overtook CSNET in 1991, and its services were discontinued.
[13] Although BITNet used IBM's NJE communications protocol, VAX/VMS systems actually constituted the majority of BITNet nodes; Unix and other systems were also supported, in addition to IBM systems running VM or MVS. BITNet was a 'store-and-forward' network. Information originating at a given BITNet-connected computer (node) was received by intermediate nodes and forwarded to its destination.

productive life, providing networking services to higher education and research. It played a major role in laying the groundwork for the widespread acceptance and use of the Internet as it proved the value of networking to higher education and motivated that community to take a leadership role in establishing NSFNet and the Internet.

BITNet provided nearly 3,000 discussion groups covering most topics of academic interest. It was also used for the transfer of data and software files, and for rapid transmission of 'interactive' messages and commands to software such as LISTSERV[14]. Gateways allowed the exchange of electronic mail between BITNet and the Internet, and also other networks.

For several years BITNet was the largest academic network in the world for computer-based communications, but by 1992-93 the number of academic organisations connected to the Internet outnumbered those using BITNet. The number of participants began to decrease in 1993 and BITNet finally ceased operating in 1996.

Discussion groups on BITNet were called *lists* because individuals joined groups by sending a message to a specified server and their email address was added to that group's subscriber list. All messages sent by each subscriber (or member) to the group were distributed automatically to the subscriber email list. Access to LISTSERV or similar software was usually the only prerequisite for the creation of a new list. As lists could be created at the whim of a single network user, a one-layer structure and a 'free-for-all' attitude characterised BITNet groups.

3.7.2. Usenet Data Source

Usenet was a world-wide distributed discussion system. It was a network of machines that hosted a shared collection of *articles* with one or more universally recognised labels, called *newsgroups*. Usenet sites included universities, businesses, home computers, and many others. There was no central authority of the Usenet.

In 1979, shortly after the release of V7 Unix with UUCP, two graduate students at Duke University, North Carolina (Tom Truscott and Jim Ellis), and a graduate student at the University of North Carolina (Steve Bellovin), developed the first version of the news software using shell scripts. At the beginning of 1980 the network consisted of just three machines. In 1981, the news software was rewritten by a graduate student at the University of California at Berkeley (Mark Horton), and a high school student (Matt Glickman) to cope with the ever increasing volume of

---

[14] LISTSERV is a software used for the management of subscription, distribution and archiving of electronic mailing lists.

news. By 1984, the increasing volume of news was becoming a concern, and the mechanism for moderated groups[15] was added to the software.

In late 1986, changes to the software included a new naming structure for newsgroups. Newsgroups were organised according to their specific areas of concentration. There were eight major[16] categories (Table 3.2).

Table 3.2. Usenet newsgroup categories

comp	Topics of interest to both computer professionals and hobbyists, including topics in computer science, software sources, and information on hardware and software systems
humanities	Groups discussing topics in the arts and humanities.
misc	Group addressing themes not easily classified into any of the other headings or which incorporate themes from multiple categories. Subjects include fitness, job-hunting, law, and investments.
news	Groups concerned with the news network, group maintenance, and software.
rec	Groups oriented towards hobbies and recreational activities.
sci	Discussions marked by special knowledge relating to research in or application of the established sciences.
soc	Groups primarily addressing social issues and socializing. Included are discussions related to many different world cultures.
talk	Groups largely debate-oriented and tending to feature long discussions without resolution and usually without appreciable amounts of generally useful information.

Since the groups are in a tree structure, the various areas are called hierarchies. Figure 3.4 illustrates how the hierarchy is structured.

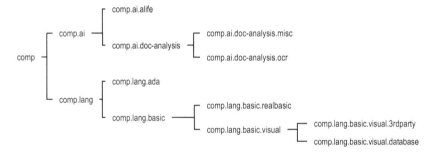

Figure 3.4. Example of Usenet newsgroup hierarchy

The transmission of Usenet news was entirely cooperative. 'Feeds'[17] were generally provided out of good will and the desire to distribute news everywhere.

---

[15] Some newsgroups insisted that the discussion remain focused and on-target. To serve this need, some groups became moderated groups. All articles posted to a moderated group were mailed to the group's moderator. He or she periodically reviewed the posts, and then either posted them individually to Usenet, or posted a composite digest of the articles for the past day or two.

[16] In addition to these major categories, there are alternative and special-purpose categories such as *alt* (true anarchy; subjects include sex, the Simpsons, and privacy), *gnu, biz, k12, iee, bionet*.

There were two major transport methods, UUCP[18] and NNTP[19]. The first was mainly modem-based and involved the normal charges for telephone calls. The second, NNTP, was the primary method for distributing news over the Internet.

Although newsgroups were circulated around the entire Usenet network, not all groups actually enjoyed world-wide distribution. For example, the European Usenet and Eunet sites took only a selected subset of the more technical groups; many sites in the US and Canada did not carry controversial 'noise'[20] groups (primarily the *talk* and *soc* classifications).

Whereas individual users could subscribe to any BITNet list and receive messages in their personal mailbox, access to newsgroups varied at each site. A site had to receive the news feed and users read messages with some kind of reader software, which nowadays is usually incorporated into MIME-encoded mailers or Web browsers. The number and types of newsgroups held, therefore, was influenced by factors such as administration and censorship policies, and amount of storage space.

The creation of new newsgroups in the *comp, humanities, misc, news, rec, sci, soc* and *talk* categories was more structured than the creation of a BITNet list. Any individual had the opportunity to create a newsgroup that was felt to be of benefit to the general readership. First, a discussion took place to address issues like the naming of the group, where in the group tree it should go (e.g. *rec.sports.charades* vs *rec.games.charades*), and whether or not it should be created in the first place. A formal Request For Discussion (RFD) was posted to *news.announce.newgroups*, and any other groups or mailing lists related to the proposed topic. The final name and charter of the group, and whether it would be moderated or unmoderated, and who the moderator would be, was determined during the discussion period. After the discussion period (which was mandatory), a Call For Votes (CFV) was posted to all the groups who received the original RFD. At the end of the voting period (between 21 and 31 days), the vote-taker posted the tally, the email addresses of votes received, and how each person voted to *news.announce.newgroups*. After the vote result was posted, there was a mandatory five-day waiting period. If there were a

---

[17] Delivery of newsgroup postings to a server on request.

[18] With UUCP, news was stored in batches on a site until a news 'neighbour' called to receive the articles, or the feed site happened to call. A list of groups that the neighbour wished to receive was maintained on the feed site.

[19] NNTP, on the other hand, offered a little more latitude with how news was sent. The traditional store-and-forward method was, of course, available. Given the 'real-time' nature of the Internet, though, other methods were devised. Programs kept constant connections with their news neighbours, sending news nearly instantaneously, handling dozens of simultaneous feeds, both incoming and outgoing.

[20] 'Noise' groups are those that have a large amount of traffic and data but little useful information.

100-vote margin and at least two-thirds of the total number of votes in favour of creation, and if there were no serious objections that might have invalidated the voting during the waiting period, then the newsgroup was created.

3.7.3. CompuServe Data Source

CompuServe was a commercial, privately-owned network. CompuServe forums had a two-layer structure: *SIGs* and *Sections*. Discussion groups were called SIGs (Special Interest Groups) and each SIG has a collection of subgroups called Sections. There were approximately 10-20 sections in each SIG on a diversity of subtopics. Creation of a new group was an expensive and complicated procedure so there was usually a substantial user base before a new group was formed.

At the time of sampling, there were approximately 1.5 million users of CompuServe and 350 forums. In addition to the forums, CompuServe offered large libraries of publicly available software. To join CompuServe in 1994, users paid a USD39.95 signup fee and USD8.95/month for unlimited access to 47 basic services (Williams, Sawyer and Hutchinson, 1995). CompuServe forums were led by professional online community leaders known as 'sysops' (Systems Operators) who worked primarily on a contract basis and were paid based on the number of hours subscribers spend in their areas.

By April 1997, although CompuServe had a 2.77 million paying customers worldwide, it lost $120 million on revenue. In a risky movement, CompuServe offered Web surfers limited access to more than 500 of its user forums. The forums were expected to attract new traffic that CompuServe could sell to advertisers. The change in business model also included a pay-per-view content and monthly subscription structure (Vonder Haar, 1997).

On 31 January 1998, a three-way deal between WorldCom (telecommunications company), America Online (AOL) and CompuServe took effect. Negotiated in the previous September, the complex transaction involved AOL acquiring CompuServe for $175 million which enabled WorldCom to sell CompuServe's consumer subscriber base of more than 2.5 million to AOL (Borzo, 1998). CompuServe and AOL, though, maintain independent online operations (Galante, 1998).

3.8. ProjectH Task

The alternatives for studying group CMC are numerous. One can use quantitative or qualitative methods. One may study societies, organisations, groups, coalitions within groups, individuals, or single messages. One may study cross-sectionally, or across time. The choice, of course, should be informed by intellectual interests and data availability, reliability and validity concerns. The ProjectH group perceived their optimal opportunity in terms of three factors:

1. The group was large.
2. One-shot, one-list studies had been done numerous times.
3. A focus on the self-reports of participants (which typifies much of the literature) needed validation from less obtrusive studies of the content of messages.

The ProjectH group chose a quantitative content analysis methodology because it was viewed as dovetailing with the large number of experimental (laboratory-based) studies of CMC, and the plethora of nongeneralisable surveys of single groups. The content analysis method is less sensitive to self-report and it focuses on the single message, the aggregate thread and the lists themselves.

The various stages of the methodology which the ProjectH group developed will now be described: (i) the conceptualisation of the nature of the project, (ii) sampling of the archived discussion groups, (iiii) coding of the data (email messages), (iv) the reliability of the coding scheme, and (v) the reliability of the coding process.

3.8.1. Conceptualisation

The initial, conceptual stage of the study involved deliberating on the unit of analysis, generating hypotheses and writing a codebook[21]. Research questions were many and varied, and included:

- What are the characteristics of longer and lasting threads?
- Does the longevity of lists relate to the number of participants, pace of discussion, interconnectedness of messages, amount and nature of meta-communication, emotic communication, interactivity, or chiming[22]?
- Are 'communities' formed on lists, and if so, how? Can social 'density' be measured? Can it be predicted, and/or manipulated by structural qualities of the list? Are any of the previously mentioned variables related to community formation? How? Can one discern the emergence of leadership on lists? Is leadership related to talkativity?
- How do 'free' or 'subsidised' lists compare with costly ones.
- Are there measurable differences between professional, academic and recreational lists.

---

[21] A codebook is a set of instructions for coding the data, i.e. a coding scheme.
[22] Chiming is intruding into a conversation on public electronic communication channels. It is not regarded as offensive or impolite.

- How does editorial intervention (moderation, collation, leadership, censorship) affect the nature of CMC?
- The gender issue: Historically, CMC studies documented almost only male participation. This has clearly (and positively) changed.
- The metacommunication concept/problem: How big is it? Is this the real downside of e-groups? Is it really a problem? How does it relate to social vs. task breakdowns of message content? How does metacommunication interact (statistically) with length of thread or intensity of social connection? Do all threads disappear down the metacommunication drain?
- What is the relative role (in collaboration, community formation, thread length) of asking vs telling, of information provision vs information demand?
- When and where does 'flaming'[23] occur? Is it dysfunctional? If so, how is it dysfunctional?
- Are there repeating patterns in the 'life' of a group, list, thread?
- How is the expression of emotion handled?
- What is the role, frequency and place of innovative forms of expression such as emoticons and smileys?

To accommodate this broad range of questions of interest, participants chose one or more of these questions and described a method for measuring the construct(s). The variables, with accompanying definition, extreme case examples, and measurement scale, were collated and formed the codebook. The codebook was pretested, assessed for reliability of measures and ambiguity of definitions and modified accordingly. The final comprehensive version of the codebook had 46 variables (Appendix A.10).

3.8.2. Sampling

Selecting a random representative sample of discussion groups was an important phase of the project. Initial discussions among the ProjectH participants revealed two divergent opinions on sampling:
- *Complete random sampling*; that is, pooling all groups from all networks and randomly selecting a sample.
- *Heavy stratification*; that is, selecting a set of strata and sample from within each stratum.

Given limited human resources and availability of accurate information on list characteristics, membership, authorship and readership, it was decided to adopt the

---

[23] Flames are messages that are intended to be hostile or aggressive. Flaming is the practice of attacking people on a personal level.

second alternative. A statement drafted by a Sampling Committee (Appendix A.8), whose members represented the spectrum of sampling persuasions within the group, recommended stratification by network and then random sampling within a restricted domain. The restricted domain excluded foreign language groups, groups on local networks, announcement groups, help/support groups for specific products, test and control groups, groups whose contents are only excerpts of other groups selected by moderators, and extremely low volume groups.

The next problem was to decide on how large a data sample should be taken from each group. List traffic is dynamic. Some groups are highly active, generating in excess of 200 messages a day; other groups are almost dormant, generating far fewer than 200 messages a year. Some groups maintain a consistent volume of traffic; other groups experience high peaks and low troughs. Sampling an equal number of messages from selected groups has the advantage of capturing threads. Sampling over an equal time period has the advantage of typifying group activity. Rather than risk having to reject a high percentage of groups because sampling happened to occur during a quiet period, a compromise was reached on a combination of numeric and time measures: 100 messages or three days worth of messages, whichever was the greater, beginning on a randomly selected Monday.

Population lists of lists, from which samples were to be selected, were collected from BITNet[24], Usenet[25] and CompuServe networks[26]. Lists clearly in the categories to be excluded were filtered out prior to random sampling (Table 3.3).

Table 3.3. Pre-filtered and post-filtered populations of lists.

	BITNet	Usenet	Compuserve	Total
Pre-filtered population of lists	3485	1868	337	5690
Post-filtered population of lists	1907	986	94	2987

A C program generated a specified number of random numbers within a specified range and matched the generated numbers against post-filtered populations of groups. With this random selection process, twenty lists from each of the three networks were selected for sampling.

The sampling period began on Monday 15 March 1993 and volunteer participants shared the task of downloading. BITNet lists were sampled using a DBase program. Internet newsgroups were downloaded from Usenet news. Articles

---

[24] A list of all known BITNet lists was obtained from Listserv@gwuvm.BITNet with a LISTS GLOBAL command.
[25] Four lists of Usenet newsgroups were FTP'd from rtfm.mit.edu.
[26] CompuServe groups presented a methodological complication. There was no available list of CompuServe sections so the CompuServe population is a list of SIGs, giving a deceptively low percentage of CompuServe groups.

were collected from news servers at the Royal Institute of Technology, Stockholm, Sweden; University of Minnesota, USA; University of Western Sydney, Nepean; and University of Sydney, Australia. Articles were collected according to the date and time of arrival at each news server.

Even with initial filtering, it was found that many of the downloaded lists did not meet the set criteria. It was therefore necessary to repeat the random selection process on filtered populations until there were 20 from each network meeting the criteria. In all, 77 BITNet lists, 39 Usenet newsgroups and 23 CompuServe SIGs[27] were selected from the filtered populations to get samples of 20 usable samples from each network.

3.8.3. Coding

Unexpectedly, few of the selected groups had 100 messages in less than three days so a standard numeric measure of 100 messages per group was used. Each batch of 100 messages downloaded from selected lists was prepared for coders. Programs were specially written to:

- split files of 100 messages into individual files
- renumber, if necessary, in numeric alphabetical order
- precode the first six variables: CODERID, LISTID, MSGNUM, AUTHORID, MSGTIME and MSGDATE
- compile a cumulative database of authors across all lists
- reassemble messages in one file

Numerous universal systems for coding were considered and rejected as coders varied in technical expertise, access to technology and Internet resources, and working style. A Technical Committee was formed to develop standard coding formats for different platforms: Hypercard stack for Macintosh, FileExpress database for DOS, and templates for text editors and wordprocessors.

After coding, data was exported as ASCII and emailed to an account dedicated to data processing. A C program and a suite of scripts verified and manipulated the data. The automatic processor involved five stages:

1. *Check if incoming mail is data.* Key strings were used to identify incoming mail as a data file. If one of the key strings were found, then the file was

---

[27] For CompuServe, the unavailability of section lists accounts for the high 'hit rate'. As each SIG contained a dozen or more subgroups, a secondary random process was applied. A section was selected from each SIG using a random number procedure. CompuServe corpora, then, were randomly selected sections from randomly selected SIGs.

processed as data. If a string were not found, the processor assumed the mail to be regular, and ignored it.

2. *Check for errors.* Each mail message determined by the processor to be data was checked for errors, e.g. values out of coding range, missing values, wrong message numbers, non-numeric codes. Data with errors were returned to the coder.

3. *Check for completeness.* As each new list was processed, a unique subdirectory was created and error-free coded messages were transferred to the subdirectory as separate files. When the list was complete (i.e. 100 error-free coded messages as 100 files), the codes were transferred to databases.

4. *Manipulate the database.* Data was added to databases of two format types - with and without comma-delimiters for fields. In each case, each line is one message.

5. *Report to coder and coordinator.* Mail with processable data generated automatic error and completion status reports; unprocessable data was returned to the coder. A copy of all reports was sent to the coordinator and the system maintained a log file of all incoming and outgoing mail.

For each list coded, a questionnaire was completed to gather descriptive information about the coders, the technology used, impressions of the list, and problems experienced.

3.8.4. Reliability of coding scheme

Reliability assesses the degree to which variations in data represent real phenomena rather than variations in the measurement process (Krippendorff, 1980). Two reliability measures were considered:

- *Test-standard:* This involves training all coders to a standard set by expert coders and accepting only those who code to the preset level of accuracy.
- *Test-test:* This involves using at least two coders for the same data to establish the reproducibility of results.

Once again, the same procedure for attaining consensus on a methodological process was followed. A Reliability Committee drafted a statement (Appendix A.9) which was subsequently adopted. Given the unprecedented nature of the project, the unavailability of an established standard, and the number of coders involved, a test-test design was adopted and each list was assigned to two coders.

For various reasons, only 45% of enlisted coders were able to code, so only 37 of the 60 selected lists were distributed. Of these 37 lists (batches of 100 messages),

20 were single coded, 12 were double coded, and 5 were not coded at all. Of the 20 single coded lists, 2 were unfinished. Of the 12 double coded lists, 2 of the duplicates were not finished, which meant these 2 lists were single coded. Hence, the final tally was 20 single coded and 10 double coded fully-coded lists. The database, therefore, has a total of 4000 coded messages, of which 3000 are unique. In addition, there are 322 coded messages from 4 unfinished lists. A breakdown by network of these figures is given in Table 3.4 and the names of single-coded, double-coded and partially-coded lists are given in Table 3.5.

It was important to maintain independence of coding, particularly those lists that were double coded. Independent coders, working in a defined (and confined) physical work context, typically are not accessible to one another on a day-to-day basis. Email access, however, bridges distances and schedule clashes, and puts coders communicatively closer to each other.

Table 3.4. Summary of coded lists and messages by network

	BITNet	Usenet	Compuserve	Total
No. of randomly selected lists	20	20	20	60
No. of coded lists (including partially coded lists)	10	14	10	34
No. of messages coded (including partially coded lists)	1128	1694	1500	4322
No. of coded lists (fully coded only)	9	11	10	30
No. of single-coded lists	8	7	5	20
No. of double-coded lists	1	4	5	10
No. of messages coded (fully coded lists only)	1000	1500	1500	4000

Table 3.5. Single-coded, double-coded and partially-coded lists

	BITNet	Usenet	Compuserve
Single coded lists	BLIND-L BONSAI BUDDHA-L CJ-L EMAILMAN HOCKEY-L LAWSCH-L LITERARY	alt.cobol alt.sexual.abuse.recovery comp.ai.genetic k12.ed.math k12.ed.comp.literacy rec.arts.startrek.current soc.college	COMIC PHOTOFORUM TELECOM UKFORUM WINEFORUM
Double coded lists	CELTIC-L	rec.folk-dancing rec.humor.funny rec.nud rec.radio.swap	CARS DISABILITIES EFFSIG FISHNET JFORUM
Partially coded lists	HOCKEY-L	comp.bbs.waffle rec.arts.startrek.current soc.veterans	

3.8.5. Reliability of the coding process

To eliminate a possible source of invalid (inflated) reliability, coders were discouraged from discussing coding problems amongst themselves or within the group. Coder queries were directed, instead, to an advisory committee of twelve members. Each advisor, or *oracle*, fielded questions on a section of the codebook, responding in a nondirective manner. The more complicated questions were discussed amongst the oracles and the leader (the *Commissioner of Oracles*) summarised the discussions and responded to the enquirer. The typical practice for complex queries was as follows:

1. A coder posts an enquiry to the oracle group.
2. The specialist oracle (or, if that oracle was unavailable, the Commissioner) posts a draft response to the oracle group for comment.
3. The oracles comment on the draft response.
4. The Commissioner summarises oracle recommendations and posts the final response to the enquirer.

Requests for oracle assistance were relatively low. Enquiries could be divided into four types: technical, confirmatory, enigmatic and interpretive. Technical questions related to the group's procedures for precoding, sampling and distribution; confirmatory questions related to apprehension about and applicability of coding categories; enigmatic questions involved some form of an apparent paradox; and interpretive questions dealt with matters of coding protocol intent. Answers were couched in analytical yet open-ended terms. The turnaround time on inquiries posted to oracles was 48-72 hours.

3.9. ProjectH Coders

In response to a call for people to voluntarily code messages (see Appendix A.4 for the "invitation to code" message), 73 responded positively (see Appendix A5 for the "welcome" message sent to people who responded to the invitation). For various reasons, 40 of these people ultimately were unable to code, which left 33 coders. After the coding was completed, a questionnaire (see Appendix A.13) was distributed to the coders in January 1994 to collect demographic information about the coders and how they coded.

3.9.1. Demographics of the coders

Responses to the questionnaire indicate that the most common coder was a middle-aged male from the United States with a PhD. Predictably, age, gender, geographic and education distribution of the coders reflected broadly the corresponding distribution of the ProjectH participants. In addition, the demographic distribution of ProjectH participants was similar to the demographic distribution of the Internet at the time. In 1992-94, the Internet was primarily a US-dominated non-commercial environment for government and educational institutions.

Figure 3.5 shows the proportion of young, middle-aged and mature-aged coders, with the middle-aged group representing 61% of the coder population. Figure 3.6 shows that three out of every five coders were male (or 58% of the coder population).

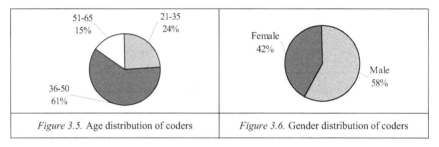

| *Figure 3.5.* Age distribution of coders | *Figure 3.6.* Gender distribution of coders |

Figure 3.7 shows that two-thirds (67%) of the coders were from the United States. After the United States, the next largest national representation was Israel (15%). The relatively large proportion of Israeli coders was no doubt due to the influence of one of the coordinators being a faculty member of the Hebrew University of Jerusalem. Other countries represented were Australia, Brazil, Canada, Sweden and the UK. Figure 3.8 indicates that all coders had at least one tertiary qualification; almost half (46%) had completed their doctoral degree.

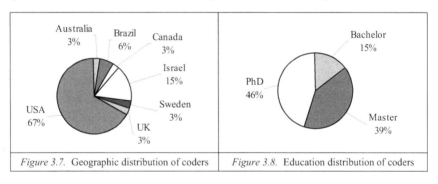

| *Figure 3.7.* Geographic distribution of coders | *Figure 3.8.* Education distribution of coders |

3.9.2. How the coders coded

The time taken by coders to code a batch of 100 messages varied considerably – from 3 hours to 80 hours (Figure 3.9), with the average being 24 hours and the mode 20 hours. This enormous difference in time could be due to: (i) the lists themselves (subscribers in some lists characteristically post longer messages); or (ii) the effectiveness of the method and technology used by the coders; (iii) or the experience of the coders.

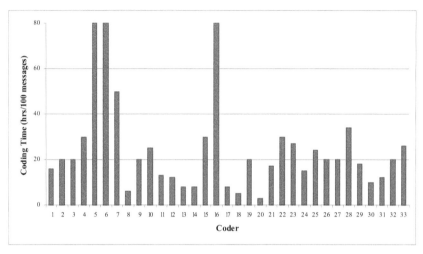

Figure 3.9. Number of hours to code a batch (100) messages.

A comparison of eight double-coded lists, however, indicates that list characteristics did not contribute greatly to the difference in coding time (Figure 3.10). In fact, in one instance, the time taken for two coders to code the same list was 6 hours for one coder and 50 hours for another coder.

Table 3.6 shows that experience appears to be related to coding time, as students took considerably longer than professors to code in most instances. Or another explanation could be that students were more careful and had more time to spend on coding.

Another variable in the time take to code could be the coders' choice of coding tool. Two ProjectH participants developed special tools for coding – FileExpress for the PC, and Hyperstack for the Macintosh. Surprisingly, one-third of the coders opted for using a basic text editor, another third chose a word processor or spreadsheet, while the remaining third utilised the FileExpress and Hyperstack (Figure 3.11).

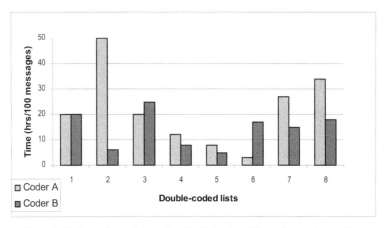

Figure 3.10. Comparison of time taken for Coder A and Coder B to code same lists.

Table 3.6. Comparison of time taken for each coder to code same list and coder's position

List	Coder A time (hrs)	Coder A position	Coder B time (hrs)	Coder B position
1	20	Nurse	20	Professor
2	50	Student	6	Assistant Professor
3	20	Assistant Professor	25	Associate Professor
4	12	Student	8	Research Associate
5	8	Lecturer	5	Professor
6	3	Research Assistant	17	Professor
7	27	Professor	15	Associate Professor
8	34	Student	18	Student

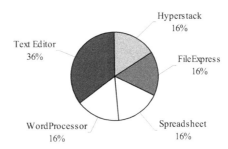

Figure 3.11. Coding methods chosen by coders.

The coding tool chosen by the coders does appear to contribute significantly to the difference in coding time. Table 3.7 shows that, in most instances, those coders who used the specially developed tools tool considerably less time to code.

Table 3.7. Comparison of time taken for each coder to code same list and coding tool

List	Coder A time (hrs)	Coder A position	Coder B time (hrs)	Coder B position
1	20	FileExpress	20	FileExpress
2	50	Text Editor	6	Hyperstack
3	20	Text Editor	25	Text Editor
4	12	Text Editor	8	Word Processor
5	8	Word Processor	5	Hyperstack
6	3	FileExpress	17	Word Processor
7	27	Text Editor	15	FileExpress
8	34	Hyperstack	18	Text Editor

3.10. ProjectH Outcomes

The ProjectH study supports, if only in case study form, the effectiveness of electronic brainstorming. The project has provided the wider network community with coded data on virtual communities, numerous publications, an annotated bibliography on CMC and a web site[28].

Research using the database is varied and ongoing. The data set compiled by the ProjectH Research Group, a cross-sectional, representative account of computer-mediated discussions, is used for research as varied as the group's participants. The results from the ongoing research are encouraging and enlightening despite the obvious limitations of the unidimensional nature of the data.

Numerous studies using the database were collected in a monograph, *Network and Netplay: Virtual Groups on the Internet*, edited by the two facilitators and one of the project participants (Sudweeks, McLaughlin and Rafaeli, 1998). Examples of studies included in the monograph are:

- *Interactivity:* The focus of this research (Rafaeli and Sudweeks, 1997; Rafaeli and Sudweeks, 1998) is an attempt to measure interactivity; that is, the degree to which communication transcends reaction. These quantitative studies demonstrate that those messages defined as 'interactive' are more opinionated, more humorous, more self-disclosing, more personal, and more likely to express agreement than non-interactive or reactive messages. In contrast to these statistical analyses of interactivity, other studies used an autoassociative neural network to construct sets of features which are typical of messages that initiate or contribute to longer lasting threads. Some of the distinguishing features identified in 'referenced' messages are medium length, factual, no questions or requests or emoticons, and addresses another

---

[28] The ProjectH web site is at http://www.it.murdoch.edu.au/~sudweeks/projecth.

person(s) (Sudweeks and Berthold, 1996; Berthold, Sudweeks, Newton and Coyne, 1997; Berthold, Sudweeks, Newton and Coyne, 1998).

- *Graphic accents:* This study explored the use of graphic accents (emotional, artistic and directional devices) as indicators of author gender. The study found that only a small proportion of network communicators include graphic accents to express emotion in their discourse but the users of these devices are primarily women (Witmer, 1998).

- *Flaming:* This study analysed the effects of flames on electronic conversations. The study found support for a consistent relationship between strategic structuring (techniques and tactics such as quoting or recounting) and conciliatory and emotional content: as emotional involvement increases, message structure declines (Mabry, 1998).

Early versions of some of the papers in the monograph were presented in a panel of six ProjectH participants at ICA'94[29], held in Sydney, Australia in May 1994.

ProjectH was a catalyst in the creation of one of the first electronic journals available on the Internet. The *Journal of Computer-Mediated Communication*[30], edited by Margaret McLaughlin and Sheizaf Rafaeli, is a refereed journal, comprised of scientific papers, online and interactive bibliographies, and book reviews.

In October 1995, the ProjectH database became publicly accessible and scores of requests were received from academics and students to use the database for their research. There was similar interest in the global research community in the communication and interactions among ProjectH participants. One research student, Marcel Allbritton (University of New Mexico, Albuquerque, New Mexico) was given permission to access and use ProjectH logs. ProjectH subsequently was the topic for Allbritton's (1996) Masters thesis, entitled *Collaborative Communication among Researchers using Computer-Mediated Communication: A Study of ProjectH.*

3.11. ProjectH Conclusions

Communication technologies and common research interests facilitated the formation of a new community that cut across social, cultural and geographic boundaries. However, those intending to embark on similar studies must be aware that an extensive coordinating overhead is necessary to resolve conflict and foster cooperation. Future studies will benefit from the knowledge that researchers are

---

[29] International Communication Association Conference.
[30] The journal website is at http://www.ascusc.org/jcmc/.

willing to engage voluntarily in collaborative groupwork. Some insights were gained from working in a virtual collaborative community.

1. The culture of online groups is typified, particularly in the popular press and magazines, as young, elitist, deviant and preoccupied with introspective and self-disclosing conversations. As a mature, eclectic, normative and task-oriented group, ProjectH did much to challenge this popular misconception.

2. The early stages of the project demonstrated that excessive traffic can create difficulties, however the organisational structure that evolved reduced traffic to approximately one-tenth of the initial volume. Given that ProjectH worked in an asynchronous environment and that communication can be processed at each participant's convenience, the time commitment for the later stages is comparable, if not less, than that required for a similar-sized group relying solely on face-to-face communication.

3. The ethics discussion illuminated the tenuous concept of consensus. Despite diverging opinions expressed emphatically over a lengthy period, only one-third of the group recorded a vote in favour of the proposed ethics policy. What of the remaining two-thirds? Were they persuaded? Were they unmotivated? Complete consensus is elusive and perhaps not even desirable in a group that values each others' expertise and experience. The approximate consensus approach adopted for ProjectH was a reasonable solution for a large online group working towards a common goal.

3.12. Summary

This chapter described the history, demographics and activities of the ProjectH Research Group – a computer-mediated collaborative group engaged in a research project that spanned a two-year period from 1992 to 1994. The project was conducted at a time when Internet technologies were at a comparatively nascent stage of development and the medium was asynchronous communication (email). The success of the project can be evaluated from the outcomes and the conclusions of the collaborative process.

In its organisation, ProjectH exhibited facets of both democracy and anarchy. The coordinators facilitated but were not appointed as controlling leaders, volunteer committee members recommended, but no individual or group had control. The participants developed a consciousness of being part of a robust environment that eventually evolved into a self-perpetuating social system.

The protracted and heated debate on the first issue to be resolved by the project participants – the ethics of using publicly archived electronic discussions intended for a defined subscriber list – was stimulating but inefficient. The discussions generated more than 300 messages over a period of eight months yet unanimous consensus was not reached. It was from this experience that the participants developed a process for optimising consensus and facilitating group cohesiveness. The various committees enabled leaders to emerge and thus the leadership became more collaborative.

As a group, ProjectH seemed to value collegiality, mutual respect, and a sense of humour, while devaluing flaming and argumentativeness. The group provided a rich environment in which people from different backgrounds 'met' and shared a common interest in list dynamics. Despite claims that text-based computer-mediated communication is a comparatively lean medium (Schmitz and Fulk, 1991), ProjectH provides a rich environment in which to study communication patterns.

In Chapter 7, the collaborative developmental and leadership characteristics of this computer-mediated group will be analysed from various data sources. The data for the analysis are the archives of all communication among the project participants, a survey, interviews with key participants and the author's participant observation.

In the next chapter, a second case study is presented. It is contrasted to the study presented in this chapter in that it spanned a two-and-half-month period, took place almost a decade after the first case study at a time when Internet technologies were at a relatively advanced stage of development, and the communication amongst participants was synchronous.

CHAPTER 4

CASE STUDY 2

The second case study discussed in this book is a unit of study, *Organisational Informatics* (OI), in the School of Information Technology at Murdoch University, Perth, Australia. The analysis of this case study is provided in Chapter 8. The data for analysis are the archives of interactions among the participants of OI, a survey for demographic information, in-depth interviews with key participants, as well as the author's own observations as a facilitator in the workshops.

The collaborative activities of OI were a series of online workshops in a virtual learning environment, and the shared creation of a web portal. In this chapter, a learning scenario designed to facilitate student construction of knowledge through participation, collaboration and reflection is described. The scenario uses a virtual learning environment for project structuring and communication.

This chapter begins with an overview of virtual learning environments, then presents a description of the OI unit and the activities of the OI participants. The chapter includes a framework which represents the pedagogical processes employed in facilitating students' collaborative learning.

4.1. Background

The extensive proliferation of computer media and networking described in Chapter 1 has opened up new opportunities for fundamental changes in the methods, models and techniques employed to educate and train students and professionals. Web-based course environments (i.e. virtual learning environments), provide an attractive interface for information dissemination (McLoughlin, 1999; D'Souza and Bunt, 2000; Curran and Devin, 2000). However, they are often adopted because of their technical innovativeness and social interest, and little thought is given to integrating the media with learning objectives and pedagogical strategies.

Most of the early web-mediated online courses were designed to complement conventional methodologies for dissemination of course materials, connecting students to various online multimedia learning materials (Stevenson, Sander and Naylor, 1996; Wilson, 1995; Ramsden, 1992). The web-mediated environments were regarded as tools for course delivery in which the students' role was primarily a passive one and their responsibility limited to daily monitoring of information spaces, downloading material, and contrived discussions on bulletin boards. These courses did not utilise the communication potential of internetworked computers and there were hardly any changes in the teaching and learning methodologies, including student monitoring and evaluation techniques.

However, perhaps more than any other teaching media, virtual learning environments have the potential to fully exploit theories of social and active learning through communication and collaboration.

4.2. Virtual Learning Environments

The term *virtual learning environment*[1] is used to describe a server software, dedicated to the design, management and administration of computer-mediated learning, including delivery of course materials, support of course communications, student management, tracking and evaluation. Virtual learning environments typically have the learning material at the centre of the system and provide a set of tools which are of use as the learner progresses through the material. In other words, these systems manage the delivery of the learning material. Examples of such commercial packages include WebCT, TopClass, Blackboard, and Lotus Learning Space (Milligan, 1999).

These new educational environments use extensive computer-mediated communication and collaboration during the learning process. The educational models used by the course developers in these environments are, however, heavily influenced by traditional distance education methodologies. The emphasis in these pedagogical methodologies is on the delivery and exchange of documents (e.g. learning materials, project assignments and research work) and on knowledge management through asynchronous communications.

Computer media, though, provide a means for extensive and detailed documentation of activities in the learning environment, including synchronous collaborative learning. This information can be employed for assisting student monitoring and evaluation. The use of virtual learning environments extends the range of supported learning designs, including:

1. *Small group learning*: workshop-style online discussions and readings.
2. *Self-paced constructivist learning*: customisable learning materials.
3. *Collaborative learning groups:* exploring, discovering and sharing online resources.

---

[1] Other terms used in the literature are *flexible learning environment, online learning environment, web-based educational environments, networked learning*, etc.

4.3. Learning Strategies

The learning strategy used in this case study was to place the learner, rather than the learning material, in the centre of the virtual environment. The environment provided learners with the facilities to manage their own learning experience. In this type of environment, learners were able to shape and develop their own knowledge and understanding in a context that was relevant to them. Kolb (1984), for example, claims that learning is a process whereby knowledge is created through the transformation of experience. This approach is based on a constructivist view of learning with values and theories including collaboration, personal autonomy, generativity, reflectivity, active engagement, personal relevance, and pluralism (Lebow, 1993).

The development of a sense of 'place' for the learner as the core of a virtual learning environment can provide the basis for an enhanced learning experience. Whereas traditional learning has been transferred to virtual environments through the distribution of learning materials such as texts and course notes, the presentation of lectures, followed by assignments and tests, the transference of *places* for learning is not as well developed. Some examples of places as learning environments are the Diversity University[2], Tappedin[3], and the Virtual Campus at the University of Sydney[4]. Many of these environments focus on the development of rooms and tools for communicating while learning. They do not yet facilitate the learner-centred approach that allows the learner to construct external representations of their knowledge space – their own 'learning place'.

The virtual learning strategies used in the OI unit have their foundation in the works of Vygotsky (1934/1987; 1981), the Russian psychologist of the early twentieth century. According to Vygotsky (1978, chap. 6), thinking and problem-solving skills are developed within a zone of proximal development (ZPD) – a zone of socio-interactive processes in which independent skills are developed through collaboration. He defines three types of skills: (i) those skills that are acquired without assistance, (ii) those skills that are never acquired even with assistance, and (iii) those skills that are learned with assistance. This somewhat simplistic construct of learning was espoused by Vygotsky shortly before he died and thus lacks the rigour of some of his earlier theories. Other scholars have expanded his account of the role of the ZPD in human development, and see the ZPD as providing a way of

---

[2] http://www.du.org/
[3] http://www.tappedin.sri.com/
[4] http://moo.arch.usyd.edu.au:7778.

conceptualising how each individual's development may be assisted by other members within the same culture (Wells, 1999; Tiffin and Rajasingham, 1995; Penuel and Wertsch, 1995).

Vygotsky claimed that human development is attained through both biological maturation (nature) and cultural inheritance (nurture). The appropriation of cultural inheritance is achieved through activity and interaction with others in a social context. To Vygotsky, society is a set of overlapping systems. The systems in contemporary developed societies are the educational system, the health system, the legal system, and so forth. Society is self-perpetuating in that it is maintained and developed by its individuals who contribute to its activity systems (Wartofsky, 1979).

Learning, therefore, is not a separate and independent activity, but an integral aspect of participation in any community of practice or any social system (Lave and Wenger, 1991). Learning is not dependent on instruction according to a set of predetermined objectives. Learning occurs when participants of a joint activity contribute to a solution to emergent problems and difficulties according to their ability to do so (Wells, 1999).

Tiffin and Rajasingham (1995) interpret ZPD as the difference between what people can do without help and what they could do with help from others more experienced than themselves. The purpose of the educational methodology is to provide that assistance to the learner. The purpose of the educational environment is to enable that provision. In this paradigm, teachers are regarded as facilitators in the students' active-learning process. Teaching is regarded as a team activity and learning as a group activity.

Studies using virtual learning environments as enhanced tools for traditional teaching techniques indicate mixed results. Ciba and Rakestraw (1998), for example, used communication tools in an unstructured way. Bulletin boards were used by instructors and students for notices and messages, and chat rooms were used for online consultations. Students considered these facilities were not useful. They did, however, find the online exam feature useful.

The results of a survey by Morss and Fleming (1998) were more favourable with 72% student satisfaction with the bulletin board, 49% satisfaction with the chat room, and 63% satisfaction with the quiz. Again, the bulletin board and chat rooms was used in an unstructured manner. Although students were enthusiastic about virtual learning environments generally, they felt the environment did not increase, or even maintain, interest in the course subject matter.

These studies do indicate that new pedagogical strategies need to be devised to fully exploit the learning potential of web-based educational environments – strategies that are directed at developing reflective construction of knowledge and active participation. Used only as an adjunct to traditional teaching methodologies, these environments do little to enhance learning efficacy.

The potential of these environments is far from being fully exploited. Networked computer media challenges traditional education methods, bringing new course models and scenarios. Two specific areas that need to be exploited far more are:

- *Reflective learning through participation*

  New pedagogical strategies need to be devised to fully exploit the learning potential of these educational environments – strategies that are directed at developing reflective construction of knowledge and active participation.

- *Student evaluation through documentation*

  The computer media provides a means for extensive and detailed documentation of activities in the learning environment. This information can be employed to assist monitoring and evaluation of student learning.

It was the need to understand how the first area, in particular, could be exploited further that provided the motivation and interest for the author to research communication patterns in virtual learning environments. The virtual learning scenario used in this case study was developed over a three-year period. It was a very different environment to that of Case Study 1, a decade earlier. The virtual learning environment was a medium for studying synchronous communication processes and strategies using the advanced technologies of the decade later.

4.4. Organisational Informatics Virtual Learning Scenario

The concept for the virtual learning scenario for OI was developed initially in 1998 for a postgraduate unit of study at the University of Sydney. In 1999, the scenario was modified for a third-year undergraduate unit of study at Murdoch University. In 2000, the scenario underwent further modifications and was used for a second-year undergraduate unit of study at Murdoch University.

4.4.1. University of Sydney

The author was one of three coordinators of a unit on Computer-Mediated Communication (CMC) in Design at the Key Centre of Design Computing and

Cognition, University of Sydney, Australia. The other two coordinators were Professor Mary Lou Maher[5] and Associate Professor Simeon Simoff[6].

Endeavouring to put "theory into practice", the CMC in Design seminars were conducted online in the University of Sydney's Virtual Campus (Figure 4.1). The Virtual Campus was a MOO[7] environment, implemented in LambdaMOO[8] with the BioGate[9] interface between the MOO database and the web server. MOOs were originally designed as spaces for online social interaction. While MOOs are similar to chat rooms, in that participants can communicate synchronously, they differ in that participants can add to this virtual world by building new rooms and other objects, and writing programs that alter their particular MOO universe in profound ways. In general, every MOO user is allowed to create objects within the MOO.

The virtual campus was organised around the presence of various buildings where each building serveed a specific function. The buildings provided office space, seminar space, and library or resource space. The instructors and students had personal offices that were either provided for them according to a style consistent with the rest of the campus, or left for each individual to design and implement his or her own office. The Virtual Campus was used for both seminar-style classes and virtual design studios.

---

[5]Dr Mary Lou Maher was Professor of Design Computing in the Department of Architectural and Design Science, University of Sydney, Australia.

[6]Dr Simeon Simoff was a Senior Research Fellow in the University of Sydney, Australia. He is currently a Professor at the University of Western Sydney, Australia.

[7]MOO stands for MUD Object Oriented. MUD is an acronym for either Multi-User Dungeon or Multi-User Dimension. Based on the concept of MUDs, MOOs come under the category of social MUDs that proliferated on the web. Many MUDs, though, have no relation to dungeons. A MUD is a form of a virtual world, a virtual meeting place which contains objects and people which behave (in principle) in a similar way to real-life equivalents. The system is based on rooms which can contain objects and where people can meet. In general, activities are restricted to the current room. MUDs weave a virtual world around the user by providing a first-person perspective of one's environment.

Originally MOOs were popular with young players of games on the Internet. Today, MOOs are increasingly recognised for their value as an educational tool. In MOOs teachers and students can meet online at scheduled times and exchange ideas, even calling up online reference materials as they participate in discussions. Educators are exploring the potential of this technology for such applications as online writing centers, electronic classrooms, netbased collaborative environments, and even complete cyberspace campuses, as in the Virtual Campus at University of Sydney.

[8] The term "LambdaMOO" refers to a piece of software and a particular site running that software. LambdaMOO, the piece of software, is a MUD server – a text-based, computer-managed, multi-user world. It is often referred to simply as "MOO". The original MOO server was written by Stephen F. White. Pavel Curtis at the Xerox Corporation's Palo Alto Research Center made some changes to the MOO software in 1990 and called it LambdaMOO to reduce confusion.

[9] The BioGate system is a set of MOO objects and associated MOO modifications that allow the MOO to function as a web server. In addition, some of the objects provided are "viewers" that allow you to see into the MOO via web pages, much like how the common telnet/client interface gives a text window into the virtual world that is the MOO. The key is that MOOs are not, as is often said, text-based virtual reality (VR). It is simply that the only means users had for perceiving their VR world was text. The BioGate system provides the tools for both adding multimedia information to MOO objects, and for allowing users to perceive those objects and their extended associated characteristics (Introductory Guide to the BioGate System, http://murfin2.tl.ed.nyu.edu/BioGate.html)

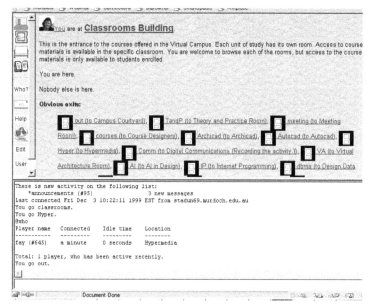

Figure 4.1. The classroom building in the University of Sydney's Virtual Campus (ndividual classrooms were in this "building")

The virtual campus approach supports flexible learning by providing a "place" (i.e. virtual space) where there is access to online course materials, other students in the course, and the instructors. The place concept is similar to the physical campus, providing the interaction and knowledge management framework of the learning space. The place concept offers a consistent frame of reference in the information space of an integrated learning environment. The learning environment supports both synchronous communication (meetings, seminars and presentations, collaborative development activities) and asynchronous communication (email and telegrams, bulletin and white boards), in addition to access to course materials, quizzes, project data, student monitoring and evaluation facilities.

The CMC in Design seminar discussions were recorded and the data were evaluated with software which provided a number of quantitative analyses of communication (Simoff and Maher, 2000).

4.4.2. Murdoch University

In 1999, the author moved from the University of Sydney to Murdoch University. The virtual campus concept, developed at the University of Sydney, was modified and trialled by the author for a new unit of study, Organisational Informatics, at Murdoch University. Nineteen third-year students were enrolled in the unit in 1999.

The customised MOO environment was not available at Murdoch University, so the concept was modified for use within the university's learning environment, WebCT (Figure 4.2).

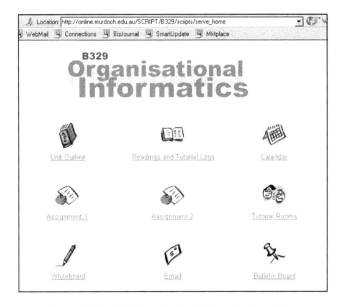

Figure 4.2. The 1999 Organisational Informatics Home Page.

WebCT is one of the major commercial products of its type. It integrates four types of learning tools: *resources* (lecture notes, assignment guidelines, readings, links to other web sites); *communication tools* (bulletin board, chat room, private email, calendar); *instructional tools* (glossary, surveys, quizzes); and *management tools* for tracking student progress and interactions. It is platform independent and is accessed using a web browser. In 2000, due to curriculum planning strategies, the third-year undergraduate unit was changed to a second-year unit. Further developments were made to the learning scenario and implemented again in WebCT at Murdoch University (Figure 4.3) with a class of 99 students.

The OI unit design had two key components:

1. a series of one-hour virtual workshops in the WebCT chat rooms
2. collaborative development of a portal as a shared resource.

Both components were designed to facilitate the students' construction of knowledge through participation and reflection.

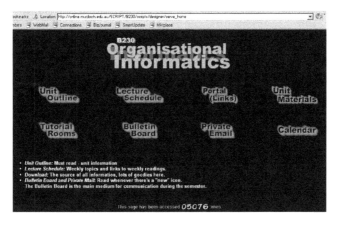

Figure 4.3. The 2000 Organisational Informatics Home Page.

4.5. Organisational Informatics Course

Organisational Informatics was a unit of study in the Information Systems Development and Information Systems Design streams within the Bachelor of Science degree.[10] The unit examined a range of contemporary information systems topics, concerning organisational, social and cultural aspects of the design and development of information systems. It covered various development methodologies, and ways of choosing between (or combining) different approaches. Current technologies and issues were considered in the context of various types of information system theories. It also included consideration of influential innovations in information systems practice and knowledge management.

The topics covered included:

1. computer mediated communication in organisations
2. organisational design and group processes
3. organisational culture
4. virtual organisations
5. sociotechnical information systems
6. computer mediated collaborative work
7. organisational decision support systems
8. analysis, design and evaluation methods, techniques and tools
9. systems theory, soft systems methodology and meta-methodologies

The aims of the unit were to:

---

[10] See Appendix B.1 for more information about the course.

1. provide the students with a range of skills associated with the organisational aspects of the design and development of information systems
2. critically assess and manage numerous issues that impact both on knowledge and knowledge workers in the context of today's organisation
3. facilitate reflective construction of knowledge
4. encourage the acquisition of cooperative and lifelong learning skills

The collaborative learning activities in which students engaged were: (i) a series of one-hour virtual (synchronous) workshops on topics that focused on the social, cultural and communication impacts of the implementation of information technology in organisations; and (ii) the development of an Organisational Informatics web portal related to these topics.

There were five areas of assessment:
1. participation in workshops
2. moderation of one workshop
3. weekly reflective journal which included: (i) a critique of specified readings, (ii) comments on a topic question related to the workshop topic, (iii) discussion of URLs relevant to the topic question and (iv) reflection on workshop discussions
4. research essay
5. exam.

4.6. Organisational Informatics Unit Design

The unit home page (Figure 4.3) was designed to simplify access and navigation. It was modelled after Oliver's (2001) framework of three interconnecting elements as critical components – learning tasks, learning resources and learning supports (see Table 4.1).

Table 4.1. Framework describing critical elements of online learning settings (Oliver, 2001, p.407)

Learning design elements	Description
Learning tasks	The activities, problems, interactions used to engage the learners and on which learning is based.
Learning resources	The content, information and resources with which the learners interact and upon which learning is based.
Learning supports	The scaffolds, structures, encouragements, motivations, assistances and connections used to support learning.

The unit design therefore featured three types of material. *Learning tasks* included tools for interactions to engage the learners (public and private forums, chat rooms, private email, shared whiteboard), and guidelines for activities (descriptive requirements for reflective journals, and research essays). *Learning resources* included content and information upon which learning is based (lecture notes, a collection of downloadable readings used for discussion topics for the workshops, transcripts of workshops, and the web portal with links to relevant websites). *Learner supports* included scaffolds and structures to support learning (course outline,[11] calendar, guidelines for communicating online,[12] guidelines for workshops moderators,[13] peer assessment form,[14] and tutors' photos and contact information (Table 4.2 and Figure 4.4).

Table 4.2. 2000 Organisational Informatics unit design modelled on Oliver (2001).

Learning design elements	Artifacts
Learning tasks	Public bulletin board, private forums, requirements for reflective journals, guidelines for research essays
Learning resources	Lecture notes, readings, transcripts of workshops, web portal.
Learning supports	Course outline, calendar, guidelines for communicating online, guidelines for workshop moderators, peer assessment form, tutors' photos and contact information.

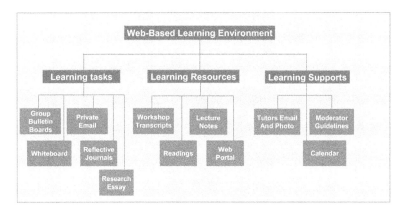

Figure 4.4. 2000 Organisational Informatics web learning environment adapted from Oliver's (2001) model.

The learning environment provided a rich set of resources for the students. The dilemma, though, was how to facilitate and motivate student participation in a group activity such as the workshop. "Hitchhiking" is a common feature of team projects,

---

[11] See a summary of the course outline in Appendix B.1.
[12] See Appendix B.2.
[13] See Appendix B.3.
[14] See Appendix B.4.

where some team members do not fulfill their responsibilities yet are awarded the same grade as their more responsible counterparts (Kaufman, Felder and Fuller, 1999). "Lurking" is a feature of discussion groups where some subscribers passively read posts but fail to contribute to the discussions. Similarly, in the virtual workshop, it is all too easy to log on and create a presence but take no active part in the group activity.

The pedagogical framework (Figure 4.5) that was used to facilitate and motivate student participation was oriented towards sustaining students' continuous engagement in discovering and applying knowledge and skills in the context of authentic problem solving.

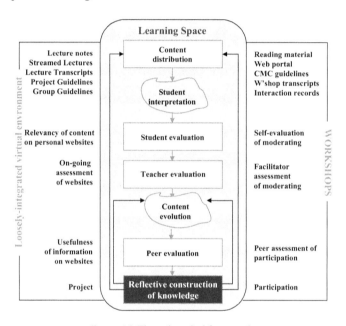

Figure 4.5. The pedagogical framework.

The aim was to create an engaging environment in which the teaching role is a facilitator in motivating students to take a proactive role, to read and think critically, and to be able to present and argue their point of view. The course design used a digital educational environment with a range of online materials that catered for diverse student learning styles and spaces. The design used the benefits of flexible learning in a manner that fostered proactive practitioners, capable of taking the initiative and responsibility in individual, cooperative and collaborative decision making. The pedagogical framework is grounded in Schön's (1983; 1991) "reflection-in-action" theory, adopting principles from Vygotsky's (1934/1987; 1981) work; that is, it used a cycle of interpretation, evaluation and reflection of content evolving into individual and shared knowledge.

4.6.1. The virtual workshop

The course design included a collection of papers covering particular topics which were used to inform a series of workshop discussions on the topics. Each workshop was devoted to a particular topic that was supported by lectures and course materials. The WebCT chat rooms were used as virtual spaces (Harasim, 1999) for the workshops.

For each workshop, each student was required to read the same two or three set papers related to the corresponding lecture topic, and a student was assigned to lead the discussions. The actors in the scenario (online synchronous workshops), therefore, were the facilitator (appointed leader), the discussion leader (moderator), and the students (participants). Guidelines for moderating, based on evaluation criteria, were available for the students to download from the web site. The students were asked to prepare a text file of a brief review of the articles, and to copy and paste a small amount of text at a time into the chat room window. They were encouraged to read the articles critically and express their own opinions. Their critique was interspersed with questions that brought out the main issues of the articles and were intended to stimulate discussions.

Transcripts of the discussions were available immediately after each workshop for students to read and reflect on in their weekly journal, and for students who were unable to attend the workshop.

The reflection on the discussions was an important feature of the workshop design as it reinforced the learning that occurred during the workshop, and provided the opportunity for self-evaluation and thus improvement in subsequent weeks. It also provided a feedback mechanism for the instructor.

4.6.2. The Portal

The second major component of the course design was the development of an Organisational Informatics portal.[15] Each week throughout the course, students responded to a topic question that addressed controversial issues related to that lecture material on the same topic. The students were required to research each

---

[15] A *portal* is a structured list of relevant web sites.

question on the web and to provide at least one relevant web page or web site. Example questions were:

"Do web cams in offices provide an unobtrusive means of maintaining communication and casual interaction among workers without mitigating privacy?"

"Are transnational communities likely to facilitate their countries of origin to 'catch up' with technological infrastructures? What effect will these communities have on their 'host' countries?"

The web references provided by individual students were evaluated initially by the facilitator and, if appropriate, added to the portal. The web references were then evaluated by all of the students and used as research material for the essay component of their assessment.

4.7. Organisational Informatics Participants

The OI course had an enrolment of 99 undergraduate students. The students were assigned to seven workshop groups of approximately 16 members. The author was the coordinator of the unit and is referred to as the facilitator.

The workshop series was a novel approach to groupwork as most of the participants had never met, either online or offline. During the first virtual workshop, the facilitator organised a schedule of moderators for the subsequent workshops.

As group members went through the process of collaborative learning and knowledge construction through discussions and citations, they built a social and intellectual foundation that strengthened and sustained the collaborative activities. Although the participant leadership was predefined, it was benign in that rotating moderators took control of each workshop. Computer-mediated synchronous communication, both public and private, was used for coordination, moderator recruitment, distribution of information, decision making, encouragement and learning.

4.8. Organisational Informatics Data Sources

The data sources for the analysis and evaluation of the virtual workshops are transcripts of the discussions in four workshop groups[16], a survey for demographic information, in-depth interviews, and the author's participation observation. This triangulation methodology, using CEDA (Sudweeks and Simoff, 1999), is the

---

[16] Although there were 7 workshop groups, the data from 3 groups were incomplete due to technical problems (server downtime during workshop sessions), so data from 4 groups were analysed for this book.

described briefly in Chapter 1 and in detail in Chapter 5. It develops further the research work carried out to evaluate the Virtual Campus at the University of Sydney (Simoff and Maher, 2000).

There were nine workshops over a period of two-and-a-half months. During this period there were two study breaks. The duration of the study breaks were one week for the first, and two weeks for the second.

The workshop discussions were automatically logged by the WebCT software. At the end of each workshop, the logs were downloaded by the instructor. Extraneous data, such as students practising the cut and paste facility, false entries and program bugs, were deleted. The cleaned file was then uploaded to the unit material archive. Transcripts were thus available to students immediately following each workshop.

The process that was developed for analysing the seminar data in the University of Sydney's virtual campus was modified for the analysis of the workshop transcripts. The methodology is described in Chapter 6 and the analyses are presented in Chapter 8.

At the end of the unit, students were asked to complete a survey to provide demographic information (age, gender, language, ethnicity) about themselves and to assess the participation level of their peers. The peer assessments were compared to both the instructor's assessments and a quantitative analysis of participation rates from the workshop transcripts. There was a significant correlation between each type of assessment (Sudweeks and Simoff, 2000; and Sudweeks, 2003). A survey was also distributed to students at the end of the semester to evaluate students' satisfaction in terms of self-determination, competence and affiliation. According to Deci and Ryan's (1985) Theory of Cognitive Evaluation, an individual's motivation is mainly determined by needs of self-determination, competence and affiliation. Feelings of self-determination are founded on an individual's perception of autonomy. Feelings of lack of self-determination are founded an individual perception of external induction of normative behaviour. The stronger the perception of self-determination, the more positive impact on motivation. An individual's perception of self-competence and affiliation[17] similarly affects motivation (Sudweeks and Simoff, 2000; Sudweeks, 2003).

Interviews were conducted with selected participants after the completion of the unit to elicit information about their perception of the group processes within the workshops as well as elaborating on the feedback provided by the survey.

---

[17] Affiliation in this sense means a feeling of belongingness to a group or community.

4.9. Summary

This chapter described the demographics and activities of the Organisational Informatics group – a computer-mediated group engaged in a collaborative learning activity that spanned two-and-a-half months. The learning environment of Case Study 2 integrated three critical aspects of online learning – tasks, resources and supports. A pedagogical framework was developed to facilitate students' reflective construction of knowledge.

The analysis of developmental and leadership characteristics of the Case Study 2 group is presented in Chapter 8. The data for the analysis are the archives of all communication that occurred among the participants, a survey eliciting demographic information, interviews with key participants and the author's participant observation.

This second case study complements the first case study in all key aspects – medium, mode, duration, leadership, formation, purpose, size, location, participants, chronology, network and process (see Table 1.1). Given the variation in these case studies and the prominent role of the author in both cases, it was necessary to develop a methodology that was flexible yet rigorous. Chapter 5 describes a CMC multimethod design – Complementary Explorative Data Analysis (CEDA). Chapter 6 describes how this CEDA methodology was applied to both case studies.

COMPLEMENTARY EXPLORATIVE DATA ANALYSIS:
A Multimethod Design

In this chapter, various traditional methodologies, and their strengths and weaknesses when applied to Internet-spawned research fields, are examined. As discussed in Chapter 1, new research environments and technologies challenge existing research assumptions and premises. To investigate the phenomena described in the case studies in Chapters 3 and 4, traditional methodologies need to be adapted to these new research environments in which communication technologies affect sociocultural norms. This chapter therefore introduces a Complementary Explorative Data Analysis (CEDA), a new methodology for Internet research. Internet research incorporates a number of separate research domains, including electronic commerce and business systems, computer-mediated communication (CMC), computer-supported collaborative work (CSCW), and distributed information systems, including mobile systems.

In the following chapter (Chapter 6), the methodology is applied to the two case studies.

5.1. Introduction

There are various methodological tools available to scientists to gain knowledge and understanding of societal and communicative phenomena. One may choose quantitative or qualitative methods; one may apply interpretive or positivist theoretical paradigms; one may study societies, organisations, groups, individuals, or single messages; one may study cross-sectionally or across time. In general, the initial hypotheses or the research questions of interest guide the choice of methodology and tools. If the unit of analysis is the individual, applying a statistical analysis of data obtained from a large sample of subjects within a population can be a rigorous method of testing predefined hypotheses and indicating generalisability of results. However, in emerging interdisciplinary fields such as Internet research in general, and computer-mediated communication (CMC) in particular, it is sometimes difficult to formulate specific hypotheses when conducting research.

The majority of CMC research has been conducted in laboratories under controlled experimental conditions, which may not present an accurate picture of the reality of virtuality. The external validity of such experiments is problematic for at least three reasons: (i) subjects are an atypically captive audience who would probably behave differently in a laboratory than they would in a "real" virtual environment; (ii) groups studied in experiments tend to be unrealistically small; and (iii) an almost natural inclination of experimental design is to compare CMC with a face-to-face standard (Rafaeli and Sudweeks, 1997; Rafaeli and Sudweeks, 1998). This comparison may be misleading.

The replication of CMC field research is difficult, if not impossible, for two main reasons (apart from the usual problems of the environment and human nature itself constantly changing). On a *technological level*, the net is perpetually changing its configuration and supporting technology. The underlying networking protocols cannot guarantee the same conditions when replicating experiments, simply because each time the path of information communication is unique, thus the time delay, and consequences connected with it, are different. On a *communication level*, the difficulties in replication come from the creative aspect of language use. Although the rules of grammar are finite, they are recursive and capable of producing infinite language (Chomsky, 1980). Novel sentences are constructed freely and unbounded, in whatever contingencies our thought processes can understand. Apart from standard clichés, sentences are rarely duplicated exactly yet each variation is generally comprehended. It follows that experiments involving text generation can rarely be repeated. Within a positivist research paradigm, this lack of replication is a violation of the initial assumptions for the application of statistical analysis.

Another aspect of CMC research is that it has to deal with heterogeneous sociocultural structures. The Internet is, of course, populated with people of many cultures. Bierstedt (1963) defines culture as a complex set of behaviours and artifacts with three major dimensions: *ideas* (traditional values and beliefs); *norms* (behaviors that adjust to the environment of traditional values and beliefs), and *material culture* (artifacts produced in the environment of traditional values and beliefs). On the Internet, cultural complexity appears to be an intractable problem. Global communication technologies bring together cultures that differ dramatically on each of Bierstedt's three dimensions.

5.2. Computer-Mediated Communication Research

As the technology changes at a pace never before experienced, CMC research is engaged in a catch-up situation. A modern CMC research methodology should take into account rapidly changing technology, social norms and communication behaviours. To be able to specify and develop such a methodology, the features specific to CMC research need to be identified. These include the features of mediation, technical knowledge, information and processing load, and sense of virtual presence. Each of these features will be discussed in the following sections.

5.2.1. Communication is computer mediated

First, and obviously, CMC differs from traditional face-to-face communication because the computer provides an interface between interlocutors. In Chapter 2, a number of aspects of computer mediation were discussed. In summary, the significant aspects as far as this research is concerned are the following.

A common practice in CMC research is to regard face-to-face as the ideal communication environment (Schudson, 1978) and CMC is rated as less than ideal. Experimental work has discovered a number of dysfunctional aspects of computer mediation including *flaming* (Mabry, 1998; Siegel, Dubrovsky, Kiesler and McGuire, 1986; Sproull and Kiesler, 1991), *unsociable behaviour* (Hiltz, Johnson and Turoff, 1986), *disinhibition* and *deindividuation* effects (Hiltz and Johnson, 1989; Matheson and Zanna, 1990), and a lack of awareness of the *social presence* of others as the environment is characterised by minimal channels for communicating (Short, Williams and Christie, 1976). Somewhat more optimistic experimental work introduced findings on *status levelling* (Dubrovsky, Kiesler and Sethna, 1991), *socioemotional connections* (Rice and Love, 1987), *consensus formation* (Dennis and Valacich, 1993), *brainstorming* (Osborn, 1941), and *collaborative productivity* (Sanderson, 1996).

5.2.2. Communication requires technical knowledge

Each communication environment requires specific knowledge. In a face-to-face environment, we learn at a very early age not only the phonetics and grammar of the language but also, for example, the management of turn taking in conversations (Herring, 1999; Sacks, Schegloff and Jefferson, 1978). In written communication, we add knowledge of orthography and a more formal use of language. In telephone communication, we learn how to search for telephone numbers, to press the right sequence of keys, and to engage in preliminary phatic conversation. Every Internet communicator, however, needs at least minimal technical knowledge of computers. To communicate, even with the simplest graphically-interfaced mailer, the user needs to know enough to compose, forward and reply to a message, and to quit the application. As computer technology is being introduced earlier into educational institutes, computer literacy will develop in parallel with linguistic literacy. In the meantime, though, computer literacy is a problem for many current and potential Internet users and affects individual levels of interactivity. Many users are content to learn sufficient technical knowledge to perform only the immediate tasks required and lack motivation to fully explore the built-in functionality of computer applications.

5.2.3. Communication is affected by information and processing overload

Mass communication is ubiquitous. We all absorb mass communication, whether it is active (television, theatre, newspapers) or passive (roadside billboards, newsstand headlines, advertising on public transport). In most instances we are able to be selective and control the amount of information absorbed. Internet communication places enormous pressures on cognitive processing. Discussion lists often generate hundreds of messages a day and to contribute to a conversation means responding immediately before the topic shifts and the sequence is lost. On the web, designers endeavour to engage the browser's attention by manipulating font type and size, text spacing, graphics, colors, backgrounds, video clips, sound bits, animation and interactive gimmicks. As discussed in Chapter 2, research has indicated that while minimal levels of novelty can stimulate and demand attention, extreme novelty leads to overstimulation, cognitive overload, distraction and ultimately impaired information processing (Mayes, Kibby and Anderson, 1990; Heylighen, 1999).

5.2.4. Communication has a sense of virtual presence

Communicating with strangers on a regular basis is not new. There have been many examples of "pen pal" relationships that have lasted for many years and romantic relationships that have led to marriage (Civin, 1999; Barnes, 2001). The sense of virtual presence in these instances, though, is not strong, as there are long delays between communication exchanges. The message exchange process on the Internet, on the other hand, can be almost instantaneous. The effect is a written correspond-ence that is like a conversation. As discussed in Chapter 2, formalities, phatic introductions, signatures, and many other features of written communication may be reduced or even eliminated (Ong, 1982). Erickson (1999) refers to mediated communication as persistent conversation:

> In CMC many of our finely honed [communication] skills become irrelevant. And the audience to whom we are used to speaking becomes largely invisible … Persistence expands conversation beyond those within earshot, rendering it accessible to those in other places and at later times. Thus, digital conversation may be synchronous or

asynchronous, and its audience intimate or vast. Its persistence means that it may be far more structured, or far more amorphous, than an oral exchange, and that it may have the formality of published text or the informality of chat.

In such a communication environment, indirect social cues are transmitted and virtual presence takes on the qualities of real presence. In fact, quite often, the mental distance between regular participants in discussion groups is less than with colleagues working in the same office.

5.3. An Internet Research System

To address the problematic aspects of researching the Internet that are discussed above, a new system, which facilitates a cyclical process of intuition, description and prediction, was developed. Figure 5.1 illustrates this cyclical process.

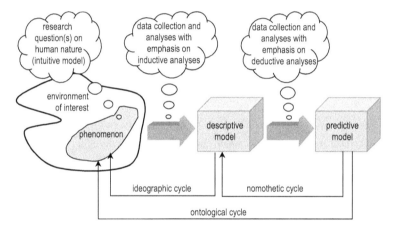

Figure 5.1. The cyclical systematic process of intuition, description and prediction in research.

Initially, there needs to be an exploration of research questions that emerge from the environment of interest (in this case, CMC), review of relevant literature, and the intuitive observations of the investigator. This initial exploration leads to data collection and primarily inductive-type analyses, which leads the investigator to posit causal relationships between variables and a tentative descriptive model of the phenomenon. The tentative descriptive model then leads to more data collection and primarily deductive-type analyses, which leads the investigator to posit a tentative predictive model of the phenomenon. As new information or new variables emerge, there are feedback loops to previous investigative stages for evaluation, refinement and identification of the causal relationships between the variables. The nomothetic cycle loops back to the inductive analyses which informed the deductive analyses.

The ideographic cycle loops back to the intuitive model (see Section 5.4 for a detailed discussion of idiography and nomology). The ontological loop is a reality check of the research questions, a process which is ongoing and cyclical (see Section 1.5 for a detailed discussion on the ontological assumptions of this book).

5.3.1. Taxonomies as the basis for understanding phenomena

There is such a variety of social processes that, in order to understand them, it is necessary to identify some regularities from observations. Regular patterns are grouped together and form taxonomies (or typologies) of human processes and behavior. Taxonomies are distinct, discrete classifications of information, which help to give order to a confusing, continuous mass of heterogeneous information. In some way, this continuum of information is divided into discrete regions, where points within each such region bear qualitative similarities to each other, whereas points in different regions bear qualitative differences to one another. The construction of meaningful taxonomies, therefore, is a fundamental ethnographic technique that enables us to understand our everyday world as well as to conduct scientific inquiries. It is an integral aspect of human thought in that representations of unique experiences or stimuli are encoded into an organised system that economises and simplifies cognitive processing (Rosenman and Sudweeks, 1995).

Organising information into categories or taxonomies has been a system used in many disparate fields. From the time of Aristotle, the process of naming, defining and categorising have undergone philosophical scrutiny. In cultural anthropology, Durkheim and Mauss (1963) analysed the ways in which the 'clan system' of the Pueblo Indians perceived concepts of orientation. In psychology, Rosch (1973) studied the way the Dani people in New Guinea categorise colour. In discourse analysis, Sacks (1972) examined transcriptions of telephone calls to the Los Angeles Suicide Prevention Center, and found that categorisation helps to explain our understanding of the human social world. In a similar vein, Schütz (1962) sees the organisation of information as a cognitive process of typification which enables us to understand our everyday world as well as to conduct scientific enquiries.

Thus, the attempt to construct empirical types within the social sciences has a long tradition, but explicit research techniques to support taxonomies of qualitative information is a comparatively new enquiry. Some notable advances in identifying patterns in social regularities while at the same time understanding these regularities has been the work of Weber (1964) and Kuckartz (1995). Weber was concerned with linking hermeneutic regularities in texts and standardisation of information, while

Kuckartz uses a case-oriented quantification model whereby taxonomies are developed from data rather than predefined. In terms of data analyses, these methodologies correspond to data-driven exploration where we do not specify what we are looking for before starting to examine case data. For example, we may parse the text in a sample of email messages looking for specific concepts that can become the basis for the development of formal models.

5.3.2. Developing an Internet multimethod design

The problems described above in choosing a research methodology to study interdisciplinary fields related to new CMC technologies appeared initially to be intractable. Numerous attempts over the past few decades to integrate quantitative and qualitative methodologies have resulted in labels such as *triangulation, micro-macro link* or *mixed methods* (Tashakkori and Teddlie, 2003; Bryman, 1988; Ragin, 1987; Tschudi, 1989). The idea is to employ a combination of research methods that are typically used to analyse empirical results or interpretations. The rationale is that the weakness of any single method - qualitative or quantitative - is balanced by the strengths of other methods.

The processes of intuition, description and prescription outlined in Figure 5.1 led the author to deliberate further about the relative strengths and weaknesses of existing methodologies. It became clear that a new methodological framework was necessary; a framework which formalised the systematic processes described in Figure 5.1. The author therefore developed a multimethod procedure specifically for Internet research. This multimethod design, the Complementary Explorative Data Analysis (CEDA) incorporates complementary use of both qualitative and quantitative methods. A preliminary outline of the CEDA methodology appeared earlier (Sudweeks and Simoff, 1999) and has been fully developed and described in detail in this book. The specific method (idiographic or nomothetic) at any particular stage of the study depends on the initial assumptions that need to be taken into consideration, thereby accommodating the features required for Internet research. CEDA takes into account the problems of validity and reliability in research associated with CMC technologies generally and case studies in particular.

In the next section, the differences between idiographic and nomothetic methodologies from various perspectives are described. Section 5.5 describes the CEDA design as a methodology for Internet research.

5.4. Idiography and Nomology

Idiography and nomology are two approaches to a common phenomenon. Idiographic and nomothetic methods are quite distinct. It is useful to explore these distinctions initially from a positivistic perspective before relating them to a postmodernist perspective.

In nomology, specifically quantitative analyses, argumentation is based on a representation of the phenomenon as a finite set of variables, and systematic statistical or other functional relations between these variables are sought. Argumentation is based on a description of the research objects or observation units, rather than on approximation of a limited number of variables. In idiography, specifically qualitative analyses, argumentation is based on a representation of the phenomenon as a set of loosely structured descriptive texts or dialogues, images and other illustrations rather than in the form of well-structured records.

Table 5.1 summarises the major distinctions between qualitative and quantitative methodologies relating to CMC research, with respect to the following aspects of scholarly enquiry: (i) the purpose of the enquiry, (ii) the formal model, (iii) the role of the researcher, (iv) the acquisition of knowledge, and (v) presentation of the research. In the following sections, these distinctions are discussed in detail.

Table 5.1. Comparison of qualitative and quantitative methods in CMC research.

Dimension	Qualitative research	Quantitative research
Purpose of the enquiry	Understand observed phenomena	Explain observed phenomena
Formal model	Descriptive model derived from intuitive knowledge of the phenomenon	Prescriptive model derived from descriptive model and apparent causal relationships between the variables.
Role of the researcher	Participatory role	Objective role
Acquisition of knowledge	Discover knowledge	Construct knowledge
Presentation of research	Data fragments, quotes	Figures, graphs, tables

5.4.1. Purpose of the enquiry

The purpose of *qualitative* research is to *understand observed phenomena*. Qualitative research begins with an area of interest or a research question drawn from an area of interest and a descriptive theory emerges through systematic data collection and analyses.

The object of enquiry for the qualitative researcher is typically a case. A case is a social practice, an integrated bounded system (Smith, 1979), which may or may not be functioning well. Case study is the study of a social practice in the context in which it takes place. Case research is defined as research in which the researcher has direct contact with the participants, and the participants are the primary source of the data. It follows, then, that the primary methods used in case research are interviews, surveys and participant observations.

The purpose of *quantitative* research is to *explain observed phenomena*. This methodology is based on the model of hypothesis testing. Research begins with a theory formulated as a set of hypotheses and the study is designed to find support for or against the initial theory. The initial step in quantitative research, therefore, is the design of the experiment. The researcher specifies the goals of the research, the initial hypotheses and respective ranges of phenomena for measuring quantified concepts. Each range defines the structure for the data collected. A key assumption in quantitative methodology is that observations and experiments can be *replicated*. Moreover, in a random experiment setup, for example, there is an assumption that all possible distinct outcomes are known in advance (Feelders, 2003). Therefore, the overall experimental schema needs to be designed in a way that ensures a higher accuracy of the estimation of these quantified values.

The idea was introduced and developed in the late 1920s and early 1930s to provide the ability to predict and control examined concepts. Consequently, these concepts need to be quantified. To do this, the researcher needs to know (or at least estimate) the form, type and range of the content of the data before the commencement of an experiment. Although there are some variations in practice, ideally the path of quantitative research is traversed from observation to generation of theoretical explanation to further testing of the theory. To a large extent, the observed phenomenon is separated from its context (Yin, 1989). Recently the overall schema has been extended with exploratory data analysis, when hypotheses are formulated and reformulated during the analysis.

5.4.2. Formal model

The formal model for primarily **qualitative** research is a descriptive model, shown in Figure 5.2. The internal structure, principles or other organisational aspects are the focus of study. The investigator selects a number of statements from participants, $s_1,...,s_k$, which are assumed qualitatively represent the phenomenon. Statements are categorised into subsets of all possible dimensions of the phenomena under investigation, $\mathbf{d}_1,...,\mathbf{d}_n$. The dimensions are usually identified during the process, so *n* may not be known in advance. Note that statements are not mutually exclusive members of a particular dimension but can be members of more than one dimension.

From the dimension subsets, the output is **D**, which is the union of all dimension subsets:

$$\mathbf{D} = \bigcup_{i=1}^{n} \mathbf{d}_i = \{d_1, d_2, ..., d_n\}$$

In other words, **D** represents all dimensions that have been discovered in the phenomenon. The aim is to formalise a model to approximate the behaviour of the phenomenon with certain accuracy, but also to explain the phenomenon based on this approximation.

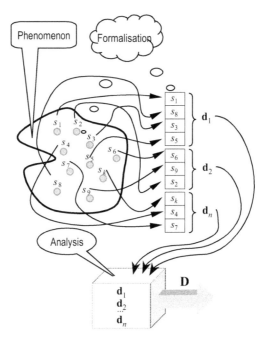

Figure 5.2. Formalised model of a qualitative Internet investigation.

The formal model for primarily quantitative research is a prescriptive model, shown in Figure 5.3. The investigator selects a finite number of variables, $v_1, ..., v_k$, which are assumed to represent the phenomenon. The independent variables are labelled $x_1, x_2, ..., x_m$; the dependent variables are labelled $y_1, ..., y_p$. The objective is not only to derive a model to approximate the behaviour of the phenomenon with certain accuracy, but also to explain and predict the phenomenon based on this approximation.

The model is not without inadequacies, though. Potential problems with such models are that they can be based on somewhat shaky assumptions, their application may not be feasible in practice, and their results may be open to misinterpretation (Nunnally, 1975).

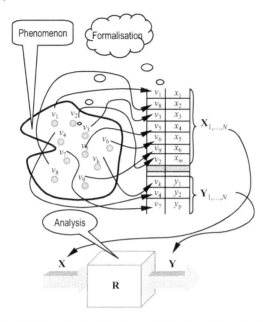

Figure 5.3. Formalised model of a quantitative Internet investigation.

5.4.3. Role of the investigator

The next step is to observe groups of people (subjects) and to record data. The role of the investigator in quantitative research is an *objective* observer. Usually the identification of variables requires substantial *a priori* empirical knowledge about the phenomenon. At this stage the experience of the investigator is critical to the adequate selection of the variables.

In the case of a passive experiment, the researcher only records the observations without setting values to "measured variables". In this scheme, there is no necessity for a preliminary division of the variables. In the case of an active experiment, the researcher may need to intrude, select the input and output variables, and set up some of the variables. The final data collection constitutes a table of the form shown in Table 5.2, where each row consists of the value of a particular variable for a particular experiment. The cell x_{11}, for example, represents the value of the variable x_1 in experiment 1.

Table 5.2. The experimental table for quantitative Internet research.

Experiment	**X**				**Y**			
	x_1	x_2	...	x_m	y_1	y_2	...	y_p
1	x_{11}	x_{21}	...	x_m	y_{11}	y_{21}	...	y_{n1}
2	x_{12}	x_{22}	...	x_{m2}	y_{12}	y_{22}	...	y_{n2}
.	.	.	.	.	.	.	.	.
.	.	.	.	.	.	.	.	.
.	.	.	.	.	.	.	.	.
N	x_{1N}	x_{2N}	...	x_{mN}	y_{1N}	y_{2N}	...	y_{nN}

The starting point for the qualitative researcher can be either the case or the question (Stake, 1995). In the former, the case presents itself as a problem and there is a need or a curiosity to learn more. Because there is a personal interest in the case, it is referred to as an intrinsic case study. In the latter, a general problem arouses interest and a particular case is chosen as a possible source for explanation. Because the case is an instrument to a general inquiry, it is referred to as an instrumental case study.

Thus, the *role* of the investigator is *participatory* and personal. Usually the identification of dimensions requires substantial *a priori* experiential knowledge about the phenomenon. The issue on which both approaches differ most is the priority that is placed on the role of interpretation during this step. All research, of course, requires some form of interpretation but, whereas quantitative research advocates the suspension of interpretation during the value-free period of experimentation, qualitative research advocates actively interpreting phenomena throughout the observation period.

In this scheme there is no division of the independent and dependent variables. All statements are evaluated and assigned to a dimension subset. The description of the final data collection can be represented as a table of the form shown in Table 5.3, where the numbers in the rows indicate if a particular statement is indicative of a particular dimension. The "1" in the matrix of $s_1.d_i$, for example, indicates that the statement s_1 is an example of the dimension d_1.

Table 5.3. The observation table.

Observation	**d_1**		**d_2**		**...**		**d_n**	
	d_i	...	d_j	d_f	...	d_p	d_f	...	d_j	d_j	...	d_p
s_1	1	...	0	0	...	1	0	...	0	0	...	0
s_2	0	...	0	0	...	0	1	...	0	0	...	1
.	.	.	.	.	.	.	.	.	.	.	.	.
.	.	.	.	.	.	.	.	.	.	.	.	.
.	.	.	.	.	.	.	.	.	.	.	.	.
s_k	0	...	0	0	...	0	1	...	1	0	...	0

5.4.4. Acquisition of knowledge

The next step in *quantitative research*, is data analysis. The selection of the appropriate data analysis method is dependent on the initial assumptions, the nature of experimental observations and the errors in these observations. Based on the established relation, **R**, the researcher has to provide some explanations for the observed behaviors, and to *construct knowledge*. These explanations are usually in the form of an approximating model. Further, either with or without refining experiments, the researcher might *generalise* these observations and propose a *theory*. Consequently, instead of trying to explain a unique event or phenomenon, the results of the research should apply to a class of cases as well. This theory could be used for building *predictive models* and become the basis for a specific research question, which is tested in a controlled manner to verify or falsify. Alternatively, a specific research question and a theory derived during qualitative research can provide *a priori* knowledge for the selection of variables. Usually this knowledge comes from the expert.

The next step in *qualitative research* is data interpretation. During this step, the typical qualitative researcher conceptualises the data and *discovers knowledge*. The conceptualisation process ranges from merely presenting the data as it was collected to avoid researcher bias, to building a theory that is grounded in the phenomenon under study. Grounded theory, for example, is a primarily inductive investigative process that emphasises research procedures (Glaser and Strauss, 1967; Glaser, 1978; Glaser, 1992; Glaser, 1998; Strauss and Corbin, 1990; Strauss and Corbin, 1994). These intuitive and interpretive processes are not regarded as less empirical than quantitative research. For example, systematic coding is important for achieving validity and reliability in analysis. Observations and data collection is rigorously systematic, occurring in natural rather than contrived contexts.

Qualitative research is not so much generalisation as extrapolation. In certain explicated respects, the results are related to broader entities. The aim is to find out what is specific and particular about the solutions adopted by these people that can be *related* to the broader population. Although the solutions adopted by the people in the case study may be regarded as isolated individual cases and as such as exceptional, some factors are very much the same for a larger population. This means it is possible to conclude indirectly (e.g. referring to other research) in which respects and to what extent the data is really an exception, in which respects it is comparable to other solutions or population groups, and what sorts of different solutions exist.

5.4.5. Presentation of research

The quantitative research results are visualised using a variety of graphing techniques that are designed to condense the vast amount of raw data. These presentation techniques usually expose some particular characteristics of the data structure and relationships between variables (Keim and Ward, 2003). The researcher has some degree of freedom to tweak the representation of the data to enhance the perception of the results. Usually each technique has one or more parameters that are sensitive to noise and smoothing. For instance, the appearance of a histogram is largely controlled by the number of bars used to depict the data. When many bars are used, the pattern of the data may look complex with fine-grained details. The reader may wonder if a simpler underlying form exists. On the other hand, the use of too few bars may obscure patterns in the data that are important to the viewer. In this case the data may look simple with course-grained details and the reader may wonder if important details are missing. Keim and Ward (2003) provide a detailed overview of information visualization and visual exploration using a classification system based on the data to be visualized, the visualization technique and the interaction technique.

Qualitative research results include a great deal of the collected data to present the researcher's interpretation of the results. Research reports usually include supporting data fragments in the form of quotes from the raw data. In this case, the researcher can slant the results towards a specific interpretation by exposing particular quotes and omitting others.

5.5. Internet Research Framework

To overcome the difficulties associated with CMC research, the Internet research framework has been developed specifically for Internet research. One step of the framework is the Complementary Explorative Data Analysis (CEDA) process. CEDA uses qualitative techniques in conjunction with quantitative techniques. Qualitative techniques are used to derive elements of a grounded theory and, from this theory, a set of hypotheses is identified for quantitative analysis. Even though the quantitative analysis has problems, such as the inability to collect identical data again (i.e. replicability), the analysis can be used to give support for a generalisation of the explanation of the phenomenon discovered in the qualitative analyses. Note that this is a different technique to triangulation in that the results of the qualitative analysis is used as a "booster" for the quantitative analysis rather than using the different methods for cross-checking information. The quantitative analysis may or may not be successful in generalising results and building a predictive model.

The Internet research framework adopts a number of steps to ensure the essence of the phenomenon under study is captured (Figure 5.4).

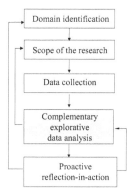

Figure 5.4. The Internet research framework.

5.5.1. Domain identification

The first step in any study is to obtain a clear understanding of the definition and boundaries of what is being studied. Internet research incorporates a number of separate research domains, including electronic commerce and business systems, computer-mediated communication (CMC), computer-supported collaborative work (CSCW), and distributed information systems, including mobile systems. Therefore the first stage is devoted to the identification of domain specifics which, in this research study, is CMC albeit in conjunction with a variety of other domains. The identified domain specifics influence the selection of the appropriate research methods and the possible scope of the research.

5.5.2. Scope of the research

A global society (or cybersociety, e.g. Jones (1995; 1997; 1998)) created by the Internet is no longer a projected vision of technocrats, it has become a reality in many senses. However, the global society is not the "global village" as envisioned by McLuhan and Powers (1986), but more like virtual neighborhoods (or cybervillages). Before the Web explosion, cybervillages were defined not by geopolitical boundaries but by listserv subscriptions or chat channels. Today, even those loosely defined boundaries are blurred as cybervillages connected to a web of hyperlinked open information space.

Only recently are communication and cultural problems associated with a global community being investigated (Ess, 1996; Jones, 1995; Jones, 1997; Jones, 1998; Smith, McLaughlin and Osborne, 1998; Voiskounsky, 1998). Global norms about privacy, freedom of speech, intellectual property, and standards of conduct are being developed. To understand new global communities, communication patterns of computer-mediated texts are investigated. In this book, the specific scope of the research relates to development and leadership characteristics of computer-mediated communities.

5.5.3. Data collection and selection of the data sets

The research for this book focuses on how the management of communication within dispersed and co-located collaborative groups can influence cohesiveness and develop a sense of consciousness which in turn contributes to both productivity and social satisfaction of group members. The communication practices of participants and subgroups within collaborative groups were observed in two case studies. This research uses a variety of data collection techniques from a number of sources to obtain diverse data sets. The data sets are from participant observation, archived electronic discussions, surveys, and in-depth interviews of key stakeholders in each study.

Marshall and Rossman (1995) list the strengths and weaknesses of various data collection methods. Table 5.4 summarises and adapts the Marshall and Rossman list for the data collection methods used in this research study, i.e. participant observation, interviews, historical data and surveys.

Table 5.4. Strengths and weaknesses of the different data collection methods.

Strengths	PO	I	HD	S
Easy to manipulate and categorise for data analysis				✓
Facilitates cooperation from research subjects	✓	✓		
Facilitates access for follow-up clarification	✓	✓	✓	
Easy and efficient to administer and manage			✓	✓
Amenable to statistical analysis				✓
Easy to establish generalisability			✓	✓
Data collected in natural setting	✓	✓		
Documents major events, crises, social conflicts			✓	
Good for obtaining data from nonverbal communication		✓		
Facilitates analysis, validity checks and triangulation	✓	✓	✓	✓
Facilitates discovery of nuances in culture	✓	✓	✓	
Provides flexibility in the formulation of hypotheses	✓	✓	✓	
Provides background context	✓	✓	✓	
Discovers "native's perspective" of organisational processes	✓	✓	✓	

Weaknesses	PO	I	HD	S
Sometimes difficult to "see the forest while observing the trees"	✓			✓
Open to misinterpretation due to cultural differences	✓	✓		✓
Open to ethical dilemmas	✓			
Difficult to replicate	✓	✓		
Open to observer effects, obtrusive and reactive	✓	✓		
Dependent on the honesty of those providing the data		✓	✓	✓
Dependent on systematic, honest, unbiased researcher	✓	✓	✓	

Adapted from Marshall and Rossman (Marshall and Rossman, 1995, pp.100-101).

Key: PO = Participant Observation; I = Interview; HD = Historical Data; S = Survey

5.5.4. Complementary explorative data analysis

Complementary Explorative Data Analysis (CEDA) can be viewed as a dynamic process that provides a valid combination of both quantitative and qualitative methods. CEDA employs qualitative methods to discover dimensions from textual data to develop a theory of the phenomenon and ensure the essence of the phenomenon is captured. Hypotheses are then extracted from the theory and a quantitative method applied to generalise the results obtained from the qualitative analyses. Figure 5.5 gives a breakdown of the CEDA process within the Internet research framework.

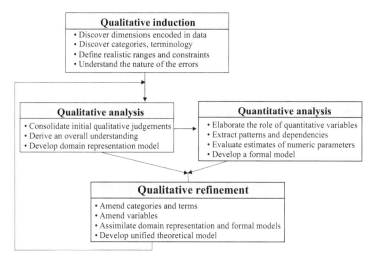

Figure 5.5. Complementary explorative data analysis (CEDA).

The first stage of CEDA is *qualitative induction*. During this initial stage, a fuzzy picture emerges from the data as categories and dimensions are discovered, appropriate constraints defined, and the extent of noise (errors) in the data is understood. The second stage is *analysis*. During this stage, the fuzzy picture that emerged in the initial stage is understood more clearly and a model is developed. The final stage is *refinement* during which any necessary adjustments are made. The final result may lead to revision of the identified domain specifics and changes in the combination of analysis methods within the Internet research framework.

Figure 5.6 illustrates the components of the CEDA step when applied to the investigation of communication in computer-mediated groups. Each of the six components, will now be described.

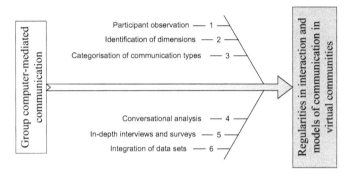

Figure 5.6. The CEDA framework for Case Study 1 and Case Study 2.

The first three steps relate to qualitative induction section in Figure 5.5. It is in these three steps that dimensions and categories are discovered. Steps 4 and 5 relate to the qualitative and quantitative analyses sections in Figure 5.5. These two analyses steps give the researcher an overall understanding of the phenomenon and enable the researcher to develop a domain representation model and a formal model. Step 6 relates to the qualitative refinement section of Figure 5.5 in which a unified theoretical model is developed based on the models developed in Steps 4 and 5.

Step 1: Participant observation. As mentioned in Section 5.5.3, the author was both participating and observing communication processes within the two case studies. Although the data was analysed after the completion of each case study, the participatory component has elements of action research. Action research can be described as a family of research methodologies which pursue action and understanding at the same time. It is an emergent process which takes shape as understanding increases; it is an iterative process which alternates between action and critical reflection. However, the participant in this case reflected and acted on the process of collaboration in light of the understanding developed at each cycle, rather than on the methods, data and interpretation that is common in action research.

Step 2: Identification of dimensions. Communication usually occurs through a system of vague agreements about the use of terms. When researching human communication, it is necessary to define the exact meaning of specific terms. The process of defining terms is conceptualisation and this involves describing aspects of a particular concept, called dimensions. Dimensions, therefore, are specifiable aspects of a concept. Specifying dimensions assists in a greater understanding of the phenomenon being researched.

Step 3: Categorisation of communication types. Communication types are categorised, or classified, according to a coding scheme. The development of the coding scheme involves three steps: (i) *initial coding*, in which significant ideas and concepts are identified; (ii) *theoretical coding*, in which the emergent relationships between codes are identified; and (iii) *selective coding*, in which only concepts and relationships relating to the research hypotheses are selected. Selective coding helps to produce a more focused theory with a smaller set of detailed concepts. Too many categories may obscure results and too few can lead to unreliable and potentially invalid conclusions. It is important, therefore, to allow the context and necessities of the research questions to influence the selection of codes. The codes can be arranged in a hierarchy, where one code is included within another (see Section 6.3.2 for a detailed explanation of how the coding scheme was developed). Conceptual analysis (or thematic analysis, see Palmquist, Carley and Dale, 1997) involves quantifying and tallying the presence of particular concepts or dimensions within a text.

Step 4: Conversation analysis. Conversation analysis, grounded in ethno-methodology (Garfinkel, 1967), is concerned with uncovering the implicit assumptions and structures in social life through a close scrutiny of the way people converse with one another. Silverman (1993), based on the work of other conversational analysis theorists and practitioners, summarised three fundamental assumptions that are relevant to this study in CMC:

1. Communication in the form of a conversation is a socially structured activity, i.e. it has established rules of behaviour which, in the case of CMC, have to comply to the limits of the underlying technology. For example, in face-to-face communication, the rule of taking turns with only one person speaking at a time may be violated, but in a text-based chat room or virtual classroom, the dialogue will always be presented as a sequence of text utterances.
2. Conversation is placed always in particular context. The same utterance may have a totally different meaning in different contexts. In this sense the context in CMC can be identified by using text analysis technique, like KWIC –

"keywords in context", where the researcher looks at the words in the neighbourhood of a selected concept or keyword.

3. Conversation analysis is based, traditionally, on the analysis of extremely accurate recordings (including bad grammatical forms, intonation, even pauses). In a similar way, in CMC, the actual transcript of a communication session is analysed not only for the content, but also for additional cues like emoticons, abbreviations (e.g. "IMHO" for "in my humble opinion"), or CMC phonetic abbreviations (e.g. "u" instead of "you").

Step 5: In-depth interviews and surveys. Although the researcher can observe by watching and participating, more active enquiry is appropriate. A qualitative interview is one in which the interviewer has a general plan of enquiry but does not use a specific set of questions – it has an overall goal but pursues specific topics raised by the respondent. The answers stimulated by the researcher's initial questions shape the subsequent questions. Surveys are a useful tool for operationalising variables. The questionnaire, in particular, elicits information that is useful for analysis. The researcher is often interested in determining the extent to which respondents hold a particular opinion or perspective. This procedure has been formalised through the creation of the Likert scale, a format in which respondents are asked to indicate the strength of an opinion from strongly agree to strongly disagree. An important purpose in constructing and conducting a questionnaire is to operationalise variables for analysis (Babbie, 2002).

Step 6: Integration of data sets. Boundaries between numerically and textually based research are becoming less distinct: data may be readily transformed from one type to another, making achievable integration of data types and analysis methods.

5.5.5. Proactive reflection-in-action

This section describes the final stage in the Internet research framework – *proactive reflection-in-action*. This stage is based on the extension and application of Schön's (1983; 1991) principles of the reflective practitioner with elements of action research (Argyris and Schön, 1989), in particular, with the integration (or embedding) of the action researcher as 'the practitioner' in Schön's schema. The action research approach extends the observational/experimental research schema by allowing researchers to bring their personal background and knowledge into the investigation cycle, which may influence the outcomes. In other words, the researcher is one of the participants, or part of the sample, rather than an independent observer.

The "reflective practitioner" was derived as Schön (1983) studied and analysed design processes. In his later work, Schön (1991) presented a number of examples of disciplines that fit a process model with characteristics similar to the design process. What is relevant to the exploratory research method described in this work is Schön's view that designers put things together and create new things in a process involving numerous variables as well as a range of obligations and limitations; that almost anything a designer does involves consequences that far exceed those expected; and that a design process one which has no unique concrete solution. The analogy to CEDA is that the researcher is compared to the designer in that the researcher puts evidential pieces of information together and creates new grounded theories in a process that involves numerous variables and methods with their limitations and initial assumptions that act as constraints. The exploratory methodology usually leads to results that exceed those expected and may change the direction of the research.

Schön also states that he sees a designer as someone who changes an indefinite situation into a definite one through a reflexive conversation with the material of the situation. By analogy, the researcher changes the complexity of the problem through the reflexive investigative iterations with the data and derived grounded theories. The reflective step is a revision of the reference framework taken in the previous step. For example, as a result of the reflective step the researcher can collect additional data to be able to address an unexpected behaviour discovered during the reflection on the analysis methods. In fact, at this stage, the researcher is faced with a problem for which he or she tries to imagine an approach to address, even a solution. The outcome may open up a range of new discoveries and consequences for the research framework, and so on.

As the researcher reflects on the direction adopted previously, branches of the problem begin to appear, along with possible consequences and options, all based on the current research results and vision that the researcher has formed. The virtuosity of the researcher is in the ability to reframe the situation in a way that the new 'frame' accommodates and does not contradict previously achieved results. This, of course, is possible when the researcher is part of the process under investigation (that is, a participant observer). The outcome of the reflection is an operative solution to the research problem (e.g. extending the coding schema or applying additional analyses, hence the methodology proposed in this book operates with an open hierarchical coding schemata, capable of accommodating such changes). The constant evaluation and refinement process of the action research approach leads, if necessary, to a reformulation of the research problem.

The stage is a proactive reflection as the process is driven by the researcher in a somewhat pre-emptive mode - the refinement process may begin even before all the results are obtained as the researcher, based on background knowledge, can extrapolate from partial results. The results of the reflection lead to an immediate action, hence "reflection-in-action". The research progresses via such iterative movements.

5.6. Summary

This chapter described a multimethod design for investigating computer-mediated environments in which traditional communication norms are challenged. CEDA is a cyclical systematic process of intuition, description and prediction. The CEDA framework involves 5 steps – domain identification, scope of the research, data collection, complementary explorative data analysis (qualitative induction, qualitative analysis, quantitative analysis, qualitative refinement) and proactive reflection-in-action. The framework takes an intuitive model of human nature and develops a descriptive model based on an initial analysis of collected data. The descriptive model guides the investigator to more data collection and analyses to develop a tentative descriptive model. Throughout the process there is an ontological loop as a reality check of the initial research questions.

The significance of this research methodology is in its flexibility and robustness. It incorporates elements of quantitative research and complementary qualitative concepts. The internal validity of quantitative research is complemented by the credibility judged by the participants themselves. The external validity of quantitative research is complemented by the applicability of the tool to a variety of cases, demonstrated in this book by its application to two very different case studies. The reliability of quantitative research is complemented by the various sets of data collected and various types of analyses applied.

The quantitative assumption of objectivity – that researcher bias is avoided – is more debatable in CEDA. However, qualitative researchers (e.g. Lincoln and Guba, 1985) point to confirmability; that is, the data can be confirmed by other observers or participants. The fact that the researcher is part of the process permits the researcher to use his or her own experience in every unique situation that is faced during the investigation. This is extremely valuable in a proactive strategy such as CEDA as it helps the researcher in seeking evaluation, refinement, formulation and reformulation of additional hypotheses as a result of the reflection.

In the next chapter, CEDA is applied to Case Studies 1 and 2 and the research design is described.

CHAPTER 6

METHODOLOGY

6.1. Introduction

The combination of several formalisms within one framework is a complex task, and even the elucidation of the relationship between them is complex. As discussed in the previous chapter, various quantitative (numerical) techniques have been developed independently, relying on different modelling assumptions and using different inference techniques. The situation with qualitative formalisms is similar. The most difficult part of the task of combining and relating formalisms in CEDA is mixing qualitative and quantitative methods. The difficulty is partly due to the fact that the two types of formalisms are intended to deal with different types of imperfect information. However, the aim of this research is to analyse messages so that it will be possible to identify communication phenomena revealed by groups and to test hypotheses derived from theories about group behaviour.

In Chapter 5, CEDA – a common research methodology combining both types of formalisms – was developed. This chapter provides a description of an application of that methodology. By using appropriate visualisations, this analysis methodology integrates data processing with the human cognitive abilities for visual exploration and pattern discovery. The CEDA methodology is applied to two significantly different case studies.

Before the research design derived from CEDA is presented in detail (qualitative reasoning, domain representation model and formal model), the participants and data used for analyses in this book are described.

6.1.1. Participants

The participants in Case Study 1 were an international voluntary group of scholars collaborating on a research project. The number of participants varied at any one time between 40 and 180 throughout the two-year period but there were 143 members who were consistently involved in the project. The participants represented a wide range of disciplines (40% from the social sciences, 35% from humanities, and 25% from applied sciences), a wide range of ages (early 20s to late 60s), and various professional levels (40% academics, 25% PhD students, 20% Masters students, 15% researchers in the private sector). Approximately two-thirds were living in the United States; the remaining one-third were spread across the globe, representing 21 countries overall (Table 6.1). The author was one of the two coordinators of the project group.

Table 6.1. Countries represented by Case Study 1 participants

Australia	Hong Kong	New Zealand
Austria	Hungary	Poland
Brazil	Ireland	Singapore
Canada	Israel	Sweden
Denmark	Japan	Switzerland
Germany	Mexico	United States
Great Britain	Netherlands	USSR

The participants in Case Study 2 were 99 undergraduate students studying Organisational Informatics at Murdoch University, and the coordinator of the course. The students were assigned to seven workshop groups of approximately 16 members. Although most students were living in Western Australia, they came from eclectic backgrounds that represented 16 nationalities (Table 6.2). The author was the coordinator of the unit and is referred to as the *facilitator.*

Table 6.2. Countries of origin represented by Case Study 2 participants

Australia	Malaysia
Brunei	Netherlands
China	Poland
Germany	Singapore
Greece	Taiwan
India	Turkey
Indonesia	United Kingdom
Kenya	Vietnam

6.1.2. Data sources

A variety of data collection techniques from a number of sources were used to obtain diverse data sets. The data sets are from participant observation, archived electronic discussions, surveys, and in-depth interviews of key stakeholders in each study.

Participation observation. Throughout the duration of each study, the author was both participating and observing communication processes within both case studies. Observation assisted in discovering underlying assumptions and dimensions of which group participants may have been unaware (Hammersley and Atkinson, 1983). Participant observation gave access to all group discussions, thus providing richness of data (Witmer, 1997).

Historical Data. In Case Study 1, members posted 1,130 messages to the project hotline. In Case Study 2, 7 groups of approximately 16 students participated in 9 hours of synchronous discussions which were automatically logged and downloaded by the author. The data from 3 of the 7 groups were incomplete due to technical problems (server downtime during workshop sessions), so data from 4 groups were analysed for this book. These two data sets (1,130 email messages of Case Study 1 and 36 hours of synchronous dialogue of Case Study 2) documenting all events and interactions, were used for conversational analysis (see Section 6.5 for a detailed description of the preprocessing and transformation of this data). Although the dialogue used for analysis is written rather than spoken, the principles of conversational analysis still apply. The texts were examined for commonalities and differences in communication management and theme (or dimension) content in order to uncover implicit assumptions and structures in collaborative and social life (Silverman, 1993). To understand linguistic form and content, it is essential to have a deep understanding of how the content is situated in the local context (Lindlof, 1995).

Surveys. A survey was distributed to Case Study 1 coders via email and was also available by FTP (see Appendix A.13). Each individual who joined the Case Study 1 project were also asked to provide a brief bio of themselves. In Case Study 2, a peer assessment form (see Appendix B.3) and a survey asking respondents for a cognitive evaluation of various aspects of the course were emailed to students. Completed forms were returned to the author. Only demographic information was extracted from all surveys for analysis in this book, however the surveys were used to collect some additional information specific to each case study (see, e.g. Sudweeks and Simoff, 2000; Sudweeks, 2003; Mabry and Sudweeks, 2003).

Interviews. In addition to participant observation, nine project members in Case Study 1 were interviewed. The semi-structured in-depth interviews took place in various locations in the United States in May 1996, each taking between one to two hours. Three students in Case Study 2 were interviewed in January 2000, each taking between half an hour and an hour. A tape recorder was used, with the permission of interviewees, and transcribed at a later date. Each interviewee agreed willingly to be available for further clarification.

6.2. Qualitative Reasoning

As mentioned in Chapter 5, the first stage of CEDA is *qualitative reasoning*. During this initial stage, a fuzzy picture emerges from the data as categories and dimensions are discovered, appropriate constraints defined, and the extent of noise (errors) in the data is understood.

Qualitative researchers generally develop prospective research questions early in the study, derived from personal experience and from relevant literature that identified problems or puzzling areas. These questions are referred to as *etic* issues; that is, issues raised external to the study, by the researcher or the wider research community (Stake, 1995). Etic issues help to structure the observations, interviews, surveys and relevant documents associated with the case studies. The questions of interest early in the study are listed below:

1. In group text-based CMC, where dramaturgical cues are weak, are there developmental processes?
2. What are the key communication processes in a computer-mediated group?
3. If communication patterns change over the life of a group, are the changes influenced by leadership strategies?
4. Do group members evolve over the life of a group?

As the study progresses, early research questions evolve. Some are refined, some are discarded and some are added. The additional issues emerge from the study itself. These questions are referred to as *emic* issues; that is, issues raised internally, from the stakeholders of the case study (Stake, 1995). In studies in which data is to be coded, the research questions need to be defined more clearly as assertions before relevant variables can be identified and understood. The research questions that evolved in this study, and finally transformed into research hypotheses, are listed in Table 6.3. The research hypotheses are divided into two broad categories which address characteristics of the developmental process of groups and the group leaders. Each of these categories of hypotheses are then divided into more specific hypotheses.

The next stage is *analysis*. During this stage, the fuzzy picture that emerged in the initial stage is understood more clearly and a model is developed. The second stage includes both qualitative and quantitative analyses and the development of domain representation model and the formal model.

Table 6.3. Research hypotheses

1.	**Developmental Characteristics:** **Do computer-mediated groups, like their traditional counterparts, display developmental processes?** 1.1. There are definable developmental stages in virtual groups. 1.2. In the early stages of development, the content of communication is more conceptual than task oriented or social. 1.3. During periods of low task activity, the content of communication is more social than task oriented. 1.4. During periods of high task activity, the content of communication is more task oriented than social. 1.5. During later developmental stages, participants engage in less disclosures about the physical and social attributes of themselves and others. 1.6. Group cohesiveness increases over the life of the group
2.	**Leadership Characteristics:** **Does leadership vary during the computer-mediated group lifecycle?** 2.1. Management intervention is more frequent during periods of high task activity. 2.2. Different management styles predominate at different developmental stages. 2.3. Leaders communicate more intensely than other participants. 2.4. Leaders emerge during the life of the group.

6.3. Domain Representation Model

There are a number of ways in which to characterise communication in time. To be able to compare the results of two dissimilar case studies, communication is viewed as a *set of utterances*, as illustrated in Figure 6.1. The representation model is derived by analogy from a model for the analysis of activities in text-based virtual worlds proposed by Simoff and Maher (2000). Simoff and Maher's representation model extends the approach taken in speech act theory (see Searle, 1969; Austin, 1962) to the description of different activities (including synchronous communication) in text-based virtual worlds only. The representation model employed in this book is focused on a uniform description of both synchronous and asynchronous CMC, and is intended to be applicable to different underlying technologies. An utterance denotes a communication unit, expressed in the format of the mediating system. In general, one physical message may have one or more utterances, as it is shown further in this chapter.

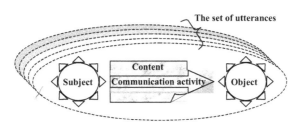

Figure 6.1. Computer-mediated communication presented as a set of utterances.

In this book, the CMC model described is based on the premise that each communication activity is composed of (i) a subject who performs the communication event, (ii) the content of the communication event, and (iii) an object(s) to whom the communication event is addressed. In other words, a subject is communicating content to an object. This general model is applicable in text-based CMC to communication activities in both *asynchronous* environments (e.g. bulletin boards, e-mail discussion lists, file-sharing workspaces) and *synchronous* environments (e.g. chat rooms, virtual worlds and shared whiteboards).

Figure 6.2 and Figure 6.3 are representations of asynchronous CMC scenarios.

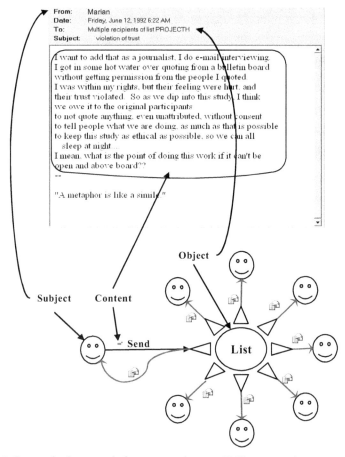

Figure 6.2. Communication scenario from an asynchronous CMC group session, supported by a list server technology.

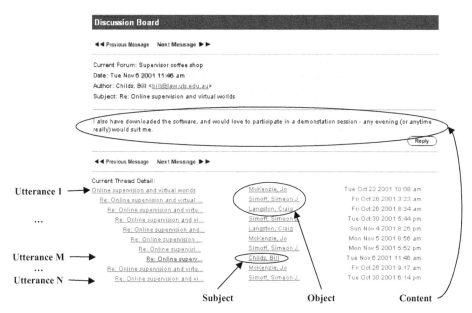

Figure 6.3. Communication scenario from an asynchronous CMC group session, supported by a bulletin board technology.

Figure 6.2 illustrates the application of the model to the asynchronous communication medium of an email discussion list. The s*ubject*[1] in this case is the sender, or the source, of the message sent to the "list". The initial (direct) recipient of the message may not necessarily be a person but may be an e-mail bot[2], another list, or an agent communicating messages. The *object* in this scenario includes all the agents (people and bots) to whom the list-serving program has permission to send messages. The *content* is the actual message content. In the content, however, there can be additional information about the *object* of the communication activity. For example, the subject may address a particular part of communicated information to a specific person(s), hence splitting the content into two (or more) parts, where part of the message is addressed to an object that is the whole list, and part of the message is addressed to an object that is one (or a few) specific person(s). To analyse messages at the utterance level, a possible way to deal with such cases is to split the message into two (or more)

---

[1] The *subject* in this model should not be confused with the "subject" field of an email message. The "subject" field is intended to specify the topic of the content.
[2] Bot is short for robot – in this instance, a program that runs automatically without human intervention.

utterances, with each utterance having the same subject, but different object and content parts.

Figure 6.3 illustrates the application of the model to another asynchronous CMC scenario – communication via a bulletin board system used for discussion purposes. Bulletin boards offer explicit means for identifying and visualising discussion threads, thus each message in the bulletin board can be considered an utterance. In general, a message may contain one or more utterances, but in reality it is unlikely. The *subject* is the person who posted the message. The *object,* in general, is the whole group in that everyone who has access to the bulletin board can read the messages; the thread structure, however, is capable of locating and localising some subgroups that are the actual object for that particular part of the communication. The *content* section is the actual content of the posted message.

Figure 6.4, Figure 6.5 and Figure 6.6 are representations of synchronous CMC scenarios. Figure 6.4 illustrates the application of the model to the synchronous communication medium of a chat room.

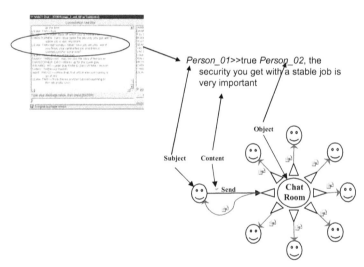

Figure 6.4. Communication scenario from a synchronous CMC group session, supported by chat server technology.

The *subject* in this case is the person who types the message in the "message" field and presses the "enter" key. The subject is identified by a name (sometimes referred to as a "handle"[3]), which is defined as that person's unique identification and is associated with a password in a protected chat environment. The *object,* in general, is the whole group participating in the chat session or it can be a specific person or subgroup of people. The *content* section is the actual content of the communication. As for the asynchronous environments, a message addressed to more than one person can be split into two or more utterances, each having a unique object. In practice, though, most messages in synchronous environments are very short and have one object – whether the group, a subgroup or a person. Even in the case where the message is to two or more people, the entire content is generally directed to those people. Hence, in these environments, each message is generally an utterance.

Figure 6.5 illustrates the application of the model to the synchronous communication medium of a text-based virtual world.

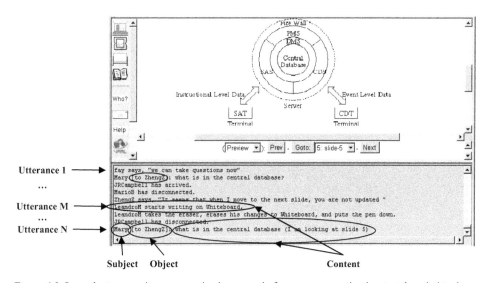

Figure 6.5. Several utterances in a communication scenario from a group session in a text-based virtual world.

The text-based virtual world includes a chat room component, similar to Figure 6.4. The *subject* in this case can be a person, a bot or the virtual world. Utterance M in Figure 6.5

---

[3] When communicating in an online environment, a handle is the name that used for identification purposes. It can be the person's real name, a nickname, or a completely fictitious name.

is an example of the virtual world as a subject, as the environment itself reports on some activity that is taking place. The text in utterance M is the content only of the communication activity. The object can include the group currently engaged in the synchronous session (see, for example, utterance 1 and M), or a specific person (see, for example, utterance N). When a specific person is the object in an utterance in such a synchronous environment, dialogues or "conversation" threads similar to a bulletin board can be identified.

Researchers in CMC have recently focused on investigating communication and interaction in 3D virtual worlds, mainly in a descriptive ("this is how we did it") and qualitative way (see, for example, Schreoder, 2002, chaps 3 and 6). The representation model proposed in this chapter offers a consistent way to present and analyse communication in these environments. Figure 6.6 is another illustration of the application of the model to a synchronous CMC environment – in this case a 3D virtual world with text-based communication.

The formal representation is similar to the text-based virtual worlds in Figure 6.5. However, the representation of each participant in the communication session as an avatar[4] influences significantly the *content* section of each utterance (Becker and Mark, 2002). For example, avatars are usually "equipped" with a set of gestures, hence, ideally, the content section of the utterance in such a virtual environment should include such information.

Avatars in computer-mediated communication introduce another dimension in the analysis. Consider the following scenarios:

1. An avatar uses a gesture(s) to communicate a message. In Figure 6.7a, for example, an avatar "waves".

2. An avatar uses a gesture(s) to clarify the meaning of a message. In Figure 6.7b, for example, an avatar asks a question and with the gesture indicates that it may not be that serious question. In Figure 6.7c, the avatar provides the answer to the question using a "smiling" gesture to clarify that this was a joke.

---

[4] *Avatar* is an ancient Sanskrit term meaning 'a god's embodiment on the Earth' (Damer, 1998). An 'avatar' is a 3D model of a person and shows where he/she is, where he/she is looking, and what gestures he/she wants to communicate. The 3D representation includes characteristics such as a verbal description, messages about movements in the place, and links to web pages and publications that help establish identity and personality. The visual presence of avatars brings a new dimension in communication in virtual places.

Subject

Utterance 1

Utterance 2

Utterance 3

Utterance 4

Utterance 5

Utterance 6

....

Content

Subject

Subject

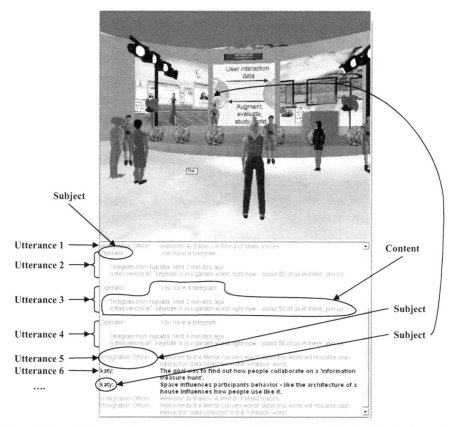

Figure 6.6. Several utterances in a communication scenario from a group session in a 3D virtual world.

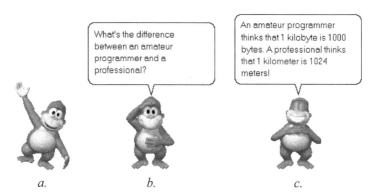

Figure 6.7. Avatar gestures as communication utterances.

3. An avatar addresses a group but uses gestures to communicate additional information to one or more people. In Figure 6.8, for example, an avatar is asking a question of the group and, using a gesture, attempts to communicate that he or she is being "facetious".

4. An avatar addresses one person in a group but gestures to one or more people in the group. In a group meeting, for example, an avatar may be answering a question while simultaneously gesturing another person to pause.

Figure 6.8. An avatar communicating to a group of avatars with a gesture that provides additional information to part of the group.

In each of these scenarios, there is communication information that is usually not recorded in conversational communication scripts. In the first scenario, the gesture is the actual communication content of the utterance. The "waving" in Figure 6.7a could be used instead of saying "hello" or "goodbye" and could be coded according to the context in which it was used, but it is a separate (silent) utterance. In the second scenario, by using a gesture, the avatar communicates additional contextual information to the group about the content of the utterance. The gesture in this case is part of the utterance and can be used at the coding stage for clarification of the actual conversational utterance. This is similar, to some extent, to when a "smiley" is used in the text of an utterance to clarify the intended meaning of the message.

The situation in the third scenario is where the avatar communicates a message to the whole group and communicates additional context information to one person or part of the group. In this case, one communication event can be split into two or more utterances, each with the same subject, but having a different object and communication content.

In the fourth scenario, the gesture is used as an alternative communication means, similar to the first scenario. Hence, similar to the approach in the third scenario, the utterance is split in two (or more, in the case of a sequence of gestures) utterances, with a common subject but different objects and communication content.

The model presented in Figure 6.1, therefore, can accommodate CMC acts that include information that augments, supports or contradicts the actual text communication. The problem in the analysis of such communication events is in data collection and data pre-processing. At the data collection stage, one has to ensure that this information is recorded in a meaningful format, including the time stamp, type of gesture, orientation of the avatar, and the closest avatars at that point of time. Such data can be part of the server log of the virtual world. At the data pre-processing stage, the time stamp can be used to relate the gesture "transcripts" to the conversational transcripts. An additional, and extremely difficult problem, is whether the information communicated with gestures has actually been seen, and interpreted, by the participants to whom it was addressed. These issues are a topic for further research and investigation and are beyond the scope of this book.

Figure 6.2-Figure 6.8 demonstrate that the CMC representation model allows researchers to derive rules for formalising and pre-processing transcripts from different CMC sources in a manner such that they can form a coherent data set. Given the diversification of CMC supporting technologies, such a model becomes an integral part of communication analysis methods and techniques. Applying this model as a data organisation model means that an utterance is considered as a *data unit* in the data set that describes the communication under consideration. Using the utterance as the unit of analysis in organising data in CMC, different types of communication scenarios in different periods of time can be compared. In this book, an asynchronous communication scenario using a list server over a two-year period is compared with a synchronous communication scenario using a chat server over a two-and-half-month period.

Another benefit is the ability to use different quantitative characteristics and measures for describing communication in terms of utterances. For example, the number of words in an utterance can be used as a characteristic of the size (or length) of an utterance in text-based communication. Such measure is applicable to the analysis of both synchronous and asynchronous communication. Quantitative measures can therefore be related to some characteristics of communication content.

6.4. Formal Model

As discussed earlier, the representation described in Figure 6.1 presents a communication activity mediated by either asynchronous or synchronous technologies. Regardless of whether the communication data is obtained from a list server, a chat server, or a virtual world, it can be reduced to a collection of utterances. Each utterance can be represented as:

$$\langle \text{Subject}, \text{Object}, \text{Content} \rangle$$

This form is referred to as a SOC-triple and the utterance can therefore be denoted as:

$$u_i = \langle s_i, o_i, c_i \rangle$$

where s_i denotes the subject that communicates the message in utterance u_i, o_i is the object of utterance u_i - the party to whom the message is addressed and c_i is the content of utterance u_i - the content of the message passed from the subject s_i to the object o_i. This model of an utterance provides a common timeless representation for both asynchronous and synchronous communication.

A set of utterances U is a sequence of SOC-triples u_i, $U = u_1, u_2, ..., u_n$, where n can be viewed as the *length* of the sequence of utterances (denoted further as Λ_U). Hence, a communication transcript that has been converted into n utterances can be called an *n*-utterance session. The sequence $U = \langle s_1, o_1, c_1 \rangle, \langle s_2, o_2, c_2 \rangle, ..., \langle s_n, o_n, c_n \rangle$ can derive the set of unique subjects $S = s^1, s^2, ..., s^m$ who are the different participants in a communication session. Further, this set of subjects is referred as a *group* where m is the number of participants. In general, a group can have subgroups or can be a part of another larger group.

Data sets in case studies vary from a single set of utterances (in the first case study) to a collection of sets of utterances (in the second case study). For example, communication transcripts from discussions that four groups have performed over 9 workshops forms a data set $D = \{ U_{g_i w_j} \}$, of 36 sets of utterances. Here, g_i, $i = 1, ..., 4$ indicates the group number, and w_j $j = 1, ..., 9$ indicates the workshop number.

Using the above presented formal representation, which reflects the model presented in Figure 6.1, researchers can apply different data pre-processing, grouping and dividing techniques to compose different data subsets that aim at discovering different communication patterns.

A *communication pattern* is a subsequence $U_{kl} = u_k, ..., u_l$, where $U_{kl} \subset U$ and $k < l$. In this framework, communication patterns can be grouped into three classes:

- *Content-independent patterns* – these patterns are statistics or utterance sequences that can be derived from an analysis of communication sequences without consideration of the content of the utterances.
- *Content-dependent patterns* – these patterns are statistics or utterance sequences that can be derived from an analysis of labelled communication sequences, where the labels belong to a predefined coding scheme, and each utterance is labelled according to its content.
- *Content-based patterns* – these patterns consist of various text statistics, term clusters, contingency analyses, and taxonomies of words, which are derived from a text analysis of the utterance content.

In this book, content-independent and content-dependent patterns will be identified and analysed only.

6.4.1. Content-independent analysis

Technically, content-independent communication patterns can be derived from tallying the *number* of utterances of communicating subjects over a period of time, or from plotting a *sequence* of utterances of communicating subjects. In the first case, content-independent analyses are used as an explorative tool for understanding the data more clearly and identifying initial points for more thorough analyses. A variety of visualisation techniques can be applied at this stage to grasp an overview of the data. For example, in group discussion data, such an analysis can reveal a high level of participation of a particular person. This highly participative person could be identified as a possible catalyst in the group development process, or identified as having a vital role in the group such as an *expert*, or an *emergent leader*. This information assists in interpreting content-dependent patterns at a later stage.

The graphs in Figure 6.9 illustrate the participation rates of a subset of group members in Case Study 2 (a series of 9 one-hour workshops), based on number of utterances of each member. Student_2 demonstrates a constant high level of participation, which is an indication that the role of this particular student in the development of the group should be examined closely. Note that at this stage it is not important whether the participation rate is a result of a high percentage of social utterances (which could indicate a core group member) or a high percentage of topic-related utterances (which could indicate an expert or emergent leader within the group). Each pie-graph can be viewed as a static group pattern for the respective workshop.

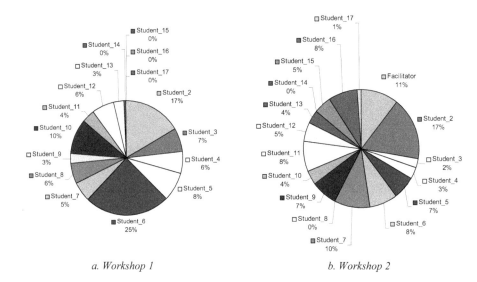

a. Workshop 1   *b. Workshop 2*

Figure 6.9. Examples of the results of a content-independent analysis of group discussions. Each visualisation shows individual participation statistics for Workshops 1 and 2 in Case Study 2.

In the second content-independent case – plotting a sequence of utterances of communicating subjects – the communication pattern U_{kl} is reduced to a sequence of subjects $S_{kl} = s_k^2, s_{k+1}^1, s_{k+2}^2 \ldots, s_l^j$ where $j \in \{1,\ldots,m\}$. A suitable form of visualisation of such patterns is a *timeline of utterances*, which show the sequences for each participant on separate axes. Timelines are built by replacing each of the subjects s_l^j with a unique numerical label (Simoff, 1996).

Figure 6.10 shows the timelines for the example presented in Figure 6.9. Each timeline can be viewed as a dynamic group pattern for the respective workshop. The timeline in Figure 6.10a shows that part of the group were engaged in the group activities only in the second half of the workshop. The participation pattern for Student_2 suggests that this participant is an emerging leader, dominating the timeline patterns in Figure 6.10a and Figure 6.10b.

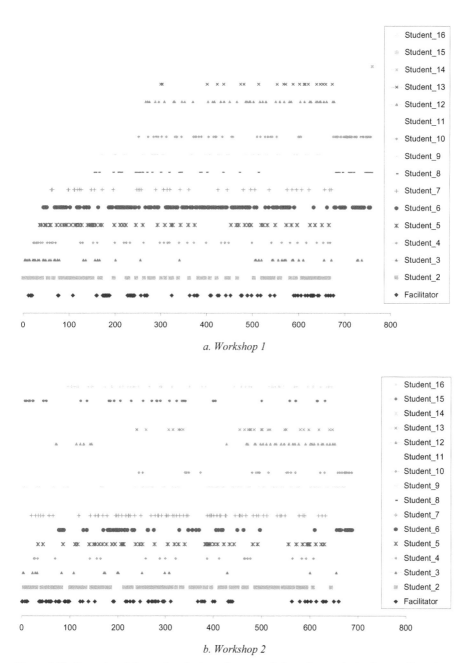

a. Workshop 1

b. Workshop 2

Figure 6.10. Examples of the results of a dynamic content-independent analysis of group discussions. Each timeline visualisation of utterance sequences (utterances are the units on the X-axis) shows the participation pattern for each participant in Workshops 1 and 2.

Note, however, that Student_2 tends to not participate in the later stages of the workshops. Student_11, on the other hand, performs at a relatively constant rate (though lower than Student_2) after a late start. This suggests that Student_11 could be a member of the core group. Similar reasoning, combined with the results in Figure 6.9, suggests that Student_9 could also be a member of the core group.

Timeline visualisation can also assist in highlighting patterns in communication that could indicate some anomalies in group behaviour. Student_10, for example, is an irregular participant but tends to increase participation towards the later stages of the discussion.

6.4.2. Content-dependent analysis

Content-dependent analysis requires the development of a coding scheme with subsequent coding of the content of each utterance. As a result of the coding, a data set of labelled utterances is obtained, which is used to estimate various quantitative *indicators* that address the research hypotheses.

In practice, coding involves the logic of consistent conceptualisation of the domain representation model and the logistics of operationalisation of the procedures that will be used to analyse those concepts. The process of developing the coding scheme is illustrated in Figure 6.11. Initially the research hypotheses are formulated. The formulation of the research questions was described in Section 6.2 and the subsequent research hypotheses listed in Table 6.3. The development of the quantitative indicators is based on the identification of codes which address the research hypotheses listed in Table 6.3. A sample of the data set is then coded and a visual representation of the coded data is examined to identify patterns of behaviour. The coding scheme is then tuned to provide the granularity required. This adaptive cycle of developing and testing of the coding scheme utilises human cognitive abilities for visual discovery of regularities in graphs and images (Keim and Ward, 2003).

Figure 6.11. Hypothesis-driven development and tuning of open hierarchical coding schemes.

Conceptualisation and creation of coding categories

To be able to implement drill-down data analysis techniques consistently, this methodology uses an open hierarchical coding scheme designed to conduct investigations with increasing levels of detail and utilising the results obtained on previous levels. This methodology is similar, to some extent, to the approaches used by Sudweeks and Allbritton (1996) and Simoff and Maher (2000).

Elaborating this approach further, the coding scheme is characterised by two independent dimensions – *feature coverage* (or 'width') and *level of detail* (or 'depth'). The feature coverage depends on the broadness of the knowledge about the communication phenomena that the researcher wants to extract from the content data set. The level of detail depends on the level of granularity with which the researcher wants to acquire and measure the phenomena within the constraints of the feature coverage.

A formal representation of the open hierarchical coding scheme is shown in Figure 6.12. The feature coverage can be characterised as the number of categories covered by the scheme at the first level of detail. In the example in Figure 6.12, the feature coverage is N. At this first level, the set of categories in the scheme is usually fairly broad. The example illustrates three levels of detail.

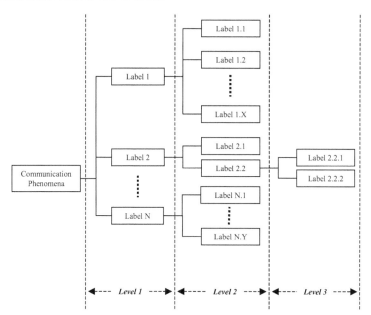

Figure 6.12. Formal representation of the open hierarchical coding scheme.

As mentioned on page 136, the development and tuning of the coding scheme is based on the research hypotheses. Coding is performed over two training sets – one sample subset from each case study data set – which should be indicative of expected trends and patterns. These patterns should be reflected in the results obtained after analysing the coded data. The results of the coding are visualised as timelines where, instead of assigning subjects a numerical label as for the content-independent analysis, the features from the coding scheme are given numerical labels.

As explained earlier, and illustrated in Figure 6.11, the researcher examines deviations from expected patterns. Such deviations can be detected visually at the pattern discovery stage. The patterns, for example, could be too coarse to capture phenomena expected from the initial qualitative reasoning described in Section 6.2. Consequently, the level of detail of the coding scheme may need to be increased or it may be necessary to extend the feature coverage of the coding scheme. Any refinement to the coding scheme is discussed with the other coders.

Coding of the data was performed by three independent coders. Each coder was given a copy of the coding scheme with examples of each variable and then trained on sample data. A level of accuracy was set and coders began coding when that standard of accuracy was attained. The open hierarchical coding scheme developed is presented in Figure 6.13. Its feature coverage includes five categories: management, reflection, content, style and interactivity. There are three levels of detail, however some categories are measured only at the second level of detail as they do not require finer granularity.

The codes developed for the two case studies, together with their definitions and examples, are shown in Table 6.4. Each code is also cross-referenced to the research hypotheses (see Table 6.3), indicating the individual hypotheses that each code (or combination of codes) is expected to test.

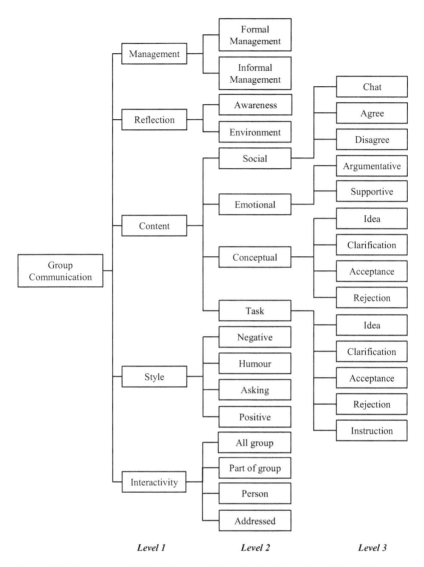

Figure 6.13. Tree representation of the open hierarchical coding scheme for studying group communication.

Table 6.4. The coding schema used for the analysis of the two case studies

Category	Code	Description	Hypothesis
Management			
Formal	FOR	Communication connected with the enforcement of rules or norms, used to manage the process of collaboration. Formal management of communication is more likely used by leaders and key stakeholders. Examples include the process of selecting committee members, moderators and enforcing time limits on discussions. Has a quality of individual or autocratic construction.	1.1, 2.1
Informal	INF	Communication connected with the collective informal creation, management, and enforcement of communication norms. Informal management of communication can be used by any participant. Has a quality of collaborative construction.	1.1, 2.1
Reflection			
Awareness	AWA	Communication connected with making knowledge of self and other participant(s) explicit to increase social awareness.	1.1, 1.5
Environment	ENV	Communication in regards to use of collaborative environment in which communication occurs.	1.1
Content			
Social	SOC	Communication content dealing with interpersonal relationships and social activities. Includes initiation of new social topics, greetings, social agreement and disagreement.	1.1, 1.2, 1.3, 1.4
Chat	*CHA*	*Communication content dealing with interpersonal relationships, social activities, greetings, farewells.*	
Agree	*AGR*	*Agreement of social (chat) comment.*	
Disagree	*DIS*	*Disagreement of social (chat) comment.*	
Emotional	EMO		1.1, 1.2, 1.6
Argumentative	*ARG*	*Communication content having the capacity to trigger or maintain an argument or conflict, having a negative emotional impact on participants.*	
Supportive	*SUP*	*Communication content having the capacity to support another member emotionally, having a positive emotional impact on participants.*	
Conceptual	CON	Conceptual communication involves the creation of mutual understandings and meanings among participants. Management of the work process as opposed to the communication process. Conceptual communication also involves the creation and prescription of shared rules to follow during the collaborative process. Includes creation or agreement about procedure to follow, creation or agreement on a common vocabulary by participants; creation or agreement of work to be completed.	1.1, 1.2, 2.1
Idea	*CID*	*Introduction of a new concept for discussion.*	
Clarification	*CCL*	*Clarification, explanation or refinement of new concept, either as a statement or question.*	
Acceptance	*CAC*	*Acceptance of a new concept. Affirmative response to new concept.*	
Rejection	*CRE*	*Rejection of new concept. Negative response to new concept.*	
Task	TSK	Communication content dealing with the collaborative activity of the group.	1.1, 1.2, 1.3, 1.4, 2.1
Idea	*IDE*	*Introduction of a new idea or issue for discussion.*	
Clarification	*CLA*	*Clarification, explanation or refinement of idea, issue or instruction, either as a statement or question.*	
Acceptance	*ACC*	*Acceptance of an idea/issue/instruction. Affirmative response to new idea/issue/instruction. Examples: "Yes", "I agree", "I'll do that."*	
Rejection	*REJ*	*Rejection of an idea/issue/instruction. Negative response to new idea/issue/instruction.. Examples: "No", "I disagree", "I can't do that".*	
Instruction	*INS*	*Specific task or instruction to other participant(s).*	

Style			
Negative	NEG	Argumentative, aggressive or any type of negative communication to achieve a goal (i.e. negative reinforcement). Its use is intended to halt or alter a communication direction, i.e. as an intervention.	2.2
Humour	HUM	Humourous communication to achieve a goal (the humour doesn't necessarily have to succeed). Its use is intended to halt or alter the communication direction, i.e. as an intervention. Often indicated by smiley or emoticon, and often used to lighten a heavy discussion.	2.2
Asking	ASK	A question asked as a management strategy to effect a change in the behaviour of an individual or group.	2.2
Positive	POS	Positive, supportive or placative communication to achieve a goal (i.e. positive reinforcement). Its use is intended to halt or alter the communication direction, i.e. as an intervention. Can be indicated by an apology. Intended to keep the peace. Can take the form of rephrasing a question or idea to be more sensitive to other participants' feelings.	2.2
Interactivity			
All	ALL	Utterance addresses whole group.	2.3
Part of a group	PAR	Utterance addresses part of the group (two or more participants)	2.3
Person	PER	Utterance addresses one individual	2.3
Addressed	ADD	Individual to whom an utterance is addressed.	2.4

Operationalisation of research hypotheses and linking to coding categories

The research hypotheses now need to be operationalised by linking to the quantitative indicators. Indicators are denoted according to the hypothesis or part of the hypothesis that they measure. For convenience, all values of indicators should be within the range $[0,1]$. Those indicators that include the total amount of utterances in the denominator (for example, Hypothesis $H_{1.5}$ – denoted as h_{15}) are within the range by default. Those indicators that do not include the total amount of utterances in the denominator (for example, Hypothesis $H_{2.2}$ – denoted as h_{22}) are normalised to the range $[0,1]$. The research hypotheses and corresponding indicators are presented in Figure 6.14.

Some notation is introduced to describe the input data and the content-dependent analysis. There is a number of ways in which coding (or labelling) of communication utterances can be implemented. In this study, a binary coding representation is used. A fragment of the coding representation is shown in Figure 6.15, where each column of the data table corresponds to a coding category c_j from the coding scheme and each row corresponds to an utterance u_i.

Hypothesis	Variable	Analysis
DEVELOPMENTAL CHARACTERISTICS		
1. Computer-mediated groups, like their traditional counterparts, display a developmental process		
1.1. There are definable developmental stages in computer-mediated groups.	FOR, INF, SOC (CHA, AGR, DIS), EMO (ARG+SUP), CON (CID, CCL, CAC, CRE), TSK (IDE+CLA+ ACC+REJ+ INS), AWA, ENV	Variables provide the means for observing the emergence of "turning points". Turning points are defined as a point in the discussions at which changes occur in the presence of a combination of variables. A turning point delineates the beginning and end of a phase in the group development. Timelines of variables illustrate changes in combinations. ANOVA statistical test. Quotes from participants and interviewees.
1.2. In the early stages of development, the content of communication is more conceptual than task oriented or social.	TSK, SOC, CON	The ratio $h_{12} = \dfrac{U_{CON}}{U_{TSK} + U_{SOC}}$ of CON utterances to TSK+SOC utterances is calculated. Quotes from participants and interviewees confirm findings from content analysis.
1.3. During periods of low task activity, the content of communication is more social than task oriented.	TSK, SOC	The ratio $h_{13} = \dfrac{U_{SOC}}{U_{TSK}}$ of SOC utterances to TSK utterances is calculated. Quotes from participants and interviewees confirm findings from content analysis.
1.4. During periods of high task activity, the content of communication is more task oriented than social.	TSK, SOC	The ratio $h_{14} = \dfrac{U_{TSK}}{U_{SOC}}$ of TSK utterances to SOC utterances is calculated. Quotes from participants and interviewees confirm findings from content analysis.
1.5. During later developmental stages, participants engage in less disclosures about the physical and social attributes of themselves and others	AWA	During the early stages, members feel the need to make explicit their physical attributes and location to create a social presence. In the later stages, members are more aware of the presence of others without the need for explicit reference. In the later stages, therefore, there is a decrease in the number of AWA utterances. The ratio $h_{15} = \dfrac{U_{AWA}}{U}$ of AWA utterances to total utterances is calculated. ANOVA statistical test. Quotes from participants and interviewees confirm findings from content analysis.

1.6.	Group cohesiveness increases over the life of the group.	SUP, ARG	Cohesiveness is described as a feeling of inclusion/exclusion and indicated by the presence of SUP utterances and absence of ARG utterances. The ratio $h_{16a} = \dfrac{U_{SUP}}{U}$ of SUP utterances to total utterances are compared. The ratio $h_{16b} = \dfrac{U_{SUP}}{U_{ARG}}$ of SUP utterances to ARG utterances are compared. ANOVA statistical test. Quotes from interviewees confirm findings from content analysis.
LEADERSHIP CHARACTERISTICS			
2.	**The role of the leader differs during the computer-mediated group developmental process**		
2.1.	Leader management is more frequent during periods of high task activity.	FOR+INF, TSK+CON	The presence of TSK and CON utterances indicate high task activity. The ratio $h_{21} = \dfrac{U_{FOR} + U_{INF}}{U_{TSK} + U_{CON}}$ of FOR+INF utterances to TSK+CON utterances is calculated. Correlation of FOR+INF with TSK+CON.
2.2.	Different leadership intervention styles (positive, negative, humour, asking) predominate at different developmental stages.	POS, NEG, HUM, ASK	The number of POS, NEG, HUM, ASK utterances by leaders in each phase is calculated.
2.3.	Leaders communicate more intensively than other participants.	ALL, PAR, PER	Activity levels of participants, including volume (number of utterances) and density (number of words and average number of words per utterance).
2.4	Leaders emerge throughout the life of the group.	ALL, PAR, PER, ADD, TSK+CON	Volume (number of utterances), length (average number of words per utterance), and TSK+CON utterances (both sent by and addressed to each participant), are used as attributes to identify which make the most important contribution in classifying participants as types of leaders. A classification tree is derived with CART and Miner3D is used to cluster the findings.

Figure 6.14. Research hypotheses and corresponding indicators.

If utterance u_i is classified as category c_j, then the corresponding element x_{ij} in the data table is assigned the value "1". For example, in Figure 6.15, the element $x_{714,5}$ is assigned "1", which means that the content of utterance 714 (u_{714}) is classified as category c_5 (CHA). Some level 2 and level 3 categories (see Figure 6.13), such as formal/informal (FOR/INF), agree/disagree (AGR/DIS), acceptance/rejection (ACC/ REJ), negative/humour/ask/positive (NEG/HUM/ASK/POS) argumentative/ supportive (ARG/SUP), competitive/convivial (COM/COV) and all/part/person (ALL/PAR/PER), are mutually exclusive but, generally, the content of an utterance can be classified into one or more categories.

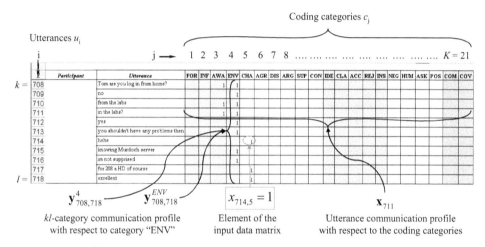

Figure 6.15. A fragment of a binary coding representation of communication utterances (participant names deleted for ethical reasons).

Each row in the data input matrix (i.e. each coded utterance) is referred to as an *utterance communication profile*. An utterance communication profile is denoted as $\mathbf{x}_i = x_{i1}, x_{i2},..., x_{iK}$, where K is the overall number of categories of the coding scheme. For example, in Figure 6.15, the utterance communication profile for utterance 711 (u_{711}) is $\mathbf{x}_{711}$, which is shown in Table 6.5. The number of categories K in this example is 21. Note that empty cells in the coded data are treated as "0".

Table 6.5. Example of utterance communication profile (from Figure 6.15).

j	1	2	3	4	5	6	7	8	9	10	11	12	13	14	15	16	17	18	19	20	21
$\mathbf{x}_{711}$	0	0	1	1	0	0	0	0	0	0	0	0	0	0	0	0	0	0	0	0	0

Each column under a category in the data input matrix is referred to as a *category communication profile*. The category communication profile with respect to category c_j is denoted as $\mathbf{y}_j = x_{1j}, x_{2j}, ..., x_{nj}$, where n is the number of utterances in a session. As different sessions usually have a different number of utterances, this type of category communication profile is useful to make comparisons between categories within the same session. More generally, though, a category communication profile can be defined as a fragment of the column between two utterances (rows). This fragment of a column is referred to as a *k,l-category communication profile*, where k and l denote the respective beginning and end row numbers of the fragment. The k,l-category communication profile with respect to category c_j is denoted as $\mathbf{y}_{k,l}^j = x_{kj}, x_{k+1j}, ..., x_{lj}$.

The k,l-category communication profile is similar to the notion of the k,l-communication pattern in the content-independent analysis. In other words, a k,l-category communication profile with respect to category c_j is the category communication profile of the communication pattern $U_{kl} = u_k, ..., u_l$. Therefore, the category profiles of patterns, identified during the content-independent analysis, can be analysed. Specific portions of a communication session (from utterance u_k to utterance u_l) can also be analysed and these portions of communication can be compared across groups. For example, in Figure 6.15, the session fragment begins at row k=708 (utterance u_{708}) and ends at row l=718 (utterance u_{718}). The 708,718-category communication profile with respect to category c_4 (ENV) is denoted as $\mathbf{y}_{708,718}^4$ (Table 6.6).

Table 6.6. Example of k,l-category communication profile (from Figure 6.15)

i	708	709	710	711	712	713	714	715	716	717	718
$\mathbf{y}_{708,718}^4$	1	1	1	1	1	1	0	1	1	0	0

Further, for convenience, the symbolic label is used instead of the numeric label (unless the numeric label for describing an analysis algorithm is needed) when referring to a category. For example, as shown in Figure 6.15, $\mathbf{y}_{708,718}^4$ is also denoted as $\mathbf{y}_{708,718}^{ENV}$. The notations used in the content-dependent analysis for Case Study 2 are presented in Table 6.7.

Overall, different components of the communication profile of a group (in different session, across all sessions) can be derived in terms of the coding scheme. The proposed utterance representation of group communication allows groups to be investigated in terms of:

- *Indicator statistics* to calculate the abovementioned quantitative indicators. These statistics are based on various total amounts in categories or combination of categories.
- *Profile comparisons* along particular categories or several categories to analyse similarities in group CMC. These comparisons are based on (dis)similarity measures that are used for dealing with so-called "symbolic data" (Bock and Diday, 2000, p.2).

Table 6.7. Summary of notation used in content-dependent analysis

Notion	Notation
Element of the data input table	group — workshop $$x_{19,3}^{1-6}$$ utterance number — category number
Utterance communication profile	group — workshop $$x_{19,3}^{1-6}$$ utterance number — category number
k,l-category communication profile	group — workshop — category $$y_{15,27}^{1-6,5}$$ number of the first utterance in the profile — number of the last utterance in the profile
k,l-category communication profile	group — workshop — category $$y_{15,27}^{1-6,CHA}$$ number of the first utterance in the profile — number of the last utterance in the profile

Indicator statistics are generated for every level of the coding scheme and for the indicators specified by the research hypotheses. These statistics are calculated for the group as a whole and for each member of the group. The former statistics are required by hypotheses related to developmental and group characteristics. The latter statistics are required by hypotheses related to leadership characteristics.

Profile comparisons (i.e. similarity analyses) address dynamic and static character-istics of computer-mediated groups. The underlying assumption is that there are some means for assessing and quantifying similarities (or dissimilarities[5]) that may exist between communication scenarios. The evaluation of similarities in group behaviour is based on:

- a visual inspection of the utterance and category communication profiles; and
- the values of similarity measures.

Visual inspection utilises timelines, which display a communication session as a symbolic array. These timelines are referred to as *categorical timelines* to distinguish them from the timelines of the content-independent analysis (illustrated previously in Figure 6.10). In categorical timelines, each category is displayed in a separate axis, parallel to the X-axis. Whereas the timelines of the content-independent analysis reveal the participation of different group members in a group communication session, categorical timelines offer a compact means for revealing and interpreting the evolution of a group over a given time period with respect to the properties stated by the coding scheme. Figure 6.16 illustrates categorical timelines that reveal some aspects of a communication profile of the same group in Case Study 2 during earlier and later stage of its development. The profiles demonstrate task, conceptual, emotional, social, informal and formal communication elements. The timelines in Figure 6.16, for example, show that there are similar trends of higher levels of social communication in the beginning and the end of each session. In addition, there is a clear increase of the overall level of social communication in the later stage of the group's development (Workshop 9) compared with the early stage (Workshop 1). The timelines also show a decline in communication management as indicated by the formal (FOR) and informal (INF) elements.

In addition to visual exploration, categorical timelines allow the identification of areas (patterns) in which to compare categorical profiles. As illustrated in the examples in Figure 6.16, such areas can be the beginning and end of a session. The length of the

---

[5] Both similarity and dissimilarity measures are referred to as *resemblance measures* (Bock and Diday, 2000, chap. 8).

pattern can be specified in a preliminary analysis. In this case, the length can be specified as 180 utterances; that is, examining the first 180 utterances and last 180 utterance. The visual "similarities" are then explored with more rigid numerical measures of similarity, discussed below.

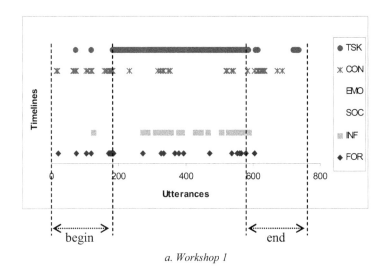

a. Workshop 1

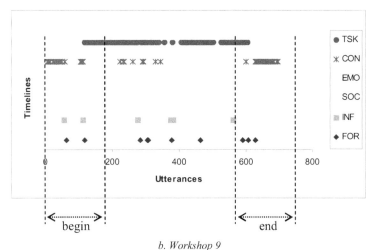

b. Workshop 9

Figure 6.16. Categorical timelines of group CMC sessions (same group, different workshops).

As discussed earlier, the comparison of communication profiles deals with categorical (binary) data. Figure 6.17 shows examples of input data for two sessions (Workshops 5 and 6) for one group (Group 1). Among all possible comparisons, the comparison of utterance communication profiles within the same session and the comparison of k,l-category profiles across different sessions are relevant to this study.

$$x_{19,3}^{1-5} = 1$$

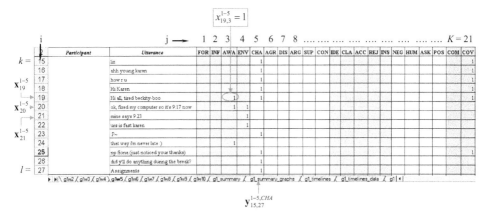

a. Coded data fragment from Case Study 2, Group 1, Workshop 5

$$x_{19,3}^{1-6} = 0$$

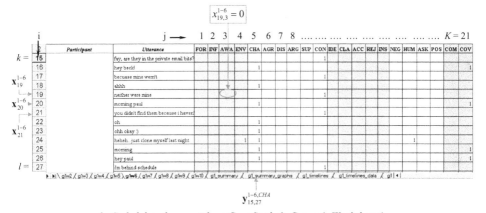

b. Coded data fragment from Case Study 2, Group 1, Workshop 6

Figure 6.17. Examples of input data generated by the coding – same group, different workshops (participant names deleted for ethical reasons)

Pair-wise comparisons

A convenient way to do the comparisons described in the previous section is to estimate pair-wise comparisons between the respective profiles. In the two case studies reported here, it was not appropriate to use this method but it is included in this section for completeness of the CEDA methodology.

The comparison of two profiles is based on matching their individual elements, thus the two profiles should have the same number of elements. Take, for example, the comparison of two utterance communication profiles p and q (the case of category profiles is similar). There are four possible cases, described in Table 6.8.

Table 6.8. Components of similarity measures.

Case	Matching criteria
a	Number of matching components where $x_{ip} = x_{iq} = 1$
b	Number of non-matching components with $x_{ip} = 1$ and $x_{iq} = 0$ (or empty cells)
c	Number of non-matching components with $x_{ip} = 0$ (or empty cells) and $x_{iq} = 1$
d	Number of matching components where $x_{ip} = x_{iq} = 0$ (or empty cells)

Let a, b, c and d in Table 6.8 denote the number of respective matches and mismatches. These numbers are the components of different similarity measures that can be used to estimate the similarity between profiles. Two basic measures listed in Bock and Diday (2000, chap. 8) are:

1. *matching coefficient* (*M*-coefficient) of Sokal-Michener

$$M_{p,q} = \frac{\text{number of matching pairs (both "1s" and "0s")}}{\text{number of all pairs in consideration}} = \frac{a+d}{a+b+c+d}$$

2. *similarity coefficient* (*S*-coefficient) of Jaccard

$$S_{p,q} = \frac{\text{number of matching pairs (only "1s")}}{\text{number of all pairs in consideration except matching "0s"}} = \frac{a}{a+b+c}$$

The *M*-coefficient is symmetric (the inversion of all categories does not change the similarity value. The *S*-coefficient is asymmetric (as the matching zeroes are not counted, it means that the assumption is that the presence of that type of code is more important than it absence).

Compare, for example, utterance communication profiles x_{19}^{1-5} and x_{20}^{1-5} from Figure 6.17a (the profiles are reproduced in Table 6.9, the matches are shaded according to the grey-scale code in Table 6.8).

Table 6.9. Utterance profiles x_{19}^{1-5} and x_{20}^{1-5} from Figure 6.17a.

j	1	2	3	4	5	6	7	8	9	10	11	12	13	14	15	16	17	18	19	20	21
x_{19}^{1-5}	0	0	1	0	1	0	0	0	0	0	0	0	0	0	0	0	0	0	0	0	1
x_{20}^{1-5}	0	0	1	1	0	0	0	0	0	0	0	0	0	0	0	0	0	0	0	0	0

Table 6.10. Values of the similarity components for the profiles in Table 6.9.

a	b	c	d
1	1	1	18

Hence the values of the similarity measures are:
1. *M*-coefficient

$$M_{19,20}^{1-5} = \frac{1+18}{1+1+1+18} = \frac{19}{21} = 0.905$$

2. *S*-coefficient

$$S_{19,20}^{1-5} = \frac{1}{1+1+1} = \frac{1}{3} = 0.333$$

These examples illustrate the sensitivity of similarity measures when calculating similarity. The value of the *M*-coefficient in this example is biased by the "0" values, i.e. the content of these two utterances is classified as only a small number of the 21 possible categories. The value of the *S*-coefficient provides a more accurate picture of the similarity in this case. The difference between the values of the coefficients depends on the "density" of the content, i.e. the number of categories into which the utterance content is classified.

The similarity analysis will benefit from the use of several similarity measures with the ability to emphasise the importance of different components (or sum of components).

The first group of measures available are the Gower-Legendre (Gower and Legendre, 1986) family of similarity measures, which generalise the M- and S- coefficients into two general formulas with a weight $w > 0$:

<table>
<tr><td>Matching coefficient</td><td>Similarity coefficient</td></tr>
<tr><td>$$M_w = \frac{a+d}{a+d+w(b+c)}$$</td><td>$$S_w = \frac{a+d}{a+w(b+c)}$$</td></tr>
</table>

The value of the weight influences the impact of the amount of mismatches ($b+c$) in the final result. If the interest is in the impact of matching cases, a smaller value for w can be selected; if the interest is in the impact of mismatching cases, then a larger value of w can be selected. Some specific instances of the family are presented in Table 6.11 and Table 6.12, respectively. The values of Gower-Legendre similarity measures for the example in Table 6.9 are shown in the right column in each table.

Table 6.11. Matching coefficients

Notation	Definition	Range	Values for the example in Table 6.9
M_1	$\dfrac{a+d}{a+d+b+c}$	$[0;1]$	$\dfrac{1+18}{1+18+1+1} = \dfrac{19}{21} = 0.905$
M_2	$\dfrac{a+d}{a+d+2(b+c)}$	$[0;1]$	$\dfrac{1+18}{1+18+2(1+1)} = \dfrac{19}{23} = 0.826$
$M_{1/2}$	$\dfrac{a+d}{a+d+0.5(b+c)}$	$[0;1]$	$\dfrac{1+18}{1+18+0.5(1+1)} = \dfrac{19}{20} = 0.95$

Table 6.12. Similarity coefficients

Notation	Definition	Range	Values for the example in Table 6.9
S_1	$\dfrac{a}{a+b+c}$	$[0;1]$	$\dfrac{1}{1+1+1} = \dfrac{1}{3} = 0.333$
S_2	$\dfrac{a}{a+2(b+c)}$	$[0;1]$	$\dfrac{1}{1+2(1+1)} = \dfrac{1}{5} = 0.2$
$S_{1/2}$	$\dfrac{a}{a+0.5(b+c)}$	$[0;1]$	$\dfrac{1}{1+0.5(1+1)} = \dfrac{1}{2} = 0.5$

As the measures range within $[0;1]$, then the dissimilarity can be calculated as $DM_w = 1 - M_w$ and $DS_w = 1 - S_w$, respectively.

Using this technique, k,l-category communication profiles can be compared across different sessions and even across different groups. Take, for example, the case of a comparison of group behaviour in terms of a single component of social communication in the early stages of two different weeks. The category communication profiles for the fragments in Figure 6.17 with to the social category component "CHA" are presented in Table 6.13.

Table 6.13. k,l-category communication profiles for $\mathbf{y}_{15,27}^{1-5,CHA}$ and $\mathbf{y}_{15,27}^{1-6,CHA}$ from Figure 6.17.

i	15	16	17	18	19	20	21	22	23	24	25	26	27
$\mathbf{y}_{15,27}^{1-5,CHA}$	1	1	1	1	1	0	0	0	1	0	1	1	1
$\mathbf{y}_{15,27}^{1-6,CHA}$	0	1	0	1	0	1	0	1	1	1	1	1	0

Table 6.14. Values of the similarity components for the category profiles in Table 6.13.

a	b	c	d
5	4	3	1

Table 6.15. Values of Gower-Legendre matching coefficients for the example in Table 6.13.

Notation	Definition	Values for the example in Table 6.13
M_1	$\dfrac{a+d}{a+d+b+c}$	$\dfrac{5+1}{5+1+4+3}=\dfrac{6}{13}=0.462$
M_2	$\dfrac{a+d}{a+d+2(b+c)}$	$\dfrac{5+1}{5+1+2(4+3)}=\dfrac{6}{20}=0.3$
$M_{1/2}$	$\dfrac{a+d}{a+d+0.5(b+c)}$	$\dfrac{5+1}{5+1+0.5(4+3)}=\dfrac{6}{9.5}=0.632$

Table 6.16. Values of Gower-Legendre similarity coefficients for the example in Table 6.13.

Notation	Definition	Values for the example in Table 6.9
S_1	$\dfrac{a}{a+b+c}$	$\dfrac{5}{5+4+3}=\dfrac{5}{12}=0.417$
S_2	$\dfrac{a}{a+2(b+c)}$	$\dfrac{5}{5+2(4+3)}=\dfrac{5}{19}=0.263$
$S_{1/2}$	$\dfrac{a}{a+0.5(b+c)}$	$\dfrac{5}{5+0.5(4+3)}=\dfrac{5}{8.5}=0.588$

These coefficients show that content-dependent analysis will benefit from including a broader spectrum of similarity measures.

6.5. Preprocessing and transformation of data

As mentioned in Section 6.1.2, the data sets (historical data) for each case study consisted of text data. For Case Study 1, the data set was a collection of time-stamped email messages; for Case Study 2, the data set was a collection of chat transcripts. Both data sets required significant preprocessing and transformation, the essence of which is described below.

First, the original data sets for each case study were transformed into a common utterance form, following the model presented in Section 6.3. An utterance is described as a *data unit* which has one subject (sender), one object (receiver) and one communication content. For Case Study 1, 1,343 utterances were generated from the original 1,130 email messages; that is, during the transformation some of the messages were split into two or more utterances. For Case Study 2, no transformation was required as each "message" was an utterance; that is, whether the object was one person, a part group or the whole group, each message addressed one object and had one communication content. In synchronous environments, participants are cognisant of the fact that the conversation needs to flow rapidly and therefore type very short messages. In fact, the participants in Case Study 2 were given guidelines for synchronous e-communication during their first meeting[6], and the guidelines included advice that longer messages should be split into 1-line lengths with 3 dots indicating that the message was incomplete and that there was more to follow.

The data set for Case Study 2 is organised around the four groups, labelled as g1, g2, g3 and g5 (data from g4, g6 and g7 were discarded as they were incomplete, see Section 6.1.2). The total number of utterances for each group in Case Study 2 is 3-5 times more than for Case Study 1, varying between 3,869 for group 5 (g5) and 5,697 for group 1 (g1). The descriptive statistics of the utterance content in both case studies is presented in Table 6.17. The statistics in Table 6.17 also illustrate the differences in the data sets with respect to the length of the utterances. In Case Study 1, where each of the utterances represents a communication act via an email message, the average length of an utterance is 776 characters (~120 words) whereas the average length of an utterance in Case Study 2 is 45-50 characters (~9-11 words). The distribution of utterances in both cases contains a number of extreme cases far from the average, which is indicated by the

---

[6] See Appendix B.1.

differences between the mean and the other measures of location – the median and the mode. The data sets in both case studies are positively (right) skewed. In Case Study 1, the range of utterance length is from 3 characters (1 word) to almost 16,000 characters (2,818 words), whereas the range of utterance length in Case Study 2 varies from 1^7 character to 909 characters. The maximum range across the groups is fairly consistent, varying between 663 and 909 (112 to 163 words). The distributions of utterance lengths in both case studies are heterogeneous, as indicated by the relatively large value of the heterogeneity factor[8].

Table 6.17. Descriptive statistics of utterances for Case Studies 1 and 2.

	Case Study 1	Case Study 2			
		g1	g2	g3	g5
Total number of utterances	1343	5697	6328	4547	3869
- In terms of characters					
Average utterance length	776	50	45	48	44
Median	401	36	33	34	32
Mode	37	3	7	3	3
Average deviation	679	35	31	35	31
Standard deviation	1,218	54	51	58	48
Range of the length	15,970	662	795	908	631
Minimum length	3	1	1	1	1
Maximum length	15,973	663	796	909	632
Characters (total)	1,041,799	285,724	287,282	218,950	171,545
Characters (without spaces)	865,414	236,864	240,638	183,298	144,757
Heterogeneity	13	12	16	16	13
- In terms of words					
Average utterance length	120	11	9	10	9
Median	67	6	7	7	6
Mode	7	1	2	1	1
Average deviation	117	7	6	7	6
Standard deviation	214	10	10	11	10
Range of the length	2817	112	116	163	112
Minimum length	1	1	1	1	1
Maximum length	2,818	113	117	164	113
Words (total)	177,932	54,486	52,934	40,185	30,590
Heterogeneity	13	11	12	15	11

---

[7] One-character words are "netspeak" contractions, e.g. "u" for "you", "k" for "ok", etc.
[8] 'Heterogeneity' is estimated as the ratio of the range to the standard deviation. Range is a very rough measure of spread. Homogeneity (small standard deviation) is indicated by a relatively small ratio of the range to the standard deviation (within 2 to 6). A result above 6 indicates a high degree of heterogeneity. Both case studies display a high degree of heterogeneity with numbers 2-3 times larger than 6.

Figure 6.18 illustrates the distribution of utterances and cumulative percentages with respect to length for Case Study 1. The majority of utterances are between 250 and 3,000 characters. Figure 6.19 illustrates the distribution of utterances and cumulative percentages with respect to length across Case Study 2 groups. The majority of utterances (about 80%) in all the groups lies below 80 characters, with one third of utterances less than 30 characters. The utterances generated during the synchronous sessions in Case Study 2, therefore, are very much shorter than the utterances in the asynchronous sessions in Case Study 1.

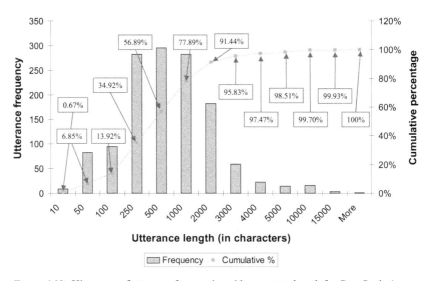

Figure 6.18. Histogram of utterance frequencies with respect to length for Case Study 1.

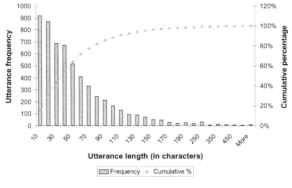

(a) Utterance histogram for group 1

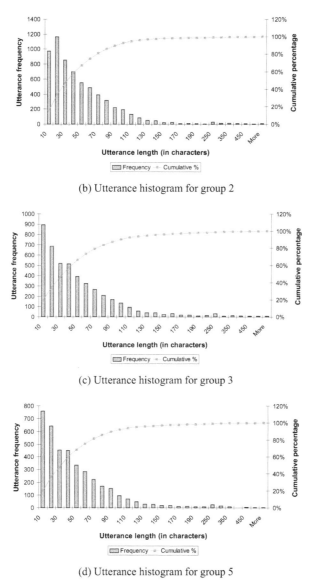

(b) Utterance histogram for group 2

(c) Utterance histogram for group 3

(d) Utterance histogram for group 5

Figure 6.19. Utterance frequencies across different groups in Case Study 2.

Figure 6.20 and Figure 6.21 illustrate fragments of the data prepared for content-independent and content-dependent analysis from Case Study 1 and Case Study 2 respectively. Data preprocessing included the elimination of sensitive data from the utterances, without losing the 'style' of the utterance. For each data set the data preprocessing procedure identified each unique participant name in a communication session and replaced it with that participant's role during the communication session. The roles in Case Study 1 are $\{Person\_N; Leader\_M\}$, where N and M are numbers assigned by the preprocessing algorithm in sequential order. The roles in Case Study 2 are $\{Person\_N; Moderator; Facilitator\}$, where N is a number assigned by the preprocessing algorithms automatically.

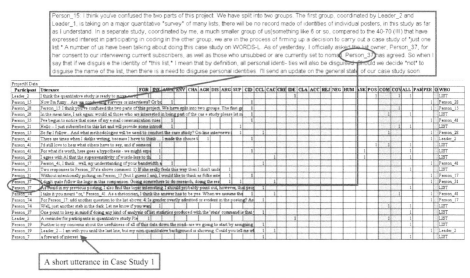

Figure 6.20. Section of preprocessed and coded data for Case Study 1.

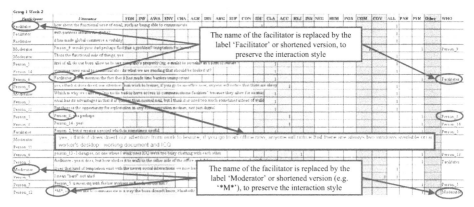

Figure 6.21. Section of preprocessed and coded data for Case Study 2.

CHAPTER 6

Once the mapping was established, further data preprocessing involved replacing sensitive information in all parts of each utterance, i.e. in the subject, the object (if necessary) and the content (see Section 6.3). This is illustrated in Figure 6.20 and Figure 6.21. The subject and the object names were replaced in the 'Participant' and 'WHO' columns respectively. The replacement of the names with the role labels in the utterance content was done in two steps. The first step was automatic, where full names were matched and replaced. The second step was part of a semi-automatic data cleaning procedure. To preserve the style of the utterance for the coder, the replacement was done as close as possible to the form used in the text. For example, in the last utterance in Figure 6.21, Person_12 originally used one letter surrounded by "*" signs to specify the name of the moderator. Hence, that letter was replaced with the letter 'M', preserving the compactness of the original style. Finally, the text of the utterances was cleaned of typographical errors in referring to the moderator or facilitator, which could have interfered with the coding process.

6.6. Summary

This chapter described the methodology used in this book. The objective of the research is to gain a better understanding of the developmental and leadership characteristics of computer-mediated groups. The two overarching research questions are:

1. Do computer-mediated groups, like their traditional counterparts, display developmental processes?
2. Does leadership vary during the computer-mediated group lifecycle?

From these research questions, ten hypotheses were formulated.

As mentioned in the introduction of this chapter, the two case studies differ significantly (see Table 1.1), especially in the communication mode and medium. The Domain Representation Model described in Section 6.3, in which the communication is viewed as a set of utterances, provides an approach that is consistent and comparable. The Domain Representation Model is presented as a Formal Model in Section 6.4. The Formal Model identified content-independent and content-dependent patterns of communication for analysis.

As the terms imply, content-independent analysis is analyses of utterances without reference to content (e.g. number of utterances); content-dependent analysis is analyses of the content of utterances (e.g. utterances related to task activity). Content-dependent analyses rely on a coding scheme to categorise utterances. In this chapter, the development of an open hierarchical coding scheme and its application to the two case studies was described.

The development of content-independent and content-dependent timelines were described. The timelines are a useful visualisation technique as well as a tool for building communication profiles.

Finally, the steps taken to preprocess and transform data sets of email (Case Study 1) and chat (Case Study 2) archives was described.

In the next two chapters, the results of the analyses of the two case studies are presented. Chapter 7 reports the findings of Case Study 1 and Chapter 8 reports the findings of Case Study 2.

CHAPTER 7

ANALYSIS OF CASE STUDY 1

7.1. Introduction

Case Study 1 was described in Chapter 3, the CEDA methodology developed for this book was described in Chapter 5, and Chapter 6 described how the methodology was applied to two different case studies. In this chapter, the results of Case Study 1 are presented as they relate to the research questions raised in Chapters 1, 2 and 6.

As explained in Chapter 3, Case Study 1 was a two-year international collaborative project, formed by a group of volunteers to collect and analyse data from email discussion groups. The medium of communication for the volunteer participants of Case Study 1 was an email mass distribution system provided by $CIOS^1$. The primary data for analysis in this chapter is the communication among the volunteer collaborators, with additional material from interviews also utilised. The research questions are concerned with two broad aspects of virtual groups – developmental and leadership characteristics. Following the CEDA methodology, the results will be presented as complementary quantitative and qualitative analyses.

7.2. Developmental Characteristics Hypotheses

The first group of hypotheses, developed in Section 2.7.1, Table 6.3, and operationalised in Section 6.4.2, are concerned with the developmental characteristics of virtual groups:

$H_{1.1}$ There are definable developmental stages in computer-mediated groups.

$H_{1.2}$ In the early phases of development, the content of communication is more conceptual than task oriented or social.

$H_{1.3}$ During periods of low task activity, the content of communication is more social than task oriented.

$H_{1.4}$ During periods of high task activity, the content of communication is more task oriented than social.

$H_{1.5}$ During later developmental stages, participants engage in less disclosures about the physical and social attributes of themselves and others.

$H_{1.6}$ Group cohesiveness increases over the life of the group.

---

[1] Communication Institute for Online Scholarship.

This group of hypotheses will be examined using the results of Case Study 1.

First, as described in Chapter 6, a categorical timeline (see explanation of content-dependent analysis in Section 6.4.2) was developed for the two-year period of Case Study 1 based on a content-dependent analysis of the 1,345 utterances exchanged among participants. Given the evidence of typical developmental phases of joining, conflict, cohesion, goal achievement and closure summarised in Chapter 2 as well as the above hypotheses proposed about developmental characteristics, one would expect particular combinations of variables to occur at particular times throughout the group's lifecycle. It would be expected, for example, that earlier phases would be focused on conceptualising the tasks to be undertaken and be more supportive, that the later phases would be more task oriented, and that there would be a period of argumentative communication. The categorical timeline of the communication profile of the project was therefore analysed to discern major turning points over the group's lifecycle with respect to the properties stated by the coding scheme (see Section 6.4.2). Table 7.1 lists the variables of interest in this section of the analysis with a brief description and the hypotheses to which they apply. All communication types (variables) are defined and described fully in Table 6.2.

Table 7.1. Communication variables used in the developmental characteristics hypotheses.

Category	Code	Description	Hypothesis
Management	**MAN**		
Formal	FOR	Communication connected with the enforcement of rules or norms, used to manage the process of collaboration. More likely used by leaders and key stakeholders..	1.1
Informal	INF	Communication connected with the collective informal creation, management, and enforcement of communication norms, used by any participant. Has a quality of collaborative construction.	1.1
Reflection	**REF**		
Awareness	AWA	Communication connected with making knowledge of self and other participants(s) explicit to increase social awareness.	1.1, 1.5
Environment	ENV	Communication in regards to use of collaborative environment in which communication occurs.	1.1
Content	**CNT**		
Social	SOC	Communication content dealing with interpersonal relationships and social activities. Includes initiation of new social topics, greetings, social agreement and disagreement.	1.1, 1.2, 1.3, 1.4
Emotional	EMO		1.1, 1.2, 1.6
Argumentative	*ARG*	*Communication content having the capacity to trigger/maintain an argument or conflict, having a negative emotional impact.*	
Supportive	*SUP*	*Communication content having the capacity to support another participant emotionally, has a positive emotional impact.*	
Conceptual	CON	Conceptual communication involves the creation of mutual understandings and meanings among participants. Involves the creation of shared rules to follow. Includes creation, agreement or disagreement about procedures to follow, a common vocabulary, work to be completed.	1.1, 1.2
Task	TSK	Communication content dealing with the collaborative activity of the group. Includes introduction, clarification, agreement or disagreement of task issues and specific task instructions.	1.1, 1.2, 1.3, 1.4

The variation in the salience of these different communication types is illustrated in Figure 7.1, which depicts the percentages of each type taken at intervals of 100 utterances.

According to Pliskin and Romm (1997), turning points are defined as points in the discussions at which significant changes occur in the nature of the communication, indicated by changes in combinations of key coding variables. These points delineate the beginning and end of major phases in the group development cycle. A high frequency of one or more types of variables indicate that such variables are characteristic of a particular developmental phase.

A visual inspection of the timeline in Figure 7.2 indicated seven regions which signalled a transition from one combination of coding variables to another combination. Subsequent detailed scrutiny of the content of utterances in those transition regions revealed one particular utterance in each case that significantly altered the dynamics of the group. These seven transition (or turning) points therefore resulted in the entire duration of Case Study 1 being broken into eight phases for more detailed analyses. For example, from u_1^2 to u_{139}, the most frequent communication categories are defined as conceptual (CON), supportive (SUP), awareness (AWA) and informal (INF), indicating communication characterised by agreement and curiosity about the environment, the project and the participants. From u_{140} to u_{446}, the most frequent communication categories are conceptual (CON), argumentative (ARG), task (TSK) and informal (INF), indicating communication that was characterised by conflict about task requirements and the project. In fact, utterance 140 introduced, for the first time, some criticisms of the project, albeit second-hand and inaccurate, as explained later in this section. Turning points for Case Study 1 are identified by vertical lines in Figure 7.2 along with the date and utterance number.

Figure 7.3 illustrates the variance of different variables in each time period (phase). Each variable is represented as a percentage of total utterances in each phase. Figure 7.4 shows the seven turning points $\{TP_1, TP_2, \ldots, TP_7\}$ and indicates the utterance numbers for each of the eight developmental phases $\{P_1, P_2, \ldots, P_8\}$.

---

[2] Utterance is referred to as "u" and the number of the utterance is indicated by the subscript.

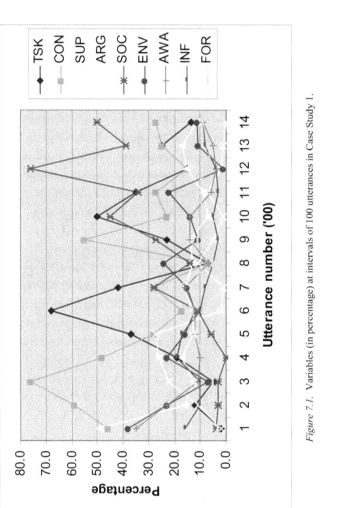

Figure 7.1. Variables (in percentage) at intervals of 100 utterances in Case Study 1.

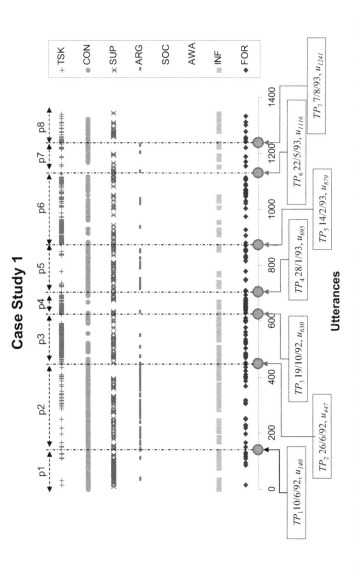

Figure 7.2. Content-dependent timeline of Case Study 1 illustrating time and utterance number of developmental turning points and phases.

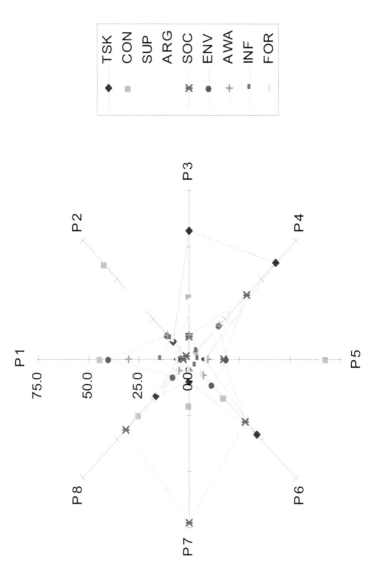

Figure 7.3. Variables (TSK, CON, SUP, ARG, SOC, ENV, AWA, INF, FOR) as percentages of total utterances for each phase (P1-P8).

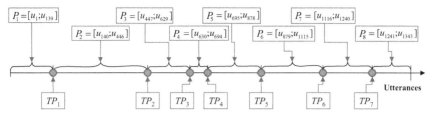

Figure 7.4. Developmental turning points and developmental phases in Case Study 1.

Figure 7.5 gives a visual representation of the length of time of each phase.

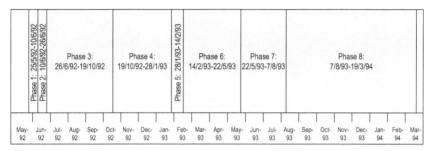

Figure 7.5. Length of developmental phases in Case Study 1.

The salient variables that characterise each phase are indicated in Table 7.2. The eight developmental phases are listed in Table 7.3.

Table 7.2. Combinations of frequent variables across eight phases of Case Study 1.

Code Name	Code Description	P_1	P_2	P_3	P_4	P_5	P_6	P_7	P_8
TSK	Task			✓	✓		✓		✓
CON	Conceptual	✓	✓	✓		✓	✓	✓	✓
SUP	Supportive	✓		✓	✓				✓
ARG	Argumentative		✓						
SOC	Social				✓	✓	✓	✓	✓
ENV	Environment	✓			✓	✓	✓		
AWA	Awareness	✓			✓				
INF	Informal	✓	✓	✓				✓	✓
FOR	Formal			✓	✓	✓	✓	✓	✓

Table 7.3. Developmental phases in Case Study 1.

Phase	Type	Utterances
P_1	Structuration	u_1; u_{139}
P_2	Tension	u_{140}; u_{446}
P_3	Reflection (on formation process)	u_{447}; u_{629}
P_4	Activity (on codebook)	u_{630}; u_{694}
P_5	Reflection (on initial activity)	u_{695}; u_{878}
P_6	Activity (on coding)	u_{879}; u_{1115}
P_7	Reflection (on the need to meet face-to-face)	u_{1116}; u_{1240}
P_8	Goal achievement and closure	u_{1241}; u_{1343}

7.2.1. Detailed Analysis of Developmental Phases

Phase 1: Structuration

The first time period, Phase 1 (u_1 to u_{139}), is visually represented by the timeline in Figure 7.6. This time period of 16 days (25 May to 10 June 1992) commenced when an email message about group dynamics was posted to a Comserve discussion list and some forty members of the list agreed to collaborate on a research study to capture the nature of online community formation. Predictably, this initial phase was characterised by a process of getting to know group members, creating a structure for the group, establishing group norms and conceptualising the collaborative task. In other words, it was consistent with the majority of the literature which describes an initial period of joining and the formation of group norms. The communication in this phase was mostly conceptual, supportive and focused on the communication environment itself.

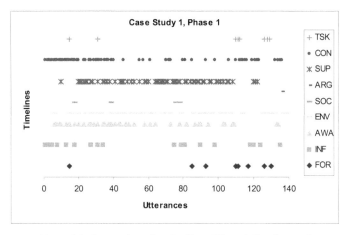

Figure 7.6. Content-dependent timeline of Phase 1 ($P_1 = [u_1; u_{139}]$)

Even though the group had agreed to collaborate on a research study, the goals, methodology and specific tasks were still being defined. It is not surprising, therefore, that almost half of the interactions were concerned with the concept of the project and defining research goals – 43.9% of all utterances included one aspect of the conceptual (CON) category of communication; that is, the subcategories of conceptual ideas (CID), clarification of ideas (CCL), acceptance of ideas (CAC) or rejection of ideas (CRE)[3] (Table 7.4).

---

[3] See Table 6.4, page 142, for explanation of coding categories.

Table 7.4. Number and percentage of communication types in Phase 1.

Code name	Code description	Number of utterances	Percentage of total P_1 utterance*
TSK	Task	8	5.8
CON	Conceptual	61	43.9
SUP	Supportive	56	40.3
ARG	Argumentative	4	2.9
SOC	Social	4	2.9
ENV	Environment	41	39.6
AWA	Awareness	41	29.5
INF	Informal	20	14.4
FOR	Formal	8	5.8

*Codes are not discrete categories, each utterance can be classified in a number of categories, hence percentages do not sum to 100.

The following extracts are examples of the conceptual type of communication typical for this phase:

> ... I think this study sounds like lots of fun, and would like very much to participate. Will you let me in? ... I propose trying to look at nature of threads in the discussions (protracted, multi-contributors, cyclical, substantive or meta-communication, etc.). I think we can come up with a fairly reliable set of measures and codebook for some of these. (u_8, 27/05/92)

> Seems that some here are qualitative/ethnography oriented, others stat-inclined, and some both. It shouldn't be hard to integrate **all** preferred research methods through the various questions and bringing appropriate methods to bear on them ... What's interesting is how "strangers" are able to plot and scheme independently, share collectively, and produce ideas and (???) maybe even some kind of final product. (u_{18}, 29/05/92)

During this phase there was little disagreement (only 2.9% interactions were classified as ARG) but almost half of the interactions were concerned with supporting (SUP=40.3%) other group members' ideas and establishing relationships by participants disclosing information about themselves. For example:

> Vivian[4], In response to your question, I think recruiting students to help with this project would be good idea ... The only problem I can think of (besides the ones already mentioned) is the time necessary for a content analysis of this nature. I have done some with television and it can be very time consuming. I would love to help if I can though (u_{10}, 27/05/92)

The level of social discussion was limited (SOC=2.9%) as participants were basically more concerned with forming the group, identifying individual strengths of the participants, and defining and allocating tasks. As can be expected with a novel

---

[4] Due to ethical reasons, participants have been given pseudonyms to protect their identity. However, the two coordinators, Sheizaf and Fay, are identified by their real names.

environment in 1992, almost half of interactions were related to the environment (ENV=39.6%) and with learning to collaborate online:

> ... Please use the quoting mechanisms of mailers sparingly. Some of us operate at 2400 baud or less, and scrolling through a lot of familiar text is a waste of time. (u_{15}, 29/05/92)

Communication management was more informal than formal (14.4% vs 5.8% of total utterances, or 71.4% vs 28.6% of utterances from coordinators and key motivators in this phase). The following extract illustrates the cooperative and informal style of communication management:

> The outline of the study sounds great. I have done some work on the topic of flaming, and would like to offer a few thoughts toward a "tighter" operationalization ... I would welcome any comments and suggestions (u_{35}, 29/5/92).

That there was a definable time period of joining, forming and planning is also supported by members' later reflections on the project. One interviewee commented:

> [The first chunk was] the conceptualisation of the project but also there was a process of organising, of us as an organisation, learning how to do this and trying to make decisions based on no guidelines because it was new and different. (Donna, 26/5/96)

And another interviewee:

> My notion of .. the early period .. [was] getting to know who's who, establishing within the group who was going to be the king of the mountain so to speak, would it be Sheizaf because he organised it, or would some other leader emerging from within this group. (Sarah, 26/5/96)

Phase 2: Tension

The second time period, Phase 2 (u_{140} to u_{446}), is visually represented by the timeline in Figure 7.7. This time period of 16 days (10 June to 26 June 1992) was a phase of heated debates mostly concerned with the ethics of using archived group discussions for research purposes. The first utterance raising the ethics issue (see u_{140} on p.172) marked the beginning of this phase of opinionated posts and aggressive interactions along with continued conceptual ideas and increased progress with the tasks of the project.

This phase was consistent with the majority of the literature which describes a phase of conflict after the initial phase of joining. This conflict phase included the day on which the highest level of messaging was reached throughout the entire course of the project – a total of 87 postings on 15 June.

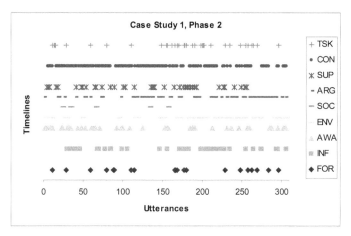

Figure 7.7. Content-dependent timeline of Phase 2 ($P_2 = [u_{140}; u_{446}]$).

Table 7.5 lists the number and percentages of different types of communication. As well as a significant number of argumentative utterances (more than one-quarter, ARG=27%), the phase was characterised by continued conceptual communication (CON=59.6%) and an increase in task-related interactions (TSK=11.1%).

Table 7.5. Number and percentage of communication types in Phase 2.

Code name	Code description	Number of utterances	Percentage of total P_2 utterance*
TSK	Task	34	11.1
CON	Conceptual	183	59.6
SUP	Supportive	39	12.7
ARG	Argumentative	83	27.0
SOC	Social	4	2.0
ENV	Environment	46	15.0
AWA	Awareness	45	14.7
INF	Informal	41	13.4
FOR	Formal	20	6.5

*Codes are not discrete categories, each utterance can be classified in a number of categories, hence percentages do not sum to 100.

More than half of the utterances in this phase were devoted to issues such as identifying theoretical constructs, privacy, ownership, attempting to explore unchartered territory, and generally how to organise an enormous collaboration with diverse people who had never met and had little in common except an interest in knowing more about group computer-mediated communication. The following is an example of conceptual communication typical for this phase:

> I am still unsure how this research question can be treated in the context of the quantitative content-analysis. Would any of you like to propose a set of variables? Remember that we are dealing with messages, discussion threads and lists as units of

analysis. Will not have individual respondents. I, for one, am interested in how (whether) you could use the content analysis for this purpose ... (u_{181}, 13/6/92)

As mentioned earlier, this phase was characterised by conflict when a number of dissidents emerged. For example:

> At this point in time, I have little confidence that projecth as a whole is capable of conducting a responsible study of any group as sensitive as [LIST]. I do have confidence in some of the individual members. My suggestion is that these very qualified individual members make some decisions about how this project is going to be run, because right now it looks like some who are not so qualified are going to be sent off to roam the net like loose cannons. (u_{422}, 25/6/92)

It eventually transpired that much of the conflict was based on a misunderstanding. Early in the planning phase of the project, there was some discussion about conducting a qualitative as well as a quantitative study. A few people eventually did complete a qualitative study offline but it was not part of the ProjectH initiative. At the time, though, the coordinators requested suggestions for discussion lists to analyse qualitatively. Among those suggested was a highly prolific discussion list in which there was some overlap in membership with ProjectH. Members of the contentious list were under the impression that ProjectH members would "eavesdrop" on their discussions and conduct a qualitative study of their list:

> I thought I should let you know that somebody mentioned the CMC project on [LISTNAME] ... Here are some excerpts from a posting this afternoon from somebody on both [LISTNAME] and this list.
>
> >>I just went back and read the two days' worth of ProjectH mail I hadn't deleted yet, and I confess to being taken aback. It was like finding out that this whole group has been talking about you and your friends behind your back, not always flatteringly. not that we deserve flattery, mind you, but it still takes the breath a little to see it happening. Unless these academo-dweebs get down and dirty with us [LIST NAME], this study is bound to be bogus from the start. Two of them are Bandwith Sissies who couldn't take the list volume. One is [name deleted—nm] (remember him? he posted his department name in the .sig of each message!) and the other is somebody whose name I can't even recall, so she must have uncloaked briefly or not at all before. [...] have kindly been looking down their noses at ... I'm highly unimpressed. They remind me of Masters and Johnson. All observation, no participation. (u_{140}, 10/6/92)

The reposting of this message to ProjectH was instrumental in much of the conflict. However, interest in a qualitative study as a group project had waned long before this phase of conflict, as pointed out by one member:

> My problem with George and especially Abigail is that they created an adversarial position where none existed by engaging in an attack on an entire group. Their attack was based on fabrications and innuendo and included some intemperate name-calling. In my view, they inflamed passions by distorting (I hesitate to use the term "lie") and misrepresenting. Despite corrections to their errors and challenges to their "facts" ...,

the pair continued their misrepresentations which they knew, or should have known, was inaccurate ... (u_{418}, 25/6/92)

In addition to the discussions on the ethics and methodology of the study, conflict arose about the ownership of the anticipated product of the collaboration, i.e. a unique and content-coded database of computer-mediated discussions:

> ... I'm not worried about privacy, I'm worried about ownership, and I'm probably being terribly anal, which is an old American custom. (u_{277}, 15/6/92)

During this difficult time period, the coding scheme for the study was being developed, which is reflected in the increased task-related discussions (TSK=11.1%):

> I think the quantitative study is ready to move on to the next stage ... Can we set as goal for the coming week, the completion of a first draft of the codebook? Looking further down, I suggest we try for a pretest of the codebook (on a sample of messages), by mid-July. I am now asking for codebook paragraphs. Please send me (directly, not to the list) definitions and coding instructions (scales) of a favorite variable or two ... (u_{199}, 14/6/92)

One of the most volatile dissidents of the project finally understood the purpose and proposed method and eventually became very much involved:

> First...I waded in here over the weekend, got into a barroom fight or two (there IS a certain amount of Dodge Citydom in the current situation), left, and was persuaded by Jeff that I was not dealing with a crew of ogres, unemployed CIA operatives, and voyeurs. In the process of getting that peace made, I learned a great deal about the genesis of the PROJECTH study, discovered, too, that I have interests of my own that might be valuable in this context, and that I too might be able to derive some additional knowledge from what happens here. (u_{441}, 26/6/92)

Apart from task-related communication, the coordinators posted infrequently to avoid becoming entangled in the conflict and also to have greater impact when emotions subsided.

Phase 3: Reflection on formation process

The third time period, Phase 3 (u_{447} to u_{629}), is visually represented by the timeline in Figure 7.8. This phase of almost four months (26 June to 19 October 1992) was primarily a time of reflecting on the argumentative discussions of the previous two weeks and collating brief biographies of participants to facilitate a more cohesive group. This humorous and disclosing post from one of the coordinators was effective in calming the group and it signalled this next phase of the project.

> Hi (or as they say around here: shalom—which also means peace) ... I am really glad the issue has come up. I think we are dealing with groundbreaking procedure, and believe we are setting precedents ... Am a bit offended that my credentials were not disputed. So, just in case anyone is interested: I have the longest, reddest, and prettiest red beard in cyberspace ... Any challenges? (u_{447}, 26/6/92)

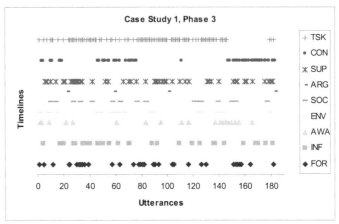

Figure 7.8. Content-dependent timeline of Phase 3 ($P_3 = [u_{447}; u_{629}]$)

It was a crucial time for the group as the focus of the project was consolidated and the codebook developed for pretesting. Four members pretested the codebook[5] while coding tools for different operating systems (DOS, UNIX, Mac) were discussed. More than half of the utterances in this phase, therefore, were task-related (56.8%) (Table 7.6). An example is:

> Greetings: Here comes the much promised codebook ... In the following message, I humbly submit a codebook proposal. To refresh all suntanned minds, we have agreed to conduct a content analysis of messages in e-mail discussion lists and groups. As I propose in the following, we should look the codebook over, react to it if necessary, and commence pretesting the codebook in a week or so. Fay and I will propose pretest texts in a few days ... Awaiting responses! (u_{470}, 7/8/92)

Table 7.6. Number and percentage of communication types in Phase 3.

Code name	Code description	Number of utterances	Percentage of total P_3 utterance*
TSK	Task	104	56.8
CON	Conceptual	50	27.3
SUP	Supportive	47	25.7
ARG	Argumentative	0	2.2
SOC	Social	18	9.8
ENV	Environment	19	10.4
AWA	Awareness	19	10.4
INF	Informal	30	16.4
FOR	Formal	33	18.0

*Codes are not discrete categories, each utterance can be classified in a number of categories, hence percentages do not sum to 100.

---

[5] There was a high correlation in the coding by the participants who pretested. The majority of item (variable) and message correlations were in the $r = 0.800$ to 1.000 range. (u_{662}, 13/1/93).

This phase was also characterised by decreased conceptual communication (CON=27.3%), and a significant increase in supportive interactions (SUP=25.7%). The following is an example of the supportive nature of this phase as participants reflected on the previous phase:

> A pity we didn't have the sanity of Kevin and Larry's comments a couple of months ago. It would have made it easier to understand (and deal with?) some of the heat generated. Oh well, hindsight's a great thing. So are summer vacations. (u_{467}, 26/8/92)

A feeling of comraderie was developing among participants. The following response to the posting of the codebook by one of the coordinators illustrates the familiarity between one of the coordinators and a member, even though they had never met:

> Heh! Speak for yourself, neo-peripatetic international jet-setter: That ain't no suntan on my mind, it's 3rd-degree sunburnout.... But, the codebook looks **great**! Nice job! (u_{472}, 7/8/92)

Given the prolonged discourse on the codebook and the coordinators' driving the coding process, not surprisingly there was a three-fold increase in formal communication during this phase (FOR=18% compared with FOR=6.5% in the previous phase).

Phase 4: Activity on codebook

The fourth time period, Phase 4 (u_{630} to u_{694}), is visually represented by the timeline in Figure 7.9. This phase had the least number of utterances of all phases but it was fairly lengthy in terms of time, spanning three months from 19 October 1992 to 28 January 1993. During this phase, the codebook was finalised following feedback from the coders who pretested in the previous phase, and practice coding was arranged for each member who volunteered to code to ensure coding consistency.

The following excerpt, recapping progress to date and heralding the release of the revised codebook, marked the turning point which initiated this phase:

> ... In a painstaking process, we collated hypotheses and variables of interest to the group. When collected, these hypotheses and variables invoked a codebook, which many of us have been testing and improving over the last months. Fay is about to uncover a much improved (and thankfully, shorter) codebook. (stay tuned!). (u_{630}, 19/10/92)

After posting various iterations of the codebook that was developed in the previous phase, there was a brief hiatus, broken by this post:

> NO, PROJECTH IS NOT DEAD   Don't trust unsubstantiated rumors!   The joint content analysis project on ProjectH has not died! We are still working along. ... Due to mid-semester blues and congestion, we have put off launching the actual coding

until early December. We are, however, soliciting any reactions to the codebook (last chance, folks!)... (u_{641}, 11/11/92)

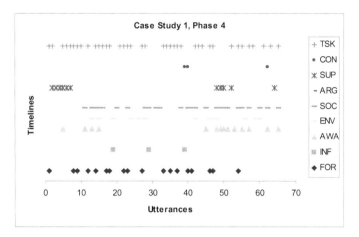

Figure 7.9. Content-dependent timeline of Phase 4 ($P_4 = [u_{630}; u_{694}]$)

Table 7.7 shows the percentages of different types of communication. Despite the slow start, the discourse during this phase was primarily concerned with tasks (TSK=60.0%). During this phase, an invitation distributed to discussion lists resulted in twelve new members, including a very talented programmer who became invaluable to the project. New members were therefore joining throughout this phase, which is reflected in the significant amount of social interactions (SOC=40.0%). There was considerably less conceptual (CON=4.6%) and supportive (SUP=16.9%) communication. Interestingly there was an increase in communication indicating an explicit awareness of the presence of others (AWA=21.5%) – almost doubling the level of the previous phase. Again, this is a reflection of new members joining and a process of "getting to know each other".

Table 7.7. Number and percentage of communication types in Phase 4.

Code name	Code description	Number of utterances	Percentage of total P_4 utterance*
TSK	Task	39	60.0
CON	Conceptual	3	4.6
SUP	Supportive	11	16.9
ARG	Argumentative	0	0.0
SOC	Social	26	40.0
ENV	Environment	14	21.5
AWA	Awareness	14	21.5
INF	Informal	3	4.6
FOR	Formal	18	27.7

*Codes are not discrete categories, each utterance can be classified in a number of categories, hence percentages do not sum to 100.

In this phase, there was an equilibrium between work and play. The coding got underway slowly, relieved by social interaction primarily of a self-disclosure nature from new members.

> I think there's a glitch in my computer: I'm not receiving any mail from ProjectH... Anybody home? (u_{657}, 12/1/93)

> No one here 'cept us burglars........ (u_{659}, 13/1/93)

> My wife ... and I have a 3 year old daughter and are expecting twins (! !) in March. Between feedings, I'll try to code samples as my contribution to the study! (u_{684}, 20/1/93)

However, the comraderie evident in the previous phase was not so obvious in this phase, no doubt being affected by new people joining the project. The dominant form of communication was formal (FOR=27.7% compared with INF=4.6%), as most interaction was task related.

Phase 5: Reflection on initial activity
The fifth time period, Phase 5 (u_{695} to u_{878}), is visually represented by the timeline in Figure 7.10. This brief phase of a little over two weeks (28 January 1993 to 14 February 1993) yielded 180 utterances. During this phase, the ethics issue that was raised initially in Phase 2 and remained unresolved, was re-visited.

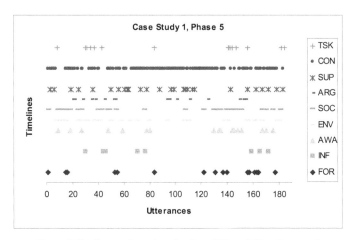

Figure 7.10. Content-dependent timeline of Phase 5 ($P_5 = [u_{695}; u_{878}]$)

Table 7.8 shows the percentages of different types of communication. This phase was the inverse of the previous one; that is, it was dominated by conceptual communication (CON=67.4%) with very little discourse devoted to actual task completion (TSK=7.6%). The only other communication types of significance were supportive (SUP=14.7%), social (SOC=16.8%) and environment-related (ENV=18.5%) communication.

Table 7.8. Number and percentage of communication types in Phase 5.

Code name	Code description	Number of utterances	Percentage of total P_5 utterance*
TSK	Task	14	7.6
CON	Conceptual	124	67.4
SUP	Supportive	27	14.7
ARG	Argumentative	16	8.7
SOC	Social	31	16.8
ENV	Environment	34	18.5
AWA	Awareness	17	9.2
INF	Informal	8	4.3
FOR	Formal	16	8.7

*Codes are not discrete categories, each utterance can be classified in a number of categories, hence percentages do not sum to 100.

The conceptual discourse focused on ethical issues associated with conducting such a survey. Four iterations of an Ethics Policy were drafted by the project coordinators in response to feedback from all members. As it was obvious that the policy was not unanimously accepted by members who had committed to coding, the coordinators called for a vote on the fourth iteration to bring the issue to closure.

> I believe the ethics issue has been given enough airtime. We need to move on. This is a call for a vote. Following this message, will be a Proposed Policy on Ethics. It is very similar to the previous 'takes', with only minor modifications. I am asking each member of ProjectH, who has committed to code, to post your vote. Please post your votes in public, to ProjectH. Please do so by Thursday, February 11. For me, a vote is valid if it is posted by Thursday, by a ProjectH member who is committed to coding. I will consider the results of the vote binding, for both the project and myself. (u_{778}, 7/2/93)

After four days, voting concluded with 38 members in favour and 3 members dissenting. The Ethics Policy (see Appendix A.6) was adopted.

> ... it's time to close the poll. With a vote of 38:3 in favour, the Ethics Policy is ratified. We consider the Copyright and Ethics Policies binding, regarding the quantitative content analysis project, on all ProjectH members. Both policies have been placed in our ftp directory. (u_{871}, 12/2/93)

Phase 6: Activity on coding

The sixth time period, Phase 6 (u_{879} to u_{1115}), is visually represented by the timeline in Figure 7.11. This phase of three months (14 February 1993 to 22 May 1993) was a very productive and interesting time of the project as the bulk of the preparatory work for coding was completed and coding began offline. Much of the task-related communication online was in the form of posts to or from the Oracles committee.

This meant that the group was being effectively led by the Oracles committee. The turning point which initiated this phase was a summary of progress to date, stimulating the group to focus on coding again.

> Here is a short summary of where we are for those troubled by the silence … (u_{879}, 14/2/93)

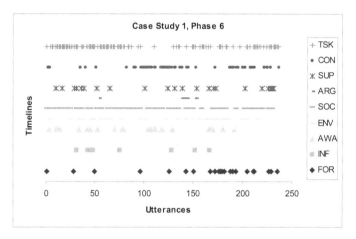

Figure 7.11. Content-dependent timeline of Phase 6 ($P_6 = [u_{879}; u_{1115}]$)

Table 7.9 shows the percentages of different types of communication. Predictably, the discourse throughout the phase alternated between "work and play"[6] (TSK=47.2%; SOC=39.1%).

Table 7.9. Number and percentage of communication types in Phase 6.

Code name	Code description	Number of utterances	Percentage of total P_6 utterance*
TSK	Task	121	47.2
CON	Conceptual	56	23.8
SUP	Supportive	8	9.8
ARG	Argumentative	0	3.4
SOC	Social	92	39.1
ENV	Environment	37	15.7
AWA	Awareness	24	10.2
INF	Informal	8	3.4
FOR	Formal	22	9.4

*Codes are not discrete categories, each utterance can be classified in a number of categories, hence percentages do not sum to 100.

---

[6] This notion of "work and play" throughout the project was the inspiration for the author of this book in her decision to give the title *Network and Netplay* to her co-edited book about ProjectH in which many chapters included analyses of the ProjectH database (Sudweeks, McLaughlin and Rafaeli, 1998).

Tasks completed in this phase included: (i) sampling and reliability strategies were finalised and statements written (see Appendices A.8 and A.9 respectively); (ii) each member who had volunteered to code was trained and accepted as a coder only when a preset level of accuracy was achieved[7]; (iii) the Oracles committee was established to advise coders on coding problems (Mabry and Sudweeks, 2003; Mabry and Sudweeks, 2004); (iv) messages for coding were downloaded from three networks; and (v) shell scripts were written to automate six of the codebook variables (coder ID, list ID, author ID, message number, message time, message date) and to verify completed coded data.

During this phase (March 1993), the two coordinators met face-to-face for the first time in Israel and the author met some of the project members in the USA. This event stimulated much of the social interaction as members were curious about the coordinators' physical appearance.

> As most know, most of us have not met each other face-to-face. A little of this is about to change. Fay is making a trip to California, Europe and Israel. I'll get to meet her! So will people in the San Francisco and Bay Area. (u_{879}, 14/2/93)

> ... first Fay was in CA, and is she still in Israel with Sheizaf? SO how long is that red beard anyway? (u_{963}, 1/4/93)

Much of the interaction, though, was a mixture of work and play, as the following post illustrates:

> Want to explain what the downloading entails? Onto where from where? I'd love to be in San Francisco with Fay and Catherine. Especially since we have a blizzard barreling down on Indiana from the west. Those of us without 4 wheel drive vehicles are dreading it. What is the acceptable error rate on intercoder reliability for the project? (u_{880}, 15/2/93)

Phase 7: Reflection on the need to meet face-to-face

The seventh time period, Phase 7 (u_{1116} to u_{1240}), is visually represented by the timeline in Figure 7.12. During this phase of just under three months (22 May 1993 to 7 August 1993), participants continued coding offline so most task-related communication online was in the form of posts to or from the Oracles committee. A natural enthusiasm for meeting project participants face-to-face emerged during this phase. The following excerpt, in which a ProjectH workshop was proposed, initiated some lively discourse and provided some distraction from the tedious coding tasks.

---

[7] The average agreement percentage among coders is a little over 87%. The agreement levels for most codebook items are over 80%. (u_{909}, 18/2/93)

Can we get a indication of how much interest there is in: (1) f2f workshop only (2) electronic conference followed by f2f workshop (3) Estes Park as a venue so that we can meet in a spectacular secluded location to ensure focused and stimulating discussions, and take full advantage of the opportunity to get to know each other. (u_{1116}, 1/4/93)

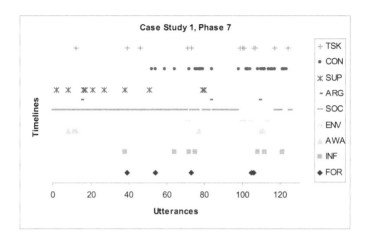

Figure 7.12. Content-dependent timeline of Phase 7 ($P_7 = [u_{1116}; u_{1240}]$)

As can be seen in Table 7.10, the discourse about the workshop is reflected in the large proportion of social communication (SOC=72.0%). This proportion of social discourse was almost twice the proportion in the previous phase.

Table 7.10. Number and percentage of communication types in Phase 7.

Code name	Code description	Number of utterances	Percentage of total P_7 utterance*
TSK	Task	12	9.6
CON	Conceptual	26	20.8
SUP	Supportive	10	8.0
ARG	Argumentative	3	2.4
SOC	Social	90	72.0
ENV	Environment	5	4.0
AWA	Awareness	6	4.8
INF	Informal	7	5.6
FOR	Formal	5	4.0

*Codes are not discrete categories, each utterance can be classified in a number of categories, hence percentages do not sum to 100.

Initially, participants were enthusiastic about the proposed workshop and meeting face-to-face, but the discussions raised another unexpected issue. The proposed venue was in Colorado, USA, and at this time there was a political upheaval in that state over discrimination of sexual minority groups:

I oppose any scheduling of *new* events in this state, until Amendment 2 is voided. For those who don't know Colorado passed a state referendum prohibiting non-discrimination laws that would protect the sexual minorities (lesbians, gay men, bisexuals, etc.). The immediate impact of the amendment will be to overturn local non-discrimination laws in five cities (including mine). The amendment earned us the title of "hate state" and sparked a boycott. (u_{1130}, 24/5/93)

The response to this post was overwhelming support for boycotting Colorado:

Thank you, Murray. I'm embarrassed to say I'd forgotten about the boycott. I vote with Murray; there are plenty of other places to have a meeting. (u_{1132}, 24/5/93)

The participants decided eventually not to go ahead with the workshop – not because of the proposed location but because they did not think it necessary to meet face-to-face:

... doesn't it strike you as significant that you want to "_meet_ the people (you) will have been working with for two years. . . ?" Haven't we already _met_? Is there something unreal or artificial about the lack of F2F contact? I think the drive to _meet_ (defined as F2F contact) expresses a profound anxiety at being unable to engage our normal appearance screening operations ... (u_{1187}, 10/6//93)

... the strength of ProjectH has been its independence of the limitations imposed by F2F collaboration, and I hate to see us slip back into the old pattern. Can't we continue to collaborate by CMC and leave the F2F to a small group of leaders/coordinators? It's not that I don't want to see you-all, but rather that I want to maintain the unique contribution of this effort. (u_{1132}, 24/5/93)

The task activities were being carried out offline, so the online task-related communication was low (TSK=9.6%), one-fifth of the proportion of task-related communication in the previous phase. One interviewee noted that, from an organisational perspective, there appeared to be a fragmentation during this phase:

... Then this kind of fragmentation that occurred. In terms of organising, I thought it was one of the more interesting things because we all went off and did our own things in singles, or pairs, or small groups, and occasionally would come back to an oracle or occasionally would come back to you or Sheizaf or somebody in a coordinating role to ask a question about data or something like that. (Donna, 26/5/96)

Phase 8: Goal achievement and closure

The eighth and final time period, Phase 8 (u_{1241} to u_{1343}), is visually represented by the timeline in Figure 7.13. This phase of more than 7 months (7 August 1993 to 19 March 1994) was lengthy but relatively quiet in terms of discourse. During this phase, coders submitted their coded data and strategies were developed for the equitable distribution of the database.

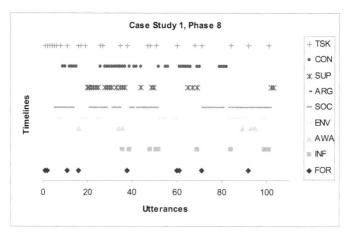

Figure 7.13. Content-dependent timeline of Phase 8 ($P_8 = [u_{1241}; u_{1343}]$)

The varied discourse is reflected in the percentages of different types of communication (Table 7.11). The discourse focused on task (TSK=23.3%), conceptual (CON=35.0%), supportive (21.4%) and social topics (SOC=43.7%).

Table 7.11. Number and percentage of communication types in Phase 8.

Code name	Code description	Number of utterances	Percentage of total P_8 utterance*
TSK	Task	24	23.3
CON	Conceptual	36	35.0
SUP	Supportive	22	21.4
ARG	Argumentative	0	0.0
SOC	Social	45	43.7
ENV	Environment	12	11.7
AWA	Awareness	7	6.8
INF	Informal	9	8.7
FOR	Formal	9	8.7

*Codes are not discrete categories, each utterance can be classified in a number of categories, hence percentages do not sum to 100.

A deadline of 13 September 1993 was set for submission of coded data. This deadline was almost met, with just a few coded lists completed a few weeks later (30 September).

> 3002 messages coded, 23 lists complete, 10 lists incomplete, 2+ lists due on 30 September … Most of the unfinished lists are just needing corrections to a few records. (u_{1300}, 30/9/93)

The group adjourned amidst self-disclosing and congratulatory posts, e.g. the birth of a third son for one of the coordinators:

> Congrats for the successful conclusion of a mutually agreed upon project, or, the
> oldest continuing collaborative project in humankind's history! If I could I would
> toast, ie: Skoal! %) ... (u_{1315}, 29/10/93)

and a forthcoming marriage of a member:

> Since it is Valentine I am pleased to announce that I will be getting married in April! I
> guess I am most excited about being 50 and finding a special love ... (u_{1336}, 14/2/94)

Information was distributed about spinoff projects, such as two ProjectH panels[8]
at the forthcoming *International Communication Association* conference, MIT
Press's acceptance of a book proposal about ProjectH edited by the coordinators[9],
and a journal about computer-mediated communication[10]. These projects ensured
that most participants maintained contact for many years after ProjectH but there was
little activity on the list.

The actual adjournment was characteristically reflective as the following
excerpts from posts illustrate:

> I find the nature of discussion in the projectH list interesting. Many of the messages
> that are sent seem very similar to messages sent to small circles of friends or co-
> workers. In particular, I think the collegiality of the list is much higher than many
> mailing lists and newsgroups that I've seen [I don't tend to see BITNET lists]. Do
> others notice this? When you send a message, do you feel as though you are sending it
> to dozens(??) of people, or just a few friends at project H? (u_{1266}, 27/8/93)

> ... [E]ven though I have not had 1:1 correspondence with everybody on ProjectH, I
> feel that I am sending to friends when I post something on here. I agree that the
> collegiality is remarkable on this list. One of my main lists in my field seems more
> like a series of battles and wars, with much backbiting and bickering. This one is
> constructive and productive. (u_{1268}, 28/8/93)

> There is a sense of cohesiveness with ProjectH exchanges that I don't apprehend on
> lists. A primary difference comes in not feeling the need to engage in self-
> credentialing (this-is-who-I-am) statements. The "this-is-what-I-know" sorts of
> statements are for the most part task-specific and volunteered in the context of
> collaborating to complete tasks rather than carry argumentative points. And, there
> definitely is a sense of "We-ness" among H-ers that may not be typical of other groups
> and lists. There is a sense of identification (and belongingness) with ProjectH that
> carries with it the same kind of psychosocial investment that one makes in f2f groups.
> That's not to say various netgroups cannot evolve similar levels of cohesiveness (I
> suspect our research will show many do). ProjectH's goals clarify members'
> purposiveness and contribute structure (vis-a-vis expectations, ongoing tasks, etc.) to

---

[8] Panel 1: *Network and Netplay: The Internet and its Users* (Chair: Fay Sudweeks; Discussant: Brenda
Danet); Panel 2: *Network and Netplay: The Uses of the Internet* (Chair: Margaret McLaughlin;
Discussant: Sheizaf Rafaeli).
[9] The proposal was accepted and is published as Sudweeks, F., McLaughlin, M. and Rafaeli, S.: 1998,
Network and Netplay: Virtual Groups on the Internet, MIT Press, Cambridge MA.
[10] *Journal of Computer Mediated Communication*, edited by M. McLaughlin and S. Rafaeli,
www.ascusc.org/jcmc/.

CHAPTER 7

their relationship in ways that less well defined groups may not achieve (or will take markedly longer to achieve) ... (u_{1269}, 28/8/93)

Eric wrote exactly what I was thinking about the collegiality of ProjectH compared to other lists. ... most of the lists have no particular task to accomplish. They are formed around a topic or area of interest, but lack the focus of ProjectH because they have no specific objectives. I suspect that one element for us may be that we've been setting benchmarks, i.e., completing an ethics statement; composing a codebook; finishing the coding --- and we have incorporated target dates. So not only has our discourse been focused on goals and objectives (as opposed to ruminations), we've been consciously moving forward in time, which, I suspect, increases the value of cooperative effort. Of course, I think that is the beginning of the phenomenon rather than the end. As a result, our interactions have created a group culture, complete with norms and values. As a group, we seem to value collegiality, mutual respect, and a sense of humor, while devaluing flaming and argumentativeness. For me, at least, that makes ProjectH a very comfortable place to pursue some interesting questions. In fact, although I subscribe to a number of lists, this is the only one on which I do much beyond lurk. Hmmmmmm. There could be an interesting study in this! ;-) (u_{1270}, 28/8/93)

7.2.2. Summary of developmental phases

The ProjectH group evolved over the lifecycle of the project. Each of the phases was distinctive in the combination of communication types. Table 7.12 gives the results of t-test on the variation of eight communication variables. In each case the variation was significant.

Table 7.12. Results of t-test for eight communication variables (by phase)

Variable	Description	t	df	p value
TSK	Task	3.370	7	0.012
CON	Conceptual	4.788	7	0.002
EMO	Emotional	5.838	7	0.001
SOC	Social	3.262	7	0.014
ENV	Environment	4.570	7	0.003
AWA	Awareness	4.568	7	0.003
INF	Informal	4.836	7	0.002
FOR	Formal	3.972	7	0.005

The early phase was characteristically concerned about establishing group norms, learning about each other, and conceptualising the collaborative activities. A period of conflict followed. Although the conflict appeared to be focused on a particular issue (ethics), there was an underlying tension related to issues such as "who are the leaders?", "who are the stakeholders?", "what needs to be done?", "who will do what?". Having established collegiality, the group reflected on the conflicts and settled down to work together. After some progress on the project, the ethics issue was raised again and resolved, which enabled the group to complete the project.

One interviewee summarised his perception of the project's lifecycle as follows:

My notion of the early period is sort of like a call for participation, this huge influx of interested people from all sorts of different backgrounds and kinda getting to know one another, exchanging biographies. ... And so, getting to know who's who, establishing within the group who was going to be the king of the mountain so to speak, would it be Sheizaf because he organised it, or would some other leader emerging from within this group.

In my mind, the next period was after the introductions were over and we were getting down to business. Getting down to business was, like, ok someone suggest some variables that ought to be coded, so these variables were coming in, and discussions of variables, whether or not this variable overlapped with another variable. And then we have people who take on ownership of different parts of the project. "I volunteer to compile a list of variables and summarise everything that's been said thus far." I feel this is the second part where work supposedly is being accomplished, we were past the introduction.

The third part, I think, was when they said, "ok now that we have our list of variables we need coders". This is going to involve some real work, not just around chatting around on a list but going and doing something. (Robin, 23/5/96)

In early phases of the project, the discourse was largely conceptual and social. As the work structure became more explicit, the discourse focused on leader directives and participant comments on individual tasks. Balancing phases of concentrated performance were phases of reflection on the interactive processes. Communication management was informal in the early phases, formal in the middle phases and a mix of both types in the later stages.

It is interesting that, after working together for more than a year, most participants did not want to meet face-to-face as they felt they already "knew" each other (see Phase 7, p.180). The degree of *awareness*, *social presence* and *connectedness* in the group, by this stage, was so high that there was little need to disclose explicit personal information. This finding supports the work on social presence by a number of researchers, such as Chapanis (1975), Short et al. (1976), Kiesler and Sproull (1986), Mantovani (1999), and Hiltz and Turoff (2002). Short et al. (1976, p.65) define social presence as the "degree of salience of the other person in a mediated communication and the consequent salience of their interpersonal interactions". Social presence involves the ability of people to be perceived as real beings despite not communicating face-to-face. As the perception of social presence increases, the ability to substitute mediated communication in collaborative activities increases. Rettie (2003) relates social presence to awareness and connectedness.

Presence is a critical social factor that is examined in both collaborative computer-mediated groups and distance or e-learning. There is some evidence that social presence increases satisfaction in an online environment, whether the task be collaborative research (Mantovani and Riva, 1999) or collaborative learning (Gunawardena and Zittle, 1997).

Figure 7.14 shows the total number of utterances of each communication type over the life of the project. As can be seen, the most persistent communication types throughout were conceptual (CON), task (TSK) and social (SOC) and emotional (SUP+ARG).

In Figure 7.15, these four main communication types (CON, TSK, SOC, EMO) are represented as proportional to each other in each development phase. In other words, the figure illustrates the percentage each communication type contributes to the total of all four types.

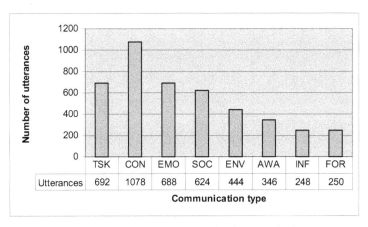

Figure 7.14. Total number of utterances of each communication type.

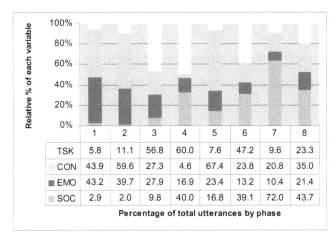

Figure 7.15. Proportion of TSK, CON, EMO and SOC in each development phase.

These four communication types can be organised as two dimensions with two constructs each: (i) *activity* which is a continuum between *task* (TSK) and *conceptual* (CON) variables; and (ii) *relationships*, which is a continuum between *social* (SOC) and *emotional* (SUP+ARG) variables. The eight phases are plotted on two axes representing the two dimensions (activity and relationships) in Figure 7.16. Figure 7.16 shows, for example, that Phase 1 has more conceptual than task communication and more emotional than social communication; Phase 3 has more task than conceptual communication and more emotional than social communication; and Phase 8 has more social than emotional communication and a little more conceptual than task communication.

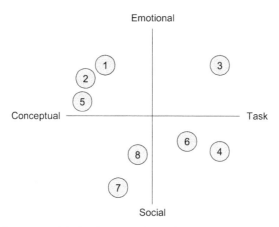

Figure 7.16. Eight developmental phases plotted on four dimensions.

7.3. Examination of Developmental Hypotheses

The previous section was a detailed analysis of each of the eight developmental phases. In this section, the hypotheses concerned with developmental characteristics will be discussed in relation to the results of the analyses.

Hypothesis H$_{1.1}$: *There are definable developmental phases in CM groups*
The analyses of the group's lifecycle demonstrate a clear developmental pattern. The timeline representations of the TSK, CON, SUP, ARG, SOC, AWA, INF and FOR variables (Figure 7.2) indicate distinct turning points (Figure 7.4) which signal a change in the development of the group. The existence of different phases is also evidenced by interviewee comments (see, e.g., p. 186). Throughout the life of

ProjectH, participants experienced periods of activity and transitional periods concerned with relationships, reflection and reassessment.

Hypothesis H$_{1.1}$, therefore, has been supported.

Hypothesis H$_{1.2}$: *In the early phases of development the content of communication is more conceptual than task oriented or social*

The timeline representations and percentages of conceptual (CON), task (TSK) and social (SOC) variables in Phases 1 and 2 (Figure 7.6, Figure 7.7, Table 7.4, Table 7.5) indicate that communication among the participants in Phases 1 and 2 was focused significantly on the conceptual aspects of the project. However, in Phase 5, participants conceptualised the aims and process of the project again, which indicates a non-sequential developmental pattern. This return to conceptualisation was precipitated by the demands of the task being undertaken in that phase, requiring re-visiting the ethics of the project and a re-assessment of methodological issues.

Figure 7.17 shows the variation in the TSK, CON and SOC variables in each development phase. The columns bars show the proportions of CON, TSK and SOC variables relative to each other; that is, the percentage each variable contributes to the total of these three variables. The figure demonstrates both the predominance of conceptual communication in the early stages and the non-sequential nature of the developmental process.

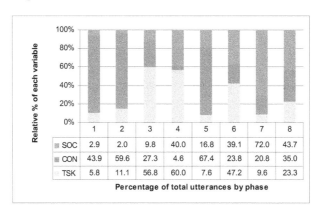

Figure 7.17. Proportion of SOC, CON and TSK variables in each development phase.

Hypothesis H$_{1.2}$, therefore, has been partly supported.

Hypotheses H$_{1.3}$ and H$_{1.4}$: *During periods of low task activity, the content of communication is more social than task oriented and vice versa*

The timeline representations and percentages of task (TSK) and social (SOC) variables in all phases (Figure 7.6-Figure 7.13, and Table 7.4-Table 7.11) indicate that in most phases when participants were focused on task activity, there was little social interaction, and vice versa. Figure 7.18 shows the variation in TSK and SOC variables in each phase. The figure illustrates the percentage each of these two variables contributes to the total of the two variables.

The high/low pattern is strong in all but Phases 4 and 6. During Phase 4 there was an influx of new members (see p.176) who responded to a general invitation, distributed to various discussion lists, to join the project. The high percentage of social communication in this phase is due to "old" members welcoming new people. In Phase 6, much of the task activity was conducted offline and communication about coding was mostly between the coders and the Oracles committee (see p.178). The TSK variable in this phase is therefore deflated.

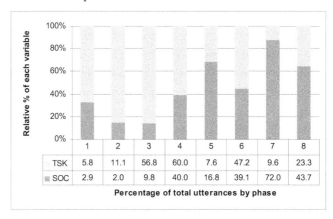

	1	2	3	4	5	6	7	8
TSK	5.8	11.1	56.8	60.0	7.6	47.2	9.6	23.3
SOC	2.9	2.0	9.8	40.0	16.8	39.1	72.0	43.7

Percentage of total utterances by phase

Figure 7.18. Proportion of TSK and SOC variables in each development phase.

Hypotheses H₁.₃ and H₁.₄ are therefore partly supported.

Hypothesis H₁.₅: *During earlier developmental stages, participants engage in more disclosures about the physical and social attributes of themselves and others.*

The timeline representations and percentages of the awareness (AWA) variable in all phases (Figure 7.6 to Figure 7.13, and Table 7.4 to Table 7.11) indicate that, throughout the lifespan of the project, participants feel the need to communicate less and less explicitly about the physical and social context of their interactions (Christiansen and Maglaughlin, 2003; Dourish and Bly, 1992). The decrease in such explicit communication indicates increased consciousness of the physical and social attributes of others, as a "taken for granted" awareness. Figure 7.19 shows the incidence of the AWA variable as a percentage of all utterances in each phase. The graph indicates that, apart from a peak in Phase 4 when there was an influx of new members, there is a general decrease in the AWA variable over the life of the project.

CHAPTER 7

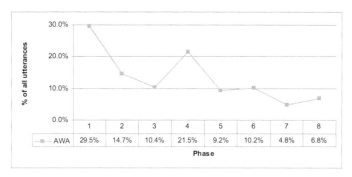

Figure 7.19. AWA variable as a percentage of total utterances in each development phase.

Hypothesis H$_{1.5}$ is therefore supported.

Hypothesis H$_{1.6}$: *Group cohesiveness increases over the life of the group*

The timeline representations and percentages of the supportive (SUP) and argumentative (ARG) variables in all phases (Figure 7.6-Figure 7.13, and Table 7.4-Table 7.11) indicate that, after some fluctuation in the early stages, there is a general trend for participants to be more supportive and less argumentative, which indicates increased group cohesiveness. This trend is also supported in participant comments in various posts (see, for example, excerpts on p.184). In addition, the graph in Figure 7.20, showing the ratio of SUP utterances to ARG utterances, illustrates this general trend towards a more supportive climate of the group in the latter phases.

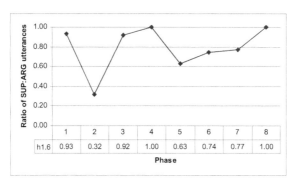

Figure 7.20. Ratio of SUP utterances to ARG utterances in each development phase.

Figure 7.21 illustrates the same trend of supportive communication as a different representation; that is, the column bars show the proportion of supportive (SUP) and argumentative (ARG) variables relative to each other.

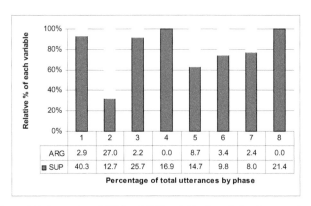

Figure 7.21. Proportion of ARG and SUP variables in each development phase.

Hypothesis $H_{1.6}$ is therefore supported.

7.4. Examination of Leadership Characteristics Hypotheses

The second group of hypotheses are concerned with the leadership characteristics of virtual groups (see Section 2.7.2 and Table 6.3):

$H_{2.1}$ Management intervention is more frequent during periods of high task activity.

$H_{2.2}$ Different management styles predominate at different developmental stages.

$H_{2.3}$ Leaders communicate more intensively than other participants.

$H_{2.4}$ Leaders emerge during the life of the group.

The importance of leadership has been argued for centuries. Leadership is part of almost every aspect of society, yet some researchers argue that leaders do not make an impact (e.g. Meindl, Ehrlich and Dukerich, 1985; Kiechel, 1998). Other researchers argue that leaders do exert considerable influence on groups and organisations (for an overview, see Bass, 1990). Predictably there are many definitions of leadership (see Sarros et al (1999) for an excellent in-depth review of leadership in the context of organisations, including an historical overview of the evolution of the concept), but for the purpose the analysis in this book, leadership is viewed as "any facilitation that moves a group closer to its outcome". Leadership considers the influence and the impact of individuals on the group. In the context of group development it can be viewed both as a property and a process. Leadership might be appointed, assigned or emergent.

In a traditional hierarchical organisational structure, group (or team) leaders are usually appointed (Katz and Kahn, 1978). Such appointment is generally by a person in a superior position in the organisation's hierarchy. Hence, appointed leadership results in another element within a hierarchical relationship. Non-appointed (assigned or emergent) leaders, on the other hand, are the result of bottom-up processes rather than a top-down command and control process. This leads to the question whether this type of leadership should be considered as a property of individuals or an emergent property of groups. This case study shows that leadership evolves as a result of group interaction, i.e. group leadership is a product of communication and interaction processes.

So far in the analysis of Case Study 1, the communication patterns have been studied at the level of the group, rather than an examination of the specifics of individual patterns. In this section on leadership, the communication patterns of specific individuals will be analysed. This study of leadership was conducted as an exploratory study to examine the unique asynchronous computer-mediated communication patterns displayed by non-appointed leaders during the two-year period of the project. Hence, these systematic patterns can be used to help identify patterns of leadership in virtual organisations (Jackson, 1999) with asynchronous communication (email, listserv, discussion boards, SMS) as a dominating communication mode.

Table 7.13 lists the variables of interest in this section of the analysis with a brief description and the hypotheses to which they apply. All communication types (variables) are defined and described in Table 6.4.

Table 7.13. Communication variables used in the leadership characteristics hypotheses.

Category	Code	Description	Hypothesis
Management	**MAN**		
Formal	FOR	Communication connected with the enforcement of rules or norms, used to manage the process of collaboration. More likely used by leaders and key stakeholders..	2.1
Informal	INF	Communication connected with the collective informal creation, management, and enforcement of communication norms, used by any participant. Has a quality of collaborative construction.	2.1
Content	**CNT**		
Conceptual	CON	Conceptual communication involves the creation of mutual understandings and meanings among participants. Involves the creation of shared rules to follow. Includes creation, agreement or disagreement about procedures to follow, a common vocabulary, work to be completed.	2.1
Task	TSK	Communication content dealing with the collaborative activity of the group. Includes introduction, clarification, agreement or disagreement of task issues and specific task instructions.	2.1
Style	**STY**		
Negative	NEG	Argumentative, aggressive or any type of negative communication to achieve a goal (i.e. negative reinforcement). Its use is intended to halt or alter a communication direction, i.e. as an intervention.	2.2

Humour	HUM	Humourous communication to achieve a goal (the humour doesn't necessarily have to succeed). Its use is intended to halt or alter the communication direction, i.e. as an intervention. Often indicated by smiley or emoticon, and often used to lighten a heavy discussion.	2.2
Asking	ASK	A question asked as a management strategy to effect a change in the behaviour of an individual or group.	2.2
Positive	POS	Positive, supportive or placative communication to achieve a goal (i.e. positive reinforcement). Its use is intended to halt or alter the communication direction , i.e. as an intervention. Can be indicated by an apology. Intended to keep the peace. Can take the form of rephrasing a question or idea to be more sensitive to other participants' feelings.	2.2
Interactivity	**INT**		
All	ALL	Utterance addresses whole group.	2.3
Part of a group	PAR	Utterance addresses part of the group (two or more participants)	2.3
Person	PER	Utterance addresses one individual	2.3
Addressed	ADD	Individual to whom an utterance is addressed.	2.4

In Case Study 1, leadership was initially assigned to two members of the group by the other participants. These leaders were assigned not by dominating the discussions or parading qualifications, but by taking the initiative and demonstrating a deep understanding of the research field. The initiatives of these two participants was acknowledged by other participants:

> We seem to be getting semi-serious about this. Maybe one tentative and fairly easy way to proceed is to appoint Sheizaf and Fay the "leaders" (not because they talk the most, but because this is already their research interest and they have some experience in it). (u_{18}, 28/5/92)

and the leading role assignment was accepted:

> OK. Here goes. I'm in this for the experience, Put my keyboard where my mouth is. I've been claiming (for ten years) that e-mail holds the potential to form communities out of thin air (thin bits?). Have been, mostly, ridiculed. So lets give it a try (u_{15}, 29/5/92).

and generally approved by participants:

> Sheizaf is doing an admirable job in moving this project along. He is not going too fast (in my view). In fact, his handling is a model for how to do a fairly unique type of research for which there are few (if any) previous exemplars ... I think both his personal style and his demonstrable methodological (and other) skills make him exceptionally suited for the leadership role into which we have placed him, albeit kicking and screaming. (u_{121}, 8/6/92)

In the following sections, the analyses of leadership is structured around the hypotheses relating to leadership characteristics. Although the analyses for this set of hypotheses are applied all participants, the hypotheses are classified as "leadership" patterns because the variables of interest relate primarily to a few participants. The first two hypotheses – management intervention and management style – are about 'group' management. But since the management group consists of the coordinators and key motivators, it is reasonable to consider these two hypotheses within this section on leadership characteristics. The last two hypotheses relate to leadership communication patterns and emergent leadership.

7.4.1. Management intervention

Management intervention in this book refers to communication that facilitates the group moving closer to its goal. Formal management communication is connected with the enforcement of rules or norms that are used to manage the process of collaboration. Although it could be used by any participant, it is more likely used by coordinators and key motivators. Informal management is connected with the collective information creation, management and enforcement of communication norms. It is more likely to be used by non-leading participants and has a quality of collaborative construction. Management intervention, therefore, is defined as the use of formal management (FOR) or informal management (INF) (see Section Table 6.4 for definitions of FOR and INF constructs).

Table 7.14 and Figure 7.22 illustrate that in Phases 3 and 4, when task activity (TSK) is high, management intervention (INF+FOR) is also high. In Phase 6, however, task activity is relatively high but management intervention does not display a similar trend, maintaining approximately the same level as in the previous phase. The reason for management intervention being less evident during this phase is that the Oracles Committee had essentially taken over the management task and much of this management was directed to individual coders who queried certain aspects of the coding tasks. This communication was offline and not part of the set of utterances used here. The Pearson correlation for management intervention (INF+FOR) and task activity (TSK), is not significantly high at $r=0.5$.

Table 7.14. Management intervention (INF+FOR) compared with task (TSK) activity (% of all utterances by phase).

Phase	Leadership management (FOR+INF)	TSK
1	20.2	5.8
2	19.9	11.1
3	34.4	56.8
4	32.3	60.0
5	13.0	7.6
6	12.8	47.2
7	9.6	9.6
8	17.4	23.3

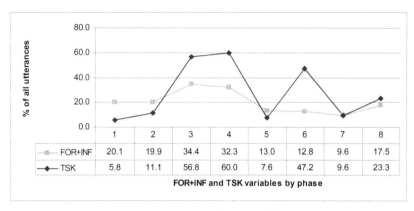

	1	2	3	4	5	6	7	8
FOR+INF	20.1	19.9	34.4	32.3	13.0	12.8	9.6	17.5
TSK	5.8	11.1	56.8	60.0	7.6	47.2	9.6	23.3

FOR+INF and TSK variables by phase

Figure 7.22. Management (FOR+INF) and task (TSK) variables compared in each phase.

It has been previously argued that the conceptual (CON) variable is related to task activity (see the discussion on TSK and CON variables as constructs of an activity dimension on p.188 and illustrated in Figure 7.16). The frequency of management intervention is therefore compared with the combination of task and conceptual (TSK+CON) variables (Table 7.15 and Figure 7.23). This comparison yielded a significantly high Pearson correlation of $r=0.79$, illustrated by the scatter plot in Figure 7.24).

Table 7.15. Management intervention (INF+FOR) compared with task (TSK+CON) activity (% of all utterances by phase).

Phase	Leadership management (FOR+INF)	TSK+CON
1	20.2	49.6
2	19.9	70.7
3	34.4	84.2
4	32.3	64.6
5	13.0	75.0
6	12.8	71.1
7	9.6	30.4
8	17.4	58.3

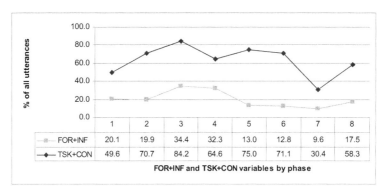

Figure 7.23. Management (FOR+INF) and activity (TSK+CON) variables compared in each phase.

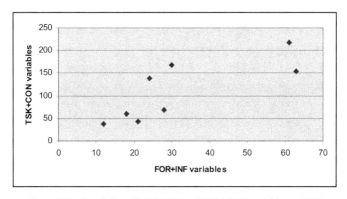

Figure 7.24. Correlation of FOR+INF and TSK+CON variables ($r=0.79$)

Comments from interviewees confirm that management intervention was more prevalent in times of high task activity to encourage productivity. One interviewee compared one coordinator's communication management in periods of low activity to a "host" (i.e. informal), and in periods of high activity to a "moderator" (i.e. formal).

> It seems that [when we were] getting down to work, deciding which variables were to be coded, that was pretty moderated to me. You know, whereas [initially it was] more like a cocktail party where Sheizaf did most of the talking and was maybe the host, it didn't seem as controlled. But with the exchange of bios and people got a feeling of who was who, … then there were already some power relationships established - we knew who was faculty, who was a grad student, who was whatever. It seemed much more ordered and moderated in my view by the organisers of ProjectH and the people they had put a blessing on as being one of the primary contributors to the project. (Brian, 27/5/96)

Another interviewee also noted the fluctuation between casual, informal intervention and a more formal intervention depending on the level of activity.

> I think you had your strategies well in hand but I think they were … [like] a moderator who is sitting back, watching, listening, very decidedly has an agenda, and who periodically appears and reflects back at the group and gives the group its next assignment, points the group in a particular direction, and gets them back on track. (Catherine, 13/7/96)

Hypothesis $H_{2.1}$, that management intervention is more frequent during periods of high task activity, is supported.

7.4.2. Management styles

Leaders adopt a variety of strategies to motivate group or team members. This section explores the communication behaviour within Case Study 1 to identify a variety of management styles that are used strategically. To determine if *different management styles predominate at different developmental stages*, four communication variables (positivity, asking, humour and negativity) will be investigated. As with management intervention, different management styles are used mostly by the coordinators and key motivators, although utterances of other group members will be investigated for comparison purposes.

In the early days of ProjectH when discussions focused on assigning a leadership role within the group, one of the participants noted that a leader should demonstrate certain qualities, including questioning in a provocative way:

> By leader I mean someone who brings up a topic which lots of people pick up on, addressing that person directly; sometimes the person is deliberately provocative, and sometimes people are unexpectedly provoked. (u_{12}, 27/5/92)

As a leadership strategy, *positivity* (giving positive comments) helps participants to focus on the task at hand and increases their confidence, *asking* questions helps to promote both confidence and a sense of ownership in participants, *humour* helps to avoid or relieve conflict, *negativity* is a harsher response but has a role in diffusing conflict situations. Humour has been related to group longevity (Scogin and Pollio, 1980) and cohesiveness (Duncan and Fieisal, 1989). These leadership strategies have also been emphasised as features of transformational leadership (see Sarros et al., 1999, Chap. 2 and Section 2.5.4 in this book). Figure 7.25 shows the frequency and timing of positive (POS), questioning (ASK), humour (HUM) and negative (NEG) styles of all participants throughout the project.

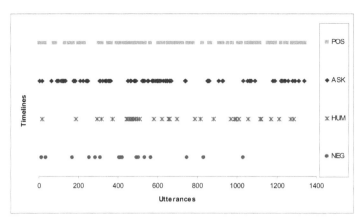

Figure 7.25. Frequency of management styles (POS, ASK, HUM, NEG) during the project period.

Table 7.16 shows the number of utterances of each management style used throughout the project period. The figures indicate that positive comments and asking questions were the most frequently used styles.

Table 7.16. Number of utterances of each type of management style (all phases combined).

Code name	Code description	Number of utterances
POS	Positive	99
ASK	Asking	93
HUM	Humour	37
NEG	Negative	16

Figure 7.26 shows the four management styles used in each development phase. Figure 7.27 shows the percentage that each of these four variables contributes to the total of the four variables.

As can be seen from Figure 7.26 and Figure 7.27, positivity and questioning are the most consistently used management styles used throughout the project period. Humour is used less often but is more prevalent in Phases 3 and 6. The reason for more humour in these phases is probably to offset the conflict that occurred in Phase 2 and, to a lesser degree, in Phase 5. This also correlates with the increased negativity figure for Phases 2, which was the most argumentative phases.

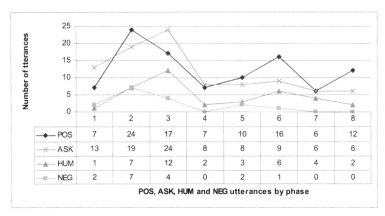

Figure 7.26. Number of utterances of each management style (POS, ASK, HUM, NEG) by phase.

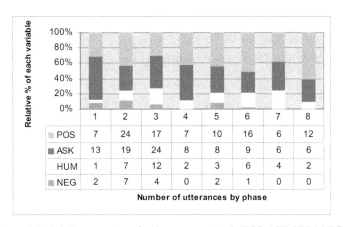

Figure 7.27. Relative percentage of each management style (POS, ASK, HUM, NEG).

When asked about their perception of the style of leadership demonstrated within the group, most interviewees commented on the transparency and 'light-handedness' of the coordinators, for example:

> For the most part, the management styles of the coordinators were transparent. ... I well recognised that the two of you ... were the coordinators, but I never felt there was a heavy handedness to it ... there were moments in time when one of the two coordinators, or both, would issue forth some instruction or new information ... so I was aware of this quiet moderation ... But it seemed that in the moments of "argumentative dialogue" ... that the coordinators were not apparent, they were transparent ... and occasionally reflective. (Brian, 27/5/96)

> I think you [Fay] had your strategies well in hand but I think they were ... [like] a moderator who is sitting back, watching, listening, very decidedly has an agenda, and who periodically appears and reflects back at the group and gives the group its next

assignment, points the group in a particular direction, and gets them back on track. (Catherine, 13/7/96)

Hypothesis $H_{2.2}$, that different management styles predominate at different developmental stages, is weakly supported.

7.4.3. Leadership communication

In face-to-face environments, research shows that leaders are identified by high participation rates in discussions (Regula and Julian, 1973; Sorrentino and Boutillier, 1975; Mullen, Salas and Driskell, 1989). This section, therefore, explores the communication behaviour within Case Study 1 to identify leadership patterns. To determine if *leaders communicate more intensely than other participants,* the number and density of utterances of all members of the group will be investigated.

Number of utterances

Figure 7.28 illustrates the activity level of different participants. The analysis of the activity level is measured as the total number of utterances over the entire period of Case Study 1. The activity level is organised in five intervals, shown in Figure 7.28 as bins. The first bin [1; 10] of the lowest number of utterances accommodates the levels of activities of typical participants; that is, 78% of the group members. The remaining 22% of the group are spread across two bins of medium levels of activity ([11; 20] and [21; 39]), one bin of a high level of activity ([40; 89]) and a fifth bin with an extremely high level of activity (more than 90 utterances). The two bins of the highest activity (more than 40 utterances), representing only 8 participants (6% of the group) are highlighted in Figure 7.28.

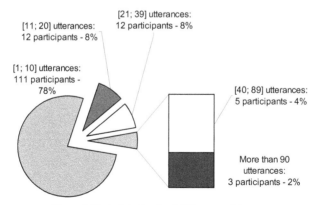

Figure 7.28. Activity levels of different participants.

Table 7.17 identifies the participants with the highest activity levels in terms of the number of utterances. Predictably, the two coordinators (assigned leaders) have the highest activity with 160 and 101 utterances. One other participant, Jeff, is also a frequent communicator with 90 utterances. This bin (or cluster) is shaded in a dark grey. There are five participants (Barbara, Catherine, Deborah, Jonathan and Eric) in the next cluster (bin [40; 89]) of utterances, which are shaded in a lighter grey. In the last cluster (bin [21; 39]) in the table, there are eleven participants.

Table 7.17. Participants with highest number of utterances.

Participant	No. of utterances	Participant	No. of utterances
Fay	160	Marian	30
Sheizaf	101	Ben	28
Jeff	90	David	27
Barbara	47	Vivian	27
Catherine	47	Brent	26
Deborah	42	Sally	26
Jonathan	42	Chloe	24
Eric	40	Tom	22
Nadia	32	Sarah	21
Donna	31		

Therefore, if based on total number of utterances only, the assigned leaders communicated more intensively than other participants.

Density of utterances

Density of utterances needs to be considered as well as total number of utterances. Density can be measured by total number of words throughout the two-year period of the project, and average utterance length in words. Table 7.20 lists the participants in Case Study 1 who posted in excess of 2000 words. Predictably, in terms of total words, the two coordinators (assigned leaders) are the most verbose (shaded in dark grey). Two other participants, Jeff and Jonathan, cluster together (shaded in lighter grey), while another two, Barbara and Eric, form a third cluster (shaded in light grey).

Table 7.18. Participants with highest total number of words.

Participants	Total words	Participants	Total words	Participants	Total words
Sheizaf	28408	Catherine	3958	Sarah	2423
Fay	22994	David	3714	Donna	2401
Jeff	16770	Deborah	3580	Jamie	2383
Jonathan	12211	Ben	3037	Brent	2285
Barbara	6863	Tom	2820	Sally	2146
Eric	5675	Daniel	2526	Carleen	2082
Nadia	3960	Marian	2490	Vivian	2066

When considering another measure, the average number of words per utterance, a very different pattern emerges. Although Sheizaf and Fay were the most verbose in terms of total number of words, Jonathan and Sheizaf have the highest average utterance length at 291 words and 281 words respectively (Table 7.19). Apart from a few utterances consisting of just one word of three letters[11], all participants tended to post lengthy messages, even if they only posted occasionally. The average utterance length of 132 words over the whole group is not substantially lower than the most verbose participants.

Although Fay had the highest number of utterances (Table 7.17), her average utterance length of 144 was not much above the average for all participants. Since Fay fielded most of the technical queries, the shorter average length for her is probably due to the high amount of quick and short responses to that type of question. Like Fay, a different pattern emerges for Jamie. Jamie, with an average utterance length of 183 words, is the participant with the fourth highest average utterance length. Yet Jamie is not among the 19 participants with the highest number of utterances (Table 7.17) and is towards the bottom of the list of 21 participants with the highest total number of words (Table 7.18). As Jamie did most of the programming to automate some of the codebook variables, it was necessary for him to give lengthy descriptions and examples of the coding process in the initial stages of coding.

Table 7.19. Participants with highest average utterance length in words.

Participants	Ave. utterance length	Participants	Ave. utterance length	Participants	Ave. utterance length
Jonathan	291	Eric	142	Brent	88
Sheizaf	281	David	138	Deborah	16
Jeff	186	Tom	128	Catherine	84
Jamie	183	Nadia	124	Marian	83
Daniel	149	Sarah	115	Sally	83
Barbara	146	Carleen	110	Donna	77
Fay	144	Ben	108	Vivian	77

The two measures of density (total number of words and average utterance length) are combined in Table 7.20 to show the high variability between these measures.

---

[11] The single word was "yes", which was in response to the call for votes on the ethics policy, see Section 3.6.1.

Table 7.20. Participants with highest total words and average utterance length.

Participants	Total words	Ave. utterance length	Participants	Total words	Ave. utterance length
Sheizaf	28408	281	Tom	2820	128
Fay	22994	144	Daniel	2526	149
Jeff	16770	186	Marian	2490	83
Jonathan	12211	291	Sarah	2423	115
Barbara	6863	146	Donna	2401	77
Eric	5675	142	Jamie	2383	183
Nadia	3960	124	Brent	2285	88
Catherine	3958	84	Sally	2146	83
David	3714	138	Carleen	2082	110
Deborah	3580	85	Vivian	2066	77
Ben	3037	108			

Figure 7.29 shows histograms of the distribution of the length of utterances in bins of words of assigned leaders (Fay and Sheizaf). Figure 7.30 shows histograms of the distribution of the length of utterances in bins of words of the next cluster of participants who communicated in excess of 5000 words; that is, Jeff, Jonathan, Barbara and Eric. The distribution in these histograms indicates that these participants have a significant number of utterances that are longer than 100 words.

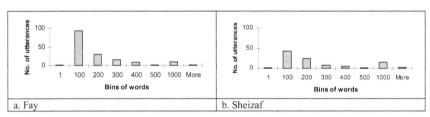

a. Fay

b. Sheizaf

Figure 7.29. Distribution of the length of the utterances (bins of words) of assigned leaders.

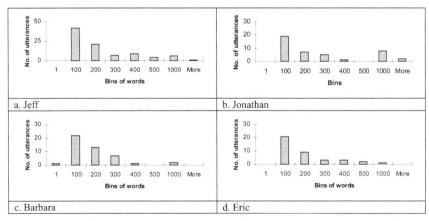

a. Jeff

b. Jonathan

c. Barbara

d. Eric

Figure 7.30. Distribution of the length (bins of words) of utterances of verbose non-assigned leaders.

Table 7.21 presents the percentage of utterances that are less than and longer than 100 words. Both assigned leaders and high communicating non-assigned leaders tend to have more than half of their utterances longer than 100 words with the exception of Fay and Eric.

Table 7.21. Percentage of shorter and longer utterances of leading participants.

Word range	Fay	Sheizaf	Jeff	Jonathan	Barbara	Eric
<100	58.7	43.6	46.7	45.2	50.0	53.8
≥100	41.3	56.4	53.3	54.8	50.0	46.2

The histograms in Figure 7.31 illustrate a sample of typical distributions of the utterance lengths for the majority of the participants in the project, where the emphasis is on shorter utterances. The longest utterances are in the 200-300 bin and the histograms in Figure 7.31 indicate the absence of the "tail" of longer utterances that were evident in Figure 7.29 and Figure 7.30. The two participants depicted in Figure 7.31, Brent and Vivian, posted 2285 and 2066 words respectively, so they were relatively active participants in the project. However, there is no evidence of these participants taking an active leading role in terms of utterance density.

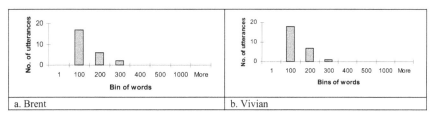

| a. Brent | b. Vivian |

Figure 7.31. Distributions of the length (bins of words) of utterances of two non-leading participants.

Table 7.22, showing the percentage of Brent's and Vivian's utterances that are more than 100 words and less than 100 words, indicates that longer utterances are far less frequent than for the assigned leaders in Figure 7.29 and the communicative non-assigned leaders in Figure 7.30. Less than one-third of the utterances of the majority of participants are more than 100 words in length.

Table 7.22. Percentage of shorter and longer utterances of two non-leading participants.

Word range	Brent	Vivian
<100	68.0	69.2
≥100	32.0	30.8

If based on density of utterances, therefore, the communication patterns of the two assigned leaders (Fay and Sheizaf) are not consistent. While both leaders posted more total words than other participants, Fay's average utterance length was less than six other participants. Four non-assigned leaders in Table 7.20 and Figure 7.30 (Jeff, Jonathan, Barbara and Eric) also communicated intensively. Other group members are far less verbose in terms of total words and tend to use shorter utterances with relatively low amounts of longer bursts.

Number and density of utterances

To assess communication intensity, number and density (with density divided into total words and average utterance length), need to be compared. Table 7.23 lists eight participants who rated the most highly in each of these criteria. There were six participants (shaded in grey) common to all criteria – the assigned leaders (Fay and Sheizaf) and four other verbose participants (Jeff, Barbara, Jonathan and Eric).

Table 7.23. Top eight participants by two intensity criteria

Number of utterances	Density	
	Total number of words	Average utterance length
Fay	Sheizaf	Jonathan
Sheizaf	Fay	Sheizaf
Jeff	Jeff	Jeff
Barbara	Jonathan	Jamie
Catherine	Barbara	Daniel
Deborah	Eric	Barbara
Jonathan	Nadia	Fay
Eric	Catherine	Eric

Number and density of utterances were effective criteria for measuring verbosity in participants. These criteria identified six participants who communicated more intensively than other participants. Two of these participants are, of course, the assigned leaders. *Hypothesis H₂.₃, that leaders communicate more intensely than other participants, is supported for the assigned leaders.* Before claiming this hypothesis is supported for the four verbose non-assigned participants, more investigation is required. These other four participants may have displayed attributes of leadership other than verbosity and may be emergent leaders. Therefore, emergent leaders may be identified by using additional criteria to number and density of utterances.

7.4.4. Emergent leadership

As mentioned in Chapter 2, research in virtual environments suggests that CMC impacts on group work in a number of ways. The communication medium is leaner (Daft and Lengel, 1986), the hierarchical structure is "flattened" (Finholt and Sproull, 1990; Dubrovsky, Kiesler and Sethna, 1991), social cues are reduced (Short et al., 1976), participants are depersonalised (Sproull and Kiesler, 1986; Watson, De

Sanctis and Poole, 1988), and overall volume of communication is less (Sarbaugh-Thompson and Feldman, 1998). Yoo and Alavi (2002) found that because of the reduced awareness of social presence and social context, the receiver of a message via CMC pays more attention to the message than the messenger.

Yoo and Alavi (2002) were particularly interested in defining emergent leaders in distributed teams. They found that emergent leaders could be identified by the number, length and content of messages. Not only did emergent leaders send more messages and longer messages, their messages were more task-oriented than other team members. Following Yoo and Alavi (2002), participants in Case Study 1 who had the most task-related utterances will be investigated to determine if content is a contributing factor in emergent leadership along with number and density of utterances.

It has been shown in the previous section that the coordinators (referred to as "assigned leaders") and key motivators communicate more intensively (more frequently and densely) than other participants. One interviewee observed anecdotally that verbosity alone does not make a leader; an observation that has since been confirmed in Yoo and Alavi's (2002) study:

> One of the things that we had some discussions on … is how leadership emerges in the environment and that sometimes we mistake verbosity for leadership - just because somebody posts a lot does not necessarily mean they are leaders or respected among the group … [T]here may have been people who posted way more, but whose messages I would read very little of, or hit the delete button, or they just weren't worth remembering, to my way of thinking. (Tom, 28/5/96)

Further, the previous section identified varying sets of highly communicative participants (apart from the assigned leaders) according to different criteria. These highly communicative participants, demonstrating leadership characteristics based on frequent and dense communication, could therefore be regarded as potential *emergent leaders*. When using the number of utterances criteria, the potential emergent leaders were Jeff, Barbara, Catherine, Deborah, Jonathan and Eric, in order of most frequent utterances. When using the total number of words criteria, the potential emergent leaders were Jeff, Jonathan, Barbara, Eric, Nadia and Catherine, in order of most words. When using the average utterance length, the potential emergent leaders were Jonathan, Jeff, Jamie, Daniel, Barbara and Eric in order of longest average utterance. In this section, to explore the *emergence of leaders in the group*, task-related content will be added as a criteria for identifying leadership characteristics.

Figure 7.32 presents a histogram of the distribution of participants according to intervals of task-related utterances. The intervals are shown as bins. The main body (85%) of participants are located in the [0; 3] bin, i.e. they have no more than 3 task-related utterances (the distribution is highly skewed towards participants with a low number of task-related utterances – kurtosis[12] = 37 and skewness = 5.4[13]). Only one participant was in the [31; 60] bin, i.e. more than 30 task-related utterances. The line graph indicates the cumulative percentage of task-related utterances at each bin.

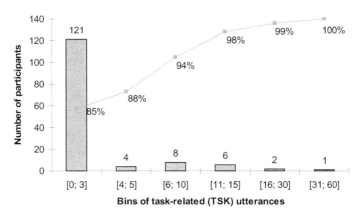

Figure 7.32. Number of task-related utterances across all participants.

Table 7.24 lists the participants who sent more than 10 task-related messages (~6% of the whole group). The two assigned leaders and one other participant, Jeff, cluster at the top of the list (bin [31; 60] shaded in dark grey and bin [16; 30] shaded in light grey). Seven participants are in the next cluster (bin [11-14]). Thus, based in this task-related utterance criteria, the only strong candidate for emergent leadership is Jeff.

---

[12] Kurtosis characterises the relative peakedness or flatness of a distribution compared to the normal distribution. Positive kurtosis indicates a relatively peaked distribution. Negative kurtosis indicates a relatively flat distribution. Normal distributions produce a kurtosis statistic of about zero; that is a mesokurtic (normally high) distribution. As the kurtosis statistic departs from zero, a positive value indicates the possibility of a leptokurtic distribution (that is, too tall) or a negative value indicates the possibility of a platykurtic distribution (that is, too flat, or even concave if the value is large enough). Values of 2 standard errors of kurtosis or more (regardless of sign) probably differ from mesokurtic to a significant degree (Brown, 1997).

[13] Skewness characterises the degree of asymmetry of a distribution around its mean. Normal distributions produce a skewness statistic of about zero. As the skewness statistic departs from zero, a positive value indicates the possibility of a positively skewed distribution amd a negative value indicates the possibility of a negatively skewed distribution. Values of 2 standard errors of skewness or more (regardless of sign) are usually skewed to a significant degree (Brown, 1997).

CHAPTER 7

Table 7.24. Participants whose task related utterances are ≥10.

Participant	Task-related utterances	Participant	Task-related utterances
Fay	53	Sally	13
Sheizaf	30	David	12
Jeff	28	Eric	11
Vivian	14	Carleen	11
Daniel	14		

However, it has been argued in this book that task (TSK) and conceptual (CON) communication are two constructs of the activity dimension[14]. So, to obtain a more accurate representation of activity-related messages, task and conceptual (TSK+CON) categories are combined for further analysis of emergent leadership.

Figure 7.33 presents a histogram of the distribution of participants according to bins of activity-related (TSK+CON) utterances. Again, the bins are shown as intervals. The main body (70%) of participants are located in the [0; 3] bin (the distribution is highly skewed towards participants with a low number of activity-related communication – kurtosis = 31.4 and skewness = 5.0). Three participants are in the [31; 60] bin and one participant is in the [60+] bin.

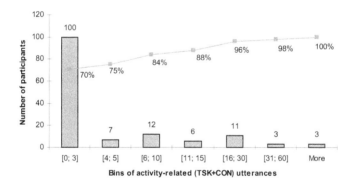

Figure 7.33. Number of activity-related (TSK+CON) utterances across all participants.

Table 7.25 lists the participants who sent more than 15 activity-related messages (~12% of the whole group). The two assigned leaders and one other participant, Jeff, cluster at the top of the list (bin [More than 60], shaded in dark grey). Three participants are in the second cluster (bin [31; 60], shaded in light grey). Eleven participants are in the third cluster (bin [16; 30]). Of the fourteen participants in the

---

[14] And the two constructs, TSK and CON, have been further subdivided into another four categories, see Table 6.4 for description of the coding scheme.

second and third cluster in Table 7.25, David, Daniel, Vivian, Sally and Eric are common to both task-related (Table 7.24) and activity-related (Table 7.25) criteria. Thus, based on the activity-related utterance criteria, the strongest candidate for emergent leader is Jeff while the other 5 (David, Daniel, Vivian, Sally and Eric) are weaker candidates.

Table 7.25. Participants whose activity- related utterances are ≥20.

Participant	Activity-related utterances	Participant	Activity-related utterances
Fay	111	Bob	20
Jeff	71	Nadia	19
Sheizaf	61	Daniel	19
Jonathan	35	Vivian	18
Barbara	33	Sarah	17
Catherine	31	Brent	17
Eric	25	Sally	17
Deborah	21	Donna	16
David	20		

Since the task (TSK) variable in this book is a subcategory of what Yoo and Alavi (2002) define as task-related content, it is the latter analysis of activity-related utterances (TSK+CON) that will be adopted in this section of leadership emergence.

What we have now are four sets of potential emergent leaders, rated according to number of utterances, density (total words and average utterance length) and content (activity-related utterances) (Table 7.17, Table 7.20 and Table 7.24). Table 7.26 combines these tables to visually compare the differences in the participants who rated highly on all criteria.

Table 7.26. Comparison of eight participants who rated highest on the number of utterances, density of utterances and activity-related content criteria

a. Number		b. Density				c. Content	
Participant	No. of utterances	Participant	Total no. of words	Participant	Average utterance length	Participant	Activity-related utterances
Fay	160	Sheizaf	28408	Jonathan	291	Fay	111
Sheizaf	101	Fay	22994	Sheizaf	281	Jeff	71
Jeff	90	Jeff	16770	Jeff	186	Sheizaf	61
Barbara	47	Jonathan	12211	Jamie	183	Jonathan	35
Catherine	47	Barbara	6863	Daniel	149	Barbara	33
Deborah	42	Eric	5675	Barbara	146	Catherine	31
Jonathan	42	Nadia	3960	Fay	144	Eric	25
Eric	40	Catherine	3958	Eric	142	Deborah	21

Table 7.26 shows that, in this combined list of the first eight participants from Table 7.23 and Table 7.25, apart from the assigned leaders (shaded in dark grey), only Jeff, Barbara, Jonathan and Eric (shaded in light grey) are common in all four

components of the table. Therefore, these four participants show evidence of emergent leadership if total number of utterances, total number of words, average utterance length and activity-related utterances are all taken into account. If any three of the four criteria are taken into account, then Catherine is also a contender. If any two of the four criteria are taken into account, then the list is extended to include Deborah as a possible emergent leader.

As Table 7.26 illustrates a different set of potential emergent leaders for each of the criteria used, there is a need for another cycle of qualitative and quantitative analyses, as described in the CEDA framework (Section 5.5.4, illustrated in Figure 5.6). Returning to the interviewee data, an interviewee mentioned that he was aware of participants, apart from the assigned leaders, being involved in facilitating the group to reach its goal:

> Well at first I thought the coordinators would be involved very heavily in the intergroup communication that was going on. I was astonished at how far outside of the group or how transparent they were, how quiet, how behind the scenes, and that a lot of the dialogue was being done by other personalities whom I didn't know and with whom I didn't understand what my relationship was other than the fact we were in this group together, and I really didn't attempt to sort that out. So I saw at times the group was being "run" by other people … I didn't see this coming from coordinators at all, but from other persons who were in the project. (Brian, 27/5/96)

This qualitative insight re-affirms the presence of emergent leaders, pointing the need to apply more quantitative analyses to the data. It is possible that an expanded set of criteria would be useful to explore emergent leadership within the group.

One of the variables in the coding scheme is the addressed (ADD) variable. This variable codes "who addresses to whom about what". An important feature of Internet communities is this connectivity (Haythornthwaite, 2003) or interactivity (Schultz, 1999; Rafaeli, 1988; Rafaeli and Sudweeks, 1997; Rafaeli and Sudweeks, 1998) among communicators. A considerable amount of research is concerned with the importance of exchanges that support work processes and their effect on social networks (Garton, Haythornthwaite and Wellman, 1997; Wellman and Berkowitz, 1997; Wasserman and Faust, 1994). These networks reveal how resources flow among individuals. The ties that are created and maintained among participants have a major impact on task completion in online collaborative groups (Haythornthwaite, 2003).

Thus, the ADD variable was used to extract the number of utterances addressed to a particular person and the number of activity-related utterances addressed to a particular person. These criteria were added to the original set of four criteria (number of utterances, total number of words, average utterance length and activity-related utterances). A more data-driven methodology was used to include this expanded set of criteria (or attributes) and the research hypothesis reformulated as a classification problem.

The task was to classify group members as one of the following participant types:

(i)   *assigned leader* (participant who has been assigned as leader explicitly or implicitly in the beginning of the project),

(ii)   *emergent leader* (participants who were identified as potential emergent leaders using the number of utterances, total number of words, average utterance length, and activity-related utterance criteria), or

(iii)   *participant* (participants identified as non-leaders).

With an appropriate inductive technique, a collection of attributes are used to ascertain which of these attributes are most important in characterising the three participant types. The collection of attributes include the four criteria used before (i.e. number of utterances, total number of words, average utterance length, activity-related).

Table 7.27 lists the set of six attributes which were used as candidates for defining *Participant Type*.

Table 7.27. Attributes used for defining *Participant Type*

Attribute	Description
Utterances	Total number of utterances
Total Number of Words	Total number of words posted by an individual
Average Length in Words	Average length of utterances in words of an individual
TSK+CON(U)	Number of activity-related utterances sent by an individual
Addressed	Number of utterances of any variable addressed to an individual
TSK+CON(A)	Number of activity-related utterances addressed to an individual

Rather than using the whole data set of 143 participants, the 31 participants who were the most active on any of the four criteria (number of utterances, total number of words, average utterance length, activity-related utterances) were selected (i.e. the top twenty in each category). These 31 participants generated 78% of the utterances throughout the project. These 31 participants represent a broader sample than the top 8 participants in each category that were depicted in Table 7.26 because it was desirable to capture all possible emergent leaders with this extended analysis.

The inductive techniques used are: (i) the CART (Classification and Regression Trees) model[15] to produce a classification tree of *Participant Type*; and (ii) visual

---

[15] CART is a non-parametric technique that selects attributes and their interactions that are most important in determining an outcome or dependent variable. If an outcome variable is continuous,

clustering[16] guided by the derived classification tree. The major goal in using CART is to understand the attributes or interaction of attributes that are responsible for a given phenomenon. It is a decision tree tool that automatically sifts through large, complex databases for significant patterns and relationships. The classification problem consists of a "dependent" variable (in this case, the target *Participant Type*) and "independent" variables (in this case, the six attributes listed in Table 7.27) (Lewis, 2000). The derived tree offers a description of the concept of *Participant Type* (i.e. *Assigned Leader*, *Emergent Leader* and *Participant*) in terms of the six attributes listed in Table 7.27. This concept of *Participant Type* can then be applied to new instances (Witten and Frank, 2000).

Therefore, this classification approach should provide a greater understanding of the relationship between the attributes that describe different aspects of computer-mediated collaboration (number and density of utterances, the importance of activity-related communication, and the impact of utterances addressed to a particular individual rather than the group).

The CART technique in building a classification tree is to split a sample into binary sub-samples based on the response to a question requiring a yes/no response (Breiman, Friedman, Olshen and Stone, 1984). Figure 7.34 shows the derived classification tree. The question used to create splits at each node is displayed at the top of the node. The first node, for example, has the question "Did the participant generate 96 or more utterance?" Each question is based on just one attribute selected from the collection of attributes in Table 7.27.

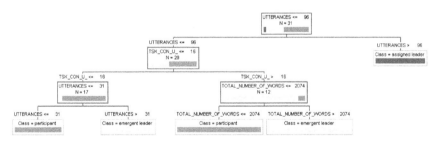

Figure 7.34. The CART classification tree for participant type.

The classification tree derived isolates each of the three participant types (assigned leaders, emergent leaders and participants). This induction technique shows that *Utterances* (number of utterances sent) is the primary attribute which

---

CART produces regression trees; if the variable is categorical, CART produces classification trees. The software is Salford Systems CART 5.0 (http://www.salfordsystems.com).

[16] The software used for visual clustering is Miner3D by Dimension 5 (http://www.miner3d.com).

splits the sample of participants into 'assigned leaders' and the rest. In the next level, the attribute *TSK+CON(U)* (activity-related utterances sent by an individual) captures a significant portion of the leadership characteristics. In the next level, the *Utterances* and *Total Number of Words* attributes split the sample into 'emergent leader' and 'participant' classes. These three attributes partitioned the data to cover all participant types in Case Study 1.

The score values in Figure 7.35 provide an estimate of the relative contributions of the *TSK+CON(U)*, *Total Number of Words*, *Utterances*, *Addressed* and *TSK+CON(A)* attributes in classifying or predicting the target class (i.e. the *Participant Type* attribute). Figure 7.35 shows that the primary attribute for splitting the data was *TSK+CON(U)*. *Total Number of Words* was also an important variable.

Variable Importance		
Variable	Scor ∇	
TSK_CON_U_	100.00	‖‖‖‖‖‖‖‖‖‖‖‖‖‖‖‖‖‖‖‖‖‖‖‖‖
TOTAL_NUMBER_OF_WORDS	90.53	‖‖‖‖‖‖‖‖‖‖‖‖‖‖‖‖‖‖‖‖‖
UTTERANCES	88.96	‖‖‖‖‖‖‖‖‖‖‖‖‖‖‖‖‖‖‖‖‖
ADDRESSED	84.19	‖‖‖‖‖‖‖‖‖‖‖‖‖‖‖‖‖‖‖
TSK_CON_A_	78.87	‖‖‖‖‖‖‖‖‖‖‖‖‖‖‖‖‖

Figure 7.35. CART attribute importance values.

The CART technique is then complemented by visual clustering. Clustering is the process of finding a partitioning of the data set into homogeneous sub-sets (clusters) (Keim and Ward, 2003). The key element in this technique is the mapping between the attributes and the corresponding visual features; in other words, this technique looks for groups of instances (individuals) that "belong together". The overall approach of this clustering technique is unsupervised learning, as the clusters are not known in advance. Figure 7.36 to Figure 7.38 show the results of visual cluster analyses performed on the data set of 31 participants and the six attributes in Table 7.27. In Figure 7.36 the X, Y and Z axes are *Utterances*, *TSK+CON(U)*, *Total Number of Words* respectively. The value of the *Average Length in Words* attribute has been used to define the size of the spheres. Guided by the classification tree, in which the *Utterances* attribute splits the data at >31 (see Figure 7.34), *Utterance* is set to '32' in Figure 7.37. This setting filters out a cluster of 23 participants. The remaining nine individuals are shown in Figure 7.37. Again, guided by the classification tree, in which the *TSK+CON(U)* attribute splits the data at >16 and the *Total Number of Words* attribute at >2074 (see Figure 7.34), these attributes are set at '17' and '2075' respectively in Figure 7.38. The same nine individuals remain; that is, two *Assigned Leaders* and seven *Emergent Leaders*.

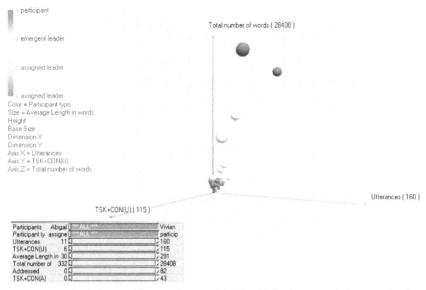

Figure 7.36. Visual clusters of data set of *Assigned Leaders* (dark spheres at top), *Emergent Leaders* (light spheres) and *Participants* (dark spheres at bottom).

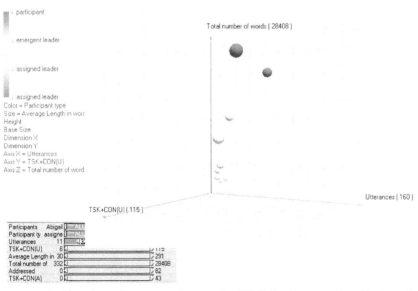

Figure 7.37. Clustering on *Utterances* attribute at value '32' (dark spheres are assigned leaders and light spheres are emergent leaders).

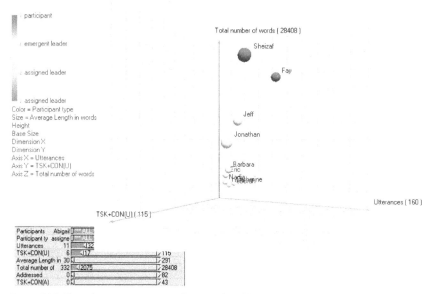

Figure 7.38. Clustering on *Utterances* attribute at value '32', *TSK+CON(U)* attribute at '17' and *Total Number of Words* attribute at value '2075' (dark spheres are assigned leaders and light spheres are emergent leaders).

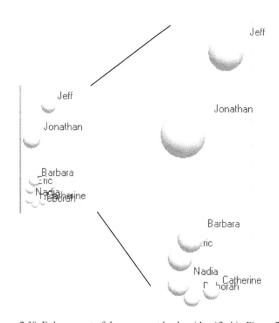

Figure 7.39. Enlargement of the emergent leaders identified in Figure 7.38.

Figure 7.39 is an enlargement of a section of Figure 7.38 showing the seven *Emergent Leaders* identified by name; that is, Jeff, Jonathan, Barbara, Eric, Catherine, Deborah and Nadia. Figure 7.40 shows that when the *Utterances* attribute is set to 97 (see Figure 7.34, which indicates that the *Utterances* attribute splits the data again at >96), Fay and Sheizaf, are identified as *Assigned Leaders*.

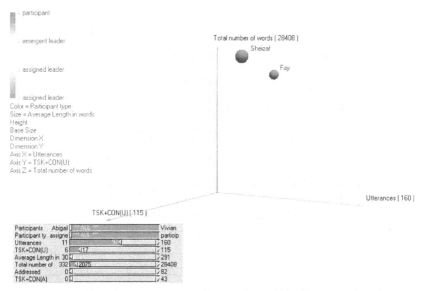

Figure 7.40. Clustering on *Utterances* attribute at value '97' identifies *Assigned Leaders*.

Hence, the CART classification tree in Figure 7.34, visualised as clusters in Figure 7.36 to Figure 7.40, show that the attributes *Utterances*, *TSK+CON(U)* and *Total Number of Words* were able to split the sample of 31 active participants into three *Participant Types* as listed in Table 7.28.

Table 7.28. Assigned leaders, emergent leaders and participants

Assigned leaders	Emergent leaders	Participants	
Fay	Jeff	Donna	Michael
Sheizaf	Jonathan	Marian	Daniel
	Barbara	Ben	Stuart
	Eric	David	Nicola
	Catherine	Vivian	Brad
	Deborah	Brent	Jamie
	Nadia	Sally	Marie
		Chloe	Andy
		Tom	Clive
		Sarah	Peter
		Carleen	Abilgail

The combination of two attributes – *Utterances* and *Addressed* – would also give a measurement of the intensity of engagement for any participant. Figure 7.41 illustrates the engagement level for the 31 participants examined in the CART model.

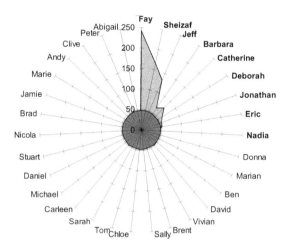

Figure 7.41. Engagement level of participants.

The circle in the middle of Figure 7.41 corresponds to the mean level of engagement across the data set of 31 participants. The graph illustrates the findings of CART (and visualised in Minder3D): the two assigned leaders (Fay and Sheizaf) have the highest level of engagement; six of the emergent leaders (Jeff, Catherine, Barbara, Deborah, Jonathan and Eric) are above the mean level of engagement. Nadia has the next highest level of engagement and was identified in the CART procedure. These nine participants are indicated in bold.

Thus, it has been demonstrated that the criteria used for descriptive statistics (number of utterances, total number of words, average utterance length, and activity-related utterances), the CART and cluster tools (number of utterances sent, total number of words, average utterance length, activity-related utterances sent, number of utterances received, activity-related utterances received), and the radar chart on engagement level (number of utterances and utterances received), all point to a set of leaders that emerged during the life of the group.

The descriptive statistics indicated four strong emergent leaders (Jeff, Barbara, Jonathan and Eric) and two weaker candidates (Catherine and Deborah). When additional criteria were added and the data analysed with the CART and cluster tools, it was found that the *TSK-CON(U)* attribute (number of activity-related utterances) contributed to the identification of the same four strong emergent leaders (Jeff, Barbara, Jonathan and Eric) and another three (Catherine, Deborah and Nadia). The engagement graph confirms the set of six emergent leaders identified by the descriptive statistics (Jeff, Barbara, Jonathan, Eric, Catherine and Deborah) with Nadia at the highest end of the mean engagement level.

$H_{2.4}$, that leaders emerge during the life of the group, is supported.

It is necessary, now, to revisit Hypothesis $H_{2.3}$ – *that leaders communicate more intensely than other participants*. It was stated in Section 7.4.3, p. 206, that Hypothesis $H_{2.3}$ was supported for the assigned leaders, and possibly four other participants who were identified as being potential emergent leaders, using the verbosity criteria of number and density (total number of words and average utterance length) of utterances. There is, of course, some circularity in this argument; that is, that emergent leaders are identified by their verbosity and that leaders communicate more intensely than other participants. To overcome this circularity, more evidence was required to evaluate the potential emergent leaders identified in Section 7.4.3.

In this section, three more factors were added to the three verbosity factors (see Table 7.27) to identify emergent leaders. The classification and cluster tools, along with the engagement measure, all provide reasonable consistency in the identification of emergent leaders. Thus it is reasonable to claim that since both verbosity and non-verbosity factors identified emergent leaders, that verbosity is a trait of emergent leadership. So there is some support for claiming that "leaders" in Hypothesis $H_{2.3}$ (*that leaders communicate more intensely than other participants*) refers to both assigned and emergent leaders and that these leaders communicate more intensely than other participants.

7.4.5. Summary of leadership

The purpose of this group of leadership hypotheses was to examine systematic differences between leaders and participants. As mentioned before, leadership is viewed as any facilitation that moves a group closer to its outcome. The first hypothesis was concerned with management intervention in periods of high task activity. A high correlation was found between two types of management – formal and informal – and two types of activity – task and conceptual.

The second hypothesis was concerned with a variety of management styles that were used during different development phases. Positive comments and questions were used consistently throughout the project. Negative comments were used during argumentative phases to diffuse conflict or reprimand argumentative participants. Humour was used in the phases following conflict periods to relieve tension, lighten the atmosphere and refocus participants on the collaborative task.

Many researchers have found that leaders communicate more than other participants and propose that verbosity is related to leadership (e.g. Regula and Julian, 1973; Sorrentino and Boutillier, 1975; Mullen et al., 1989; Yoo and Alavi, 2002). Researchers have also found that verbosity alone does not make a leader (e.g. Sorrentino and Boutillier, 1975; Strickland, Guild, Barefoot and Paterson, 1978). The third leadership hypothesis attempted to illuminate these conflicting findings. Two criteria were used for verbosity – number of utterances and density of utterance (total number of words and average length in words). These two criteria identified six participants (Fay, Sheizaf, Jeff, Jonathan, Barbara and Eric) who communicated more frequently and longer than other participants.

Research in emergent leadership in computer-mediated environments is almost non-existent. Yoo and Alavi (1996; 2001; 2002) are the prominent researchers in this area. According to Yoo and Alavi (2002), leadership in distributed teams emerges as a consequence of frequent and lengthy task-related utterance. These findings were explored in the fourth leadership hypothesis. Using a classification tree model and cluster visualisation techniques, number of utterances was the only criteria of nominated by Yoo and Alavi that contributed to identifying emergent leaders. The other criteria of importance was the number of utterances addressed personally to participants. Six emergent leaders (Jeff, Eric, Barbara, Catherine, Deborah and Jonathan) were identified using these techniques. It is interesting to note also that the participants who exhibited leadership at the time of this project have been successful in their careers. Table 7.29 lists the positions of the assigned and emergent leaders in 1992 and their positions more than a decade later.

Table 7.29. Changes in position of emergent leaders and participants since 1992

Participant	Position in 1992	Position in 2004
Fay	PhD candidate	Emeritus Associate Professor
Sheizaf	Senior Lecturer	Professor
Jeff	Professor	Professor
Barbara	Associate Professor	Emeritus Professor
Eric	Associate Professor	Associate Professor
Catherine	Masters student	Social Worker
Deborah	Professor	Professor
Jonathan	Consultant	Director of Curriculum Development
Nadia	Associate Professor	Professor
Donna	PhD Candidate	Professor
Jamie	PhD Candidate	Associate Professor
Daniel	Researcher	Chief Executive Officer, International Organisation

7.5. Summary

This chapter is the first of two analysis chapters. This chapter reports the results of Case Study 1 analyses. The analyses are structured in two main sections: (i) the developmental characteristics hypotheses; and (ii) the leadership characteristics hypotheses.

Using the coding scheme described in Chapter 6, the coded data of 1,345 Case Study 1 utterances yielded a content-dependent timeline that identified eight developmental phases. Descriptive statistics, timelines and extracts from participant communication and interview responses were used to analyse each phase. It was found that each phase could be described in terms of *activity* (task and conceptual communication) and *relationship* (social and emotional communication) dimensions. The developmental stages have been described as structuration, tension, reflection (on formation process), activity (on codebook), reflection (on initial activity), activity (on coding), reflection (on the need to meet face-to-face), and goal achievement and closure.

The absence of social presence is a known quality of computer-mediated groups (see, e.g. Tu, 2002; Gunawardena and Zittle, 1997; Rettie, 2003; Biocca, Harms and Burgoon, 2001). To compensate, the Case Study 1 participants engaged in self-disclosures early in the project as evidenced by the high proportion of awareness (AWA) communication in the early phases relative to the later phases. Furthermore, the physical and social information that was disclosed appeared to be sufficient to create a group culture, complete with group norms and values. As one participant perceptively observed: "There is a sense of cohesiveness with ProjectH exchanges" (u_{1169}, 28/8/93). The degree of cohesiveness was evidenced by the high proportion of supportive (SUP) communication in the later phases.

Four aspects of leadership were investigated –intervention strategies, style, communication and emergence. "Management" (defined as assigned leaders and key motivators) intervened more frequently during periods of high task activity, as evidenced by the significant correlation of formal and informal management communication (FOR+INF) and task and conceptual (TSK+CON) activity. It was also found that leaders used a range of intervention styles, however the most frequent styles throughout the lifespan of the group were positive comments and questioning. A questioning atmosphere can foster curiosity and build confidence or it can cause people to feel threatened. In Case Study 1, the evidence shows that the participants were stimulated to activity when leaders asked questions.

The most significant finding in this case study was the emergence of leaders. Using descriptive statistics, the non-parametric technique and a visual clustering tool, six emergent leaders were identified. Furthermore, both assigned and emergent leaders characteristically were more verbose and engaged in more task-related communication. Table 7.30 lists the findings for Case Study 1 hypotheses.

Table 7.30. Results of Developmental Hypotheses, Case Study 1

No.	Hypothesis	Finding
$H_{1.1}$	There are definable developmental stages in computer-mediated groups.	Supported
$H_{1.2}$	In the early phases of development, the content of communication is more conceptual than task oriented or social.	Partly supported
$H_{1.3}$	During periods of low task activity, the content of communication is more social than task oriented.	Partly supported
$H_{1.4}$	During periods of high task activity, the content of communication is more task oriented than social.	Partly supported
$H_{1.5}$	During earlier developmental stages, participants engage in more disclosures about the physical and social attributes of themselves and others.	Supported
$H_{1.6}$	Group cohesiveness increases over the life of the group.	Supported
$H_{2.1}$	Management intervention is more frequent during periods of high task activity.	Supported
$H_{2.2}$	Different management styles predominate at different developmental stages.	Weakly supported
$H_{2.3}$	Leaders communicate more intensively than other participants.	Supported
$H_{2.4}$	Leaders emerge during the life of the group.	Supported

In summary, six of the ten hypotheses were supported while the other four were weakly or partly supported. These findings are relevant specifically to the context of this study; that is, large collaborative computer-mediated groups using asynchronous communication.

CHAPTER 8

ANALYSES OF CASE STUDY 2

8.1. Introduction

Case Study 2 was described in Chapter 4. The CEDA methodology developed for this book was described in Chapter 5, and Chapter 6 described how the methodology was applied to two different case studies. In this chapter, the results of Case Study 2 are presented as they relate to the research questions raised in Chapters 1, 2 and 6.

As explained in Chapter 4, this case study consisted of nine one-hour online (synchronous) workshops for students over a three-month period. Each workshop was devoted to critiquing two required readings (book chapter, article, paper, etc.) to facilitate active learning through collaboration. The discussions were facilitated by the course coordinator (facilitator) and moderated by different participants each week. All workshops were conducted in a chat room of a learning management environment (WebCT). As for Case Study 1, the research questions are concerned with two broad aspects of virtual groups – developmental and leadership characteristics. Following the CEDA methodology, the results will be presented as complementary quantitative and qualitative analyses.

There were 99 participants in Case Study 2 and they were assigned to seven groups. Of these seven groups, the data from three groups were incomplete due to various organisational and technical problems. The remaining four groups (Groups 1, 2, 3 and 5) were coded with the same coding scheme as used for Case Study 1 (see Table 6.2). The total number of utterances in each workshop for each of the four groups is shown in Table 8.1.

Table 8.1. Total number of utterances in Groups 1, 2, 3 and 5 by workshop.

Workshop	Number of utterances in Group 1	Number of utterances in Group 2	Number of utterances in Group 3	Number of utterances in Group 5
1	756	555	474	574
2	687	761	802	608
3	586	771	363	409
4	685	835	490	473
5	678	858	497	414
6	432	806	415	196
7	591	556	517	493
8	735	601	505	362
9	547	585	484	340
Total	**5697**	**6328**	**4547**	**3869**

Table 8.2 shows the percentages of category types for each group throughout the period of Case Study 2.

Table 8.2. Percentage of category types in four groups of Case Study 2.

Code name	Code Description	% of total Group 1 utterances	% of total Group 2 utterances	% of total Group 3 utterances	% of total Group 5 utterances
TSK	Task	49.2	47.4	51.4	61.6
CON	Conceptual	8.0	5.4	13.9	9.7
SUP	Supportive	3.7	2.1	5.6	3.4
ARG	Argumentative	2.6	0.1	1.3	0.8
SOC	Social	31.0	20.9	22.4	15.6
ENV	Environment	3.2	2.5	2.6	2.7
AWA	Awareness	6.7	4.5	3.8	2.3
INF	Informal	1.8	5.9	4.4	1.3
FOR	Formal	1.9	5.1	2.4	2.4
POS	Positive	4.0	3.8	3.6	1.8
ASK	Asking	5.7	5.9	6.2	3.2
HUM	Humour	2.3	2.6	2.4	0.9
NEG	Negative	1.3	1.5	0.9	0.5

A visual inspection of the descriptive statistics in Table 8.2 indicates that the communication pattern in all four groups is very similar, so quantitative analyses were applied to verify the strength of the similarity. A correlation of the four groups confirmed the descriptive statistics with values between $r=0.94$ and $r=0.98$ (Table 8.3). An ANOVA test on all variables for all workshops for the four groups also confirms no significant difference for eleven of the thirteen variables (Table 8.4).

Table 8.3. Correlation of communication variables between four groups.

	Group 1	Group 2	Group 3	Group 5
Group 1	1			
Group 2	0.97	1		
Group 3	0.97	0.98	1	
Group 5	0.94	0.97	0.98	1

Table 8.4. Results of ANOVA on thirteen variables for four groups (by workshop)

Variable	Description	F	df	p value
TSK	Task	1.62	8	0.17
CON	Conceptual	0.74	8	0.65
SOC	Social	0.89	8	0.54
SUP	Supportive	0.53	8	0.82
ARG	Argumentative	0.70	8	0.69
ENV	Environment	3.40*	8	0.01
AWA	Awareness	3.15*	8	0.01
INF	Informal	0.29	8	0.97
FOR	Formal	1.56	8	0.18
POS	Positive	0.70	8	0.69
ASK	Asking	0.83	8	0.59
HUM	Humour	1.20	8	0.34
NEG	Negative	1.26	8	0.31

Therefore, given the very high degree of similarity between the groups, the focus in this case study will be on one group only, since this alone involves a detailed analysis of 4,547 utterances. Group 3 is selected as being the most representative of the four groups as it has the most consistent correlation with the other three groups (Group 1: $r=0.97$; Group 2: $r=0.98$; and Group 5 and $r=0.98$). For simplicity, from this point on, Case Study 2 will refer to Group 3 only.

Group 3 initially had 18 participants. After the first workshop, one participant transferred to another group (Group 6). Another participant attended Workshop 2 only, and then discontinued the unit. The data for both of these participants is included in the analyses as it was considered that they are similar to participants of Case Study 1 who left the project or who subscribed but decided not to take an active role.

8.2. Examination of Developmental Characteristics Hypotheses

The first group of hypotheses developed in Section 2.7.1 and Table 6.3, are concerned with the developmental characteristics of computer-mediated groups. They are:

$H_{1.1}$ There are definable developmental stages in computer-mediated groups.

$H_{1.2}$ In the early phases of development, the content of communication is more conceptual than task oriented or social.

$H_{1.3}$ During periods of low task activity, the content of communication is more social than task oriented.

$H_{1.4}$ During periods of high task activity, the content of communication is more task oriented than social.

$H_{1.5}$ During later developmental stages, participants engage in less disclosures about the physical and social attributes of themselves and others.

$H_{1.6}$ Group cohesiveness increases over the lifecycle of the group.

This group of hypotheses will be examined in this chapter using the results of Case Study 2.

Table 8.5 lists the communication variables used for the developmental characteristics hypotheses with a brief description and the specific hypothesis(es) to which they apply. All communication types (variables) are defined and described fully in Table 6.2.

Table 8.5. Communication variables used in the developmental characteristics hypotheses.

Category	Code	Description	Hypothesis
Task	TSK	Communication content dealing with the collaborative activity of the group. Includes introduction, clarification, agreement or disagreement of task issues and specific task instructions.	1.1, 1.2, 1.3, 1.4
Conceptual	CON	Conceptual communication involves the creation of mutual understandings and meanings among participants. Involves the creation of shared rules to follow. Includes creation, agreement or disagreement about procedures to follow, a common vocabulary, work to be completed.	1.1, 1.2
Supportive	SUP	Communication content having the capacity to support another participant emotionally, has a positive emotional impact.	1.1, 1.2, 1.6
Argumentative	ARG	Communication content having the capacity to trigger/maintain an argument or conflict, having a negative emotional impact.	1.1, 1.2, 1.6
Social	SOC	Communication content dealing with interpersonal relationships and social activities. Includes initiation of new social topics, greetings, social agreement and disagreement.	1.1, 1.2, 1.3, 1.4
Environment	ENV	Communication in regards to use of collaborative environment in which communication occurs.	1.1
Awareness	AWA	Communication connected with making knowledge of self and other participants(s) explicit to increase social awareness.	1.1, 1.5
Informal	INF	Communication connected with the collective informal creation, management, and enforcement of communication norms, used by any participant. Has a quality of collaborative construction.	1.1
Formal	FOR	Communication connected with the enforcement of rules or norms, used to manage the process of collaboration. More likely used by leaders and key stakeholders..	1.1

In Case Study 1, it was necessary to identify major turning points over the group's lifecycle with respect to the properties stated by the coding scheme. For Case Study 2, though, the group's lifecycle of two-and-a-half months is already naturally divided into nine discrete sections defined by the one-hour synchronous workshop meetings each week. Figure 8.1 indicates the utterance range in each workshop $\{W_1, W_2, \ldots, W_9\}$. Utterances are numbered as a complete set covering workshops 1-9.

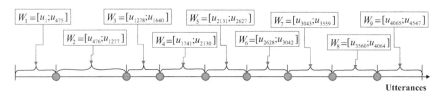

Figure 8.1. Number of utterances in each of the nine workshops of Case Study 2.

Even though the workshops were of the same duration of one hour, the number of utterances in each workshop differed, ranging from 363 utterances in Workshop 3 to 802 utterances in Workshop 2 (see the workshop utterance figures for Group 3 in Table 8.1).

Table 8.6 lists the nine communication types described in Table 8.5 as percentages of total utterances for each workshop.

Table 8.6. Percentage of communication types in Workshops 1-9.

Code name	Code description	Percentages of utterances in each workshop								
		W_1	W_2	W_3	W_4	W_5	W_6	W_7	W_8	W_9
TSK	Task	39.2	48.0	46.6	50.2	63.6	50.4	56.7	52.5	55.4
CON	Conceptual	28.1	15.7	19.8	18.4	3.6	13.7	11.0	8.1	8.1
SUP	Supportive	4.9	3.6	6.6	4.3	6.4	6.3	4.6	5.5	9.7
ARG	Argumentative	0.0	1.1	0.3	2.4	0.6	4.3	0.4	1.0	1.7
SOC	Social	18.6	23.3	17.1	21.0	20.7	22.4	19.0	32.5	25.2
ENV	Environment	1.3	3.5	8.3	1.0	2.4	1.9	3.5	2.2	0.2
AWA	Awareness	8.0	6.5	4.1	3.0	3.6	2.2	2.5	1.0	1.9
INF	Informal	4.6	4.0	6.1	3.1	5.2	4.6	3.5	4.8	4.1
FOR	Formal	5.1	1.9	3.6	3.9	1.2	2.7	2.1	1.4	0.8

*Codes are not discrete categories, each utterance can be classified in a number of categories, hence percentages do not sum to 100.

These percentages are converted to min-max normalised values, which preserve the relationship between the values but re-scales each value for a clearer representation in graph form (see Figure 8.2). The minimum and maximum values of the scale are set at 1 and 2 respectively. Figure 8.2 shows that there is not as much variability across Case Study 2 as for Case Study 1 (compare with Figure 7.3). This is to be expected given the two very different scenarios for the case studies. Case Study 1 was a continuous two-year international asynchronous collaboration among 143+ participants; a period in which, as the coordinators noted, "the sun always sets on at least one part of ProjectH but work never ceases" (Sudweeks and Rafaeli, 1996). Case Study 2, on the other hand, was a (mostly) local synchronous collaborative series of workshops for 16 participants for just one hour on nine occasions. These differences enable the hypotheses to be tested in an alternative type of collaborative online environment.

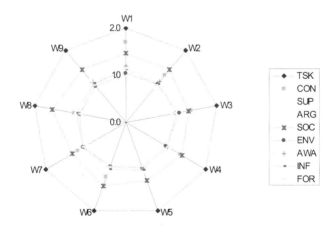

Figure 8.2. Communication variables (min-max normalised values) in each workshop (W1-W9).

Since each workshop had the same aim of learning through a collaborative activity, it could be that the nine workshops represent a group's lifecycle repeated nine times. Or it could be that there are some effects over the period of the nine workshops (for example, note the variation in the percentage of conceptual (CON) communication in Table 8.6). In other words, developmental effects may be evident both within and across workshops. Therefore, the workshops will be analysed for both short-term (within workshops) and long-term (across workshops) developmental characteristics.

All nine workshops were analysed in detail and displayed similar characteristics. In Section 8.3, the analysis of the short-term developmental characteristics of Workshop 1 will be presented in detail. In Section 8.4, a summary of the short-term developmental characteristics of Workshops 1-9 will be presented. The full analyses of Workshops 2-9 are presented in Appendix C. A summary of the developmental characteristics for Workshops 2-9 is also included in Appendix C.3. In Section 8.5, the analysis of long-term developmental effects is presented.

8.3. Analysis of Developmental Characteristics within Workshop 1

In this section, short-term developmental characteristics within Workshop 1 will be examined. The hypotheses, re-phrased to account for short-term effects in Case Study 2, are:

$H_{1.1}$ There are definable developmental stages in each workshop.

$H_{1.2}$ In the early phases of each workshop, the content of communication is more conceptual than task oriented or social.

$H_{1.3}$ Within each workshop, during periods of low task activity, the content of communication is more social than task oriented.

$H_{1.4}$ Within each workshop, during periods of high task activity, the content of communication is more task oriented than social.

$H_{1.5}$ During later developmental stages within workshops, participants engage in less disclosures about the physical and social attributes of themselves and others.

$H_{1.6}$ Group cohesiveness increases during the period of each workshop.

8.3.1. Workshop 1

A total of 474 utterances were exchanged by participants throughout the one-hour topic discussions in the first workshop on 26 July 2000. Table 8.7 shows the number and percentages of different types of communication in this first workshop. This workshop was characterised by a significant amount of task (TSK=39.0%), conceptual (CON=28.1%) and social (SOC=18.6%) communication. In addition, approximately one in twelve utterances were concerned with explicit self-disclosure or knowledge about other participants (AWA=8.0%). Generally the group was more supportive than confrontational (SUP=4.9% compared with ARG=0.0%). Small but approximately equal amounts of informal and formal management of communication were used (INF=4.6%, FOR=5.1%).

Table 8.7. Number and percentage of communication types in Workshop 1.

Code name	Code description	Number of utterances	Percentage of total W_1 utterance*
TSK	Task	185	39.2
CON	Conceptual	133	28.1
SUP	Supportive	23	4.9
ARG	Argumentative	0	0.0
SOC	Social	88	18.6
ENV	Environment	6	1.3
AWA	Awareness	38	8.0
INF	Informal	22	4.6
FOR	Formal	24	5.1

*Codes are not discrete categories, each utterance can be classified in a number of categories, hence percentages do not sum to 100.

Much of the conceptual communication was concerned with explaining the procedure for the workshops and with organising moderators for subsequent workshops. The usual procedure for appointing moderators in this unit of study was that the facilitator would randomly select one or two participants in each group and contact them by email about a week before the first workshop, requesting them to take on the moderator's role for the first workshop. During the first workshop, moderators would be appointed for subsequent workshops. As there was an average of 16 participants in each group and nine workshops, in most weeks there were two participants assigned to the moderator role for each workshop.

For this particular group, though, the facilitator did not get a response to her email request to moderate the first workshop, so she asked for a volunteer at the beginning of the first workshop.

> [Fay]: ... i haven't had a response from the nominated person(s) (u_8) [1]
> [Fay]: would someone like to take the tute[2] this morning ... (u_{12})

---

[1] All utterance examples are exact reproductions and therefore include original spelling and grammatical errors.
[2] The workshops were referred to by different terms by participants, e.g. "tute", "seminar", "meeting".

One of the participants "volunteered", with some gentle persuasion from the facilitator, as she had disclosed that she had already written discussion notes on some of the readings, and hence felt somewhat prepared to take the moderator's role.

Expected communication norms in a chat environment were outlined by the facilitator and readily accepted by the participants, e.g.:

[Fay]: Keep comments as short as possible to allow everyone the opportunity to "talk". (u_{134})
[Doug]: fair enough (u_{135})
[Fay]: Be polite and don't interrupt. (u_{136})
[Fred]: thats cool (u_{142})

The workshop communication is visualised by the timeline in Figure 8.3. The timeline illustrates that, at the commencement and conclusion of the workshop, the participants engaged in social, conceptual and awareness communication. Almost all task-oriented communication was confined to the middle section of the workshop, along with some supportive comments. The timeline therefore indicates two obvious regions which signal a transition from one general style of communication (combination of coding variables) to another combination. Subsequent detailed scrutiny of the content of utterances in those transition regions revealed particular utterances that significantly altered the communication of the group.

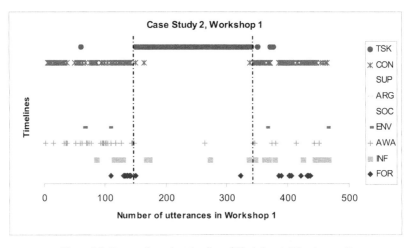

Figure 8.3. Content-dependent timeline of Workshop 1 ($W_1 = [u_1; u_{474}]$)

The first transition (i.e. the point between Phase 1 and Phase 2) was at utterance u_{151}. The moderator, who was unaware before the session that she would take this role, but had prepared notes on some of the readings, announced that she would lead the discussions on two articles of her choice, thus focusing everyone's attention on the workshop task:

> [Sandy]: Ok...well I have choosen a reading from week 1 and also 1 from week 2...I'l start with... (u_{151})

The second major transition occurred with the discussions becoming more reflective at utterance u_{338} when a participant made the following comment:

> [Duncan]: Would this disscussion go better if we were all in the same room talking (u_{338})

The changes in the nine communication variables in the three development phases of Workshop 1 are shown in Figure 8.4. The graph represents the percentage of each variable with respect to the total number of utterances in each phase.

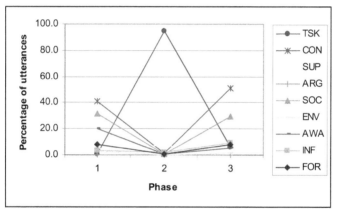

Figure 8.4. Percentages of each communication variable in three phases of Workshop 1.

Since three of the variables are clustered at the top of the scale and six variables are clustered at the bottom, Figure 8.5 and Figure 8.6 illustrate these variables separately for improved visualisation and include data tables showing the percentage figures. Figure 8.5 shows that when the group was engaged in task-related communication, there was almost no conceptual or social communication. In Phase 1 and Phase 3, when task activity was low, there was increased conceptual and social communication.

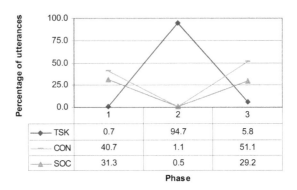

Figure 8.5. Percentages of the three most frequent communication variables (TSK, CON and SOC) in three phases of Workshop 1.

Figure 8.6 shows that each phase varies in the proportion of each of the six less frequent variables. The awareness (AWA) communication occurs mostly in Phase 1; formal management (FOR) occurs in Phases 1 and 3; and supportive (SUP) communication occurs mostly in Phase 2.

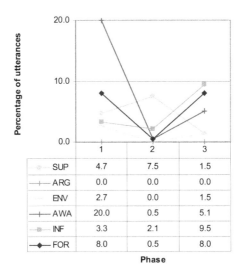

Figure 8.6. Percentages of the six less frequent communication variables (SUP, ARG, ENV, AWA, INF, FOR) in three phases of Workshop 1.

Predictably, since this was the first workshop of the series and most of the participants had never met each other, the communication included disclosures about themselves to increase social awareness of each other. The facilitator, who had previously considered she had some expertise in "netspeak", found there was much more to learn. It became obvious that some of the participants were experienced ICQ users as they disclosed information about their physical location.

[Doug]: sorry I was afk (u_{16})

[Fay]: ah, another new "word", what's afk? (u_{18})

[Doug]: away from keyboard (u_{20})

[Fay]: where are you? at home? (u_{34})

[Doug]: yeah ... (u_{36})[3]

[Doug]: I wish i could take uni from home all the time ... (u_{37})

[Doug]: I had to take my car up for a service this morning so there was no way i could have come to uni anyway (u_{39})

[Kirk]: I love this, i can drink coffee and listen to music whilst attending a tute heheh (u_{75})

[Duncan]: I am at home...in my pajamas drinking coffee hehehehehe...this is so sweet (u_{102})

[Kevin]: i am much more comfortable on a pc rather than talking to a group of ppl... (u_{346})

Case Study 2 exhibited three developmental phases in the first workshop. Broadly, the first phase was concerned with "getting to know you" (SOC, AWA) and pattern establishment (i.e. establishing norms of communication behaviour) (CON). The second phase was concerned with "getting on with the task" (TSK). The third phase was concerned with "this is what we did"; that is, reflecting on the task process (CON) and social interaction (SOC) to build integration and cohesiveness. These three most frequent communication types (TSK, CON and SOC) are represented in Figure 8.7 as proportional to each other in each phase; that is, the figure illustrates the percentage each communication type contributes to the total of all three types.

---

[3] In Case Study 2, utterances are generally very short, often consisting of phrases of sentences. The guidelines to participants for communicating in a synchronous environment (chat room) recommended: "If you want to say more than a line, enter the first line followed by three dots (...) to indicate there is more to come. Press enter to "send" this line to everyone. Repeat this until you have finished communicating your comment. Absence of three dots means that you have finished your comment." (see Appendix C.1) This technique keeps the conversation flowing. However, in the transcripts of the conversations, a phrase from one participant is very often interspersed with phrases from other participants.

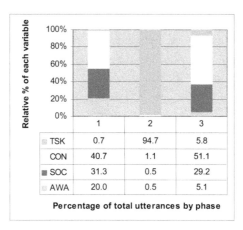

	1	2	3
TSK	0.7	94.7	5.8
CON	40.7	1.1	51.1
SOC	31.3	0.5	29.2
AWA	20.0	0.5	5.1

Percentage of total utterances by phase

Figure 8.7. Proportion of TSK, CON, SOC and AWA in each development phase of Workshop 1.

There was a small amount of supportive and no argumentative communication in this workshop. What little supportive communication there was, occurred mostly in Phase 2, and took the form of concurring with other participants' comments, for example:

[Adrian]: i think sandy has a point ... (u_{220})
[Sandy] i agree doug ... (u_{311})
[Doug]: that's a good point duncan (u_{337})

8.3.2. Examination of Developmental Hypotheses within Workshop 1

In this section, the developmental hypotheses will be evaluated for short-term (within workshops) effects for Workshop 1.

Hypothesis H$_{1.1}$: *There are definable developmental phases in Workshop 1*
The timeline representations of the TSK, CON, SUP, ARG, SOC, ENV, AWA, INF and FOR variables identify distinct turning points (Figure 8.3), verified by specific utterances. These turning points indicate changes in the development of the group within this first workshop. Figure 8.4 shows considerable variation between these three phases in the TSK, CON, SOC and AWA variables in particular. *Hypothesis H$_{1.1}$ has been supported for Workshop 1.*

Hypothesis H$_{1.2}$: *In the early phase of the development of Workshop 1, the content of communication is more conceptual than task-oriented or social*
The timeline in Figure 8.3 and the graph in Figure 8.5 show that there is more conceptual communication than task communication in the first phase. There is less social communication in this early phase. Even though the last phase is almost a

replication of the pattern of communication in the first phase, it can be stated that in the early phase of development there is a higher percentage of conceptual communication than task or social communication. *Hypothesis $H_{1.2}$ is therefore supported for Workshop 1.*

Hypotheses $H_{1.3}$ and $H_{1.4}$: *In Workshop 1, during periods of low task activity, the content of communication is more social than task oriented; during periods of high task activity, the content is more task oriented than social*

The timeline in Figure 8.3 and the graph in Figure 8.5 show that in Phase 2, when the communication is almost totally devoted to the task activity, there is very little social communication. In Phases 1 and 3, when there is very little task-oriented communication, the participants engage in a moderate level of social communication. *Hypotheses $H_{1.3}$ and $H_{1.4}$ are therefore supported for Workshop 1.*

Hypothesis $H_{1.5}$: *During earlier developmental stages of Workshop 1, participants engage in more disclosures about the physical and social attributes of themselves and others*

The graph and figures in Figure 8.6 and the relative percentages in Figure 8.7 show that there is a significant decrease of awareness communication from Phase 1 (20%) to Phase 3 (5.1%). *Hypothesis $H_{1.5}$ is supported for Workshop 1.*

Hypothesis $H_{1.6}$: *Group cohesiveness increases over the period of Workshop 1.*

The graph and figures in Figure 8.6 show that, although supportive communication increased from Phase 1 (4.7%) to Phase 2 (7.5%), it decreased in Phase 3 (1.5%). There was no argumentative communication in this workshop. *Hypothesis $H_{1.6}$ is not supported for Workshop 1.*

8.4. Analysis of Developmental Characteristics within Workshops 1-9

Analyses of Workshops 2-9 is given in Appendix C. In this section, a summary of Workshops 2-9 is included with the results of Workshop 1.

8.4.1. Workshops 1-9

Figure 8.3 showed the timeline for Workshop 1, and Figure 8.8 shows "thumbnail" timelines for Workshops 2-9 (see Appendix C for larger images of timelines for these workshops) with turning points indicated by dotted lines.

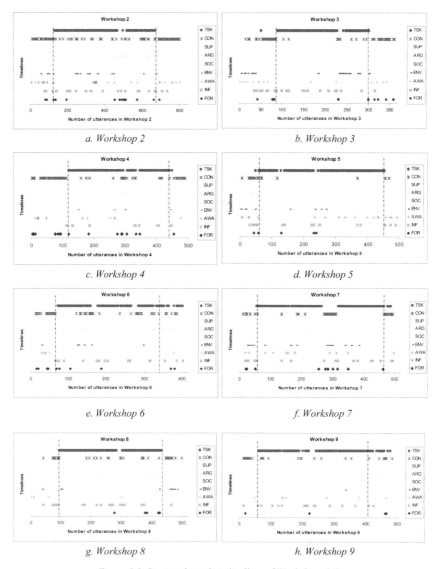

Figure 8.8. Content-dependent timelines of Workshops 2-9.

All timelines in Figure 8.8 indicate similar communication patterns to Workshop 1 (Figure 8.3); that is, an initial period of "getting to know you" (SOC) and establishing norms of communication behaviour) (CON); a middle period of "getting on with the task" (TSK); and a final period of reflecting on the task process (CON) and social interaction (SOC) to build integration and cohesiveness.

The only workshop that exhibited a slightly different pattern was Workshop 7. As explained in Appendix C.2.11, the middle of Phase 2 has a short period in which the communication pattern changed from primarily task to primarily conceptual and environment communication. But as this was a distraction initiated by the facilitator it has been discounted as an artifact of that particular workshop.

Table 8.8 is a summary of the three most frequent variables (TSK, CON, SOC) in each workshop, showing percentages of utterances in each development phase with means and standard deviations.

Table 8.8. Summary of three most frequent variables (%) in each development phase in Workshops 1-9.

	Task (TSK)			Conceptual (CON)			Social (SOC)		
	P1	P2	P3	P1	P2	P3	P1	P2	P3
W1	0.7	94.7	5.8	40.7	1.1	51.1	31.3	0.5	29.2
W2	0.0	70.6	0.0	31.2	7.0	37.1	44.0	13.0	46.2
W3	1.2	78.8	1.5	45.3	4.7	35.4	30.2	3.8	43.1
W4	0.8	76.0	10.9	45.9	6.1	27.3	41.8	9.9	38.2
W5	1.8	78.9	0.0	19.6	1.3	4.8	48.2	11.0	76.2
W6	0.0	67.6	32.0	30.8	10.5	10.7	50.8	13.8	29.3
W7	0.0	69.2	13.5	13.5	9.4	21.2	65.4	9.7	46.2
W8	0.0	77.4	1.4	10.0	6.2	14.9	84.4	9.5	75.7
W9	14.7	72.4	25.3	28.0	2.8	10.8	57.3	13.8	41.0
Mean	2.1	76.2	10.0	29.4	5.5	23.7	50.4	9.5	47.2
SD	4.7	8.1	11.7	13.2	3.4	15.2	17.0	4.5	17.4

The means of the three most frequent variables are shown in graphic form in Figure 8.9. This figure illustrate the average communication pattern in the developmental phases for all nine workshops in Case Study 2.

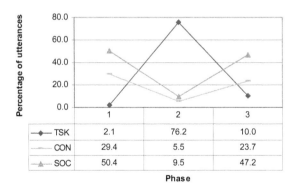

Figure 8.9. Percentage means of TSK, CON and SOC for all workshops.

Figure 8.9 shows numerical data supporting the broad description of the development of each phase mentioned earlier (i.e. an initial period of "getting to know you" and establishing norms of communication behaviour; a middle period of "getting on with the task"; and a final period of reflecting on the task process and social interaction to build integration and cohesiveness).

Table 8.9 is a summary of the six less frequent variables (SUP, ARG, ENV, AWA, INF, FOR) in each workshop showing percentages of utterances in each development phase with means and standard deviations.

Table 8.9. Summary of six less frequent variables (%) in each development phase in Workshops 1-9.

	Supportive (SUP)			Argumentative (ARG)			Environment (ENV)			Awareness (AWA			Informal (INF)			Formal (FOR)		
	P1	P2	P3	P1	P2	P3	P1	P2	P3	P1	P2	P3	P1	P2	P3	P1	P2	P3
W1	4.7	7.5	1.5	0.0	0.0	0.0	2.7	0.0	1.5	20.0	0.5	5.1	3.3	2.1	9.5	8.0	0.5	8.0
W2	0.0	2.4	12.1	0.8	1.5	0.0	7.2	3.3	0.8	17.6	4.0	6.1	3.2	4.2	3.8	2.4	2.0	0.8
W3	3.5	3.8	20.0	1.2	0.0	0.0	14.0	8.0	1.5	10.5	0.9	6.2	8.1	6.6	1.5	4.7	0.9	10.8
W4	1.6	4.5	9.1	0.8	3.5	1.8	0.0	1.3	1.8	7.4	1.6	1.8	1.6	3.5	3.6	9.0	2.2	1.8
W5	5.4	6.3	9.5	3.6	0.3	0.0	14.3	1.0	0.0	7.1	2.5	4.0	12.5	3.8	4.0	1.8	1.3	0.0
W6	0.0	7.6	6.7	1.5	1.5	18.7	3.1	2.2	0.0	12.3	0.0	1.3	0.0	5.8	4.0	7.7	1.5	2.7
W7	0.0	3.9	15.4	0.0	0.2	1.9	13.5	2.7	0.0	3.8	2.4	1.9	7.7	2.9	3.8	5.8	1.9	0.0
W8	3.3	5.6	8.1	0.0	1.5	0.0	1.1	0.9	9.5	4.4	0.3	0.0	7.8	4.7	1.4	0.0	2.1	0.0
W9	0.0	8.6	22.9	0.0	2.1	1.2	0.0	0.3	0.0	1.3	2.1	1.2	6.7	4.0	2.4	1.3	0.3	2.4
Mean	2.1	5.6	11.7	0.9	1.2	2.6	6.2	2.2	1.7	9.4	1.6	3.1	5.7	4.2	3.8	4.5	1.4	2.9
SD	2.2	2.1	6.7	1.2	1.2	6.1	6.2	2.4	3.0	6.3	1.3	2.3	3.9	1.4	2.4	3.3	0.7	3.9

The means of these six less frequent variables are shown in graphic form in Figure 8.10.

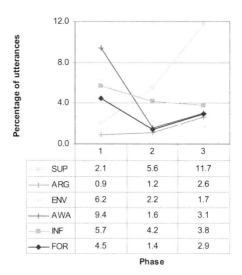

	1	2	3
SUP	2.1	5.6	11.7
ARG	0.9	1.2	2.6
ENV	6.2	2.2	1.7
AWA	9.4	1.6	3.1
INF	5.7	4.2	3.8
FOR	4.5	1.4	2.9

Phase

Figure 8.10. Percentage means of SUP, ARG, ENV, AWA, INF and FOR for all workshops.

Figure 8.10 shows developmental trends with the less frequent communication types. The most obvious trends, over the one-hour period of each workshop, are an increase in supportive communication, a decrease in awareness and environment communication, and a decrease in both formal and informal management of communication.

Table 8.10 gives the results of a one-way ANOVA test on the variation in the three most frequent variable means (TSK, CON and SOC) between phases for the nine workshops. For each of these three variables, Phase 1 is significantly different to Phase 2, and Phase 2 is significantly different to Phase 3. However, Phase 1 is not significantly different to Phase 3.

Table 8.10. Results of ANOVA for three most frequent variables in nine workshops (by phase)

Variable	Description	F	df	p value
TSK	Task	198.11*	2	<.01
CON	Conceptual	10.18*	2	<.01
SOC	Social	22.78*	2	<.00

A one-way ANOVA test on the variation of the six less frequent variable means (SUP, ARG, ENV, AWA, INF, FOR) between phases is shown in Table 8.11. Between phases, there are significant differences in the SUP and AWA variables. Table 8.12 shows the significant differences between each phase. The significant differences in the SUP variable are between Phase 1 and Phase 3 (P1-P3) and Phase 2 and Phase 3 (P2-P3). The significant differences in the AWA variable are between P1-P2 and P1-P3. There is also significant differences in the ENV variable between P1-P3, and the FOR variable between P1-P2.

Table 8.11. Results of ANOVA for six less frequent variables in nine workshops (by phase)

Variable	Description	F	df	p value
SUP	Supportive	11.82*	2	<.01
ARG	Argumentative	0.59	2	.56
ENV	Environment	3.12	2	.06
AWA	Awareness	9.81*	2	<.01
INF	Informal	1.16	2	.33
FOR	Formal	2.49	2	.11

Table 8.12. Mean differences between phases for six less frequent variables in nine workshops

Variable	Description	Between P1 and P2	p value	Between P2 and P3	p value	Between P1 and P3	p value
SUP	Supportive	-3.52	.09	-6.12*	<.01	-9.64*	<.01
ARG	Argumentative	-0.30	.86	-1.44	.41	-1.74	.32
ENV	Environment	4.02	.05	0.51	.79	4.53*	.03
AWA	Awareness	7.79*	<.01	-1.48	.44	6.31*	<.01
INF	Informal	1.48	.27	0.40	.76	1.88	.16
FOR	Formal	3.11*	.04	-1.53	.28	1.58	.27

8.4.2. Examination of Developmental Hypotheses within Workshops 1-9

In this section, the development hypotheses will be evaluated for developmental effects within each workshop. Table 8.13 summarises the findings of the hypotheses in Workshops 1-9.

Table 8.13. Summary of developmental results for Workshops 1-9

Work-shop	$H_{1.1}$	$H_{1.2}$	$H_{1.3}$	$H_{1.4}$	$H_{1.5}$	$H_{1.6}$	Ref*
1	Supported	Supported	Supported	Supported	Supported	Not supported	8.3.2
2	Supported	Partly	Supported	Supported	Supported	Supported	C.2.2
3	Supported	Supported	Supported	Supported	Partly	Supported	C.2.4
4	Supported	Weakly	Supported	Supported	Supported	Supported	C.2.6
5	Supported	Partly	Supported	Supported	Supported	Supported	C.2.8
6	Supported	Partly	Supported	Supported	Supported	Not supported	C.2.10
7	Supported	Partly	Supported	Supported	Weakly	Supported	C.2.12
8	Supported	Not supported	Supported	Supported	Weakly	Supported	C.2.14
9	Supported	Partly	Supported	Supported	Not supported	Supported	C.2.16

*See section referred to for details of the results of the hypotheses.

Hypothesis $H_{1.1}$: *There are definable developmental phases within each workshop*
The timeline representations of the TSK, CON, SUP, ARG, SOC, ENV, AWA, INF and FOR variables identify distinct turning points (Figure 8.3 and Figure 8.8), verified by specific utterances. These turning points indicate changes in the development of the group within all workshop. The summary statistics in Table 8.8 and Table 8.9 and the graphs of the means in Figure 8.9 and Figure 8.10 show considerable variation between these three phases in all variables. The ANOVA tests (Table 8.10, Table 8.11, Table 8.12) show the variation in TSK, CON and SOC, SUP and AWA variables is statistically significant. *Hypothesis $H_{1.1}$ has been supported.*

Hypothesis $H_{1.2}$: *In the early phase of the development within each workshop, the content of communication is more conceptual than task-oriented or social*
The timeline representations of each workshop (Figure 8.3 and Figure 8.8), the graph in Figure 8.9, and the figures in Table 8.8 show that there is more conceptual than task communication but not more than social communication in the first phase. The last phase shows a similar pattern of communication as in the first phase. However, it can be stated that in the early phase of development there is significantly more conceptual communication than task-oriented communication. *Hypothesis $H_{1.2}$ is therefore is partly supported.*

Hypotheses H₁.₃ and H₁.₄: *In each workshop, during periods of low task activity, the content of communication is more social than task oriented; during periods of high task activity, the content is more task oriented than social*

The timeline representations of each workshop (Figure 8.3 and Figure 8.8), the graph in Figure 8.9, and the figures in Table 8.8, show that in Phase 2, when the communication is almost totally devoted to the task activity, there is very little social communication. In Phases 1 and 3, when there is very little task-oriented communication, the participants engage in a moderate level of social communication. *Hypotheses H₁.₃ and H₁.₄ are therefore supported.*

Hypothesis H₁.₅: *During earlier developmental stages of each workshop, participants engage in more disclosures about the physical and social attributes of themselves and others*

The graph and mean figures for the AWA variable in Figure 8.10 show that there is a decrease of awareness communication from Phase 1 to Phase 3. The ANOVA tests (Table 8.11, Table 8.12) show this variation in the AWA variable is statistically significant. *Hypothesis H₁.₅ is therefore supported.*

Hypothesis H₁.₆: *Group cohesiveness increases over the period of each Workshop*

The graph and mean figures for the SUP variable in Figure 8.10 show that there is an increase in supportive communication from Phase 1 to Phase 3. The ANOVA tests (Table 8.11, Table 8.12) show this variation in the SUP variable is statistically significant from Phase 1 to Phase 3 and from Phase 2 to Phase 3. Apart from Phase 3 in Workshop 6, there was very little argumentative communication, so the ratio of SUP:ARG is not relevant. *Hypothesis H₁.₆ is therefore supported.*

8.5. Analysis of Developmental Characteristics across Workshops

In this section, long-term developmental characteristics (across workshops) will be examined.

8.5.1. Developmental phases

To analyse the first hypothesis concerned with developmental characteristics – *that there are definable developmental phases in computer-mediated groups* – a categorical timeline, similar to that developed for Case Study 1 (see Figure 7.2), was developed for the period of Case Study 2. This timeline, shown in Figure 8.11, is based on a content-dependent analysis of the 4,547 utterances exchanged among the members of the group for the duration of nine workshops. The commencement of each workshop is indicated by vertical dotted lines.

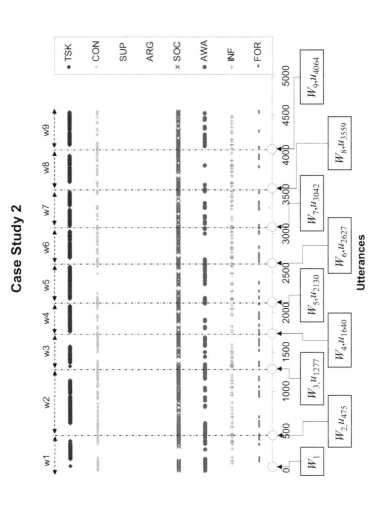

Figure 8.11. Content-dependent timeline of Case Study 2, illustrating beginning of each weekly workshop

In terms of development across the nine workshops, the timeline does not reveal as much information as the timeline for Case Study 1 (Figure 7.2). This is to be expected for two reasons:

1. The "turning points" in Case Study 2 were predefined by discrete periods dictated by the length of each workshop.
2. Strong developmental effects were identified in each workshop so, for most variables, the communication pattern is repeated for each workshop.

The variables are therefore converted to percentage of total utterances in each workshop and plotted as line graphs in Figure 8.12 and Figure 8.13 to be able to examine trends more clearly.

Figure 8.12 shows trends for the three most frequent variables (TSK, CON and SOC) across each workshop. The trend for task communication is to increase over the period, apart from a high point in the middle. The trend for conceptual communication is to decrease over the period, apart from a low point in the middle. The trend for social communication is to increase over the period.

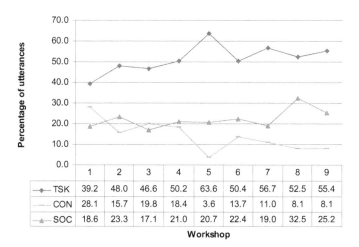

Figure 8.12. Percentage of TSK, CON and SOC utterances in each workshop.

Figure 8.13 shows trends for the six less frequent variables (SUP, ARG, AWA, ENV, INF, FOR) across each workshop. The trend for supportive communication is to increase over the period. The trend for awareness communication is to decrease over the period. The trend for formal communication is to decrease over the period. There are no discernible trends for the argumentative, environment and informal communication.

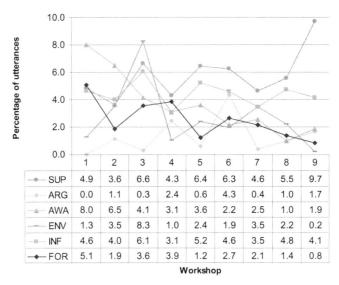

	1	2	3	4	5	6	7	8	9
SUP	4.9	3.6	6.6	4.3	6.4	6.3	4.6	5.5	9.7
ARG	0.0	1.1	0.3	2.4	0.6	4.3	0.4	1.0	1.7
AWA	8.0	6.5	4.1	3.1	3.6	2.2	2.5	1.0	1.9
ENV	1.3	3.5	8.3	1.0	2.4	1.9	3.5	2.2	0.2
INF	4.6	4.0	6.1	3.1	5.2	4.6	3.5	4.8	4.1
FOR	5.1	1.9	3.6	3.9	1.2	2.7	2.1	1.4	0.8

Workshop

Figure 8.13. Percentage of SUP, ARG, ENV, AWA, INF and FOR utterances in each workshop.

8.5.2. Conceptual communication

The second developmental hypotheses proposed that the conceptual communication was more prevalent than task-oriented or social communication in the early phase of development. Figure 8.12 shows there is a trend for more conceptual communication in the early phases of the long-term development of this group. Although there is more task communication in all stages (workshops), and there is less social communication only in the first stage (first workshop), the ratio[4] for $H_{1.2}$ ($U_{CON}/U_{TSK+SOC}$) (Figure 8.14) confirms a definite trend of more conceptual communication in the early phase. The high proportion of conceptual communication in Workshop 1 is explained in Section 8.3.1, page 229; that is, during the first workshop it was necessary to explain the workshop procedure, organise moderators and outline expected communication norms.

---

[4] See Figure 6.15 for description of analyses for each hypothesis.

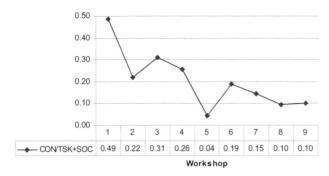

Figure 8.14. Ratio of CON and TSK+SOC variables.

8.5.3. Communication and task activity

The next two developmental hypotheses are concerned with communication content and task activity. The third hypothesis proposes that during periods of low task activity the communication is more social than task oriented. The fourth hypothesis proposes that during periods of high task activity the communication is more task oriented than social. The two variables of interest in this hypothesis – TSK and SOC – are plotted in the line graph of Figure 8.15. Figure 8.15 shows that the percentage of task utterances is always higher than social utterances. In the early workshops (phases), task and social communication follow similar patterns, but in the later workshops, there is a trend for task and social communication to diverge. The ratio[5] for $H_{1.3}$ (U_{SOC}/U_{TSK}) and $H_{1.4}$ (U_{TSK}/U_{SOC}) (Figure 8.16) shows the highest difference between the two variables is in Workshops 5 and 7.

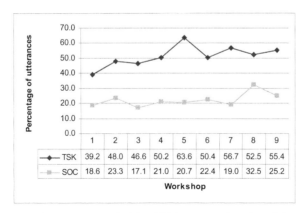

Figure 8.15. Percentage of TSK and SOC utterances in each workshop.

---

[5] See Figure 6.15 for description of analyses for each hypothesis.

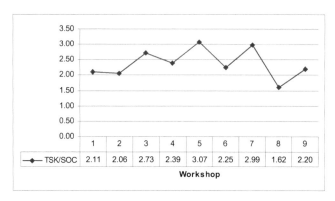

Figure 8.16. Ratio of TSK and SOC variables in each workshop.

8.5.4. Participant disclosures

The fifth developmental hypothesis proposes that participants engage in more disclosures about the physical and social attributes of themselves and others during earlier developmental stages. The variable that relates to this hypothesis is awareness (AWA). The degree of awareness or social presence of a virtual group is measured by the amount of communication concerned with making knowledge of self and other participant(s) explicit. It would be expected that, in the early stages of development, there would be a greater need for this type of disclosure either about oneself or others. Given the absence of physical and social cues that are available in a face-to-face environment, such disclosures contribute to a higher degree of "social presence", or the ability of people to be perceived as "real" beings (Short, Williams and Christie, 1976; Kiesler and Sproull, 1986; Mantovani and Riva, 1999; Hiltz and Turoff, 2002). As a group develops and participants learn more about each other, there is an increased consciousness of the physical and social attributes of others, so there is a decreased need to make such disclosures. The following are examples of awareness communication:

[Gail]: I am sitting at my desk at home ... (u_{545})
[Fred]: eyah.... i eman working wit summone for so long but not having met them is quite interesting (u_{817})
[Leah]: Good morning, Off to get coffee back at 9.30 - chat amongst yourselves :-) (u_{1277})
[Doug]: irc got boring for me (u_{891})
[Duncan]: They are also used as a tag and such like my smile ;o), it's slightly different. (u_{1014})
[Gail]: duncan, you must have nice teeth (u_{1016})
[Adrian]: Well i only attend this class to get and education, I don't really need it but I want it. I already earn a million dollars a year. (u_{1048})
[Joe]: brb (u_{3972})

As in Case Study 1, this group were not keen to meet each other in person. When the facilitator suggested a face-to-face workshop, there was not one person who expressed a desire to change from an online to a face-to-face mode. The following is an extract from a conversation thread in Appendix C.2.11 (Workshop 7):

[Fay]: i guess the question is, is anyone really keen to have a ftf tutorial ... (u_{3320})
[Leah]: sorry i wld prefer online (u_{3336})
[Gail]: nope (u_{3339})
[Monica]: i prefer online (u_{3341})

Figure 8.17 shows the ratio of awareness communication (U_{AWA}/U) as a percentage of total utterances in each workshop. Apart from slight fluctuations in Workshops 5, 7 and 9, there is a significant decrease in communication across the nine workshops (F=3.16, df=8, p=0.01).

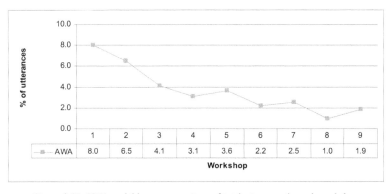

Figure 8.17. AWA variable as a percentage of total utterances in each workshop.

8.5.5. Group cohesiveness

The last developmental hypothesis proposes that group cohesiveness increases over the life of the group. The variables that relate to this hypothesis are supportive (SUP) and argumentative (ARG). Most of the research on group development describes a period of conflict in an early stage of a group's lifecycle, and a steady increase in agreement and engagement towards the final stages (e.g. Tuckman, 1965; Wheelan and Hochberger, 1996). The degree of cohesiveness or connectedness (Sproull and Kiesler, 1991; Haythornthwaite, 2003; Rettie, 2003) of a virtual group is therefore measured by the ratio of supportive to total utterances (U_{SUP}/U) and the ratio of supportive to argumentative utterances (U_{SUP}/U_{ARG}) across the nine workshops.

Figure 8.18 shows that there is a trend towards a more supportive environment across the workshops, peaking in the last workshop.

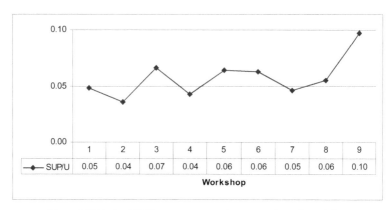

Figure 8.18. Ratio of SUP utterances to total utterances in each workshop.

Figure 8.19 shows the ratio of supportive to argumentative utterances, with values normalised for improved visualisation. Maximum values indicate maximum supportiveness. The graph therefore shows that, despite the small number of argumentative utterances in this case study, the group did exhibit some tension in Workshops 2, 4 and 6.

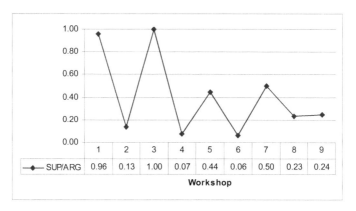

Figure 8.19. Ratio of SUP and ARG utterances in each workshop.

8.6. Examination of Developmental Hypotheses across Workshops

In this section, the developmental hypotheses will be evaluated for effects across workshops.

Hypothesis H$_{1.1}$: *There are definable developmental phases in computer-mediated groups*

The analyses of the long-term developmental effects of Case Study 2, demonstrate that there is some variation across the workshops (Figure 8.12 and Figure 8.13). The variation, though, is not as distinctive as for the short-term developmental effects. In the early phases of the workshop series, the communication pattern of the group was a combination of task, conceptual and formal type utterances. In other words, a significant part of the first workshop (phase) was devoted to the facilitator formally advising the participants what was to be expected throughout the workshop series. As the series progressed, the group became more social and supportive. The task activity of the group increased to a high peak in the middle of the series and then tapered off towards the end. *Hypothesis H$_{1.1}$ has been weakly supported across the workshops.*

Hypothesis H$_{1.2}$: *In the early phase of development, the content of communication is more conceptual than task-oriented or social*

Figure 8.12 and Figure 8.14 show that the group was engaged in more conceptual than social communication in the early phase (Workshop 1). Conceptual communication decreased over the period of the workshop series. However, there was consistently more task than conceptual communication. *Hypothesis H$_{1.2}$ is therefore is partly supported across the workshops.*

Hypotheses H$_{1.3}$ and H$_{1.4}$: *During periods of low task activity, the content of communication is more social than task oriented; during periods of high task activity, the content is more task oriented than social*

Although towards the latter part of the workshop series, the pattern of task and social communication were divergent, Figure 8.15 and Figure 8.16 show that in all phases (workshops), there was more task than social communication. *Hypotheses H$_{1.3}$ and H$_{1.4}$ are therefore not supported across the workshops.*

Hypothesis H$_{1.5}$: *During earlier developmental phases, participants engage in more disclosures about the physical and social attributes of themselves and others.*

Figure 8.17, showing the percentage of awareness communication across all workshops, indicates a definite trend of decreasing awareness communication and thus concomitant increase in the physical and social attributes of others. In other words, awareness communication occurs more frequently in the initial stage of the workshop series. *Hypothesis H$_{1.5}$ has therefore been supported across the workshops.*

Hypothesis H$_{1.6}$: *Group cohesiveness increases over the life of the group.*

Figure 8.18, showing the percentage of supportive communication, and Figure 8.19, showing the ratio of supportive and argumentative communication across all workshops, indicates a trend of increasing supportive communication and thus concomitant increase in the cohesiveness of the group. *Hypothesis H$_{1.6}$ is therefore supported across workshops.*

8.7. Summary of Developmental Characteristics

The developmental characteristics have been analysed for short-term (within workshops) and long-term (across workshops) effects.

The first hypothesis proposed that there are developmental phases in computer-mediated groups. Both qualitative and quantitative analyses demonstrated a strong short-term developmental effect in which the communication in the early and late phases was primarily social and conceptual while the middle phase was task-oriented. The developmental effect was not as strong across workshops but there was a trend for more task and conceptual communication in the early phases of the workshop series and a trend for more social and supportive communication in the later phases. The weaker effect across workshops is no doubt due to the structured process and environment of the series of nine one-hour workshops. There was a defined commencement and conclusion point for each workshop and very little contact among participants in the time between workshops. This meant that participants needed a short period of "getting to know you (again)" at the start of each workshop. However, as there were developmental trends across the workshop series, as well as within workshops, the first hypothesis was supported overall for Case Study 2.

The second developmental hypothesis proposed that in the early phases of development, participants focus on conceptual aspects of the group activity rather than engage in task-oriented or social communication. The results indicate that this was partly supported for phases within workshops. While conceptual communication was more common in the early phase than task communication, social communication was also more common than task communication. The results also indicate that this hypothesis was partly supported across workshops. While conceptual communication decreased, and task and social communication increased over the workshop series, the proportion of task communication was consistently higher than conceptual or social communication. Again, we need to look at the structure of these workshops to explain this pattern. The activity task was well defined at the commencement of the workshop series and the participants had only one hour to complete that particular workshop activity, so less time was needed to conceptualise the collaborative task.

The third and fourth developmental hypotheses were also concerned with the relative proportion of communication types. These hypotheses proposed that there is an inverse relationship between social and task-oriented communication. The results indicate that, within workshops, there was minimal social communication during periods of high task activity, and a high proportion of social communication during periods of low task activity. However, this hypothesis did not hold for across workshops as there was consistently more task than social communication.

The fifth developmental hypothesis addressed the issue of social presence (or lack thereof) in virtual environments. The hypothesis proposed that in earlier developmental stages, participants communicate more about the physical and social attributes of themselves and others. The measurement used to test this hypothesis was the proportion of communication that included some personal disclosure. The decrease in this type of communication both within and across workshops was statistically significant so this hypothesis is supported.

The last developmental hypothesis related to group cohesiveness, which was measured by the pattern and relative proportions of supportive and argumentative communication. The hypothesis proposed that an increase in supportive communication and a decrease in argumentative communication is an indicator of group cohesiveness. There was very little argumentative communication throughout the workshop series so this variable was deemed to be irrelevant. However, there was an increase in supportive communication both within and across workshops. The result within workshops was significant and there was a definite trend across workshops so this hypothesis is supported.

8.8. Examination of Leadership Characteristics Hypotheses

The second group of hypotheses are concerned with the leadership characteristics of virtual groups (see Section 2.7.2 and Table 6.3):

$H_{2.1}$ Management intervention is more frequent during periods of high task activity.

$H_{2.2}$ Different management styles predominate at different developmental stages.

$H_{2.3}$ Leaders communicate more intensively than other participants.

$H_{2.4}$ Leaders emerge during the life of the group.

This group of hypotheses will be discussed for Case Study 2.

So far in the analysis of Case Study 2, the communication patterns have been studied at the level of the group, rather than an examination of the specifics of individual patterns. In this section on leadership, the communication patterns of specific individuals will be analysed. This study of leadership was conducted as an exploratory study to examine the unique synchronous computer-mediated communication patterns displayed by non-appointed leaders during the two-and-a-half month period of the workshop series. Hence, these systematic patterns can be used to help identify patterns of leadership in virtual organisations (Jackson, 1999) using a synchronous communication mode.

As mentioned in Chapter 7, in a traditional hierarchical organisational structure, group (or team) leaders are usually appointed (Katz and Kahn, 1978). Such appointment is generally by a person in a superior position in the organisation's hierarchy. Non-appointed leaders, on the other hand, are the result of bottom-up processes rather than a top-down command and control process. In Case Study 2, the facilitator was appointed by the university. Each participant moderated in one workshop and was assigned to that role by the facilitator; that is, although the moderator was an assigned to a leading role, that role was for one workshop only. Each participant would therefore be expected to dominate discussions in the workshop which they moderated. Hence, the participation pattern would be a large number of utterances in one workshop and a smaller number of utterances in the remaining eight workshops. Thus, the contributions to the discussions from each participant were potentially equalised across the period of the nine workshops.

Table 8.14 lists the variables of interest in this section of the analysis, with a brief description and the hypotheses to which they apply. All communication types (variables) are defined and described in Table 6.4.

In the following sections, the analyses of leadership is structured around the hypotheses relating to leadership characteristics across all nine workshops; that is, the long-term effects where each workshop represents a development stage (see Section 8.5). The analyses for this set of hypotheses are applied to all participants.

As mentioned in Section 8.1, p.225, one participant (Sandy) transferred to another group and another participant (Ellen) discontinued the unit. Although the hypotheses are classified as "leadership" patterns, they apply to all participant as all participants (except Ellen) took on a moderator role in one workshop. The first two hypotheses – management intervention and management style – are about 'group' management. But since the management group consists of the facilitator and a rotating member(s) of the group (the moderator), it is reasonable to consider these two hypotheses within this section on leadership characteristics. The last two hypotheses relate to leadership communication patterns and emergent leadership.

Table 8.14. Communication variables used in the leadership characteristics hypotheses

Category	Code	Description	Hypothesis
Formal	FOR	Communication connected with the enforcement of rules or norms, used to manage the process of collaboration. More likely used by leaders and key stakeholders..	2.1
Informal	INF	Communication connected with the collective informal creation, management, and enforcement of communication norms, used by any participant. Has a quality of collaborative construction.	2.1
Conceptual	CON	Conceptual communication involves the creation of mutual understandings and meanings among participants. Involves the creation of shared rules to follow. Includes creation, agreement or disagreement about procedures to follow, a common vocabulary, work to be completed.	2.1
Task	TSK	Communication content dealing with the collaborative activity of the group. Includes introduction, clarification, agreement or disagreement of task issues and specific task instructions.	2.1
Negative	NEG	Argumentative, aggressive or any type of negative communication to achieve a goal (i.e. negative reinforcement). Its use is intended to halt or alter a communication direction, i.e. as an intervention.	2.2
Humour	HUM	Humourous communication to achieve a goal (the humour doesn't necessarily have to succeed). Its use is intended to halt or alter the communication direction, i.e. as an intervention. Often indicated by smiley or emoticon, and often used to lighten a heavy discussion.	2.2
Asking	ASK	A question asked as a management strategy to effect a change in the behaviour of an individual or group.	2.2
Positive	POS	Positive, supportive or placative communication to achieve a goal (i.e. positive reinforcement). Its use is intended to halt or alter the communication direction , i.e. as an intervention. Can be indicated by an apology. Intended to keep the peace. Can take the form of rephrasing a question or idea to be more sensitive to other participants' feelings.	2.2
All	ALL	Utterance addresses whole group.	2.3
Part of a group	PAR	Utterance addresses part of the group (two or more participants)	2.3
Person	PER	Utterance addresses one individual	2.3
Addressed	ADD	Individual to whom an utterance is addressed.	2.4

8.8.1. Management intervention

As mentioned in Chapter 7, management intervention in this book refers to communication that facilitates the group moving closer to its goal. Formal management communication is connected with the enforcement of rules or norms that are used to manage the process of collaboration. Although it could be used by any participant, it is more likely used by the facilitator and moderator. Informal management is connected with the collective information creation, management and enforcement of communication norms. It is more likely to be used by non-leading participants and has a quality of collaborative construction. Management intervention, therefore, is defined as the use of formal management (FOR) or informal management (INF) (see Table 6.4 for definitions of FOR and INF constructs).

Table 8.15 shows that when task (TSK) activity is high, management intervention (FOR+INF) is low. There is a significant negative correlation between TSK and FOR+INF (r=-0.71 p=0.03), as indicated in the scatter plot in Figure 8.20.

Table 8.15. Management intervention (INF+FOR) compared with task (TSK) activity (% of all utterances by workshop).

Workshop	Leadership management (FOR+INF)	TSK
1	9.7	39.2
2	5.9	48.0
3	9.7	46.6
4	7.0	50.2
5	6.4	63.6
6	7.3	50.4
7	5.6	56.7
8	6.2	52.5
9	4.9	55.4

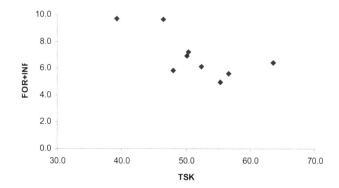

Figure 8.20. Management (FOR+INF) and task (TSK) variables in each workshop.

A negative correlation between management intervention and task activity is, of course, contrary to Hypothesis $H_{2.1}$. The reason for the negative correlation in Case Study 2 could be due to the structured nature of the workshops. There is a trend for management intervention to be higher in the earlier workshops. It was during the earlier workshops that expectations for the moderator role were explained. After witnessing how moderators handled the workshop procedure in the earlier part of the workshop series, the interactions of all participants needed less management.

It was argued in Chapter 7 that the conceptual (CON) variable is related to task activity (see Section 7.2.2). The frequency of management intervention is therefore compared with the combination of task and conceptual (TSK+CON) variables (Table 8.16). This comparison shows a trend towards high management intervention when task activity is high. The correlation, however, is not significant (r=0.37, p=0.32), as indicated in the scatter plot in Figure 8.21.

Table 8.16. Management intervention (INF+FOR) compared with
task (TSK+CON) activity (% of all utterances by workshop).

Workshop	Leadership management (FOR+INF)	TSK+CON
1	9.7	39.2
2	5.9	48.0
3	9.7	46.6
4	7.0	50.2
5	6.4	63.6
6	7.3	50.4
7	5.6	56.7
8	6.2	52.5
9	4.9	55.4

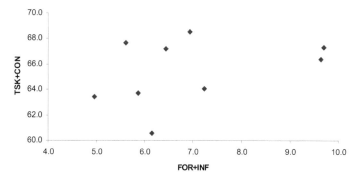

Figure 8.21. Management (FOR+INF) and activity (TSK+CON) variables in each workshop.

Hypothesis $H_{2.1}$, that management intervention is more frequent during periods of high task activity, is not supported.

8.8.2. Management styles

Leaders adopt a variety of strategies to motivate group or team members. This section explores the communication behaviour within Case Study 2 to identify a variety of management styles that are used strategically. To determine if *different management styles predominate at different developmental stages*, four communication variables – positivity, asking, humour and negativity – will be investigated. As with management intervention, different management styles are used mostly by the facilitator and moderators.

As mentioned in Chapter 7, *positivity* (giving positive comments) helps participants to focus on the task at hand and increases their confidence, *asking* questions helps to promote both confidence and a sense of ownership in participants, *humour* helps to avoid or relieve conflict, *negativity* is a harsher response but has a role in diffusing conflict situations. Humour has been related to group longevity (Scogin and Pollio, 1980) and cohesiveness (Duncan and Fieisal, 1989).

Table 8.17 shows the number of utterances of each management style used throughout the workshop series. The figures indicate that asking questions and positive comments were the most frequently used styles.

Table 8.17. Number of utterances of each type of management style (all workshops combined).

Code name	Code description	Number of utterances
POS	Positive	164
ASK	Asking	284
HUM	Humour	110
NEG	Negative	40

Figure 8.22 shows the relative percentages of the four different management styles used in each workshop. Figure 8.23 shows the percentage that each of these four variables contributes to the total of the four variables.

As can be seen from Figure 8.22 and Figure 8.23, asking and positivity are the most consistently used management styles used throughout the workshop period. Humour is used less often but is more prevalent in Workshops 2, 6 and 9. Negativity is rarely used.

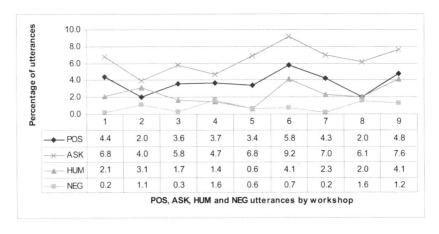

Figure 8.22. Percentage of utterances of management styles (POS, ASK, HUM, NEG) by workshop.

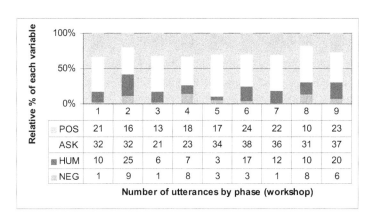

	1	2	3	4	5	6	7	8	9
POS	21	16	13	18	17	24	22	10	23
ASK	32	32	21	23	34	38	36	31	37
HUM	10	25	6	7	3	17	12	10	20
NEG	1	9	1	8	3	3	1	8	6

Number of utterances by phase (workshop)

Figure 8.23. Relative percentage of each management style (POS, ASK, HUM, NEG).

The two most frequently used management styles (POS and ASK) are significantly correlated (r=.81, p=.01). This means that the relative proportions of positive and asking management styles are reasonably consistent across all workshops. There is also a trend for the relative proportions of the other management styles to be consistent with the exception of positive and negative styles. POS and NEG are negatively correlated, though not significantly (r=-0.42, p=0.26). Overall, the variation in management styles across the nine workshops do not show much relationship to phases, perhaps because the phases are not strongly defined.

Hypothesis $H_{2.2}$, that different management styles predominate at different developmental stages, is not supported.

8.8.3. Leadership communication

In face-to-face environments, research shows that leaders are identified by high participation rates in discussions (Regula and Julian, 1973; Sorrentino and Boutillier, 1975; Mullen, Salas and Driskell, 1989). This section, therefore, explores the communication behaviour within Case Study 2 to identify leadership patterns. To determine if *leaders communicate more intensely than other participants,* the number and density of utterances of all members of the group will be investigated.

Number of utterances

Figure 8.24 illustrates the activity level of different participants. The analysis of the activity level is measured as the total number of utterances over the entire period of Case Study 2. The activity level is organised in five intervals, shown in Figure 8.24 as bins. Almost half (47%) of the participants fall within the bin of the second lowest number of utterances [100; 199]. The next most populated bin is the third lowest number of utterances [200; 299] with 21% of the participants. The remaining three bins ([1; 99], [300; 499], [500; 800]) account for 11% of participants in each.

Table 8.18 identifies the participants with the highest activity levels in terms of number of utterances. Predictably, the facilitator (Fay) has the highest activity with 743 utterances. One other participant, Gail, clusters at the top with Fay. The next cluster identified as a bin ([300; 499]) in Figure 8.24 has two participants (Doug and Lorna). The next cluster ([200; 299] has four participants (Henry, Kirk, Leah and Joe).

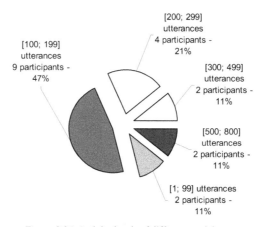

Figure 8.24. Activity levels of different participants.

Table 8.18. Participants with highest number of utterances.

Participant	No. of utterances	Participant	No. of utterances
Fay	743	Monica	184
Gail	626	Donald	180
Doug	410	Duncan	172
Lorna	317	Fred	135
Henry	256	Ruth	130
Kirk	225	Louis	112
Leah	209	Sandy	108
Joe	205	Kevin	84
Adrian	189	Ellen	78
Susan	184		

Therefore, if based on total number of utterances only, the appointed leader and Gail communicated most intensively, with Doug and Lorna communicating more than the other fifteen participants.

Density of utterances

Density of utterances needs to be considered as well as total number of utterances. Density can be measured by total number of words throughout the workshop series, and average utterance length in words. Table 8.19 shows the total number of words for each participant. Although Table 8.18 showed that Fay (the facilitator) had the most number of utterances, Table 8.19 indicates that another participant, Gail, actually posted more total words than Fay. While Doug, Henry and Lorna are among the highest clusters in terms of both measures (number of utterances and total number of words), Duncan has moved from the thirteenth highest in the number of utterances measure to the fifth highest in the total number of words measure.

Table 8.19. Total number of words for each participant.

Participants	Total words	Participants	Total words
Gail	7039	Louis	1390
Fay	5743	Fred	1376
Doug	3834	Sandy	1365
Henry	2688	Ruth	1096
Duncan	2583	Susan	1048
Lorna	2328	Monica	870
Joe	1849	Adrian	850
Kirk	1807	Kevin	451
Leah	1767	Ellen	426
Donald	1676		

The other measure for leadership communication, the average number of words per utterance, is not as informative as for Case Study 1 since the range for Case Study 2 is from 1 to10 words (Table 8.20) compared with 1 to 291 words for Case Study 1. What this measure does highlight is the very different style of communication in a synchronous compared with an asynchronous environment. Utterances in a synchronous environment are short, often abbreviated, or acronyms, e.g. "ROTFL" meaning "rolling on the floor laughing". Acronyms such as ROTFL reduces the actual number of words from 5 to 1.

At the top of the narrow range are: Gail, Henry and Duncan with an average utterance length of 10 words; Fay, with an average of 8 words; and Leah and Donald, with an average of 7 words. Of course, this division of higher and lower communicators at 7 words is somewhat arbitrary as there is very little difference between an average of 7 words and an average of 6 words. However, the cut-off point at 7 words results in six participants at the top of the range rather than the ten participants with an average of 6 or more words.

Table 8.20. Average utterance length in words for each participant.

Participants	Ave. utterance length	Participants	Ave. utterance length
Gail	10	Lorna	5
Henry	10	Susan	5
Duncan	10	Monica	5
Fay	8	Fred	5
Leah	7	Ruth	4
Donald	7	Adrian	3
Kirk	6	Kevin	2
Louis	6	Sandy*	1
Doug	6	Ellen**	1
Joe	6		

*Sandy attended only one workshop and then transferred to another group.
**Ellen attended only one workshop and then discontinued the unit.

Of particular interest in this measure of verbosity is Duncan, who is at the top of the range (average utterance length of 10 words). Duncan was among the participants with the highest total number of words but he was towards the bottom of the range on the total number of utterances. Duncan therefore tended to communicate less frequently than other participants but when he did he had more to say.

Another interesting case is Doug who rated third highest on the other two measures but is in the middle of the range of the average utterance length (6 words). Doug therefore tended to communicate frequently but his utterances were short.

The two measures of density (total number of words and average utterance length) are combined in Table 8.21 to show the variability between these measures.

Table 8.21. Total words and average utterance length of each participant.

Participants	Total words	Ave. utterance length	Participants	Total words	Ave. utterance length
Gail	7039	10	Louis	1390	6
Fay	5743	8	Fred	1376	5
Doug	3834	6	Sandy	1365	1
Henry	2688	10	Ruth	1096	4
Duncan	2583	10	Susan	1048	5
Lorna	2328	5	Monica	870	5
Joe	1849	6	Adrian	850	3
Kirk	1807	6	Kevin	451	2
Leah	1767	7	Ellen	426	1
Donald	1676	7			

Figure 8.25 shows histograms of the distribution of the length of utterances in bins of words of the most verbose participants (those who communicated in excess of 2000 words). Fay (appointed leader) and Gail cluster at the top, while Doug, Henry, Duncan and Lorna are in the next cluster. The distribution in these histograms

indicates that the length of these verbose participants' utterances are mostly in the 5-15 word range.

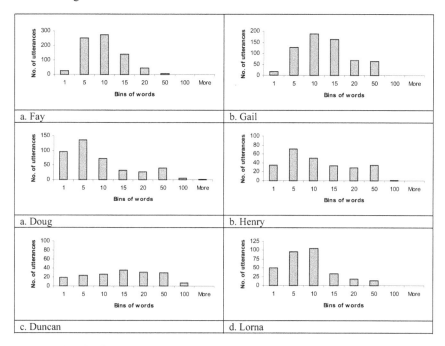

Figure 8.25. Distribution of the length (bins of words) of utterances of most verbose participants.

Table 8.22 presents the percentage of utterances that are less than and longer than 10 words. Except for Doug, more than half of the utterances from high communicating participants are more than 10 words.

Table 8.22. Percentage of shorter and longer utterances of most verbose participants.

Word range	Fay	Gail	Doug	Henry	Duncan	Laura
<10	37.4	22.8	56.1	41.4	25.0	46.4
≥10	62.6	77.2	43.9	58.6	75.0	53.6

The histograms in Figure 8.26 illustrate the typical distributions of the utterance lengths for the low communicating participants. The figure indicates that almost all utterances cluster in the short utterance range. Figure 8.25, on the other hand, showed that the utterances of the high communicating participants were spread over the range from very short to comparatively long utterances.

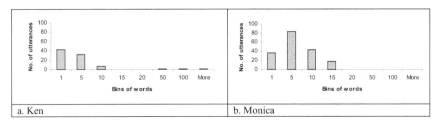

| a. Ken | b. Monica |

Figure 8.26. Distributions of the length (bins of words) of utterances of two non-leading participants.

Table 8.23, showing the percentage of Ken's and Monica's utterances that are more than 10 words and less than 10 words, indicates that longer utterances are far less frequent than for the high communicating participants in Figure 8.25.

Table 8.23. Percentage of shorter and longer utterances of low communicating participants.

Word range	Ken	Monica
<10	88.1	66.5
≥10	11.9	33.5

If based on density of utterances, therefore, the communication pattern of the appointed leader, Fay, indicates that she was less verbose than Gail. Fay's total number of words and average length was less than Gail's, although the number of utterances were higher than Gail's.

Number and density of utterances

To assess communication intensity, number and density (with density divided into total words and average utterance length), need to be compared. Table 8.24 lists eight participants who rated the most highly in each of these criteria. There were four participants (shaded in grey) common to all criteria – Fay (appointed leader), Gail, Henry and Kirk.

Table 8.24. Top eight participants by two intensity criteria

	Density	
Number of utterances	Total number of words	Average utterance length
Fay	Gail	Gail
Gail	Fay	Henry
Doug	Doug	Duncan
Lorna	Henry	Fay
Henry	Duncan	Leah
Kirk	Lorna	Donald
Leah	Joe	Kirk
Joe	Kirk	Louis

Number and density of utterances were effective criteria for measuring verbosity in participants. These criteria identified four participants who communicated more intensively than other participants. One of these participants is the appointed leader. *Hypothesis $H_{2.3}$, that leaders communicate more intensely than other participants, is supported for the appointed leader.* Before claiming this hypothesis is supported for the other three verbose participants, more investigation is required. These other three participants may have displayed attributes of leadership other than verbosity and may be emergent leaders. Therefore, emergent leaders may be identified by using additional criteria to number and density of utterances.

8.8.4. Emergent leadership

It has been shown in the previous section that the facilitator (referred to as an "appointed leader") and three participants communicated more intensively (more frequently and densely) than other participants. Further, the previous section identified varying sets of highly communicative participants (apart from the appointed leader) according to different criteria. These communicative participants, demonstrating leadership characteristics based on frequent and dense communication, could therefore be regarded as potential *emergent leaders*. When using the number of utterances criteria, the potential emergent leaders were Gail, Doug, Lorna, Henry, Kirk, Leah and Joe, in order of most frequent utterances. When using the total number of words criteria, the potential emergent leaders were Gail, Doug, Henry, Duncan and Lorna, in order of most words. When using the average utterance length, the potential emergent leaders were Gail, Henry, Duncan, Leah and Donald, in order of longest average utterance. In this section, to explore the *emergence of leaders in the group*, task-related content will be added as a criteria for identifying leadership characteristics.

Figure 8.27 presents a histogram of the distribution of participants according to intervals of task-related utterances. The intervals are shown as bins. The majority of participants (63%) are located in two bins ([50; 99] and [100; 149]). The line graph indicates the cumulative percentage of task-related utterances at each bin. The distribution is skewed towards participants with a lower number of task-related utterances (kurtosis = 4.1, skewness = 1.8).

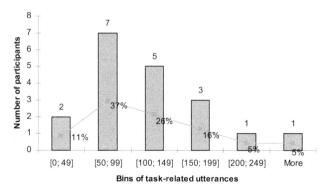

Figure 8.27. Number of task-related utterances across all participants.

Table 8.25 lists the participants who sent 150 or more task-related messages (~26% of the whole group). Gail and Fay cluster at the top of the list (bins [More] and [200; 249]), shaded in grey. Three participants are in the next cluster (bin [150; 199]). Thus, based in this task-related utterance criteria, Gail is astrong candidate for emergent leadership while Lorna, Doug and Henry are possible candidates.

Table 8.25. Participants whose task related utterances are ≥10.

Participant	Task-related utterances
Gail	380
Fay	240
Lorna	199
Doug	174
Henry	166

However, it has been argued in this book that task (TSK) and conceptual (CON) communication are two constructs of the activity dimension[6]. So, to obtain a more accurate representation of activity-related messages, task and conceptual (TSK+CON) categories are combined for further analysis of emergent leadership.

Figure 8.28 presents a histogram of the distribution of participants according to bins of activity-related (TSK+CON) utterances. Again, the bins are shown as intervals. More than half the participants (52%) are located in two bins ([50; 99] and [100; 149]). The line graph indicates the cumulative percentage of task-related utterances at each bin. The distribution is skewed towards participants with a lower number of task-related utterances (kurtosis = 3.2 and skewness = 1.9).

---

[6] And the two constructs, TSK and CON, have been further subdivided into another four categories, see Table 6.4 for description of the coding scheme.

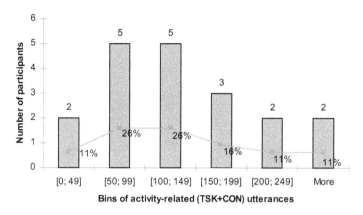

Figure 8.28. Number of activity-related (TSK+CON) utterances across all participants.

Table 8.26 lists the participants who sent 150 or more activity-related messages (~38% of the group). Fay and Gail cluster at the top of the list (bin [More than 249]), shaded in dark grey. Two participants are in the second cluster (bin [200; 249], shaded in light grey. Three participants are in the third cluster (bin [150; 199]). Of the seven participants in Table 8.26, Fay (appointed leader), Gail, Doug, Lorna and Henry are common to both task-related (Table 8.25) and activity-related (Table 8.26) criteria. Thus, based on the activity-related utterance criteria, the strongest candidate for emergent leader is Gail while the other three (Doug, Lorna and Henry) are weaker candidates.

Table 8.26. Participants whose activity- related utterances are ≥150.

Participant	Activity-related utterances
Fay	471
Gail	432
Lorna	228
Doug	225
Henry	180
Leah	166
Kirk	158

Since the task (TSK) variable in this book is a subcategory of what Yoo and Alavi (2002) define as task-related content, it is the latter analysis of activity-related utterances (TSK+CON) that will be adopted in this section of leadership emergence.

What we have now are four sets of potential emergent leaders, rated according to number of utterances, density (total words and average utterance length) and content (activity-related utterances) (Table 8.18, Table 8.21 and Table 8.25). Table 8.27

combines these tables to visually compare the differences in the participants who rated highly on all criteria.

Table 8.27. Comparison of eight participants who rated highest on the number of utterances, density of utterances and activity-related content criteria

a. Number		b. Density				c. Content	
Participant	No. of utterances	Participant	Total no. of words	Participant	Average utterance length	Participant	Activity-related utterances
Fay	743	Gail	7039	Gail	10	Fay	471
Gail	626	Fay	5743	Henry	10	Gail	432
Doug	410	Doug	3834	Duncan	10	Lorna	228
Lorna	317	Henry	2688	Fay	8	Doug	225
Henry	256	Duncan	2583	Leah	7	Henry	180
Kirk	225	Lorna	2328	Donald	7	Leah	166
Leah	209	Joe	1849	Kirk	6	Kirk	158
Joe	205	Kirk	1807	Louis	6	Susan	133

Table 8.27 shows that, in this combined list of the first eight participants from Table 8.24 and Table 8.26, apart from the appointed leader (shaded in dark grey), only Gail, Henry and Kirk (shaded in light grey) are common in all four components of the table. Therefore, these three participants show evidence of emergent leadership if total number of utterances, total number of words, average utterance length and activity-related utterances are all taken into account. If any three of the four criteria are taken into account, then Doug, Lorna and Leah are also a contenders.

As Table 8.27 illustrates a different set of potential emergent leaders for each of the criteria used, there is a need for another cycle of qualitative and quantitative analyses, as described in the CEDA framework (Section 5.5.4, illustrated in Figure 5.6). As explained in Chapter 7, an expanded set of criteria would be useful to explore emergent leadership within the group. The addressed (ADD) variable was used to extract the number of utterances addressed to a particular person and the number of activity-related utterances addressed to a particular person. These criteria were added to the original set of four criteria (number of utterances, total number of words, average utterance length and activity-related utterances). A more data-driven methodology was used to include this expanded set of criteria (or attributes) and the research hypothesis reformulated as a classification problem.

The task was to classify group members as one of the following participant types:

(i)   *appointed leader* (participant who has been appointed as leader),

(ii)   *emergent leader* (participants who were identified as potential emergent leaders using the number of utterances, total number of words, average utterance length, and activity-related utterance criteria), or

(iii)   *participant* (participants identified as non-leaders).

With an appropriate inductive technique, a collection of attributes were used to ascertain which of these attributes are most important in characterising the three participant types. The collection of attributes include the four criteria used before (i.e. number of utterances, total number of words, average utterance length, activity-related).

Table 8.28 lists the set of six attributes which were used as candidates for defining *Participant Type*. As the whole data set includes only 19 participants, all participants were used because it was desirable to capture all possible emergent leaders with this extended analysis.

Table 8.28. Attributes used for defining *Participant Type*

Attribute	Description
Utterances	Total number of utterances
Total Number of Words	Total number of words posted by an individual
Average Length in Words	Average length of utterances in words of an individual
TSK+CON(U)	Number of activity-related utterances sent by an individual
Addressed	Number of utterances of any variable addressed to an individual
TSK+CON(A)	Number of activity-related utterances addressed to an individual

As in Chapter 7, the inductive techniques used are: (i) the CART (Classification and Regression Trees) model to produce a classification tree of *Participant Type*; and (ii) visual clustering guided by the derived classification tree. Figure 8.29 shows the classification tree. The predictors for the tree are the attributes listed in Table 8.28.

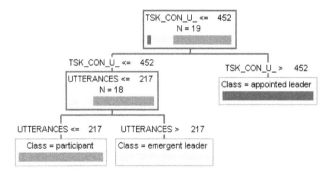

Figure 8.29. The CART classification tree for participant type.

The classification tree derived isolates each of the three participant types (appointed leader, emergent leaders and participants). This induction technique shows that *TSK+CON(U)* (activity-related utterances sent by an individual) is the primary attribute which splits the sample of participants into 'appointed leader' and the rest. The attribute *Utterances* (number of utterances sent) splits the sample into the 'emergent leader' and 'participant' classes. These two attributes partitioned the data to cover all participant types in Case Study 2.

The score values in Figure 8.30 provide an estimate of the relative contributions of the *Utterances, TSK+CON(U), Addressed, TSK+CON(A), Total Number of Words* and *Average Length in Words* attributes in classifying or predicting the target class (i.e. the *Participant Type* attribute). Figure 8.30 shows that the primary attribute for splitting the data was *Utterances. TSK+CON(U)* was also an important variable.

	Variable Importance	
Variable	Scc ∇	
UTTERANCES	100.00	‖‖‖‖‖‖‖‖‖‖‖‖‖‖‖‖‖‖‖‖‖‖‖‖‖
TSK_CON_U_	93.23	‖‖‖‖‖‖‖‖‖‖‖‖‖‖‖‖‖‖‖‖
ADDRESSED	87.97	‖‖‖‖‖‖‖‖‖‖‖‖‖‖‖‖‖‖‖
TSK_CON_A_	87.97	‖‖‖‖‖‖‖‖‖‖‖‖‖‖‖‖‖‖‖
TOTAL_NUMBER_OF_WORDS	71.58	‖‖‖‖‖‖‖‖‖‖‖‖‖‖
AVERAGE_LENGTH_IN_WORDS	36.18	‖‖‖‖‖‖

Figure 8.30. CART attribute importance values.

The CART technique is then complemented by visual clustering (see Section 7.4.4 for a description of visual clustering). Figure 8.31 to Figure 8.34 show the results of visual cluster analyses performed on the data set of 19 participants and the six attributes in Table 8.28. In Figure 8.31, the X, Y and Z axes are *TSK+CON(U), Utterances* and *Addressed* respectively. The value of the *Total Number of Words* attribute has been used to define the size of the spheres.

Guided by the classification tree, in which the *Utterances* attribute splits the data at >217 (see Figure 8.29), *Utterance* is set to '218' in Figure 8.32. This setting filters out a cluster of 13 participants. The remaining six individuals; that is, one *Appointed Leader* and five *Emergent Leaders* are shown in Figure 8.32. Figure 8.33 is an enlargement of a section of Figure 8.32 showing the five *Emergent Leaders* identified by name; that is Gail, Doug, Henry, Kirk and Lorna.

Figure 8.34 shows that when the *TSK+CON(U)* attribute is set to 453 (see Figure 8.29, which indicates that the *TSK+CON(U)* attribute splits the data again at >452), Fay is identified as an *Appointed Leader*. Hence, the CART classification tree in Figure 8.29, visualised as clusters in Figure 8.31 to Figure 8.34, show that the attributes *Utterances* and *TSK+CON(U)* were able to split the 19 participants into three *Participant Types* as listed in Table 8.29.

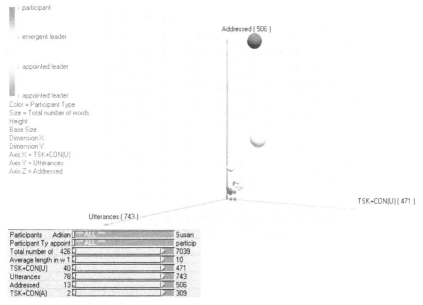

Figure 8.31. Visual clusters of data set of *Appointed Leader* (dark spheres at top), *Emergent Leaders* (light spheres) and *Participants* (dark spheres at bottom).

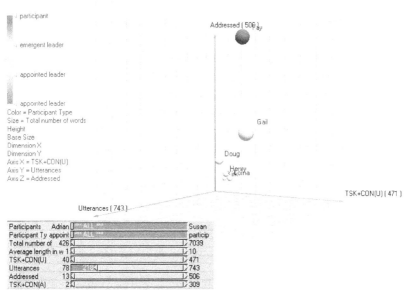

Figure 8.32. Clustering on *Utterances* attribute at value '218' (dark sphere at top is assigned leader and light spheres are emergent leaders).

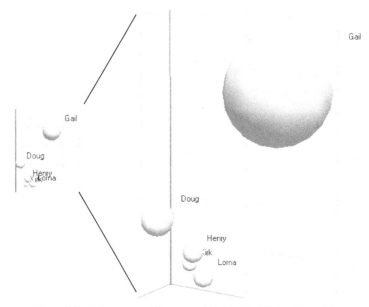

Figure 8.33. Enlargement of the emergent leaders identified in Figure 8.32.

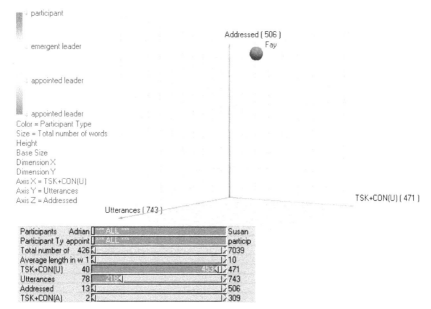

Figure 8.34. Clustering on *TSK+CON(U)* attribute at value '453' identifies the *Appointed Leader.*

Table 8.29. Appointed leader, emergent leaders and participants

Appointed leader	Emergent leaders	Participants	
Fay	Gail	Duncan	Susan
	Doug	Joe	Monica
	Henry	Leah	Adrian
	Kirk	Donald	Kevin
	Lorna	Louis	Sandy
		Fred	Ellen
		Ruth	

The combination of these three important attributes (*Utterances*, *TSK+CON(U)* and *Total Number of Words*) would also give a measurement of the intensity of engagement for any participant. Figure 8.35 illustrates the engagement level for the 19 participants examined in the CART model.

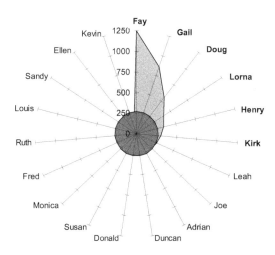

Figure 8.35. Engagement level of participants.

The circle in the middle of Figure 8.35 corresponds to the mean level of engagement across the data set of 19 participants. The graph illustrates the findings of CART (and visualised in Minder3D): the appointed leader (Fay) has the highest level of engagement and five emergent leaders (Gail, Doug, Lorna, Henry and Kirk) are above the mean level of engagement. These six participants are indicated in bold. Leah is just above the mean level of engagement and was identified as a potential emergent leader in the descriptive statistics, so she is a borderline emergent leader.

Thus, it has been demonstrated that the criteria used for descriptive statistics (number of utterances, total number of words, average utterance length, and activity-related utterances), the CART and cluster tools (number of utterances sent, total number of words, average utterance length, activity-related utterances sent, number of utterances received, activity-related utterances received), and the radar chart on engagement level (number of utterances sent and number of utterances received), all point to a set of leaders that emerged during the life of the group.

The descriptive statistics indicated three strong emergent leaders (Gail, Henry and Kirk) and three weaker candidates (Doug, Lorna and Leah). When additional criteria were added and the data analysed with the CART and cluster tools, it was found that the *Number of Utterances* attribute contributed to the identification of the same three strong emergent leaders (Gail, Henry and Kirk) and two of the weaker candidates (Doug and Lorna). The engagement graph confirms the set of five emergent leaders identified by the descriptive statistics and the CART and cluster tools.

Hypothesis $H_{2.4}$, that leaders emerge during the life of the group, is supported.

It is necessary, now, to revisit Hypothesis $H_{2.3}$ – *that leaders communicate more intensely than other participants*. It was stated in Section 8.8.3, p.263, that Hypothesis $H_{2.3}$ was supported for the appointed leader, and possibly three other participants who were identified as being potential emergent leaders, using the verbosity criteria of number and density (total number of words and average utterance length) of utterances. There is, of course, some circularity in this argument; that is, that emergent leaders are identified by their verbosity and that leaders communicate more intensely than other participants. To overcome this circularity, more evidence was required to evaluate the potential emergent leaders identified in Section 8.8.3.

In this section, three more factors were added to the three verbosity factors (see Table 8.28) to identify emergent leaders. The classification and cluster tools, along with the engagement measure, all provide reasonable consistency in the identification of emergent leaders. Thus it is reasonable to claim that since both verbosity and non-verbosity factors identified emergent leaders, that verbosity is a trait of emergent leadership. So there is some support for claiming that "leaders" in Hypothesis $H_{2.3}$ (*that leaders communicate more intensely than other participants*) refers to both appointed and emergent leaders and that these leaders communicate more intensely than other participants.

8.9. Summary of Leadership Characteristics

As mentioned in Chapter 7, the purpose of this group of leadership hypotheses was to examine systematic differences between leaders and participants.

The first hypothesis was concerned with management intervention in periods of high task activity. This hypothesis was not supported in Case Study 2. It was argued in Section 8.8.1 that the workshops were more structured than the amorphous project of Case Study 1 so there was less need for management intervention.

The second hypothesis was concerned with a variety of management styles that were used during different development phases. As it was explained in Section 8.2, each workshop was considered a phase in terms of long-term effects, so the management styles were compared across workshops. It was found that there were similar proportions of positive comments and questions in each workshop. The pattern of negative comments and humour was less consistent but these styles were used less often. This hypothesis was not supported in Case Study 2, which makes sense considering that there was little management intervention anyway and not strong developmental stages across workshops.

The third leadership hypothesis attempted to determine if leaders communicate more intensively than other participants. Two criteria were used for verbosity – number of utterances and density of utterances (total number of words and average utterance length). These criteria identified the appointed leader (Fay) and three other participants (Gail, Henry and Kirk) who communicated more frequently and longer than other participants. The hypothesis was supported for the appointed leader but further criteria were added to verify that the three verbose participants are emergent leaders.

The fourth leadership hypothesis was concerned with identifying emergent leaders. Using the criteria for the third leadership hypothesis (number of utterances, number of words, average utterance length) plus three more criteria (number of utterances addressed to each participant, number of activity-related utterances sent by each participant, number of activity-related utterances addressed to each participant), five participants (Gail, Doug, Henry, Kirk and Lorna) were identified as emergent leaders. These emergent leaders were confirmed by applying an interaction measure (number of utterances sent and number of utterances received by each participant). Thus, the fourth hypothesis was confirmed – leaders did emerge. Further, these emergent leaders were verbose, so the third hypothesis holds for both appointed and emergent leaders.

8.9.1. Leadership Outcomes

Whereas Case Study 1 was concerned with a large collaborative computer-mediated group using asynchronous communication, Case Study 2 is concerned with the effectiveness of learning strategies for a small collaborative computer-mediated group using synchronous communication.

In Chapter 4 (Section 4.3), learning strategies in online environments were described. Of particular importance in e-learning is the use of reflective learning through social (group) activity and social interaction. The learning strategies described in Chapter 4 were applied to the online workshops. It is therefore of interest to determine the effectiveness of these learning strategies.

Table 8.30 lists the 5 emergent leaders and 13 participants with their course assessment (research essays, workshop journals, workshop moderation and exam). The course coordinator (appointed leader) is, of course, not included. Assessments for Sandy and Ellen are not applicable since Sandy transferred to another workshop group and Ellen discontinued the unit. It can be seen that, in most instances, the emergent leaders performed at the top of the assessment range.

Table 8.30. Course assessment for emergent leaders and participants.

Participant	Participant Type	Assessment
Gail	Emergent leader	91.9
Doug	Emergent leader	78.2
Lorna	Emergent leader	70.0
Henry	Emergent leader	84.7
Kirk	Emergent leader	73.4
Leah	Participant	78.0
Joe	Participant	54.5
Adrian	Participant	73.9
Duncan	Participant	61.0
Donald	Participant	58.1
Susan	Participant	76.0
Monica	Participant	72.4
Fred	Participant	57.0
Ruth	Participant	49.5
Louis	Participant	69.9
Sandy	Participant	N/A
Ellen	Participant	N/A
Kevin	Participant	45.0

The assessment scores of the 16 participants were then correlated with different criteria used for the leadership characteristics: (i) engagement (number of utterances sent and number of utterances received by each participant); (ii) total number of words; (iii) total number of utterances; and (iv) activity-related utterances (number of task and conceptual utterances sent by each participant). Table 8.31 shows that in each case, the correlation was significant. In other words, the more interactive the participants were, the more likely they performed well in all assessment types. It is not claimed that the correlation suggests a direct causal effect between interactivity and performance; rather, it could be that interactivity is a co-effect of another untested attribute. It does appear, though, that interactivity in this type of environment could be used as a predictor of performance.

Table 8.31. Correlation of leadership criteria with assessment scores.

Criterion	Correlation with assessment score	p value
Engagement (Utterances sent + Utterances received)	.692*	.003
Total number of words	.610*	.012
Number of utterances	.702*	.002
Activity-related utterances (TSK+CON)	.744*	.001

8.10. Summary

This chapter is the second of two analysis chapters. This chapter reports the results of Case Study 2 analyses. The structure of this analysis chapter differs from the Case Study 1 analysis chapter because of Case Study 2 group's structure. In Case Study 2, the archives of synchronous discussions of four groups of approximately 16 participants were coded with the same coding scheme as for Case Study 1. However, because of the brevity of synchronous communication, the discussions resulted in 20,441 utterances. When the coded data of the four groups were compared, it was found that there was no significant difference for 11 of the 13 variables. One group was therefore selected as being the most representative of the four groups and was subjected to further analyses. It is assumed that, given the similarity of the four groups, that the findings for one group could be generalised to all four groups.

Another variation from the analyses of Case Study 1 is that the developmental hypotheses in this case study were examined for both short-term and long-term effects. Case Study 2 was a series of 9 one-hour workshops, each with the same aim of learning through a collaborative task, so the rationale was that developmental effects could be discerned both within and across workshops. As the analyses of each workshop were lengthy and yield similar results, only the short-term effects for Workshop 1 were presented in this chapter. The short-term analyses of Workshops 2-9 are presented in Appendix C.

So, the analyses in this chapter was structured in three main sections: (i) the developmental hypotheses within Workshop 1; (ii) the developmental hypotheses across all workshops; and (iii) the leadership characteristics hypotheses.

Each workshop exhibited three distinct developmental phases: an initial "getting to know you" phase; a "getting on with the task" phase; and a final "this is what we did" reflecting phase. Descriptive statistics, timelines and extracts from participant communication and interview responses were used to analyse each phase. It was found that developmental phases across the nine workshops were less distinct than within each workshop. The effects across workshops were strongest for the last two developmental hypotheses. Participants engaged in more self-disclosure at the commencement of the workshop series and became more supportive at the conclusion of the workshop series.

Four aspects of leadership were investigated – intervention strategies, style, communication and emergence. Because of the structured procedure of the workshops, there was little need for leader intervention. What little intervention occurred was in the form of positive comments and questions.

Using descriptive statistics, a non-parametric technique and a visual clustering tool, five emergent leaders were identified. It was found that both appointed and emergent leaders characteristically were more verbose and engaged in more task-related communication.

Table 8.32 summarises the findings for Case Study 2 hypotheses.

Table 8.32. Results of hypotheses, Case Study 2

No.	Hypothesis	Short-term effects	Long-term effects
$H_{1.1}$	There are definable developmental stages in computer-mediated groups.	Supported	Weakly supported
$H_{1.2}$	In the early phases of development, the content of communication is more conceptual than task oriented or social.	Partly supported in the majority of workshops	Partly supported
$H_{1.3}$	During periods of low task activity, the content of communication is more social than task oriented.	Supported	Not supported
$H_{1.4}$	During periods of high task activity, the content of communication is more task oriented than social.	Supported	Not supported
$H_{1.5}$	During earlier developmental stages, participants engage in more disclosures about the physical and social attributes of themselves and others.	Supported in the majority of workshops	Supported
$H_{1.6}$	Group cohesiveness increases over the life of the group.	Supported in the majority of workshops	Supported
$H_{2.1}$	Management intervention is more frequent during periods of high task activity.	N/A	Not supported
$H_{2.2}$	Different management styles predominate at different developmental stages.	N/A	Not supported
$H_{2.3}$	Leaders communicate more intensively than other participants.	N/A	Supported
$H_{2.4}$	Leaders emerge during the life of the group.	N/A	Supported

In summary, five of the six developmental hypotheses were supported for short-term effects and two of the six developmental hypotheses were supported for long-term effects. Two of the four leadership hypothesis were supported. These findings are relevant specifically to the context of this study; that is, small collaborative computer-mediated groups using synchronous communication.

CHAPTER 9

DISCUSSION AND CONCLUSIONS

This book began with the overarching question: "How do computer-mediated collaborative communities develop and grow?". Or more broadly, "How do groups function in a complex social system mediated by information and communication technologies". Two specific processes of computer-mediated groups were explored in this research: (i) their *developmental characteristics*; and (ii) their *leadership characteristics*. These processes were explored through qualitative and quantitative analyses of communication data from two cases studies.

Case Study 1 was a large international group of volunteer researchers who collaborated on a research study over a two-year period in the early 90s, using asynchronous communication. The author was in the privileged position of participating and coordinating this unique collaborative project in the early days of information and communication technologies.

By the year 2000, Internet technologies had developed and diffused into most countries at a rate not envisioned in the early 90s. Were computer-mediated collaborative groups essentially the same or were there significant differences? To understand how collaborative groups may have changed, Case Study 2 was selected as another window on computer-mediated collaboration. Case Study 2 took place almost a decade after Case Study 1 with a small group of students who collaborated on a learning activity over a two-and-a-half month period, using synchronous communication. Again, the author was a participant and coordinator in the collaboration.

In this final chapter of the book, the first section discusses the rationale and validity of the research design, the next section discusses findings in relation to the research hypotheses, the third section discusses the implications of the research in relation to group theory, and the final section discusses future directions in this research.

9.1. Validity of the Research Design and CEDA Methodology

In both case studies, the author was not only a participant observer but had a leading role. The research reported here, therefore, has elements of action research in that there was a systematic cycle of planning, evaluation, reflection and refinement.

Action research can be described as a family of research methodologies and the aim was to utilise both qualitative and quantitative approaches. However, current mixed methodologies were found to be lacking in rigour, particularly when applied to Internet research. Internet research requires a set of assumptions relating to ontology, epistemology, human nature and methodological approach that differs from traditional research assumptions. A research framework for Internet research – Complementary Explorative Data Analysis (CEDA) – was therefore developed and applied to the two case studies. Thus, CEDA is a significant outcome of this research.

CEDA incorporates principles of triangulation. Triangulation has been an emerging trend in research over the past few decades. Triangulation in research refers to a combination of two or more theories, data sources, methods or investigators in studying a phenomenon (Massey, 1999) with the goal of convergence and completeness (Knafl and Breitmayer, 1989). In this book, triangulated data, methods and analyses were used:

- *multiple data sources* – communication archives, surveys, interviews, participant observation;
- *multiple methods* – qualitative, quantitative;
- *multiple analyses* – conversational analyses, descriptive statistics, parametric statistics, non-parametric statistics.

Using both quantitative and qualitative methodological approaches was not simply to combine the strengths of each, but rather an attempt to complement them to counteract weaknesses in the validity of each. A complementary approach captures a more complete and contextual picture and reveals more of the complexity of interrelated dimensions of the phenomenon under study.

The various methodologies and analyses contributed to a thorough exploration of the research puzzle and minimised any researcher bias. A framework such as CEDA, though, requires more data preparation time and more expertise than a single methodology, whether it be quantitative or qualitative. Analytical issues need to be resolved such as how to combine numerical and linguistic data, whether numerical data should be normalised, whether data sources should be weighted, and how to interpret divergent results. Where appropriate, statistical procedures were used. However, it must be pointed out that the significance of the research reported here is not based on the statistical significance of the findings. Rather, the statistical results are a function of contextual and theoretical factors that complemented qualitative interpretation and guided the direction of the research.

Although CEDA was applied to asynchronous and synchronous text-based computer-mediated communication in this research, it can be extended to other research environments. Text-based and 3D virtual words, described in the Domain Representation Model (Section 6.3), offer rich research opportunities. The units of analyses in these environments could be other communication elements such as avatar gestures, which are not recorded in conversational archives. The range of analyses can be also be expanded. The Case Study 1 data, for example, has been analysed using an associative neural network (Berthold and Sudweeks, 1995; Sudweeks and Berthold, 1996; Berthold, Sudweeks, Newton and Coyne, 1997; Berthold, Sudweeks, Newton and Coyne, 1998).

As with any methodology, though, CEDA has its limitations. Its application is more suited to understanding complex social systems.

9.2. Discussion of Hypotheses

This section discusses the results of the hypotheses related to the group processes which were the focus of this research – developmental and leadership characteristics. Table 9.1 summarises the support for each hypothesis in each case study (see also Tables 7.30 and 8.32).

Table 9.1. Summary of strength of findings of Case Studies 1 and 2 hypotheses.

No	Hypothesis	Case Study 1	Case Study 2
$H_{1.1}$	There are definable developmental stages in computer-mediated groups.	Supported	Supported short-term Weakly supported long-term
$H_{1.2}$	In the early phases of development, the content of communication is more conceptual than task oriented or social.	Partly supported	Partly supported short-term and long-term
$H_{1.3}$	During periods of low task activity, the content of communication is more social than task oriented	Partly supported	Supported short-term Not supported long-term
$H_{1.4}$	During periods of high task activity, the content of communication is more task oriented than social.	Partly supported	Supported short-term Not supported long-term
$H_{1.5}$	During later developmental stages, participants engage in less disclosures about the physical and social attributes of themselves and others.	Supported	Mostly supported short-term Supported long-term
$H_{1.6}$	Group cohesiveness increases over the lifecycle of the group	Supported	Mostly supported short-term Supported long-term
$H_{2.1}$	Management intervention is more frequent during periods of high task activity.	Supported	N/A short-term Not supported long-term
$H_{2.2}$	Different management styles predominate at different developmental stages.	Weakly supported	N/A short-term Not supported long-term
$H_{2.3}$	Leaders communicate more intensively than other participants.	Supported	N/A short term Supported long-term
$H_{2.4}$	Leaders emerge during the life of the group.	Supported	N/A short term Supported long-term

9.2.1. Developmental stages in computer-mediated groups

It was hypothesised that *there are developmental stages in computer-mediated collaborative groups* (Hypothesis $H_{1.1}$). This hypothesis was supported for Case Study 1 and within each workshop in Case Study 2 (short-term). However, there was only weak support for across workshops in Case Study 2 (long-term).

A content analysis of utterances of Case Study 1 identified eight developmental phases: structuration, tension, reflection (on formation process), activity (on codebook), reflection (on initial activity), activity (on coding), reflection (on the need to meet face-to-face), and goal achievement and closure. These eight phases displayed two prominent dimensions – *activity* and *relationships*. Throughout the lifespan of the group, periods of activity were interspersed with transitional periods. During these transitional periods, participants engaged in reflection about relationships and tasks. From the analysis of these phases, a developmental framework can be created. The phases generally alternate between activity and transitional phases as illustrated in Figure 9.1.

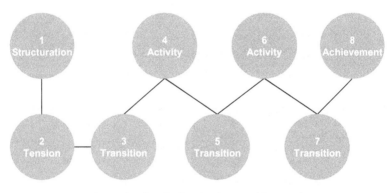

Figure 9.1. Case Study 1 developmental framework.

This is a generic framework as the transitional phases can be in the form of reflection on conflicts and relationships, or simply reassessing tasks and the work progress. This temporal rhythm of activity interspersed with periods of reflection throughout the development of the group most closely follows the punctuated equilibrium model of Gersick (1988; 1991), described in Section 2.4.1. There was, however, an early phase characterised by intense argumentation, supporting many of the face-to-face models of group stages (e.g. Tuckman, 1965; Wheelan and Hochberger, 1996; Schutz, 1966) also discussed in Section 2.4.1. The groups that Gersick studied were organisational *ad hoc* groups, with lifespans ranging from seven days to six months. These groups were formed for one specific task, similar to the Case Study 1 group. However, this pattern of punctuated equilibrium may not be seen in continuing task groups. Collaborative groups such as Case Study 2, engaging in task activity on a regular and continuing basis, may not exhibit this pattern of development for each task but eventually develop their own individual approach to task performance.

The Case Study 2 group did, in fact, develop a very strong developmental pattern within each workshop, which indicates that each workshop could be regarded as one collaborative task activity. A content analysis of each workshop identified a three-phase pattern in which the first phase was primarily concerned with conceptual and social matters, the second phase was mainly task activity, and the final phase was a reflection on relationships and tasks. As in Case Study 1, the period of task activity is intermixed with periods of conceptualisation and reflection, as is illustrated in Figure 9.2.

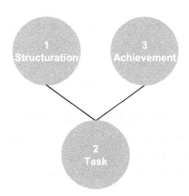

Figure 9.2. Case Study 2 developmental framework.

There are, of course, both similarities and differences between the development of the two case study groups. Both collaborative groups do have definable developmental phases which alternate between periods of task activity and periods of reflection. Given that Case Study 1 was a two-year project and Case Study 2 was a one-hour workshop repeated nine times, it is obvious that the first group would take longer to reach goal achievement than the second group. However, it is not only the differential time factor involved. The most crucial factor that contributes to the different pattern is the repetitive nature of the Case Study 2 task. Over the period of the nine workshops, although the pattern in each workshop was similar, the second group became more efficient, spending proportionately more time on task activity and less on conceptual activity. Another factor that contributes to the different developmental pattern between the two case studies is the mode of communication. The participants of Case Study 1 used asynchronous communication (email) and the participants of Case Study 2 used synchronous communication (chat room). Synchronous communication requires brief (usually one-line) comments, abbreviated as much as possible to compensate for slow typing speed, high degree of concentration to follow multiple conversation threads, and explicit references to managing turn taking. Asynchronous communication facilitates lengthy thoughtful comments and less need for explicit reference to conversation management. The rapid communication interactions of Case Study 2 therefore contributed to a much faster developmental process.

9.2.2. Conceptual communication

The second developmental hypothesis (Hypothesis $H_{1.2}$) proposed that *the content of communication in the early phases of development is more conceptual than task oriented or social*. The support for this hypothesis depends on the interpretation of the hypothesis. While there was strong support for a higher proportion of conceptual communication in the early phases of Case Study 1, as well as within and across workshop in Case Study 2, there was also a significant amount of this type of communication in Phase 5 of Case Study 1 and the last phase of each workshop in Case Study 2. So, while the highest proportion of conceptual communication did occur in the early developmental phases, there was also an increase in other phases throughout the groups' lifespan.

This finding highlights again that the development of a collaborative group is a recurring pattern rather than a linear process. Even though much of the communication regarding conceptual aspects of the task activity occurred in the early phases, there were later periods when the groups needed to re-visit and re-conceptualise the task to be undertaken.

9.2.3. Task and social communication

The next two developmental hypothesis (Hypotheses $H_{1.3}$ and $H_{1.4}$) were concerned with the relationship between task and social types of communication and level of task activity. It was proposed that *when task activity is low, the content of communication is more social than task oriented*, and that *when task activity is high, the content of communication is more task oriented than social.*

This high/low pattern was evident in six of the eight phases of Case Study 1. In two phases (Phases 4 and 6), however, task and social communication were close to similar proportions. These two deviations from the regular pattern in the other six phases can be attributed to unusual events. In Phase 4, although the group was focused on task activities, there was an influx of new people who responded to a general invitation, circulated on the Internet by the coordinators, to join the collaborative project. The welcome messages to each new participant generated a substantial amount of social communication during this period of high task activity. In Phase 6, much of the task activity (coding) was conducted offline and any communication about the task was addressed to a committee of experts to avoid having coding issues discussed publicly. The committee was set up specifically to help coders and to preserve coding integrity. Apart from the two anomalous phases, there was strong support for these two hypotheses for Case Study 1.

Within the Case Study 2 workshops, there was very strong support for these two hypotheses. Participants engaged in social communication in Phases 1 and 3 and were very focused on task activity in the middle phase. However, when examined across workshops, there was consistently more task than social communication and the short-term overall pattern was not evident. This is not surprising since the group was engaged in a series of regular but discrete task activities which were completed for each workshop.

Once again, this finding highlights the nonlinear developmental nature of collaborative groups. Collaborative groups are, by definition, formed for the purpose of accomplishing a task. However, if collaborative groups were to concentrate only on task completion, they would fail to establish an environment that encourages trust and validation among group members and thus eventually perform poorly. Satisfying the social and emotional needs of participants makes a group more cohesive and ultimately more functional. This supports Bales (1950) contention that both task and socioemotional needs must be addressed in groupwork.

9.2.4. Disclosures

The next developmental hypothesis (Hypotheses $H_{1.5}$) proposed that *during earlier developmental stages, participants engage in more disclosures about the physical and social attributes of themselves and others*. There was strong support for this hypothesis in Case Study 1 and both within and across the workshops of Case Study 2.

Social presence is a concept used by a number of researchers (e.g. Short, Williams and Christie, 1976; Walther and Burgoon, 1992; Sproull and Kiesler, 1986) to describe the salience (or lack thereof) of other participants in mediated environments. Rourke et al. (1999) identify self-disclosure as one of the characteristics of social presence. The awareness coding category used in this research is communication connected with making knowledge of self and other participant(s) explicit. It was found that in the early phases of the groups' lifespans, awareness-type communication was much more prevalent than in the later phases. It is therefore reasoned that participants establish a sense of social presence in the early phases to compensate for the lack of context cues that are normally associated with face-to-face interactions. In a face-to-face situation, group members are usually reticent about disclosing personal information until a communication rapport is established. However, virtual groups need to make that personal connection explicit. Once social presence is established there is a decreased need for disclosure in later phases.

9.2.5. Cohesiveness

The last developmental hypothesis (Hypotheses $H_{1.6}$) proposed that *group cohesiveness increases over the lifecycle of the group.* There was strong support for this hypothesis in Case Study 1 and both within and across the workshops of Case Study 2.

A cohesive group has been described one that 'sticks together', but what is the glue? Cohesiveness is generally measured by how attractive its members perceive the group. This measure, of course, becomes somewhat difficult in a mediated environment in which physical cues are absent. The ratio of supportive to argumentative communication was used in this research to gauge cohesiveness. It is, of course, only one of many measures that could be used. Other group characteristics, such as self-disclosure, gender issues, leadership styles, resolution of conflicts and group structure (Cragan and Wright, 1990), also impact on cohesiveness. However, comments extracted from the online conversations and from interviewee responses also support that the groups in both case studies developed a high degree of cohesiveness.

9.2.6. Management intervention

The first leadership hypothesis (Hypotheses $H_{2.1}$) proposed that *management intervention is more frequent during periods of high task activity.* There was strong support for this hypothesis in Case Study 1 but no support in Case Study 2.

Management intervention in this book was measured by the frequency of formal or informal communication. Both communication types were concerned with creation and enforcement of rules and norms. In the former case, the communication was more likely to be used by coordinators and key participants; in the latter case, the rules and norms are created collectively.

The differences in the support for this hypothesis is no doubt due to the differences in the structure of the groups. Case Study 1 was an *ad hoc* group, formed for a unique and specific collaborative task. There was no precedence or model to follow in terms of norms and processes, so there was a need for a significant amount of management-type communication to establish working guidelines and standard operating procedures. Case Study 2, though, was a highly structured group for which guidelines and procedures were explicitly outlined prior to commencement. In effect, the management communication occurred in the form of documents available to all participants before the formation of the group, e.g. moderator guidelines, e-communication guidelines, topic discussions, etc.

9.2.7. Management style

The second leadership hypothesis (Hypotheses $H_{2.2}$) proposed that *different management styles predominate at different developmental stages*. There was weak support for this hypothesis in Case Study 1 but no support in Case Study 2.

Four types of management styles were explored: positivity, or giving positive comments; asking questions to encourage a sense of ownership among the participants; negativity, or giving negative comments; and humour. These leadership styles are by no means an exhaustive taxonomy but they are associated with transformation leadership (e.g. Sarros, Densten and Santora, 1999).

In both case studies, positivity and asking were used most frequently in all phases by both leaders and key participants as a means of managing communication and the task activities. In most cases, humour was used as a deliberate strategy for diffusing tension or resolving conflict.

9.2.8. Leadership communication

The third leadership hypothesis (Hypotheses $H_{2.3}$) proposed that *leaders communicate more intensely than other participants*. There was strong support for this hypothesis in both Case Study 1 and Case Study 2.

The criteria used for verbosity was number of utterances, total number of words and average length of utterances. As to be expected, the two coordinators (assigned leaders) in Case Study 1 and the coordinator (appointed leader) in Case Study 2 were at the top of the range when these criteria were measured for all participants. Other verbose participants were flagged as potential emergent leaders and this hypothesis was re-visited after the next (and last) leadership hypothesis.

9.2.9. Emergent leadership

The fourth leadership hypothesis (Hypotheses $H_{2.4}$) proposed that *leaders emerge during the life of the group*. There was strong support for this hypothesis in both Case Study 1 and Case Study 2.

Three criteria were added to the above verbosity criteria to identify emergent leaders: number of utterances addressed to an individual, number of activity-related utterances sent by an individual; and number of activity-related utterances addressed to an individual. In both case studies, a non-parametric technique and a visual clustering tool identified a small group of participants who emerged as leaders. In Case Study 1, three attributes were instrumental in categorising assigned leaders, emergent leaders and participants: number of utterances sent, number of activity-related utterances sent; and total number of words. In Case Study 2, two attributes categorised appointed leaders, emergent leaders and participants: number of activity-related utterances sent; and number of utterances sent.

These findings give further support for Yoo and Alavi's (1996; 2002) work on emergent leaders in virtual teams. It can be stated that not only do leaders send more messages but the messages are more likely to be task-related. In other words, sheer volume of words does not make a leader but frequent messages with topic-related content does contribute to leadership qualities.

9.3. Theoretical Implications

The aim of this research was not to add yet another prescriptive group development model to the plethora of models already in the literature. Rather the research in this book has provided a greater understanding of the dynamics of computer-mediated collaborative groups in terms of developmental and leadership characteristics and assessed existing models.

Since the early 90s, technologies have been increasingly woven into the fabric of our everyday lives. Concerns about the negative impacts of technologies appear to be dissipating as the general populace embraces their apparent benefits (see, e.g. Kraut, Patterson, Lundmark, Kiesler, Mukophadhyay and Scherlis, 1998; Kraut, Kiesler, Boneva, Cummings, Helgeson and Crawford, 2002). With such widespread acceptance of the role of technologies in our communities, one would expect to see concomitant changes in work and social interactions. Some of the differential findings between the two case studies in this research such as the faster developmental process, and the prolific use of acronyms and abbreviations in communication, can be contributed in part to such changes.

9.3.1. Group Development

This research has confirmed that collaborative groups do progress through a development process throughout their lifespan. Goal achievement for computer-mediated collaborative groups can be described in three main steps: (i) a period of structuration in which participants engage in social interaction, disclose personal information to increase social presence, and conceptualise the task to be undertaken; (ii) a period of activity in which the task is undertaken; and (iii) a period of achievement, an almost mirror-image of the first step in which participants conceptualise the task completed, demonstrate support for each other, and engage in social interaction. Depending on many other external factors, such as the time available, the technological medium, the mode of communication, the structure of the group, the number of participants, there are transitional stages which can involve tension, some activity and some reflection (Figure 9.3). These transitional phases occurred in Case Study 1 but not in Case Study 2, where the duration and nature of the tasks did not precipitate them.

This research has demonstrated that computer-mediated collaborative groups are highly adaptive to the aim of the collaboration, the specific task to be completed, and the medium in which they collaborate. In the organisational setting, it has been found that virtual teams can devise and complete a collaborative task entirely online. It may be an advantage, but it is certainly not mandatory to have preliminary face-to-face discussions. What is more important is to ensure that time is allowed for an initial period of structuration which involves social interaction to develop a social presence and eventually cohesiveness.

The growing popularity of e-learning has resulted in an interest in the application of virtual teams to education. Educators, like management, must realise that the way that technologies is used depends largely on how humans interact and form communities. In the educational setting, a collaborative community increases pedagogical effectiveness. Providing collaborative projects and interdependent tasks promotes constructivist learning and a strong foundation for understanding how to collaborate in the global workplace. Again, this research has demonstrated that students can collaborate entirely online, although more pedagogical scaffolding may be required than in the organisational setting. The importance of initial social interaction to foster a sense of presence and community in a mediated environment has also been highlighted. This is needed at the start of each interaction session, although its duration can decrease as the group matures.

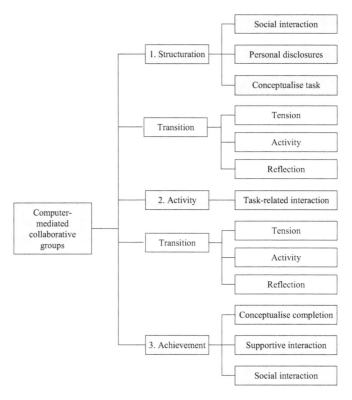

Figure 9.3. Steps to reach goal achievement in computer-mediated collaborative groups

9.3.2. Leadership

Effective leadership and facilitation practices require communication skills, task competence, flexibility, trustworthiness, and the capability to initiate and accept influence in support of cooperative goals. Clearly, these attributes are similar to the attributes advanced by various leadership theories (e.g. Stogdill, 1974; Blake and Mouton, 1964; Bass, 1990; Fiedler, 1964; Frey, 1994). However, the degree of leadership intervention and type of leadership required are dictated by situational factors, such as the specific task being undertaken, the amount of time available to complete the task, the group's expertise, and the particular environment for the collaboration. The research reported here indicates that the degree of leadership or management intervention required is also dictated by the extent of structure or scaffolding that is integrated in the group's collaborative task. The more explicit the guidelines and procedures, the less leadership intervention is required.

Leadership is about motivating and inspiring a group to achieve its goal. This research has demonstrated that motivation and inspiration can be achieved with consistent positive feedback and prompts in the form of questions. It has also been shown that humour, when used in a timely and transparent manner, is also an effective leadership strategy.

The notion of leadership emerging from a virtual collaborative group may seem counter-intuitive because leadership is typically thought of as a property of an individual or an organisational position, not as a group's beneficial task. This research supported Yoo and Alavi's (1996; 2002) findings that the characteristics of emergent leaders' messages include both verbosity and task-related content. However, this research was able to provide more fine-grained results identifying emergent leaders' content being activity-related. In other words, content includes both task and conceptual content. Furthermore, frequency of messages is more critical than lengthy messages in identifying emergent leaders. This finding is important in both the organisational and educational setting, as the emergent leadership criteria can be used in the initial step of a computer-mediated collaborative task for management and educators to identify key people with leadership ability.

9.4. Future Research Directions

While the results described in this book have provided a deeper understanding of computer-mediated collaborative groups, there is still more to be explored. The research approach and methodology can be applied towards a number of different research scenarios in studies of technology-mediated groups.

9.4.1. Further research issues in group development

CEDA has been applied to two case studies using computer-mediated communication. The methodology should be implemented in other fields to verify its validity. Group interaction has been explored in this book but in most instances groups have defined boundaries. A group is only one type of social network. Other social networks disrupt boundaries and are much more complex social systems. To help analyse such circumstances, CEDA could be extended to include techniques such as *social network analysis*. Social network analysis focuses on patterns of relationships between people, organisations, information processing systems, and so forth, to extract prominent patterns, trace flows of information and discover the effects of such relations on ever-widening social networks.

This research has explored extensively the development of computer-mediated collaborative groups. Understandably, industry and academic institutions are cautious about implementing computer-mediated collaboration, claiming there is no substitute for face-to-face collaboration. However, when the richness of group interaction is desired with people who cannot easily meet face-to-face due to geographical, temporal, individual preferences, etc., then online collaboration is a viable alternative. Computer-mediated groups do exhibit characteristics of their face-to-face counterparts, such as a developmental process, personal disclosures and cohesiveness. There are many group characteristics that were not addressed in this research, such as age, gender and culture. Much more needs to be known about how these *human factors impact on computer-mediated collaborative groups*. For example, do older group members take longer to get to know each other? do women talk more than men? do women disclose personal information more than men? do groups comprised of cultures that are typically high-context communicators (Hall, 1981) have a different developmental pattern?

The outcomes of this research can also provide the basis for further research in the area of *visualisation of group development and evolution*. Mapping group features to visual attributes is the key step in this direction. In this book, timelines were used to visualise group communication, relating each utterance type to the time it appeared. An alternative way to visualise group interaction is to investigate representations of the flow of ideas in either synchronous or asynchronous communication. Further research will be necessary to identify which visualisation attributes can be used to convey meaning, importance, emergence of leadership or other relationships between group members.

Awareness is an intrinsic part of interaction. Context awareness is a fundamental concern in the area of ubiquitous computing. Much of the research in the field is focused on unveiling each others external activities. In virtual worlds, where each person is represented (embedded) by an avatar these include different indicators of presence, including position, orientation, direction of movement, gestures. These indicators assist in so-called self-awareness, where group members are not only aware of others, but also of themselves within the virtual world and, to some extent, how others perceive them. Utterances in virtual worlds was described in Chapter 6. An interesting research issue is concerned with *identifying communication patterns that relate to the awareness of group members in the virtual world* and how these patterns evolve with the group development. The methodology proposed in the book would allow different data (e.g. movements, gestures) to be related.

9.4.2. Further research issues in leadership

While this research identified communication characteristics that define emergent leaders, further investigation could focus on the *contingency attributes* of these utterances. In Case Study 1, for example, the posts that were catalysts in changing the direction of the process of the project were invariably from either assigned or emergent leaders.

The widespread adoption of advanced communication technologies in organisations has brought about an increased "flattening" {Sproull, 1986 #86} of organisational structures, which leads to the emergence of informal groups. Knowing the structure of such emergent groups and their emergent leaders is invaluable for management. The development of methods for identifying such structures and emergent leaders is one of the future directions that stems from this research. These methods could incorporate elements of *social network analysis for discovering and analysing hidden "structures"* in mediated groups and identifying potential leaders. The research presented used a coding scheme to identify utterances that were addressed to an individual or group and utterances that were received by particular individuals. The extraction of such information can be automated to a greater extent, using the "To" and "From" fields. If the frequency of email exchange between two individuals is above a certain threshold over a period of time, then it can be assumed that these individuals are linked. The resultant network model of group would reveal a structure in which each individual would be represented by a node. Potential leaders could be identified by the values of node statistics and further validated by the methodology proposed in the book.

9.4.3. Further research issues in computer-mediated (online) learning

Methods and research techniques developed in this book have been tested on a case study from the area of computer-mediated (online) learning. Group development is one of the key components of social learning in online learning strategies. The research approach and techniques presented here are appropriate for conducting detailed study of social learning in virtual learning environments. The initial hypotheses of such study and the coding scheme for data analysis could be based on different aspects of social learning identified by Salomon and Perkins (1998), e.g.:

- *pro-active social mediation of individual learning* – investigating how group members help each other in the learning process
- *social mediation as participatory knowledge construction* – the investigation of this aspect will treat the individual and the social mediation of learning as an integrated and highly situated system in which communication utterances within the group are the "socially shared vehicles of thought";
- *cultural aspects of social mediation* – investigating the impact of cultural norms in collaborative learning as some cultures tend to be more collaborative than others (Hofstede, 1980; 1991).
- *the social learner and the group as a learning system* – investigating strategies for learning to learn in groups or organisations as a collective entity for knowledge acquisition and the impact of the group culture on understanding of learning materials and development of different skills;
- *the impact of learning social content* – extending the content-dependent analysis technique described in this book to further investigate how group members use different strategies in resolving conflicts and reaching consensus in decision making.

9.5. Summary

This research proposed ten hypotheses, nine of which were supported for Case Study 1, and eight of which were supported for Case Study 2. This represents significant progress towards understanding computer-supported collaborative groups. In particular, the following contributions to knowledge in this area are highlighted:

- A new methodology – Complementary Explorative Data Analysis (CEDA) – was developed which enabled Internet research to be explored vigorously. CEDA takes into account research assumptions that are specific to Internet studies and provides an iterative design of intuition, description and prediction in research. It provides for a synergistic combination of qualitative and quantitative methods of analysis.
- An understanding of how computer-mediated collaborative groups develop through recurrent phases of activity and reflection.
- A set of criteria to identify potential emergent leaders in computer-mediated collaborative groups.

The implications for theories relating to virtual teams in organisations and virtual communities in education have been discussed and several directions for future research have also been identified.

CASE STUDY 1 DOCUMENTS

A.1. Bad email posters drive out good ("Levine's Law")

The post entitled "Bad email posters drive out good", reproduced below in full, was the inspiration for the ProjectH study. This post initiated a long thread which eventually developed into the research project.

```
Date: Mon, 25 May 1992 13:40:00 PDT
Sender: "Computer Mediated Communication"
<CMC%RPIECS.BITNET@pucc.Princeton.EDU>
From: LEVINE2%UCBCMSA.BITNET@pucc.Princeton.EDU
Subject: Bad email posters drive out good
To: Multiple recipients of list CMC <CMC%RPIECS.BITNET@pucc.Princeton.EDU>

This posting describes the immodestly titled "Levine's Law": Bad postings
drive out good.  That is, as an electronic conversation becomes more
popular, those people who have too much time on their hands will make a
disproportionate fraction of the postings.  These postings, in turn, will
drive out those who have more intersting things to contribute.

Consider a scenario.  A few interesting people begin a conversation on the
network.  By virtue of being  interesting, most of them have a high marginal
value of their time.  (The correlation is not perfect.  Some very
interesting people are isolated, and have high relative value of
communication time.  Such folk will contribute many interesting postings.)

Being busy, these folk post an average of one message / week.  Because of
the high density of interesting postings, many new people listen, and begin
to contribute occasionally.

Some of the newcomers are not busy, and begin to contribute more and more.
On average, the less busy are also less interesting.  (This holds only _on
average_, since lots of very interesting people have time to spare.)

As the proportion of postings from non-busy rises, it is no longer worth the
while of some of the busy folk to contribute.  They drop out, further
lowering the proportion of their (on average interesting) contributions.

This process continues until the conversation falls prey to Levine's Law.
What Gresham described for the currency of his day (Bad money drives out
good, referring to gold and silver), I propose for the information-currency
of today.
```

The typical reader of this posting participates in electronic conversations,
and views his or her own time as valuable. Thus, it will be hard to
convince readers of this posting of the merits of this law. All you must do
is note either (1) you   are in the early stages of a conversation,
before the less interesting have noticed it; (2) your conversations are
isolated by medium or topic from the less interesting; or (3) you are one of
the minority who is both interesting and has lots of time of time.

Comments on this posting, particularly concerning cases where it has played
out, or reasons why it (sometimes) is avoided, are greatly appreciated.

A.2. Straw man proposal

Date: Fri, 29 May 1992 00:27:16 IST
Sender: "Computer Mediated Communication"
<CMC%RPIECS.BITNET@pucc.Princeton.EDU>
From: "Sheizaf Rafaeli 02-827676 (Israel)"
<KBUSR%HUJIVM1.BITNET@pucc.Princeton.EDU>
To: Multiple recipients of list CMC <CMC%RPIECS.BITNET@pucc.Princeton.EDU>

THINGS TO DO - "straw man" outline.
IN RE: Study of discussions on e-mail

OK. Here goes. I'm in this for the experience. Put my keyboard where my
mouth is. I've been claiming (for ten years) that e-mail holds the
potential to form communities out of thin air (thin bits?). Have been,
mostly, ridiculed. So lets give it a try.

I will be travelling a lot this summer, but will be next to a modem at most
times. So... lets try: All are invited to add, take away, and, mostly,
sign their names to working out, investigating and/or reporting on any
of the following items.

I broke the tasks down to four categories: Generating hypotheses,
codebook, identification of lists, and actual coding. I am sure there
will be many volunteers for analysis...

I am untroubled by the qualitative/quantitative rift. Let a thousand
methods blossom.

Standing proposal: Let's see if we can sustain discussion of the
following points for a few weeks, and aim for crystallized codebook
and sample within a month or two?

1) Generate Hypotheses
   Conceptually, what are we looking for?

   Dependent measures include:
      a. Length of threads: number of "turns taken", spread over time,
         time-intervals between exchanges.
      b. Variability of threads: # of "new ideas", # of different
         participants, extent of verbalized 'agreement' generated.
      c. Spates of protest, flaming, "resignations".
         OTHERS?

Hypotheses mentioned so far:
  a. "Levine"s original: bad postings drive out good.
  b. Contribution level (ratio of posters to lurkers) predicts longevity.
    b(1). Talkativity predicts leadership.
  c. Gender differences among posters, social position of posters.
  d. Related to (c): gender _balance_ may have an effect.
  e. The presence of a moderator affects length of discussion.
  f. Status: students vs. faculty, etc. makeup of participants
  g. Too-Long posts are (reading and) discussion killers.
  h. Too interesting posts generate 'break-off' phenomena.
  OTHERS?

2) Generate CodeBook
  - Should, of course be based on hypotheses, but hypotheses
    are also constrained by what is possible here.
  - Code specific messages, headers, threads?
    Can we identify writers, status, location?
    Identify length of messages, # of "new" ideas", time of posting
  - identify back-references to same discussion
  - identify references to external sources: sci. journals, newspapers, tv,
    personal communication, etc.
        OTHERS?

3) Identify list of LISTS to sample from and agree on sampling scheme
  - What is an acceptable minimum sample size: in list numbers, thread
    numbers, etc.?
  - Need to identify accessible, archived lists (I think both
    Bitnet and Usenet, if possible Compuserve SIGS, Genie, Freenet, Bix,
    Fidonet, (others ?) should be included, as long as they comply with
    being accessible and archived over some period).
  - Need to decide on sampling frame (one week, six months...?)
  - Stratify the sample (?), to ensure representation of:
        - moderated vs. unmoderated lists?
        - technical vs. nontechnical?
        - "old", established vs. new or forming?
        - "technical", vs. humanities, soc. sciences?
        - academic vs. general interest
        - subsidized vs. 'expensive'
        - selective vs. open
        - lists that have 'code of ethics' vs. those that do not?
  - Shall we insist on using only lists that publish or make available
    lists of users? (Alternatively, we can use the stats only for those
    lists that provide such info).
    OTHERS?

4) Divide coding effort among participants:
  - attention to some overlap, to get mesasure of reliability of coding
  - set time frame for work completed

  Expressed interest so far:

  Brenda Danet, Hebrew Univ., KCUBD@HUJIVM1
  Jim Thomas,   , TK0JUT1@niu.bitnet
  "Levine"" ?
  Johannes van Veen (Amsterdam)
  Jim McGregor
  Ruth *** (Alaska)
  *don't remember name (from Victoria, Australia)
  Valerie Wagoner, (?), wagovs@morekypr (?)
  Doug Brent, Calgary (?),

Sheizaf Rafaeli, Hebrew Univ., KBUSR@HUJIVM1 or sheizafr@shum.huji.ac.il
        OTHERS?

Sorry, I haven't kept track of all e-mail addresses. Please help. Please use
the quoting mechanisms of mailers sparingly. Some of us operate at 2400 baud
or less, and scrolling through a lot of familiar text is a waste of time.

A.3. Poll to CMC-L

Date: Sat, 6 Jun 1992 09:15:58 +0200
Sender: "Computer Mediated Communication"
   <CMC%RPIECS.BITNET@pucc.Princeton.EDU>
From: sheizaf rafaeli <sheizafr@SHUM.HUJI.AC.IL>
Subject: E-group poll
To: Multiple recipients of list CMC <CMC%RPIECS.BITNET@pucc.Princeton.EDU>

In the interests of furthering a collaborative quantitative study, we'd like
to take a poll on four practical questions. Responses are necessary to help
plan the sampling strategy, and realize which hypotheses are answerable by
the data we'll collect.

To respond to this poll, please mail your answers to either
fays@archsci.arch.su.oz.au, or sheizafr@shum.huji.ac.il, or
KBUSR@HUJIVM1.bitnet.

Please do not respond to the list. We will collect, collate and report.

We are assuming a joint effort to content-analyze a cross section, cross-
time sample of discussions on e-mail lists and groups. We are further
assuming an attempt to share the work.

1. Are you willing to take part in the work involved in a quantitative
    study?

2. How much time do you anticipate you will be able to contribute between
    now and 30 September?
    (a)   8 hours
    (b)   4 days
    (c)   1 week
    (d)   2 weeks
    (e)   1 month or more

3. Which of the following do you prefer?
    (a)   Stay on CMC: let the discussion be open to more joiners,
          suggestions, and public scrutiny.
    (b)   Break off into a separate group. The congestion on CMC and
          suggestions from non-participants are counterproductive.
    (c)   I have no preference.

4. Following, is a list of suggested items for the codebook. Please feel
    free to add to these. For each of the items on the list (including your
    additions), please do two things:
    (a)   Rank the items. Use #1 to mark the item that is most important to
          you, down to #25 (?) to indicate that this is the first item you
          would toss, in the interests of brevity.
    (b)   Indicate at least two items for which you will be willing to
          tackle the task of writing a codebook definition and your
          hypothesis(es). We'll need a few paragraphs for each item

remaining on our list, including examples and 'critical cases', that will serve as coding instructions for all of us.

Don't send these yet. We'll have to see if there is enough interest first.

Note that some of the item titles may be ambiguous. For each item, If you think the ambiguity can be straightened out, say so. Otherwise, mark it as a candidate for deletion.

* Length of messages (in words)
* Timing (from header, compared to some base line)
* Language of message
* Location of author (continent, country, university)
* Presence and nature of subject header
* Presence and nature of stylized signature
* Writer status
* Writer gender
* Use of humor? (or finer: sarcasm, mockery, self-deprecation.)
* Dependency on previous messages (pointer to most recent relevant post)
* Use of quotes from previous posts
* Reference, quote or cross posting to/from other lists?
* Reference to external communication sources (journals, mass media)
* Mobilizing communication, (that is, call for action by others)
* Classification of message to content category (probably need specific categories for each list analyzed).
* Tone (sarcasm, information, plea, threat, support, 'lecture')
* Use of questions, challenges
* Extent of use of nonverbal cues in message (emoticons, smilies)
* Presence of "flames"
* Metacommunication, that is communication about communication
* Is there a personal interest vested in message?
* Discussion of 'ownership' or proprietary nature of info on list?
* Use of the plural "we" (and other forms of expressing community)
* Use of greetings for newcomers
* Disclosure of self or intimate info: introductions.

As noted above, please respond to either fays@archsci.arch.su.oz.au, or sheizafr@shum.huji.ac.il, or KBUSR@HUJIVM1.bitnet.

Thanks,

Sheizaf Rafaeli, Hebrew University, Jerusalem
and Fay Sudweeks, University of Sydney

A.4. Invitation to Join Ongoing Research Project

This is an invitation to join an exciting ongoing research project, on the use of electronic mail discussion lists. A large group of scholars, from numerous universities, is engaged in a collaborative study of discussion lists. This is a last-chance offer to jump on the bandwagon.

For over eight months, a group of several dozen researchers has been discussing the state of computer-mediated discussion groups, and the state of research on such groups. We are now collaborating in a large, comparative survey of such groups. The method of choice is content analysis of a representative sample of messages, groups and discussion threads, across different networks.

The project has produced, so far:

> ** A unique research experience:*
>> A large group of previously unaffiliated researchers has undertaken (and is carrying out) a collaborative study. The research is run, so to speak, on stage.
> ** A joint bibliography:*
>> Hundreds of citations about the subject matter have been collected and are shared.
> ** Hypothesis list:*
>> A rather elaborate set of theories and hypotheses has been formulated regarding the experience, quality, longevity, nature structure and impact of computer-mediated groups, and their structural and social characteristics.
> ** Policy deliberations:*
>> We have painstakingly developed treatments of such thorny issues as the ethics of studying online public lists, the ownership of data resulting from such collaboration, sampling procedures in the study of online groups, etc.
> ** Some financial support from industry.*
> ** A pretested codebook.*
> ** Several conference papers.*

But the best is yet to come. We are about to begin the full-fledged data collection stage. Thus, now is probably the latest oppportunity to join in.

Take part in the data collection and analysis phases. If the computer-mediated exchange of ideas is a process that intrigues you, if you have ideas about what makes online groups tick (or sick), if you think this is a topic ripe for empirical, content-analysis comparative study, and if you would like to join work in this project, please contact one of us:

Sheizaf Rafaeli
Hebrew University of Jerusalem
sheizafr@shum.cc.huji.ac.il

Fay Sudweeks
University of Sydney
fays@arch.su.edu.au

A.5. Welcome to the Project

Thanks for responding to our invitation and for your interest in the content analysis project.

We have been using a "private" hotline, through COMSERVE, to "meet". This hotline is called ProjectH on Rpitsvm. To subscribe, you need to send a message to LISTSERV@RPITSVM or listserv@vm.its.rpi.edu containing a single line:

Subscribe ProjectH Your Name

Please note that this "hotline" is private. This is not to be secretive. In fact, the archives of discussions are available to all. We just want to establish the workgroup, task-oriented nature of the list.

If you wish to leave the hotline at any time, send a message to LISTSERV@RPITSVM or listserv@vm.its.rpi.edu containing a single line:

 Signoff ProjectH

You can catch up on recent activities by accessing the archives of ProjectH. To do so, simply send the commands REVIEW, HELP, INDEX, or GET to LISTSERV@RPITSVM or listserv@vm.its.rpi.edu. You can also catch up on our activities over the past twelve months by transferring the following files from our ftp site:

FTP:	archsci.arch.su.edu.au
Directory:	pub/projectH
Files:	ethics.policy
	copyright.policy
	sampling.statement
	reliability.statement
	projecth.bib.4-93
	projecth.bios.2-93

A prerequisite to coding is a pretest. The purpose of the pretest is to provide each coder with an opportunity to complete a practice run, ask questions and realise problems. Each coder must code the same nine messages using a pretest version of the codebook. The messages and codebook are also stored on our ftp site:

Files:	pretest.messages
	pretest.codebook

If you have difficulty in retrieving the files by ftp, please let us know and we'll mail them to you. Send your completed pretest to fays@archsci.arch.su.edu.au and then a batch of 100 messages, and other necessary material will be sent to you.

We are at different stages of the coding process - some are still pretesting, some have begun real coding, some have completed coding full lists. On our immediate agenda are: (1) completing the full coding process, (2) organising "on site" and "net" workshops, and (3) maintaining an annotated bibliography on CMC. We have so far maintained a very encouraging cordial and supportive tone. We hope to keep both that and the pace of progress.

We ask that you complete the following form and send it back along with a short (a paragraph is sufficient) bio. Then once you've joined ProjectH, please just jump in and introduce yourself to the list. As you'll need to catch up with other coders, you should ftp the pretest files, and complete the pretest as soon as possible.

We think we have something quite special going here. We're glad to have more people involved, delighted to have you involved. Looking forward to your participation in both the discussions and actual coding!

Fay and Sheizaf
fays@archsci.arch.su.edu.au
sheizafr@shum.cc.huji.ac.il

PROJECTH PARTICIPATION

When you have completed the pretest, a batch of messages and the final version of the codebook will be sent to you. The codebook has a written set of instructions including definitions, examples and measurement scales. Please let us know how much time you will be able to contribute to this stage of the project.

[ ]   I am willing to take part in the coding for the quantitative content analysis study. I anticipate being able to contribute:
[ ] 2 days (code approximately 100 messages)
[ ] 4 days (code approximately 200 messages)
[ ] 1 week (code approximately 300 messages)
[ ] more than 1 week (code approximately 500 messages)

during the following period:
[ ] _____

Please fill in and send to fays@archsci.arch.su.edu.au.

A.6. Copyright Policy

The content analysis data produced by the collaboration of ProjectH members is subject to the following conditions.
1. The processed data, defined as the data that is pulled together, cleaned, and in any way compiled from the raw data, is the result of considerable effort by members of the ProjectH Research Group, and is the intellectual property of ProjectH members participating in the work.
2. The data is copyright to "ProjectH Research Group" and included in the copyright notice will be the full list of current members.
3. Any individual or group who uses the processed data, either in part or in full, must acknowledge the source of the data as "ProjectH Research Group".
4. Initial access to the processed data is dependent upon participation rate. Access is granted as follows:
    * *Senior ProjectH members* have immediate access to and use of data, subject to conditions 3 and 5. Senior membership is achieved by substantial contribution to the quantitative research project. Substantial contribution is deemed to be coding a complete list sample (100 messages) in addition to pretest coding, development of codebook and/or membership of a ProjectH committee.
    * *Junior ProjectH members* have access to and use of data six months after the data set is finalized, subject to conditions 3 and 5. Junior membership is achieved by minimal contribution to the quantitative research project. Minimal contribution is deemed to be participation in pretest coding, development of codebook and/or membership of a ProjectH committee.
    * *ProjectH members* who have not contributed to the quantitative research project have access to and use of data eighteen months after the data set is finalized, subject to conditions 3 and 5.
    * The data will be made available for public access and use twenty-four months after the data set is finalized subject to conditions 3 and 5.
5. ProjectH members who have access privileges may release data to their graduate research students or collaborators, subject to condition 3.
6. Access by person(s) other than specified in conditions 4 and 5 is considered on a case-by-case basis by the Copyright Committee. Appeals against Copyright Committee decisions are brought before the current ProjectH members and decisions overruled by 60% of members.
7. The processed data is stored on an ftp site with restricted (non-anonymous) access.
8. Any participant(s) who is about to commence a research project based solely or principally on the data, is required to register the general nature of the research with the ProjectH coordinators. A list of current research projects and principal investigators will be available for

FTP with updates sent to ProjectH monthly. If requested by principal investigators, and approved by the coordinators, details of the research project can be kept confidential. Neither coordinators, nor ProjectH, may censor or censure any topic, or in any way interfere or hinder the academic freedom of any investigator.

9. Any person producing a paper, article, chapter, report, monograph or book from the processed data, either in part or in full, is to notify the ProjectH Research Group. In addition, it is requested that any or all papers based on this data be submitted in ASCII and/or postscript to the ftp repository.

10. The codebook, which is the product of considerable effort by members of the ProjectH Research Group, is the intellectual property of all ProjectH members. The codebook is copyright to "ProjectH Research Group" and included in the copyright notice a list of current members. Any individual or group who uses the codebook must acknowledge the source as "ProjectH Research Group".

11. The annotated bibliography, which is the product of considerable effort by members of the ProjectH Research Group, is the intellectual property of all ProjectH members. The annotated bibliography is copyright to "ProjectH Research Group" and included in the copyright notice is a list of current members.

A.7. Ethics Policy

1. Members of the ProjectH Research Group acknowledge and affirm the individual rights of informed consent, privacy, and intellectual property. We are all committed to reducing censorship and prior restraint. We believe the issue of informed consent of authors, moderators and/or archiving institutions does not apply to the ProjectH quantitative content analysis, as we intend to analyze only publicly available text. We believe public posts are public and their use is governed by professional and academic guidelines.

2. Each member of ProjectH will ensure that his/her participation in this project, data collection and analysis procedures does not violate the standards of his/her own institution's Human Subjects Committee or equivalent.

3. In this project, we will use only texts that are posted to public lists and are publicly available

4. In the quantitative content analysis data collection process, the ProjectH group as a whole will observe the following policy regarding 'writers' (authors of messages in our sample), 'messages' (obvious), and 'groups' (the collections of contributors and readers of content in computer-mediated contexts.

   - Informed consent will not be sought in advance for the quantitative content analysis of publicly available messages.
   - No individual writer will be identified by name in either data collection or data set, unless that writer has been contacted, and her/his consent was obtained in writing.
   - Except for short excerpts of 1 or 2 sentences, no messages will be quoted, in any data set, paper or publication, unless the author of the message was contacted and her/his approval was obtained in writing.
   - Statements and findings about groups of contributors will avoid identifying individuals.

5. We will take all measures necessary to separate names of authors and groups from any data collected, measured, or assessed. Individual authors will be identified only by a number. The association of person and identifying number will be kept confidential.

A.8. Sampling Statement

Objectives and Constraints

The objectives of the sampling strategy are many and conflicting. The more critical objectives are:

1. Maintaining enough randomness to allow conclusions about as broad a range of CMC as possible.
2. Obtaining enough data from each group (newsgroup or list) to draw conclusions about the group.
3. Sampling a wide range of groups with diverse characteristics. Among the characteristics of interest to some of us are:
   * readership and authorship
   * list volume (messages per day or week)
   * average number of concurrent threads
   * average duration of threads
   * type of group (i.e., technical, recreational, etc.)
   * type of distribution (i.e., free vs. paid)
4. Learning about CMC and human interaction.

At the same time, we operate under certain constraints:

1. Limited human resources both for coding and for analysis of the types of groups.
2. Limited availability of data, both list contents and list statistics.

The Sampling Continuum

A sampling strategy, given the objectives stated above, lies on a continuum between random selection and stratification. We believe that the constraints posed above will limit us to 50 or 60 groups. We considered two extreme proposals:

1. *Complete random sampling.* Just pick any groups from any of the lists. This has the advantage of randomness, but the disadvantage of likely leading to the selection of inappropriate groups (perhaps groups with only announcements, automated postings, or test messages), and might well result in a sample that is poorly representative of the entirety of the networked experience. This is particularly the case on Usenet, for example, where there are relatively many low-volume groups and relatively few high-volume ones.
2. *Heavy stratification.* Select a set of strata and sample from within the strata. For example, given 60 groups, we would be sure to select 30 high-volume and 30 low-volume. Perhaps 20 each from Compuserve, Bitnet, and Usenet. And so forth. This has the clear problem that we would be unable to select much randomly, and even a few strata would lead to unacceptably few measures per category.

Accordingly, we examined the following compromises:

1. *Weighted random sampling with a weighting factor based on the volume, authorship, and readership.* We concluded that we did not yet know enough about the domain to derive a meaningful weighting function that would capture the "normality" of a group.
2. *Purely random sampling.* This had the problem that we would not be likely to sample enough groups from certain domains (i.e., Compuserve) to draw conclusions about the difference between pay and free services.
3. *Random sampling over a more restricted domain with stratification by the type of list.* This strategy limits the groups under consideration to exclude:
   * foreign language lists
   * local lists
   * announcement lists
   * help/support lists for specific products
   * test and control groups
   * lists whose contents are only excerpts of other lists selected by moderators

- extremely low volume lists (i.e., lists with fewer than 25 messages and 3 authors during a selected test month)
4. The stratification will select equal numbers of lists from Compuserve, Bitnet, and Usenet. If the number of lists is not a multiple of three, the extra lists will be selected randomly from all groups.

It is this final strategy which we propose to adopt.

We propose to select randomly from all lists and reject those meeting the exclusion criteria above. Where possible, this rejection will be accomplished in advance by not considering clearly inappropriate groups. Otherwise, groups will be rejected as they are chosen. Lists that are primarily flames or other "degenerate" cases will be accepted and coded as long as they meet these criteria on the grounds that they too hold interesting scientific results and may be reflective of a segment of the CMC experience.

Once lists are selected, we will sample 100 messages or 3 days worth of messages, whichever is greater. This is to allow us to observe and code threads with sufficient time for e-mail lag and response. The selection period shall begin on a randomly selected Monday for which message data is available. While we considered pure random selection, we consider it unwise to try to compare weekend data with weekday data until we have a better understanding of the domain. Weekend data will be included in most low and medium volume groups. In addition, we will pre-process an additional 100 messages or 3 days worth of messages, whichever is greater, BEFORE the sampling region to provide extra thread and author information for coding.

Precoding

To assist coders and provide greater information, we will be pre-coding messages, including both messages in the sample and those before it, to identify authors and subject classifications. With each batch of messages, coders will get a list of authors with author ID numbers and a list of subjects with subject ID numbers. These numbers will be unique across the entire study to allow us to exploit the opportunity should authors participate in multiple lists or should a thread exist in or move across several lists. To the extent possible, this process will be automated and will simplify coding for each coder.

List Statistics

In addition to the message coding statistics, we will attempt to obtain list statistics. Of particular interest are the following, though additional ones are likely to be added:

1. Average number of postings per day in a one-month period
2. Number of authors in a one-month period
3. Number of readers in a one-month period
4. Average message length
5. Average thread length (# of messages)
6. Average length of threads longer than 2 messages
7. Average thread duration (# of days)
8. Average duration of threads longer than 2 messages
9. % of messages in threads
10. Editorial status (moderated, unmoderated)
11. Topic (Academic, Technical, Social, etc.)
12. Age of List (New, Old)

A.9. Reliability Statement

The following statement on reliability represents a month of intense discussions and a compromise among the many and varied opinions of the "reliability group". We consider, however, it is sufficiently flexible to satisfy both casual inquirers and restrictive publishing standards.

There are a number of ways to collect reliability data. We considered two that are proposed by Klaus Krippendorff (*Content Analysis*, Sage, 1980):

1. *Test-standard:* "The degree to which a process functionally conforms to a known standard." This involves training all coders to a standard set by "expert" coders and accepting as coders only those who code to the preset level of accuracy.
2. *Test-test:* "The degree to which a process can be recreated under varying circumstances." This involves using at least two coders for the same data to establish the reproducibility of results.

Given the unprecedented nature of our project, the unavailability of an established standard, and the number of coders involved, we propose to adopt a test-test design as follows.

1. Each coder must code the nine pretest messages using the pretest codebook. Completion of the pretest is a prerequisite for real coding. The purpose of this is to provide all an opportunity to complete a practice run, ask questions, realize problems, etc.
2. Everything will be coded twice. In other words, each 'list' (or batch) of 100 messages will be coded by two coders. We now have sufficient coding power (participants) to do this. It is crucial that each coder codes independently. Communication among coders introduces errors and makes data appear more reliable than they are. Independence of coding will be maintained as follows:

   - each 'list' (batch of 100 messages) will be randomly assigned to two coders
   - the list assignment will be kept confidential
   - each coder will receive assigned lists privately
   - guidelines will be posted to ProjectH for avoiding coding discussions that threaten reliability
   - everyone is requested to ensure specific comments or quotes from messages are avoided in discussions with other group members, except "oracles" (see 4 below), either privately or publicly.

   These strategies will provide us with full reliability figures.

3. We will set a threshold for an acceptable level of bi-coder agreement. In cases where this threshold is not reached, we will have a third coder deal with corpora/data. In other words, while all messages get double coded, we'll set a tolerable level of ambiguity. Any list (or pair of coders) that does not achieve that level of agreement, will be given to a third "blind" coder who will code the divergent variable(s). If the third coder codes the problematic variable(s) in a way that coincides with one of the two previous coders, then we accept the two consistent data. If the third coder's coding is different from both of the two previous coding attempts, we will use the original two coders' data and mark as 'unagreed'.

4. We will recruit a small number of "oracles" for sets of variables. Questions on the codebook will be directed privately to the oracle for that question. The question to the oracle may be specific and include quotes but the oracle will respond with a summary of general comments to ProjectH. We will also appoint a "Commissioner of Oracles" to coordinate this effort.

A.10. Codebook

Date: April 1993.
Copyright (C) ProjectH
This codebook has been developed by participants of ProjectH. It is the product of much work and we take the copyright notice seriously.

Included here are:
* Methodology
* Coding formats
* Information about coding questionnaire
* Long description of variables
* A short one-page description of variables

METHODOLOGY

You will be given batches of 100 messages. The first six variables will be precoded for you:

CODERID
LISTID
MSGNUM
AUTHORID
MSGTIME
MSGDATE

You will code the remaining variables for each message. For coding, you may use a hypercard stack on the Macintosh, a database on DOS, or any text editor or wordprocessor. Instructions and programs for these formats are available by anonymous ftp from archsci.arch.su.edu.au. Codes may be entered directly into one of these programs or written on paper first. A codeform is available if you prefer to work this way.

Each list will be coded by two people. It is important for the reliability of our data that each coder codes independently. If you need clarification on coding or variable descriptions, you should contact an "oracle" privately. Questions to the oracle may be specific and include quotes but the oracle will respond with a summary of general comments to ProjectH.

If there is absolutely no way you can code a variable, use 9 (except the 4-column DEPEND2, which will be coded 9999 as indicated). Make a note in the codebook questionnaire (see separate file) for every time you've chosen this drastic measure.

CODING FORMATS

You may use one of the following formats to enter data:
1) Hypercard stack for the Macintosh
2) File Express database for DOS
3) Text editors/wordprocessors for any platform
4) Codeform for pen and paper

1) HYPERCARD STACK (for the Macintosh)

Retrieve these files by anonymous ftp from archsci.arch.su.edu.au (in the directory pub/projectH):
coding-stack.hqx [ascii]

hypercard.doc [ascii]

Note: if you have problems with the coding-stack.hqx file, type "binary" at the ftp> prompt and then transfer again. Reset ftp for ascii files by typing "ascii".

+ "coding-stack.hqx" is a HyperCard stack in binhex 4 format.

+ "hypercard.doc" contains instructions for installing the stack and using it for recording your ProjectH data.

If you transferred these files onto a mainframe you will have to use a communications program to get them onto a Macintosh.

To use this method you must have a Macintosh computer with HyperCard 2.1, AND a program which can decode files from binhex 4. Some programs that do this include Compact Pro, Stuffit Expander (or Stuffit Classic or Stuffit Deluxe), DownLine, and dehqx-2.

If you have not downloaded files to a Macintosh before, you might want to ask some help from your local computing services staff.

2) FILE EXPRESS (database for DOS)

(To use File Express you must have an IBM or IBM compatible computer with DOS and a hard drive.)

Use anonymous ftp to get these files from archsci.arch.su.edu.au (in directory pub/projectH)
fileE.zip [binary]
pkunzip.exe [binary]
fileE.doc [ascii]

Note: to get a binary file, type "binary" at the ftp> prompt before getting the file. To reset ftp for ascii files, type "ascii".

+ "fileE.zip" is the File Express program, compressed with the pkzip utility

+ "pkunzip.exe" is the utility for uncompressing File Express from the fileE.zip file.

+ "fileE.doc" contains instructions for installing File Express on your hard drive and using it for data entry.

3) TEXT EDITORS & WORD PROCESSORS (any platform)

Get these files by anonymous ftp from archsci.arch.su.edu.au:
ed-template [ascii]
editor.doc [ascii]
codeform.txt [ascii]

Save them anywhere on your computer system that is convenient for you.

+ The "editor.doc" file contains instructions for how to use a text editor or word processor to enter your data for ProjectH.
It describes two formats for entering data; use whichever one you like best.

+ "ed-template" is a template file for data entry; you will need to make copies of it to type your data in if you are using the first format described in "editor.doc".

4) CODEFORM (for entering codes on paper first)

Get this file by anonymous ftp from archsci.arch.su.edu.au:
codeform.txt [ascii]

+ "codeform.txt" is a form you can print and reproduce if you want to write your coding on paper before entering the data on the computer.

CODING QUESTIONNAIRE

In addition to message coding statistics, we are attempting to obtain information about individual coders, the technology being used by coders, impressions of the lists being coded, and problems experienced. Please complete the Coding Questionnaire (available by anonymous ftp from archsci.arch.su.edu.au) for every list you code.

LONG DESCRIPTIONS OF VARIABLES

Code No.	Code Label	Column No	Code Description
1	CODERID	1-4	Your coder ID number. THIS IS GIVEN TO YOU.
2	LISTID	5-8	List id number. All messages in a batch will have the same list number. We will designate the number for each list. THIS IS GIVEN TO YOU.
3	MSGNUM	9-12	Message number. The messages will be numbered sequentially. THIS IS GIVEN TO YOU.
4	AUTHORID	13-16	Each author will be identified with a unique number. If the current author has already appeared in the sample on this list, the number used earlier will be reused. Otherwise, since this is a new author, the next number will be used. If the current author includes a message from another person, it will still be coded as the current author. (Note: If you find an error in the automatic coding, either one author given two AUTHORIDs or or two authors given the same AUTHORID, please note this error in the accompanying "comments" file.) THIS IS GIVEN TO YOU.
5	MSGTIME	17-20	The hours and minutes of the message (e.g. 1246) from the Date: field. THIS IS GIVEN TO YOU.
6	MSGDATE	21-26	The month, day and year of message (e.g. 033093) from the Date: field. THIS IS GIVEN TO YOU.
7	MSGLINES	27	Number of lines in the message. Count only lines that contain original (non-quoted) characters. Do not include: automatically appended headers, automatically generated introduction (e.g. "On Thu, 11 Mar 93 Joe said:"), subject line, routing information, verbatim quotes from previous messages or other sources, blank lines between paragraphs, or signatures. Count partial lines as complete lines. In other words, count only lines that contain original (non-quoted) characters. 1 - 1-10 lines of original text (short message) 2 - 11-25 lines of original text (medium message) 3 - 26-100 lines of original text (long message) 4 - 100+ lines of original text (very long message)
8	SUBJECT	28	Is the subject line appropriate? 1 - No 2 - Yes 3 - There is no subject line
9	NOISE	29	Is this message not intended for this list, i.e. is it misdirected (e.g. intended to be a private message or for a listserv or another list), or is it intended for the list but not a regular message (e.g. 'this is a test')? 1 - Not intended for this list, it is misdirected. 2 - This is a regular message. 3 - Intended for the list but not a regular message.
10	FIRSTPER	30	Does the message contain any verbal self disclosure, introduction, admission, or any other "personalizing" content (e.g. "I like opera", "I'm an email junkie",

			"My hair is black" but not "My mother's hair is black" or "My cat is black")? To code YES for this variable, there needs to be a reference to first person "I, me, my, mine". Do not code Yes for "we" or "us". (Note: FIRSTPER is a statement by the author about the author; OPINION is a statement by the author about things/persons other than the author.) 1 - No 2 – Yes
11	OPINION	31	Does this message state (or contain a statement of) an opinion by the author. To be an OPINION, the statement must indicate first person, directly or indirectly, e.g. "I think chocolate is the best flavour ice cream", "Chocolate is a favourite flavour of mine". If first person is not indicated, it is a statement of FACT. 1 - No 2 - Yes, but it's not a main item of content 3 - Yes, it is a main item of content
12	FACT	32	Does this message state (or contain a statement of) a fact? If there is a reference to first person, then code as an OPINION. (Note: to code YES, the fact doesn't have to be accurate, it can be a statement that the writer considers to be a fact, e.g. "The association of Santa Claus with Memorial Day festivities is a Jewish tradition that began in 1994".) 1 - No 2 – Yes
13	APOLOGY	33	Does the message contain any form of apology (e.g. "I am sorry I said what I said", "I take my words back", etc.)? 1 - No 2 - Yes, but only mild, mostly "manner of speech". 3 - Yes, the writer is clearly apologizing.
14	QUESTION	34	Does the message contain a question or request? 1 - No 2 – Yes
15	ACTION	35	Does this message call for action on the part of readers? (e.g. write your congressman, include this in your classes, go see this movie, etc.). (Note: to code YES, the action is generally disjoint from the list. If the action refers to the discussion itself, then code as METACOMM.) 1 - No 2 - Yes, but it's not a main item of content. 3 - Yes, it is a main item of content.
16	CHALLENG E	36	Does the message contain a challenge, dare, bet, or some such (e.g. "I challenge you to support that statement"). 1 - No 2 – Yes
17	HUMOUR	37	Does the message contain (even if only an attempt at) humour (do not judge success)? 1 - No 2 – Yes
18	METACOM M	38	Does the message contain metacommunication, i.e. is its content about how, when, where, what, who or why one should or could communicate? (Examples -- how: "will you please QUIT USING CAPS in your messages, it sounds like shouting"; where: "is this the appropriate list for this?"; what: "what Sheizaf said really should not be allowed on this list"; why: "this is really a waste of bandwidth") 1 - No 2 - Yes, but it's not a main item of content. 3 - Yes, it is a main item of content.
19	FORMAT	39	Is this message formatted with appropriate and consistent use of paragraphs, tabs and spacing, and words not broken at ends of lines? (Note: code short, appropriately formatted messages of one paragraph as "minimal formatting".) 1 - Unformatted (dense, no paragraphs, no tabbing) 2 - Minimal formatting (consistent and regular use of paragraph(s)) 3 - Mostly formatted (consistent and regular use of paragraph(s) paragraphs, tabs, spaced) 4 - Overformatted (too much space, too many paragraphs)
20	STYLE1	40	Does the text of the message under-utilise or over-utilise upper case letters? (If

			caps are used as a device to indicate emphasis or shouting, code as "regular capitalisation") 1 - minimal or no caps 2 - regular capitalisation 3 - mostly or all caps
21	STYLE2	41	Does this message use "colloquial" spelling, e.g. "gotcha", 41 "dunno", "hiya", "'cos". 1 - No 2 – Yes
22	NATURE	42	Here, address the overall nature of the message. Is it: 1 - Primarily providing information 2 - Primarily requesting information 3 - Primarily persuasive 4 - Primarily opinionated 5 - Mixed style
23	EMOTICON	43	Does the BODY OF THE MESSAGE contain icons to express emotion, e.g. :-), :-{), 8-) (also include "stage directions" which are used for the same purpose, e.g. <sigh>, <grin>). 1 - No 2 - One only 3 - More than one
24	EMODEVIC E	44	Does the BODY OF THE MESSAGE contain punctuation devices or capitalisation to express emotion, e.g. CAPS; !#@%$, ..., !!!!!!. (Note: To code in the affirmative, there needs to be an IRREGULAR use of the punctuation/capitalisation specifically to convey a feeling or emotion. The use of one exclamation mark or devices for emphasis or elipses to indicate missing text is not considered irregular.) 1 - No 2 - One only 3 - More than one instance
25	ARTICON	45	ARTICON Does the BODY OF THE MESSAGE contain icons (symbols, signs, drawings, lines, arrows) that are artistic, expressing other than emotion, e.g. -->, @->---, illustrations depicting cats, trains, trees, etc. Do NOT include punctuation, e.g. ..., !#@$. 1 - No 2 - One only 3 - More than one
26	GENDER1	46	GENDER1 Is the writer female or male? (If the writer's name is ambiguous, you can use a combination of clues from the batch of messages you have, e.g. a previous reference to the writer, identifying pronouns, words, comments.) 0 - Can't tell 1 - Female 2 – Male
27	GENDER2	47	GENDER2 How does the writer identify her/his own gender? 47 (Examples: "being a female", "from a male point of view" (directly) or "when I was pregnant", "my wife thinks I should..." (indirectly)) 1 - Does not identify 2 - Name/signature 3 - Directly 4 - Indirectly 5 - Mixture of 2, 3 and 4
28	GENDER3	48	Does the message include any of the following: gender 48 identifications of others either on or off this list (e.g. use of gender specific terms like she/her/Sally he/his/Harry) or ask for gender cues (e.g. "Is <name> male or female?") or include consciously non- specific gender language (e.g. "Whatever s/he thinks")? 1 - No 2 – Yes
29	GENDER4	49	Does the message deal with gender identification as an issue? 1 - No 2 – Yes
30	QUOTE1	50	Is any text (a full sentence or more), quoted VERBATIM from the discussion on THIS list? (Note: count *total* number of quoted lines of text in the message, including single lines and blocks.)

			1 - No discussion quoted (or less than one sentence). 2 - Yes, 1-10 lines 3 - Yes, 11-25 lines 4 - Yes, 26+ lines
31	QUOTE2	51	Is any text (a full sentence or more) quoted VERBATIM from another computer mediated source? (Note: count *total* number of quoted lines of text in the message, including single lines and blocks.) 1 - No discussion quoted (or less than one sentence). 2 - Yes, 1-10 lines 3 - Yes, 11-25 lines 4 - Yes, 26+ lines
32	QUOTE3	52	Is any text (a full sentence or more) quoted VERBATIM from any non-computer-mediated source (books, journals, TV, movies, etc.) (Note: count *total* number of quoted lines of text in the message, including single lines and blocks.) 1 - No discussion quoted (or less than one sentence). 2 - Yes, 1-10 lines 3 - Yes, 11-25 lines 4 - Yes, 26+ lines
33	DEPEND1	53	Does the message contain any reference, directly or indirectly, to previous message(s) on this list (by name, general subject matter, or author)? (Reference can be verbatim AND/OR paraphrased. Code affirmative even if you've already coded YES for QUOTE1.) 1 - Not at all 2 - Yes, one message is referenced. 3 - Yes, more than one message is referenced. 4 - Yes, a SEQUENCE of messages is referenced.
34	DEPEND2	54-57	Indicate the MSGNUM of the LAST message referenced. Use leading zeros (e.g. 0087). If you are unable to indicate the last MSGNUM, code: 0000 - If none is referenced. 9999 - If the last message referenced precedes the batch of messages you have.
35	DEPEND3	58	Does the message contain any reference, directly or indirectly, to the manner in which a previous message(s) related to those preceding it(them)? (i.e. is there any reference to how or whether earlier messages were RESPONSIVE, HELPFUL, ARGUMENTATIVE, QUICK, STUPID, NUMEROUS, etc..) (Note: for a positive response here, the current message should say something about how two or more earlier messages related to each other.) 1 - No 2 – Yes
36	DEPEND4	59	Does the message introduce a new topic? 1 - No, it's clearly part of an ongoing thread. 2 - Yes, with no reference to previous discussion. 3 - Yes, with reference to previous discussion.
37	COALIT1	60	Is there "coalition formation" evident in this message, 60 i.e. does the message include indications of agreement with another person or statement previously appearing on this list (whether IN the sample or PRECEDING it)? (Note: if this is the first message of a batch or a thread, code "No indication".) 1 - Primarily strong agreement 2 - Primarily mild agreement 3 - No indication, only citations or otherwise neutral reference 4 - Both agreement and disagreement 5 - Primarily mild disagreement 6 - Primarily strong disagreement
38	COALIT2	61	Is there use of first person plural, i.e. "we", "us", etc., to refer to others on the list in addition to the author (e.g. "we really should be careful about the ethics of this")? 1 - No 2 – Yes
39	COALIT3	62	Does the message directly address another person(s) on the list (e.g. "Sally, ...", "In your last message, you said ..." but NOT automatically generated introductions such as "On Thu 13 Mar 93, Sally said:")? 1 - No 2 – Yes

40	EXTCOAL	63	Is there "coalition formation" in a broader sense, outside the list, evident in this message, i.e. does the message include indications of agreement with persons, opinions, ideologies, organizations OUTSIDE of the list? (Note: if this is the first message of a batch or a thread, code "No indication".) 1 - Primarily strong agreement 2 - Primarily mild agreement 3 - No indication, only citations or otherwise neutral reference 4 - Both agreement and disagreement 5 - Primarily mild disagreement 6 - Primarily strong disagreement
41	FLAME1	64	How argumentative is the message? This variable asks for an assessment of the opinionated tone of the MESSAGE. (Note: a friendly opinion doesn't contradict another person's opinion; a diverging opinion contradicts another person's opinion without referring directly to the other person.) 1 - Neutral or no opinion 2 - Friendly: opinion given in friendly tone 3 - Diverging: different opinion voiced. 4 - Disagreeing: in direct reference to opposition. 5 - Tension: attacking opposing argument 6 - Antagonistic: attacks opposing participant(s) 7 - Hostile: profanity, tirades, to the point of ignoring original issue.
42	FLAME2	65	Would a "normal" reader conclude that the message contains abusive or coarse LANGUAGE? (Abusive or coarse language includes swearing, insults, name calling, obscene words, and hostile comments.) 1 - There is no abusive language. 2 - Yes, the abusive language is about content only. 3 - Yes, the abusive language is about a person. 4 - Yes, but not about persons or comments on this list (e.g. about the writer her/himself, or generalized others) 5 - Mixed (combination of 1, 2, 3 and 4).
43	FLAME3	66	Does this message state an intention to keep tension from arising, or to calm or alleviate ongoing 'flames', tensions, or arguments? 1 - No 2 - Yes, tries to keep tension from arising 3 - Yes, tries to calm ongoing tension
44	STATUS	67	Does the message (either the header, body of the message or the signature) explicitly identify the personal status of the writer? e.g. The Right Hon. Sheizaf Rafaeli, PhD; Dr Fay Sudweeks III, Chair, Society for the Preservation of the Monarchy. 1 - No 2 – Yes
45	SIGNAT1	68	Signatures are a means of adding `personality' to CMC. A simple signature is a name and/or email address(s). Stylised signatures include nicknames, computer-generated art, additional address information (e.g. fax/phone numbers, postal address) and the use of quotations. Is there a signature? 1 - No 2 - Yes, a simple one (name and/or email address(es)) 3 - Yes, a complex one (text plus name and/or email address(es)) 4 - Yes, a stylised one (articon, whether or not there is text in addition to name and/or email address(es)
46	SISNAT2	69	Is there an ending quotation attached to the signature? 1 - No 2 - Yes

SHORT DESCRIPTIONS OF VARIABLES

No	Variable	Brief Description	Rating Scale
1	CODERID	Supplied	
2	LISTID	Supplied	
3	MSGNUM	Supplied	
4	AUTHORD	Supplied	

5	MSGTIME	Supplied	
6	MSGDATE	Supplied	
7	MSGLINES	No. of lines?	1=1-10, 2=11-25, 3=26-100, 4=100+
8	SUBJECT	Is it appropriate?	0=?, 1=N, 2=Y, 3=NONE
9	NOISE	Misdirected msg?	1=MISDIR, 2=REG, 3=INTENDED
10	FIRSTPER	Self disclosure?	1=N, 2=Y
11	OPINION	Opinion?	1=N, 2=SOME, 3=MOSTLY
12	FACT	Fact?	1=N, 2=Y
13	APOLOGY	Apology?	1=N, 2=MILD, 3=Y
14	QUESTION	Question/request?	1=N, 2=Y
15	ACTION	Action?	1=N, 2=SOME, 3=MOSTLY
16	CHALLENGE	Challenge/dare?	1=N, 2=Y
17	HUMOUR	Humour?	1=N, 2=Y
18	METACOMM	Metacommunication?	1=N, 2=SOME, 3=MOSTLY
19	FORMAT	Format of msg	1=NONE, 2=MIN, 3=MOSTLY, 4=OVER
20	STYLE1	Caps?	1=MIN, 2=REG, 3=MAX
21	STYLE2	Colloq. spelling?	1=N, 2=Y
22	NATURE	Overall style	1=PROV, 2=ASK, 3=PERS, 4=OPIN, 5=MIX
23	EMOTICON	Icon for emotion?	1=N, 2=ONE, 3=ONE+
24	EMODEVICE	Device for emotion?	1=N, 2=ONE, 3=ONE+
25	ARTICON	Other than emotion	1=N, 2=ONE, 3=ONE+
26	GENDER1	Male/female? 0=?,	1=F, 2=M
27	GENDER2	How identify?	1=NOT, 2=N/SIG, 3=DIR, 4=INDIR, 5=MIX
28	GENDER3	Gender cues?	1=N, 2=Y
29	GENDER4	Gender issues?	1=N, 2=Y
30	QUOTE1	From this list?	1=N, 2=1-10, 3=11-25, 4=26+
31	QUOTE2	From other CMC?	1=N, 2=1-10, 3=11-25, 4=26+
32	QUOTE3	From non-CMC?	1=N, 2=1-10, 3=11-25, 4=26+
33	DEPEND1	Ref to prev msg?	1=N, 2=ONE, 3=ONE+, 4=SEQ
34	DEPEND2	Msg no referenced?	MSGNUM, 0000=NONE, 9999=?
35	DEPEND3	Ref to how related?	1=N, 2=Y
36	DEPEND4	New topic?	1=N, 2=Y/NOREF, 3=Y/REF
37	COALIT1	Agree---disagree	1=SA, 2=MA, 3=NONE, 4=BOTH, 5=MD-5, 6=SD
38	COALIT2	Use of "we/us"	1=N, 2=Y
39	COALIT3	Directly address	1=N, 2=Y
40	EXTCOAL	Agree---disagree	1=SA, 2=MA, 3=NONE, 4=BOTH, 5=MD, 6=SD
41	FLAME1	Tone?	1=NEUT, 2=FRI, 3=DIV, 4=DIS, 5=TEN, 6=ANT, 7=HOST
42	FLAME2	Coarse lge?	1=NONE, 2=CON, 3=PER, 4=OTH, 5=MIXED
43	FLAME3	Avoid tension/calm?	1=N, 2=Y/AVOID, 3=Y/CALM
44	STATUS	Status of author?	1=N, 2=Y
45	SIGNAT1	Signature?	1=N, 2=Y/SIMPLE, 3=Y/COMPLEX, 4=Y/STYL
46	SIGNAT2	Quotation?	1=N, 2=Y

A.11. Access to ProjectH Data

This note is coming to you NOT on ProjectH, but directly and personally. You are being contacted as one of the coders, who is now eligible to have first access at the data.

Access to the data set is limited for the first six months to members who have coded at least 100 messages. The unique data set is the result of considerable effort so untimely spreading of the data or news of its location will be harmful to both faculty and graduate students who have worked hard to code the messages.

To ensure, as much as possible, that you adhere to the ethics/copyright policies and do not inappropriately disclose identity of lists and authors, we ask that you re-read the ethics and copyright policies (included below) and request access to the data and accompanying files by completing and returning the form at the end of this note to the "coding" account (coding@archsci.arch.su.edu.au).

The following will be available from our ftp site (archsci.arch.su.edu.au or 129.78.66.1) with access restricted to "senior" members for the first six months:

1) Database in two different formats (with/without delimiters)
2) Data index (explanation of col/row numbers)
3) List id, coder id (identifying number, not coder name), list names, and network
4) Corpora (each list of 100 messages that has been coded)
5) List of author ids and matching author names
6) Coder questionnaires for individual analysis
7) Technical Report which summarises the methodology of sampling, precoding, coding, and reliability calculations. Included will be ProjectH policies and statements.

Here are the latest figures on the database:

| 38 complete lists | 3800 messages |
6 incomplete lists	401 messages
44 lists	4201 messages

These have been coded as follows:

12 coded by 2 people
20 coded by 1 person
----
32 unique lists

There are 199 records outstanding. We are still hoping lists will be completed while we are preparing the Technical Report. If lists are still incomplete when all documents are ready, data from incomplete lists will not be included in the database, but will be available as a separate file.

When released, the data-set will be the full and complete product of phase 1 of ProjectH. This is an important statement, because it places a lid on (and frame around) what will henceforth be termed ProjectH phase 1 data set: the first (and so far only) representative sample of international, public group CMC.

ProjectH Coordinators:
Sheizaf Rafaeli, Fay Sudweeks

Distribution Committee:
Bob Colman, Joe Konstan, Ed Mabry, Peggy McLaughlin, Diane Witmer

A.12. ProjectH Agreement Form

Please complete this form and return to coding@archsci.arch.su.edu.au.

CODER ID:

LIST ID:

NAME:_____

ADDRESS:_____

_____

_____

TELEPHONE:_____ FAX: _____

EMAIL ADDRESS:_____

Type "x" between brackets to indicate an affirmative response
to all the following.

[ ]   I have read and agree to comply with the ethics policy.

[ ]   I have read and agree to comply with the copyright policy.

[ ]   I will ensure that any graduate student or collaborator with
      whom I work, and who will have access to ProjectH data, will
      agree to comply with the policies.

[ ]   I will take reasonable precautions to protect the ProjectH
      data, and especially author-identifying information.

[ ]   I will maintain proper security for computer-stored documents.

[ ]   I request access to the database and accompanying documents.

Please summarise briefly how you intend to maintain confidentiality
of lists and authors when using the data:

_____

_____

_____

A.13. Questionnaire for ProjectH Coders

Date: April 1993.
This document is available via anonymous ftp.
Host: archsci.arch.su.edu.au (129.78.66.1)
File: /pub/projectH/codebook.questionnaire

In addition to message coding statistics, we are attempting to obtain information about individual coders, the technology used by coders, impressions of the lists being coded, and problems experienced. This data will provide supplementary information to the content analysis. Please complete this Coding Questionnaire for every list you have coded. If you prefer not to disclose personal information, you may choose to leave any part or all of question 3 unanswered.

1. CODERID:
(Note: if you are a student or research assistant coding for another ProjectH member, please provide the name of your advisor/supervisor also.)

2. LISTID:

3. PERSONAL DETAILS ABOUT CODER (optional):
Age: <20   [ ]
          21-35   [ ]
          36-50   [ ]
          51-65   [ ]
          >65   [ ]
Sex: Male   [ ]
          Female   [ ]
Place of birth (city/state/country):
Place of residence (city/state/country):
Educational Qualifications:
Occupation/Position:

4. TIMING:
Approximately how long did it take for you to code this list of 100 messages?

5. TECHNOLOGY:
What kind of computer did you use?
          [ ]   Mac
          [ ]   Workstation
          [ ]   PC
          [ ]   Other (please specify):

6. CODING FORMAT:
What format did you use?
          [ ]   Hyperstack
          [ ]   File Express
          [ ]   Spreadsheet
          [ ]   Word Processor
          [ ]   Text Editor
          [ ]   Other (please specify):

7. CODING METHOD:
How did you enter code?
          [ ]   On paper first
          [ ]   Directly on the computer

How did you read the messages?
  [ ]   Print the messages and read hard copy
  [ ]   Read the messages online

8. OTHER LIST INFORMATION:
What are your impressions of the list:
(a) Editorship
  [ ]   Moderated
  [ ]   Unmoderated
(b) Topic
  [ ]   Academic
  [ ]   Technical
  [ ]   Social
  [ ]   Other (please specify):
(c) Membership (on a scale of 1 --> 5)
  [ ]   Homogeneous --> Heterogeneous
(d) Tone (on a scale of 1 --> 5)
  [ ]   Informal --> Formal
  [ ]   Verbose --> Brief
  [ ]   Leisurely --> Serious
  [ ]   Supportive --> Unsupportive
(e) Utility (on a scale of 1 --> 5)
  [ ]   High noise --> High signal

9. Why was it necessary to code 9 *(repeat for each variable coded 9)*:
     MSGNUM:
     Variable:
     Reason:

10. Problems:
(note here any errors in automatic coding, etc.)

General comments:

APPENDIX B

CASE STUDY 2 DOCUMENTS

B.1. Summary of Unit Outline

B.1.1. Unit aims and objectives

The aim of this unit is to provide you with a range of skills associated with the organisational aspects of the design and development of information systems, including development methodologies, CMC, CSCW, group dynamics, groupware and organisational culture. You will be able to critically assess and manage numerous issues that impact both on knowledge and knowledge workers in the context of today's organisation.

Part of the lecture time will be devoted to discussions in which all students are expected to participate actively. In addition to required reading, students are encouraged to extend their knowledge with additional suggested reading. Assessments are intended to encourage the development of written and oral communication skills, group skills, and research skills.

B.1.2. Lectures

There is one three-hour lecture each week. The lecture schedule is in Table B.1.

Table B.1. Lecture schedule.

Topic	Date	Lecture Topic
1	21 July	Introduction to the unit and Organisational Informatics
		History and cognitive impacts of computing and communication technologies
2	28 July	Computer-mediated communication in organisations
3	4 August	Organisational design and group processes
4	11 August	Organisational culture
One non-teaching week beginning 18 August		
5	25 August	Managing knowledge workers
		Virtual organisations
6	1 September	Sociotechnical information systems
7	8 September	Computer-mediated collaborative work
8	15 September	Organisational decision support systems
9	22 September	Analysis, design and evaluation methods, techniques and tools
Two non-teaching weeks beginning 29 September		
10	13 October	Systems theory

B.1.3. Workshops

There is a one-hour workshop each week. The workshop is conducted online in the WebCT chat room in a seminar format. The computer lab SC2.31 is available to log on to WebCT, but students are encouraged to log on from work or home. You should attend one workshop only. The workshop schedule is in Table B.2.

Table B.2. Workshop schedule.

Day	Time	Group Number
Tuesday	09:30-11:20	Group 1
Tuesday	11:30-13:20	Group 2
Wednesday	09:30-11:20	Group 3
Wednesday	11:30-13:20	Group 4
Wednesday	13:30-15:20	Group 5
Wednesday	15:30-17:20	Group 6
Wednesday	17:30-19:20	Group 7

B.1.4. Unit assessment

This unit will be assessed by a research essay, moderation of two workshops, a workshop journal, participation in discussions, and a final examination. The assessments have the following weights:

Research essay	30%
Workshop moderation	15%
Workshop journal	20%
Discussion participation	5%
Examination	30%

In order to pass this unit you must complete **all** assessment components (including discussion participation) **and** achieve an aggregate mark of 50% or higher. Failure to comply with any component of the unit will result in a failure in the unit. Final unit grades will be awarded using the approximate scale:

Notation	Grade	Notional Percentage Scores
HD	High Distinction	80-100%
D	Distinction	70-79%
C	Credit	60-69%
P	Pass	50-59%
N	Fail	Below 50

B.1.5. Research essay

The research essay is to be 2,000 words. It is individual work and it is marked out of 100. You will be given a list of topics from which to choose, or you may choose any topic from the unit reader. The assignment topics and requirements will be available on WebCT. The assignment is to be handed in by 17:00 on Friday 13 October. If an assignment is handed in late without an approved extension, a penalty will apply. Late work will attract a penalty in the form of a reduction in the mark given for your assignment. The penalty is 5 marks deducted each day for the first three days after the due date, and then 2 marks each and every day thereafter (including each weekend day). For further details about assessment, see the current *University Handbook and Calendar*.

B.1.6. Workshop moderation

Each student will be required to moderate discussions on two set readings. This involves a brief prepared discussion of the key points of the reading (maximum 15 minutes). The moderator will summarise the reading, identify key points, relate to lecture material and/or additional readings, and lead the group in discussions. It is recommended that you prepare your discussion in Word (or similar) and "cut and paste" text into the chat window. Pause frequently to allow questions and comments. Assessment will be based on a clear summary, knowledge of the topic, and efforts to stimulate discussion.

B.1.7. Workshop journal

You are required to keep a weekly "journal" throughout the semester. The weekly entries consist of three parts: (i) a brief summary of one of the week's readings from the unit reader; (ii) comments on a weekly workshop question, including at least one relevant reference from the web; and (iii) a reflection on the workshop discussions.

The purpose of keeping the journal is twofold: (i) to identify the main points/issues of each week's topic; and (ii) to comment on your feelings about and the usefulness of the questions and discussions. The purpose of the summaries is to provide a mechanism for encouraging more knowledgeable participation in the discussions, as well as to extend a courtesy to the workshop presenter. Obviously, the reading summary should be completed before the workshop presentation and the reflection should be completed after the presentation.

The weekly workshop question will be posted on WebCT each week. The web references provided by students will be added to an ongoing Organisational Informatics portal on WebCT, which will available to everyone. Each week's entry should be kept brief – approximately 500 words – and submitted in the B230 assignment box by 17:00 on the Wednesday of the following week (e.g. the entry for Week 2 is due on Wednesday of Week 3). A copy of each week's entry is to be kept by you and a completed journal is to be submitted by 17:00 on Wednesday 1 November.

B.1.8. Discussion participation

Assessment for participation will be based on both quantity and quality of interactions. Marks will be awarded for active and thoughtful participation in discussion sessions. Students who attend regularly but make little or no contribution to the discussion should not expect a pass mark in this component of the assessment.

B.1.9. Examination

The examination will be a short-answer, closed-book examination covering all aspects of the unit.

B.1.10. Lecture notes and other unit materials

Lecture notes, assignments, workshop questions, and other information are available from WebCT. To log into WebCT:

B.1.11. Course Readings

Every student should read at least the required readings before the workshop each week to allow full participation. If you are moderating a workshop, you should read at least the required and recommended readings. Another category of readings – additional readings – have been added for students interested in exploring the topic further and/or as a resource for assignments.

B.1.12. Information distribution

Information will be distributed via the Bulletin Board in WebCT and your student email address. For this reason, you should check the Bulletin Board and your email every day.

B.2. Guidelines for Communicating in a Synchronous Environment

1. If you want to say more than a line, enter the first line followed by three dots (…) to indicate there is more to come. Press enter to "send" this line to everyone. Repeat this until you have finished communicating your comment. Absence of three dots means that you have finished your comment.
2. Keep comments as short as possible to allow every the opportunity to "talk".
3. It helps to indicate who you are responding to, e.g. "Peggy, why do you think that?"
4. Abbreviations can be used to save typing, such as:
   imho – in my humble (honest) opinion
   btw – by the way
   lol – laughing out loud
   rofl – rolling on the floor laughing
   np – no problems
   brb – be right back
   wb – welcome back
   u – you
   r – are
5. It is quite acceptable to use lower case at all times as it saves time (and is also more friendly and casual).
6. Shouting is usually indicated by upper case letters, so avoid upper case unless you mean to shout.
7. Emoticons are very popular to convey expression:
   :-) to indicate a smile
   :-(to indicate displeasure or being unhappy about something
   ;-) to indicate a wink

B.3. Guidelines for Workshop Moderators

1. Workshops are online and conducted in the WebCT Chat Rooms - log on to WebCT and go to your designated workshop "room" about 5 minutes before the workshop is due to start. **All** students (both external and internal) are expected to attend workshops each week.
2. You will moderate discussions of **two** readings from the list of required readings for the week. Note that the topic list starts from Topic 1 and workshops start in Week 2. So if you are moderating discussions in Week 6, for example, you will prepared comments on two readings from Topic 5. The list of readings on WebCT (go to "Workshops" then click on "Readings") indicates both the topic number and the week number. I will also announce the topic number each workshop on the calendar so be sure to check that also.
3. For some weeks, there are more than two required readings given so you will have a choice. For most weeks, however, there are only two required readings so you will **not** have a choice. If there are more than two required readings, advise your group members **before** your workshop via your group's forum (bulletin board) which readings you will be discussing. Private forums for each workshop group will be created once workshop groups are finalised.
4. As there are only 9 workshops and an average of 16 people per workshop, most weeks there will be two people moderating.
5. If there are two people moderating, each moderator is required to prepare two presentations but actually present only one. The second prepared discussion will be posted to your group's forum. The two moderators should also liaise before the workshop and ensure that each one moderates a different article.

6. If there is only one person moderating, aim to have about 20 minutes of prepared comments on the articles; that is, about 10 minutes per article. The remaining time should be used for discussions among the group.
7. If there are two people moderating, aim to have about 10 minutes presentation and 20 minutes discussion each.
8. You can assume that everyone in your workshop group has read the required readings so it's not necessary to summarise the readings. Rather, you should review or critique each reading. Highlight the main issues addressed in each reading and give your opinions on the issues. Your opinions may agree or disagree with the author's research. Support your opinions, where possible, by referring to other literature or documented examples. I advise you to read at least one other reading from the "recommended" or "additional" reading list for the workshop in which you are moderating discussions to give you a broader knowledge of the topic.
9. Include in your discussion some questions to stimulate comments from workshop group members. Although you will have prepared about 10 minutes of comments on each article, do not present all comments in one block as a monologue. Intersperse your comments with questions for the group to discuss so that the workshop becomes more interactive and the group maintains interest in the topic.
10. Prepare your discussion in a text file (e.g. in NotePad). Have the prepared file opened in one window of your computer and the chat room in another window. Copy a paragraph at a time from your prepared file and paste into the message field of the chat room window (where it says "Type your message below and press [enter]").
11. Moderating includes leading the the group discussions. This means that you will need to keep the discussions flowing and coherent. If there is a lag in the discussions, you may need to ask another question; if too many people want to "talk", you may need to interrupt and stipulate an order. It is best to ask a question of the whole group, however if you find that some group members are not participating, you may need to address them individually in order to draw them into the discussions.
12. In the first workshop, your facilitator will be organising moderators for the workshop series. This process should take 10-15 minutes so there will be less time for discussion.

B.4. Organisational Informatics Peer Assessment Form

ABOUT YOU

Your name

Please put an X against the appropriate category.
Your age:
[ ] <25   [ ] 25-35   [ ] 35-45   [ ] >45

Your native language:
[ ] English   [ ] Other than English

Your ethnic background:
[ ] Australian   [ ] European   [ ] Asian   [ ] African

[ ] Other (please specify)_____

Your gender:
[ ] Male   [ ] Female

YOUR ASSESSMENT OF GROUP MEMBERS

Please rate the degree to which each member of Group 1 fulfilled his/her responsibilities in participating in the discussions. The possible ratings are:

Excellent   Consistently went above and beyond, carried more than his/her fair share
Very good   Consistently did what he/she was supposed to do, very well prepared, cooperative
Satisfactory   Usually did what he/she was supposed to do, acceptably prepared and cooperative
Ordinary   Often did what he/she was supposed to do, minimally prepared and cooperative
Marginal   Sometimes failed to show up, rarely prepared
Deficient   Often failed to show up, rarely prepared
Unsatisfactory   Consistently failed to show up, unprepared
Superficial   Practically no participation
No show   No participation at all

These rating should reflect each individual's level of participation and effort and sense of responsibility, not his or her academic ability.

Group member	*Rating*

ANALYSIS OF CASE STUDY 2 WORKSHOPS

C.1. Introduction

A detailed analysis of Workshop 1 and a summary of Workshops 2-9 were given in Chapter 8. The following sections provide detailed analyses of Workshops 2-9. The hypotheses, re-phrased to address short-term effects in Case Study 2, are

$H_{1.1}$ There are definable developmental stages in each workshop.

$H_{1.2}$ In the early phases of each workshop, the content of communication is more conceptual than task oriented or social.

$H_{1.3}$ Within each workshop, during periods of low task activity, the content of communication is more social than task oriented.

$H_{1.4}$ Within each workshop, during periods of high task activity, the content of communication is more task oriented than social.

$H_{1.5}$ During later developmental stages within workshops, participants engage in less disclosures about the physical and social attributes of themselves and others.

$H_{1.6}$ Group cohesiveness increases during the period of each workshop.

In this appendix, all these hypotheses relate to short-term (within workshop) developmental effects. Long-term characteristics of $H_{1.5}$ and $H_{1.6}$ are analysed in Chapter 8.

In Chapter 8, the analysis of Workshop 1 identified three developmental phases: (i) a beginning section, in which the communication was mostly conceptual (CON) and social (SOC); (ii) a middle section, in which the communication was mostly task (TSK); and (iii) an ending section, in which the communication returned to mostly conceptual (CON) and social (SOC)[1]. It was found that these three frequent communication types were the primary indicators of turning points in the workshop.

In this appendix, the other eight workshops will be analysed to determine if they exhibit similar short-term developmental effects to the first workshop. The three most frequent communication types (TSK, CON, SOC) will be examined, along with the six less frequent communication types (SUP, ARG, ENV, AWA, INF and FOR), for trends within individual workshops.

---

[1] All communication types (variables) are defined and described fully in Table 6.2.

C.2. Analysis of Development Characteristics of Workshops 2-9

C.2.1. Workshop 2

A total of 802 utterances were exchanged by participants throughout the one-hour topic discussions in the second workshop on 2 August 2000. Table C.1 shows the number and percentages of different types of communication in this second workshop. Compared with the first workshop, there was an increase in the proportion of task communication (from 39% to 48%), a decrease in conceptual communication (from 28.1% to 15.7%), an increase in social communication (from 18.6% to 23.3%), and a decrease in formal communication (from 5.1% to 1.9%).

Table C.1. Number and percentage of communication types in Workshop 2.

Code name	Code description	Number of utterances	Percentage of total W_2 utterance*
TSK	Task	385	48.0
CON	Conceptual	126	15.7
SUP	Supportive	29	3.6
ARG	Argumentative	9	1.1
SOC	Social	187	23.3
ENV	Environment	28	3.5
AWA	Awareness	52	6.5
INF	Informal	32	4.0
FOR	Formal	15	1.9

*Codes are not discrete categories, each utterance can be classified in a number of categories, hence percentages do not sum to 100.

The higher task and lower conceptual communication indicates that participants were more familiar with the norms expected of them and the management of the work activities so they were able to devote more time to the actual tasks. There was less need for the facilitator to manage the process.

Some of the conceptual communication was a result of one participant being absent for the previous workshop, so the process was explained to him by another participant:

> [Joe]:[2] do we get to pick which week we want to do it in? (u_{495})
> [Doug]: yeah.... (u_{496})[3]
> [Doug]: we picked them last week (u_{499})
> [Joe]: i couldnt get in last week (u_{501})[4]

---

[2] All names are aliases to avoid any possibility of identification of participants.
[3] In Case Study 2, utterances are generally very short, often consisting of phrases of sentences. The guidelines to participants for communicating in a synchronous environment (chat room) recommended: "If you want to say more than a line, enter the first line followed by three dots (...) to indicate there is more to come. Press enter to "send" this line to everyone. Repeat this until you have finished communicating your comment. Absence of three dots means that you have finished your comment." (see Appendix C.1) This technique keeps the conversation flowing. However, in the transcripts of the conversations, a phrase from one participant is very often interspersed with phrases from other participants.

Figure C.1 is a visualisation of Workshop 2 communication with transition regions identified.

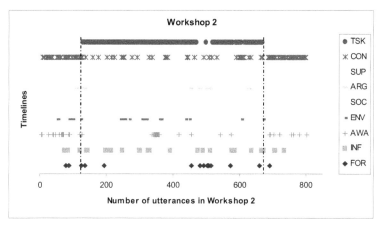

Figure C.1. Content-dependent timeline of Workshop 2 ($W_2 = [u_{475}; u_{1276}]$)

A detailed examination of the content of utterances in the transition regions revealed particular utterances that significantly altered the communication of the group. At utterance u_{600},[5] the moderator indicated that he was ready to lead the discussions about one of the articles, which focused everyone's attention on the activity:

> [Doug]: here goes nothing :) (u_{600})

At utterance u_{1145}, the discussions turned to the environment (ENV) when one of the participants asked a question about talking to someone privately[6]:

> [Gail]: what is private mode again? (u_{1145})

For the first time, tension was introduced in this workshop when the moderator became impatient. The participants were getting distracted with side issues and not concentrating on the task:

---

[4] All utterance examples are exact reproductions and therefore include original spelling and grammatical errors.
[5] All utterance numbers are numbered from the first utterance of the first workshop to the last utterance of the last workshop; that is, they are continuous across all workshops. The utterances shown on the X axis are the number of utterances in that particular workshop.
[6] In the chat room environment, there is a list displayed of all users who have logged on. By clicking on one of the names, any text that is entered is seen by that particular user only. This is referred to as being in "private mode". To "speak" to everyone again, the user needs to be in "public mode" again. This is done by clicking again on the name of the person to whom he/she was talking privately to de-select the "private mode".

[Doug]: read my last posting and talk about that instead!!!! (u_{987})

The changes in the nine communication variables in the three development phases of Workshop 2 are shown in Figure C.2.

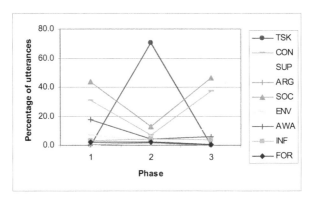

Figure C.2. Percentages of each communication variable in three phases of Workshop 2.

Since three of the variables are clustered at the top of the scale and six variables are clustered at the bottom, Figure C.3 and Figure C.4 illustrate these variables separately for improved visualization and include data tables showing the percentage figures. Figure C.3 shows that when the group was engaged in task-related communication, there was little conceptual or social communication. In Phase 1 and Phase 3, when task activity was low, there was increased conceptual and social communication.

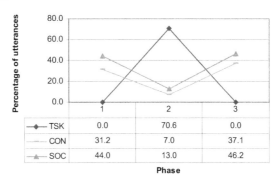

Figure C.3. Percentages of the three most frequent communication variables (TSK, CON, SOC) in three phases of Workshop 2.

Figure C.4 shows that each phase varies in the proportion of each of the six less frequent variables. The awareness (AWA) and environment (ENV) communication occurs mostly in Phase 1 (17.6%) and supportive (SUP) communication occurs mostly in Phase 3 (12.1%).

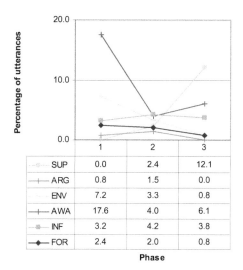

	1	2	3
SUP	0.0	2.4	12.1
ARG	0.8	1.5	0.0
ENV	7.2	3.3	0.8
AWA	17.6	4.0	6.1
INF	3.2	4.2	3.8
FOR	2.4	2.0	0.8

Phase

Figure C.4. Percentages of the six less frequent communication variables (SUP, ARG, ENV, AWA, INF, FOR) in three phases of Workshop 2.

An example of awareness (AWA) communication in the first phase was one of the participants revealing to everyone that it was her first experience in a chat room (she was not able to attend the first workshop):

[Gail]: Good morning everyone, you may have to bear with me, this is my first time. (u_{540})

Later in the workshop, the same participant disclosed her preferred name (which was different to the enrolled name that appeared by default in the chat room environment):

[Gail]: … my preferred name is Gail (u_{561})

This disclosure prompted similar disclosures from other participants:

[Kevin]: mine is Kevin (u_{564})
[Kirk]: my preferred name is Kirk (u_{562})
[Henry]: MY IS JUST HENRY (u_{572})

In the final phase, there were further disclosures such as the following, but they were not as frequent as in the first phase:

[Joe]: back to my bed hahahahaha (u_{1165})

The following are some examples of supportive (SUP) communication:

[Joe]: duncan that's gd haha (u_{1056})
[Gail]: extremely good question David (u_{1100})

The supportive feeling strengthened throughout the workshop period and was quite strong in Phase 3, as indicated in the graph in Figure C.4.

C.2.2. Examination of Development Hypotheses for Workshop 2

The development hypotheses will be evaluated for short-term (within workshops) effects for Workshop 2.

Hypothesis H$_{1.1}$: *There are definable developmental phases in Workshop 2*
The timeline representations of the nine variables identify distinct turning points (Figure C.1), verified by specific utterances. These turning points indicate changes in the development of the group within the second workshop. Figure C.2 shows considerable variation between these three phases in the TSK, CON, SOC and AWA variables in particular. *Hypothesis H$_{1.1}$ has been supported for Workshop 2.*

Hypothesis H$_{1.2}$: *In the early phase of the development of Workshop 2, the content of communication is more conceptual than task-oriented or social*
The timeline in Figure C.1 and the graph in Figure C.3 show that there is more conceptual communication than task communication in the first phase. However, there is more social communication than conceptual communication in this early phase. Although the last phase is almost a replication of the pattern of task, conceptual and social communication in the first phase, it can be stated that, in the early phase of development, there is a much higher percentage of conceptual communication than task-oriented communication. *Hypothesis H$_{1.2}$ is therefore partly supported for Workshop 2.*

Hypotheses H$_{1.3}$ and H$_{1.4}$: *In Workshop 2, during periods of low task activity, the content of communication is more social than task oriented; during periods of high task activity, the content is more task oriented than social*
The timeline in Figure C.1 and the graph in Figure C.3 show that in Phase 2, when the communication is mostly concerned with the task activity, there is very much less social communication. In Phases 1 and 3, when there is very little task-oriented communication, almost half the interactivity is social. *Hypotheses H$_{1.3}$ and H$_{1.4}$ are therefore supported for Workshop 2.*

Hypothesis H$_{1.5}$: *During later developmental stages of Workshop 2, participants engage in less disclosures about the physical and social attributes of themselves and others.*

The graph and figures in Figure C.4 show that there is a significant decrease of awareness communication from Phase 1 (17.6%) to Phase 3 (6.1%). *Hypothesis H$_{1.5}$ is supported for Workshop 2.*

Hypothesis H$_{1.6}$: *Group cohesiveness increases over the period of Workshop 2.*

The graph and figures in Figure C.4 show that there is a significant increase in supportive communication from Phase 1 (0%) to Phase 3 (12.1%) of Workshop 2, with very little argumentative communication in any phase. *Hypothesis H$_{1.6}$ is supported for Workshop 2.*

C.2.3. Workshop 3

A total of 363 utterances were exchanged by participants throughout the one-hour topic discussions in the third workshop on 9 August 2000. Table C.2 shows the number and percentages of different types of communication in this third workshop. Compared with the previous workshop, there was a slight decrease in task (from 48% to 46.6%), an increase in conceptual (from 15.7% to 19.8%), a decrease in social (from 23.3% to 17.1%), an increase in environment (from 3.5% to 8.3%) and a slight increase in both informal (from 4.0% to 6.1%) and formal (from 1.9% to 3.6%) communication. Generally, though, the relative percentages of different types of communication are similar to the previous two workshops.

Table C.2. Number and percentage of communication types in Workshop 3.

Code name	Code description	Number of utterances	Percentage of total W$_3$ utterance*
TSK	Task	168	46.6
CON	Conceptual	72	19.8
SUP	Supportive	24	6.6
ARG	Argumentative	1	0.3
SOC	Social	62	17.1
ENV	Environment	30	8.3
AWA	Awareness	15	4.1
INF	Informal	22	6.1
FOR	Formal	13	3.6

*Codes are not discrete categories, each utterance can be classified in a number of categories, hence percentages do not sum to 100.

An interesting change from the previous workshop was the more supportive (SUP=6.6%) nature of the communication. In particular, participants expressed their support to the moderator:

[Duncan]: I spose I'll just muddle through and see how it goes... (u_{1323})

[Donald]: take ur time (u_{1324})

Another interesting change was the increased focus on the environment. The WebCT system downloads enrolled students' names from a central server. The names displayed in the chat room are therefore official names. Many students have nicknames or, in the case of Asian students, Western names which they choose to add to their given names. The facilitator had added these preferred names in brackets to assist and personalize the communication flow. The following comment by one of the participants initiated a discussion about the chat room environment:

[Gail]: By the way Fay, it is great to have the preferred names in brackets (u_{1304})

Figure C.5 is a visualisation of Workshop 3 communication with transition regions identified.

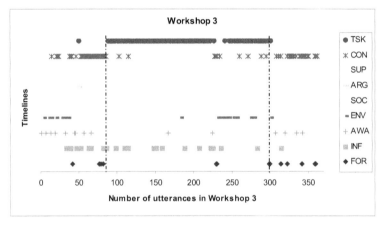

Figure C.5. Content-dependent timeline of Workshop 3 ($W_3 = [u_{1277}; u_{1639}]$)

A detailed examination of the content of utterances in the transition regions revealed particular utterances that significantly altered the communication of the group. In this workshop, the nominated moderator had prepared notes for the wrong article so another participant volunteered to swap moderator times. The commencement of Phase 2 was at utterance u_{1363}, when the facilitator acknowledged the graciousness of the volunteer and asked her to if she was ready to discuss the correct article. This focused everyone's attention on the activity.

[Fay]: ok, gail, thanks for filling in, ready to go? (u_{1363})

The commencement of Phase 3 was at utterance u_{1575}, when it was necessary for the facilitator to conclude the discussions.

[Fay]: well i think it's time to close ... (u_{1575})

Communication, however, continued for some time. Because of the confusion with the article to be discussed in this workshop, the participants felt it necessary to confirm their nominated time and article:

[Joe]: hey adrian which one r u doing? (u_{1606})

The changes in the nine communication variables in the three development phases of Workshop 3 are shown in Figure C.6.

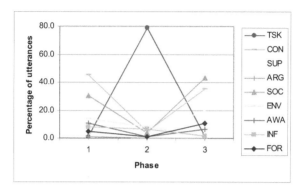

Figure C.6. Percentages of each communication variable in three phases of Workshop 3.

Figure C.7 and Figure C.8 illustrate the three most frequent variables and the six less frequent variables respectively for improved visualization and include data tables showing the percentage figures. Figure C.7 shows that when the group was engaged in task-related communication, there was little conceptual or social communication. In Phase 1 and Phase 3, when task activity was low, there was increased conceptual and social communication.

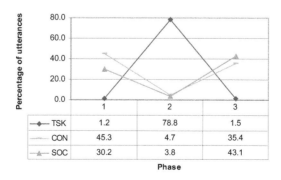

	1	2	3
TSK	1.2	78.8	1.5
CON	45.3	4.7	35.4
SOC	30.2	3.8	43.1

Figure C.7. Percentages of the three most frequent communication variables (TSK, CON, SOC) in three phases of Workshop 3.

Figure C.8 shows that each phase varies in the proportion of the six less frequent variables. As in the last workshop, awareness (AWA) and environment (ENV) communication occur mostly in Phase 1 and there is a high proportion of supportive (SUP) communication in Phase 3. Informal (INF) management decreases over the three phases, while formal (FOR) management increases.

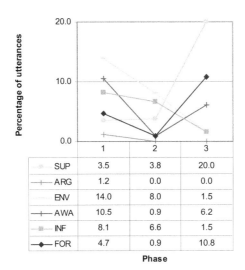

	1	2	3
SUP	3.5	3.8	20.0
ARG	1.2	0.0	0.0
ENV	14.0	8.0	1.5
AWA	10.5	0.9	6.2
INF	8.1	6.6	1.5
FOR	4.7	0.9	10.8

Phase

Figure C.8. Percentages of the six less frequent communication variables (SUP, ARG, ENV, AWA, INF, FOR) in three phases of Workshop 3.

An example of awareness (AWA) communication in the first phase was when one of the participants asked the nominated moderator what he was doing as he was taking a while to take over:

[Gail]: mmmm, what's happening Duncan? (u_{1321})
[Duncan]: i'm getting ready (u_{1322})

The following are some examples of how the facilitator and the participants appreciated and supported the way the moderator led the discussions:

[Fay]: Excellent!! (u_{1578})
[Doug]: well done (u_{1585})
[Leah]: good for u (u_{1588})

The supportive feeling strengthened throughout the workshop period and was quite strong in Phase 3, as indicated in the graph in Figure C.8.

C.2.4. Examination of Developmental Hypotheses for Workshop 3

The development hypotheses will be evaluated for short-term (within workshops) effects for Workshop 3.

Hypothesis $H_{1.1}$: *There are definable developmental phases in Workshop 3*
The timeline representations of the nine variables identify distinct turning points (Figure C.5), verified by specific utterances. These turning points indicate changes in the development of the group within the third workshop. Figure C.6 shows considerable variation between these three phases in the TSK, CON, SOC and AWA variables in particular. *Hypothesis $H_{1.1}$ is supported for Workshop 3.*

Hypothesis $H_{1.2}$: *In the early phase of the development of Workshop 3, the content of communication is more conceptual than task-oriented or social*
The timeline in Figure C.5 and the graph in Figure C.7 show that, in Phase 1, almost half of the interactions are conceptual, there is less social and almost no task communication. Although the last phase exhibits a similar pattern of task, conceptual and social communication as in the first phase, it can be stated that, in the early phase of development, there is a much higher percentage of conceptual communication than task or social communication. *Hypothesis $H_{1.2}$ is supported for Workshop 3.*

Hypotheses $H_{1.3}$ and $H_{1.4}$: *In Workshop 3, during periods of low task activity, the content of communication is more social than task oriented; during periods of high task activity, the content is more task oriented than social*
The timeline in Figure C.5 and the graph in Figure C.7 show that in Phase 1 and 3 when there is very little task activity, the communication is more social. In Phase 2, when the communication is mostly concerned with the task activity, there is very little social communication. *Hypotheses $H_{1.3}$ and $H_{1.4}$ are supported for Workshop 3.*

Hypothesis $H_{1.5}$: *During later developmental stages of Workshop 3, participants engage in less disclosures about the physical and social attributes of themselves and others.*
The graph and figures in Figure C.8 show that there is a decrease of awareness communication from Phase 1 (10.5%) to Phase 3 (6.2%), although there was even less in Phase 2 (0.9%). *Hypothesis $H_{1.5}$ is partly supported for Workshop 3.*

Hypothesis $H_{1.6}$: *Group cohesiveness increases over the period of Workshop 3.*
The graph and figures in Figure C.8 show that there is a significant increase in supportive communication from Phase 1 (3.5%) to Phase 3 (20.0%) of Workshop 3, with very little argumentative communication in any phase. *Hypothesis $H_{1.6}$ is supported for Workshop 3.*

C.2.5. Workshop 4

A total of 490 utterances were exchanged by participants throughout the one-hour topic discussions in the second workshop on 23 August 2000. Table C.3 shows the number and percentages of different types of communication in this fourth workshop. Comparing with the previous workshop, there was an increase in task (from 46.6% to 50.2%), and social (from 17.1% to 21.0%) communication, and a slight decrease in supportive (from 6.6% to 4.3%) communication.

Table C.3. Number and percentage of communication types in Workshop 4.

Code name	Code description	Number of utterances	Percentage of total W_4 utterance*
TSK	Task	245	50.2
CON	Conceptual	90	18.4
SUP	Supportive	21	4.3
ARG	Argumentative	12	2.4
SOC	Social	103	21.0
ENV	Environment	5	1.0
AWA	Awareness	15	3.0
INF	Informal	15	3.1
FOR	Formal	19	3.9

*Codes are not discrete categories, each utterance can be classified in a number of categories, hence percentages do not sum to 100.

An interesting change from the previous workshop was the significant decrease in communication related to the environment (from 8.3% to 1.0%, and a similar percentage to Workshop 1), indicating that the participants were now familiar with the chat-room environment.

The percentage of informal communication halved compared to the previous workshop (from 6.1% to 3.1%). One reason for this decrease was the moderator for this workshop displayed a high degree of competence in leading the discussions so there was less need for the conversation to be managed, either formally or informally.

Also of interest in this workshop was that, for the first time, there was some tension amongst the participants, reflected in the increased argumentative (ARG=2.4%) communication. Most of the argumentative communication was due to one of the participants typing with the caps lock on.[7] About half-way through the workshop, other participants expressed their irritation. The offender, though, was unaware of what uppercase letters signify in e-communication. Part of the conversation is reproduced below (replacing real names with aliases):

[Lorna]: henry can you please stop yelling (u_{1928})

---

[7] In written communication, uppercase letters usually signify emphasis. A norm in written e-communication is to use uppercase letters to mean shouting.

[Henry]: WHO IS YELLING, NOT ME. (u_{1930})
[Kirk]: its your caps (u_{1932})
[Henry]: WHAT CAPS. (u_{1934})
[Lorna]: the capital letters (u_{1936})
[Kirk]: CAPITAL LETTERS!!!! (u_{1937})
[Joe]: YOU HAVE THE CAPS LOCK ON!!! (u_{1938})
[Kirk]: use lower caps (u_{1939})

The tension was relieved by a humorous comment from another participant:

[Gail]: capital comments, eh what? (u_{1941})

Figure C.9 is a visualisation of Workshop 4 communication with transition regions identified.

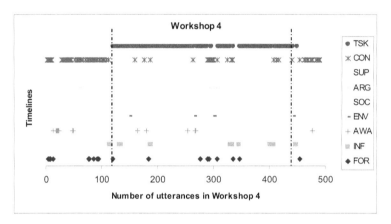

Figure C.9. Content-dependent timeline of Workshop 4 ($W_4 = [u_{1640}; u_{2129}]$)

A detailed examination of the content of utterances in the transition regions revealed particular utterances that significantly altered the communication of the group. This workshop was the first one after a one-week study break so much of the conversation revolved around what everyone had been doing during the break. The following exchange, for example, was between one of the participants and the facilitator:

[Gail]: so how was the eastern seaboard Fay? (u_{1713})
[Fay]: gail, nice rest in broken hill and canberra (u_{1721})
[Gail]: Fay, lunch with Pro Hart? (u_{1724})
[Fay]: gail, i could think of more interesting people, even in bh (u_{1730})

The moderator brought everyone's attention to the task, which signaled the commencement of Phase 2 at utterance u_{1726}.

[Lorna]: Welcome everyone to week five and our tutorial. (u_{1726})

The discussions during this workshop were excellent, with each participant contributing ideas and opinions. The session began to dissolve, however, when a fire drill commenced in the building in which the computer laboratories are located. Although the majority of participants were logged on to the chat room from their home or office, a few were using the computers in the laboratories. One participant announced:

[Donald]: oh no the fire alarm has gone off (u_{2075})
[Donald]: i betta log off... dont want to die (u_{2082})

This prompted a few others to say they had to leave. Although discussions on the topic reading continued, the enthusiasm diminished and eventually the workshop session concluded. Thus utterance u_{2075} signaled the commencement of Phase 3.

The changes in the nine communication variables in the three development phases of Workshop 4 are shown in Figure C.10.

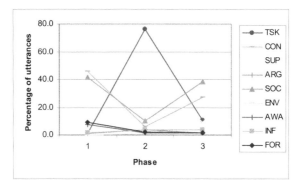

Figure C.10. Percentages of each communication variable in three phases of Workshop 4.

Figure C.11 and Figure C.12 illustrate the three most frequent variables and the six less frequent variables respectively and include data tables showing the percentage figures. Figure C.11 shows that when the group was engaged in task-related communication, there was little conceptual or social communication. In Phase 1 and Phase 3, when task activity was low, there was increased conceptual and social communication.

Figure C.12 shows that each phase varies in the proportion of the six less frequent variables. There is less awareness communication than the previous two workshops, but it does occur mostly in Phase 1. Unlike the previous two workshops, there is almost no communication about the environment. The interactions became increasingly supportive over the period of the workshop, but there was some argumentative communication in Phase 2. Informal (INF) management increases slightly over the three phases, while formal (FOR) management decreases, which is the opposite trend to the previous workshop.

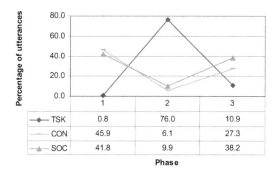

	1	2	3
TSK	0.8	76.0	10.9
CON	45.9	6.1	27.3
SOC	41.8	9.9	38.2

Phase

Figure C.11. Percentages of the three most frequent communication variables (TSK, CON, SOC) in three phases of Workshop 4.

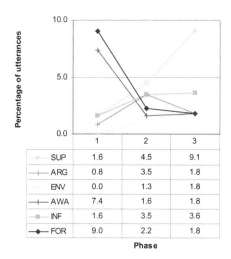

	1	2	3
SUP	1.6	4.5	9.1
ARG	0.8	3.5	1.8
ENV	0.0	1.3	1.8
AWA	7.4	1.6	1.8
INF	1.6	3.5	3.6
FOR	9.0	2.2	1.8

Phase

Figure C.12. Percentages of the six less frequent communication variables (SUP, ARG, ENV, AWA, INF, FOR) in three phases of Workshop 4.

The following excerpt of a conversation is an example of awareness (AWA) communication in the first phase of this workshop and illustrates how participants liked to "locate" each other:

[Kirk]: are you at home? (u_{1657})
[Ruth]: no I am at uni (u_{1658})
[Kirk]: where? (u_{1659})
[Ruth]: ps lab (u_{1661})
[Kirk]: I'm at ecl lab. (u_{1662})
[Ruth]: o i c cool (u_{1663})

As in the last workshop, the participants expressed appreciation and support of how the facilitator led the activities:

[Henry]: well done (u_{2091})
[Kirk]: good work (u_{2095})

The supportive feeling strengthened throughout the workshop period and was quite strong in Phase 3, as indicated in the figures and graph in Figure C.12.

C.2.6. Examination of Developmental Hypotheses for Workshop 4

The development hypotheses will be evaluated for short-term (within workshops) effects for Workshop 4.

Hypothesis $H_{1.1}$: *There are definable developmental phases in Workshop 4*

The timeline representations of the nine variables identify distinct turning points (Figure C.9), verified by specific utterances. These turning points indicate changes in the development of the group within the fourth workshop. Figure C.10 shows considerable variation between these three phases in the TSK, CON, SOC and AWA variables in particular. *Hypothesis $H_{1.1}$ is supported for Workshop 4.*

Hypothesis $H_{1.2}$: *In the early phase of the development of Workshop 4, the content of communication is more conceptual than task-oriented or social*

The timeline in Figure C.9 and the graph in Figure C.11 show that, in Phase 1, almost half of the interactions are conceptual, but there is almost as much social communication. Although the last phase exhibits a similar pattern of task, conceptual and social communication as in the first phase, it can be stated that, in the early phase of development, there is a much higher percentage of conceptual communication than task communication and slightly higher percentage of social communication. *Hypothesis $H_{1.2}$ is weakly supported for Workshop 4.*

Hypotheses $H_{1.3}$ and $H_{1.4}$: *In Workshop 4, during periods of low task activity, the content of communication is more social than task oriented; during periods of high task activity, the content is more task oriented than social*

The timeline in Figure C.9 and the graph in Figure C.11 show that in Phase 1 and 3 when there is very little task activity, the communication is more social. In Phase 2, when the communication is mostly concerned with the task activity, there is very little social communication. *Hypotheses $H_{1.3}$ and $H_{1.4}$ are supported for Workshop 4.*

Hypothesis $H_{1.5}$: *During later developmental stages of Workshop 4, participants engage in less disclosures about the physical and social attributes of themselves and others.*

The graph and figures in Figure C.12 show that there is a considerable decrease of awareness communication from Phase 1 (7.4%) to Phase 3 (1.8%). *Hypothesis $H_{1.5}$ is supported for Workshop 4.*

Hypothesis H$_{1.6}$: *Group cohesiveness increases over the period of Workshop 4.*
The graph and figures in Figure C.12 show that, although there was some argumentative communication in Phase 2, there is a significant increase in supportive communication from Phase 1 (1.6%) to Phase 3 (9.1%) of Workshop 4. *Hypothesis H$_{1.6}$ is supported for Workshop 4.*

C.2.7. Workshop 5

A total of 497 utterances were exchanged by participants throughout the one-hour topic discussions in the fifth workshop on 30 August 2000. Table C.4 shows the number and percentages of different types of communication in this fifth workshop. Compared with the previous workshop, there was an increase in task (from 50.2% to 63.6%) and a decrease in conceptual (from 18.4% to 3.6%) communication. These figures represent the highest percentage of task communication and the lowest percentage of conceptual communication of all nine workshops. These figures indicate that, as this workshop was the midpoint in the series, the participants were familiar with each other, with the environment, and with the process. In other words, there was little distraction and all participants focused on the activity.

The only other variation from the previous workshop was in the communication management with an increase in informal (from 3.1% to 5.2%) and a decrease in formal (from 3.9% to 1.2%) communication, indicating less need for leadership intervention.

Table C.4. Number and percentage of communication types in Workshop 5.

Code name	Code description	Number of utterances	Percentage of total W$_5$ utterance*
TSK	Task	316	63.6
CON	Conceptual	18	3.6
SUP	Supportive	32	6.4
ARG	Argumentative	3	0.6
SOC	Social	103	20.7
ENV	Environment	12	2.4
AWA	Awareness	18	3.6
INF	Informal	26	5.2
FOR	Formal	6	1.2

*Codes are not discrete categories, each utterance can be classified in a number of categories, hence percentages do not sum to 100.

Figure C.13 is a visualisation of Workshop 5 communication with transition regions identified.

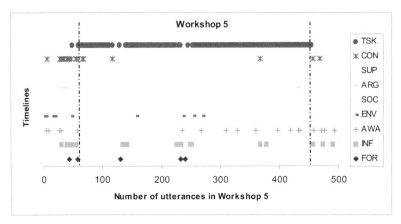

Figure C.13. Content-dependent timeline of Workshop 5 ($W_5 = [u_{2130}; u_{2626}]$)

A detailed examination of the content of utterances in the transition regions revealed particular utterances that significantly altered the communication of the group. The topic discussions in this workshop got underway early and the participants were focused throughout most of the session. The moderator outlined her task at utterance u_{2186}:

> [Ruth]: I will be going through very briefly every topic that is covered in the article. (u_{2186})

Even when the moderator had technical problems, discussions continued amongst the participants.

> [Susan]: ruth is MIA[8] (u_{2364})
> [Fay]: oh, just noticed ruth's not here, must have got kicked off (u_{2366})

When she returned, the moderator explained the problem:

> [Ruth]: ohhh sorry the com got Frozen have to restart the com sorry (u_{2399})
> [Ruth]: sorry about that :(((((((((((((((((((((u_{2402})
> [Monica]: its ok regha... (u_{2404})

Another participant eventually initiated the commencement of the last phase with his comment at utterance u_{2585}

> [Susan]: times up for guys....see ya next week...cheers (u_{2585})

The changes in the nine communication variables in the three development phases of Workshop 5 are shown in Figure C.14.

---

[8] MIA is shorthand notation for "missing in action".

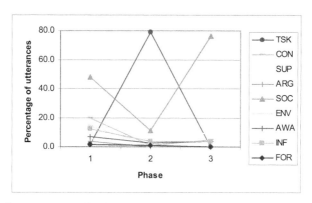

Figure C.14. Percentages of each communication variable in three phases of Workshop 5.

Figure C.15 and Figure C.16 illustrate the three most frequent variables and the six less frequent variables respectively and include data tables showing the percentage figures. Figure C.15 shows that, in Phases 1 and 3, when task activity was low, the interactions were mostly social, particularly in the last phase. In Phase 2, when task activity was high, there was little conceptual and social communication. Conceptual communication occurred mostly in Phase 1.

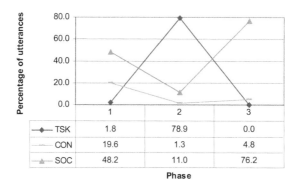

	1	2	3
TSK	1.8	78.9	0.0
CON	19.6	1.3	4.8
SOC	48.2	11.0	76.2

Phase

Figure C.15. Percentages of the three most frequent communication variables (TSK, CON, SOC) in three phases of Workshop 5.

Figure C.16 shows that each phase varies in the proportion of the six less frequent variables. Phase 1 was characterised by awareness and environment communication. Of interest in this workshop is that more than one in every ten utterances was intended to informally manage the communication process. The workshop group became more supportive over the period of the workshop.

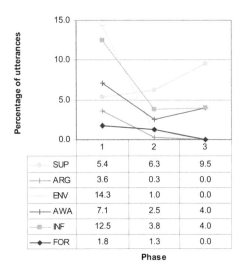

	1	2	3
SUP	5.4	6.3	9.5
ARG	3.6	0.3	0.0
ENV	14.3	1.0	0.0
AWA	7.1	2.5	4.0
INF	12.5	3.8	4.0
FOR	1.8	1.3	0.0

Phase

Figure C.16. Percentages of the six less frequent communication variables (SUP, ARG, ENV, AWA, INF, FOR) in three phases of Workshop 5.

The following is an example of awareness (AWA) communication in the first phase of this workshop when one of the participants advised disclosed some information about himself:

[Doug]: hehehehhe ...i gotta work next two weeks on wednesdays ... (u_{2138})

In the last phase, participants expressed approval and support of the facilitator's suggestion:

[Fay]: we have a couple of minutes left, let's go back to that real estate example (u_{2586})
[Ruth]: good idea fay (u_{2590})
[Kevin]: ok great (u_{2095})

The supportive feeling strengthened throughout the workshop period, as indicated in the figures and graph in Figure C.16.

C.2.8. Examination of Hypotheses H$_{1.1}$-H$_{1.4}$ for Workshop 5

The first four development hypotheses will be evaluated for short-term (within workshops) effects for Workshop 5.

Hypothesis H$_{1.1}$: *There are definable developmental phases in Workshop 5*
The timeline representations of the nine variables identify distinct turning points (Figure C.13), verified by specific utterances. These turning points indicate changes in the development of the group within the fifth workshop. Figure C.14 shows

considerable variation between these three phases in the TSK, CON, SOC and AWA variables in particular. *Hypothesis $H_{1.1}$ is supported for Workshop 5.*

Hypothesis $H_{1.2}$: *In the early phase of the development of Workshop 5, the content of communication is more conceptual than task-oriented or social*
The timeline in Figure C.13 and the graph in Figure C.15 show that, in Phase 1, about one in five utterances related to conceptual activity, but there was more than double that amount of social communication. It can be stated, therefore, that in the early phase of development, there is a much higher percentage of conceptual communication than task communication but not social communication. *Hypothesis $H_{1.2}$ is partly supported for Workshop 5.*

Hypotheses $H_{1.3}$ and $H_{1.4}$: *In Workshop 5, during periods of low task activity, the content of communication is more social than task oriented; during periods of high task activity, the content is more task oriented than social*
The timeline in Figure C.13 and the graph in Figure C.15 show that in Phase 1 and 3 when there is very little task activity, the communication is more social. In Phase 2, when the communication is mostly concerned with the task activity, there is very little social communication. *Hypotheses $H_{1.3}$ and $H_{1.4}$ are supported for Workshop 5.*

Hypothesis $H_{1.5}$: *During later developmental stages of Workshop 5, participants engage in less disclosures about the physical and social attributes of themselves and others.*
The graph and figures in Figure C.16 show that there is a decrease of awareness communication from Phase 1 (7.4%) to Phase 3 (4.0%). *Hypothesis $H_{1.5}$ is supported for Workshop 5.*

Hypothesis $H_{1.6}$: *Group cohesiveness increases over the period of Workshop 5.*
The graph and figures in Figure C.16 show that, although there is some argumentative communication in Phase 1, there is a steady increase in supportive communication from Phase 1 (5.4%) to Phase 3 (9.5%) of Workshop 5. *Hypothesis $H_{1.6}$ is supported for Workshop 5.*

C.2.9. Workshop 6

A total of 415 utterances were exchanged by participants throughout the one-hour topic discussions in the sixth workshop on 6 September 2000. Table C.5 shows the number and percentages of different types of communication in this sixth workshop. Compared with the previous workshop, there was a decrease in task (from 63.6% to 50.4%) and an increase in conceptual (from 3.6% to 13.7%) communication. In other words, these communication types reverted to similar proportions as for Workshop 4.

All other communication types were similarly represented, except for an increase in argumentative communication (from 0.6% to 4.3%), which is explained on page 345.

Table C.5. Number and percentage of communication types in Workshop 6.

Code name	Code description	Number of utterances	Percentage of total W_6 utterance*
TSK	Task	215	50.4
CON	Conceptual	53	13/8
SUP	Supportive	26	6.3
ARG	Argumentative	13	4.3
SOC	Social	92	22.4
ENV	Environment	7	1.9
AWA	Awareness	9	2.2
INF	Informal	19	4.6
FOR	Formal	11	2.7

*Codes are not discrete categories, each utterance can be classified in a number of categories, hence percentages do not sum to 100.

Figure C.17 is a visualisation of Workshop 6 communication with transition regions identified.

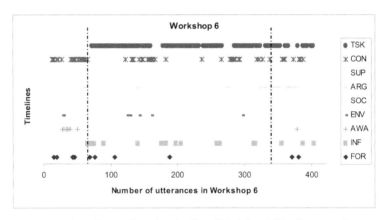

Figure C.17. Content-dependent timeline of Workshop 6 ($W_6 = [u_{2627}; u_{3041}]$).

For this workshop, two moderators had been nominated. The conceptual communication in the early part of the workshop was related to the clarification of each moderator's role. Despite being instructed to contact each other before the workshop, they had not done so. The topic discussions and the second phase eventually began at utterance (u_{2692}) when the facilitator suggested a procedure:

[Fay]: well, how about duncan starts, fred chimes in whenever, and fred also talks about the second article? (u_{2692})
[Fred]: soundz good if eveyone like it (u_{2696})
[Gail]: adore it (u_{2697})

The third phase commenced at utterance (u_{2967}) when the discussions got off the topic with a personal observation from one of the participants about another participant and the conversation between them became argumentative. The discussions had been focused on the topic of leadership in online environments, and how much control a leader has in a chat room compared with a face-to-face environment.

[Duncan]: Well yeah.. Gail by sheer weight of conversation has established herself as a leader .. (u_{2967})
[Gail]: oh, not picking on me again duncan (u_{2968})
[Duncan]: See ... Gerry responds to my attempt to knock her off the top and thus conflict ensues.. (u_{2976})
[Duncan]: … I find Gerry to have annoyingly relevant points of view.... (u_{2991})
[Gail]: annoyingly? (u_{2993})

Although the conversation among most of the participants was still on track, the moderator attempted to bring everyone in line by "shouting":

[Fred]: AS PRESENTER I AM USING MY POWER (u_{2996})
[Monica]: whoa...talk about abuse of power!! (u_{2996})

The changes in the nine communication variables in the three development phases of Workshop 6 are shown in Figure C.18.

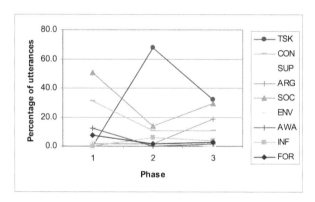

Figure C.18. Percentages of each communication variable in three phases of Workshop 6.

Figure C.19 and Figure C.20 illustrate the three most frequent variables and the six less frequent variables respectively and include data tables showing the percentage figures. Figure C.19 shows that, in Phase 2, when the group was engaged in task-related communication, there was little conceptual or social communication. In Phase 1, when task activity was low, there was more conceptual and social communication. However, unlike the previous workshops, Phase 3 comprised about equal amounts of task and social communication.

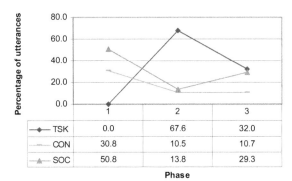

	1	2	3
TSK	0.0	67.6	32.0
CON	30.8	10.5	10.7
SOC	50.8	13.8	29.3

Phase

Figure C.19. Percentages of the three most frequent communication variables (TSK, CON, SOC) in three phases of Workshop 6.

Figure C.20 shows that each phase varies in the proportion of the six less frequent variables. Awareness communication occurs mostly in Phase 1. Unlike the previous workshops, there is a high proportion (almost one in five utterances) of argumentative communication in Phase 3. The communication was managed formally in the initial phase and informally in Phases 2 and 3.

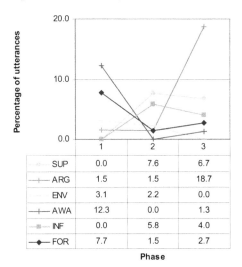

	1	2	3
SUP	0.0	7.6	6.7
ARG	1.5	1.5	18.7
ENV	3.1	2.2	0.0
AWA	12.3	0.0	1.3
INF	0.0	5.8	4.0
FOR	7.7	1.5	2.7

Phase

Figure C.20. Percentages of the six less frequent communication variables (SUP, ARG, ENV, AWA, INF, FOR) in three phases of Workshop 6.

As in most of the other workshops, the participants disclosed information about their physical location at the beginning of the session, this time with some humour:

[Monica]: where are you henry? (u_{2659})
[Henry]: here (u_{2660})
[Monica]: hmm that helps a lot (u_{2661})
[Gail]: that's funny I'm here too (u_{2662})
[Henry]: commerce building (u_{2664})
[Gail]: well I'm at home nice and snug (u_{2666})

Even though there was a significant proportion of argumentative utterances in the last phase of this workshop (as described above), it was offset by supportive comments in the second phase:

[Fred]: once again my bad if im off track ok (u_{2945})
[Ruth]: you're right on track … (u_{2946})
[Gail]: that was extremely nice of you Fred to do all the work for us (u_{2952})

Figure C.21 shows the ratio of supportive to argumentative utterances in Workshop 6. It indicates clearly that the environment of this particular workshop was more supportive in the middle of the session.

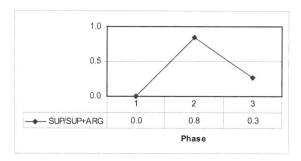

Figure C.21. Ratio of SUP and ARG utterances in each phase of Workshop 6.

C.2.10. Examination of Developmental Hypotheses for Workshop 6

The development hypotheses will be evaluated for short-term (within workshops) effects for Workshop 6.

Hypothesis H₁.₁: *There are definable developmental phases in Workshop 6*
The timeline representations of the nine variables identify distinct turning points (Figure C.17), verified by specific utterances. These turning points indicate changes in the development of the group within the sixth workshop. Figure C.18 shows considerable variation between these three phases in the TSK, CON, SOC and AWA variables in particular. *Hypothesis H₁.₁ is supported for Workshop 6.*

Hypothesis H$_{1.2}$: *In the early phase of the development of Workshop 6, the content of communication is more conceptual than task-oriented or social*

The timeline in Figure C.17 and the graph in Figure C.19 show that, in Phase 1, almost a third of the interactions are conceptual, but there is even more social communication. It can be stated, therefore, that in the early phase of development, there is a much higher percentage of conceptual communication than task but not social communication. *Hypothesis H$_{1.2}$ is partly supported for Workshop 6.*

Hypotheses H$_{1.3}$ and H$_{1.4}$: *In Workshop 6, during periods of low task activity, the content of communication is more social than task oriented; during periods of high task activity, the content is more task oriented than social*

The timeline in Figure C.17 and the graph in Figure C.19 show that in Phase 1, when there is very little task activity, the communication is more social. In Phase 2, when the communication is mostly concerned with the task activity, there is very little social communication. However, in Phase 3, there are similar amounts of both task and social communication. *Hypotheses H$_{1.3}$ and H$_{1.4}$ are partly supported for Workshop 6.*

Hypothesis H$_{1.5}$: *During later developmental stages of Workshop 6, participants engage in less disclosures about the physical and social attributes of themselves and others.*

The graph and figures in Figure C.20 show that there is a significant decrease of awareness communication from Phase 1 (12.3%) to Phase 3 (1.3%). *Hypothesis H$_{1.5}$ is supported for Workshop 6.*

Hypothesis H$_{1.6}$: *Group cohesiveness increases over the period of Workshop 6.*

Figure C.20 and Figure C.21 show that, although there is an increase in supportive communication from Phase 1 (0%) to Phases 2 and 3 (7.6% and 6.7%) there is also a significant increase in argumentative communication from Phase 1 (1.5%) to Phase 3 (18.7%). *Hypothesis H$_{1.6}$ is not supported for Workshop 6.*

C.2.11. Workshop 7

A total of 517 utterances were exchanged by participants throughout the one-hour topic discussions in the seventh workshop on 13 September 2000. Table C.6 shows the number and percentages of different types of communication in this seventh workshop. Compared with the previous workshop, there was an increase in task (from 50.4% to 56.7%), a slight decrease in conceptual (13.7% to 11.0%) and supportive (from 6.3% to 4.6%), and a decrease in argumentative communication (from 4.3% to 0.4%). Otherwise there was little variation from the previous workshop in the relative total percentages of each communication type.

Table C.6. Number and percentage of communication types in Workshop 7.

Code name	Code description	Number of utterances	Percentage of total W_7 utterance*
TSK	Task	293	56.7
CON	Conceptual	57	11.0
SUP	Supportive	24	4.6
ARG	Argumentative	2	0.4
SOC	Social	98	19.0
ENV	Environment	18	3.5
AWA	Awareness	13	2.5
INF	Informal	18	3.5
FOR	Formal	11	2.1

*Codes are not discrete categories, each utterance can be classified in a number of categories, hence percentages do not sum to 100.

Figure C.22 is a visualisation of Workshop 7 communication with transition regions identified.

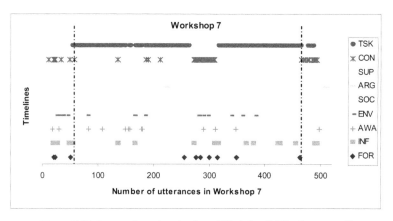

Figure C.22. Content-dependent timeline of Workshop 7 ($W_7 = [u_{3042}; u_{3558}]$)

It is interesting to note, that although three phases are identified here, the second phase in this particular workshop could actually be further divided into three phases. Phase 2 is interrupted by about 50 utterances with a different communication pattern, comprising an absence of task communication and the presence of conceptual and environment communication. This brief hiatus was initiated by the facilitator who asked if anyone would feel more comfortable with a face-to-face workshop rather than the current chat room environment. The following is an excerpt from that conversation thread:

[Fay]: i guess the question is, is anyone really keen to have a ftf tutorial … (u_{3320})
[Gail]: one off or for ever? (u_{3327})
[Leah]: sorry i wld prefer online (u_{3336})
[Gail]: nope (u_{3339})

[Monica]: i prefer online (u_{3341})
[Donald]: looks like its online then (u_{3343})
[Gail]: saves a ton of makeup (u_{3347})

Because this was only one of nine workshops with this distinct pattern and because this divergence was initiated by the facilitator, the middle section will be considered as one phase.

In the first phase, together with the usual conceptual and social communication, there was some discussion about the environment of the chat room. It was during this phase that one of the participants noticed that it was possible to enter a URL into a special field and send it to the group. The URL pops up as a separate window with an active link.

[Gail]: just by the by, you more knowledgeable folks, with the send url key on the right of the screen, who would you send it to and maybe for why? (u_{3066})
[Gail]: Ah, thank you Fay, lesson by example (u_{3074})
[Henry]: YES, BUT WHAT IS IT? (u_{3075})
[Fay]: if you want to direct everyone to a relevant url, that's how you do it, henry (u_{3078})

However, the moderator was anxious to discuss the topic article and so initiated the commencement on Phase 2 at utterance (u_{3094})

[Henry]: start now? (u_{3094})

Phase 3 commenced at utterance (u_{3508}) when the facilitator praised the moderator:

[Fay]: excellent conclusion (u_{3508})

The changes in the nine communication variables in the three development phases of Workshop 7 are shown in Figure C.23.

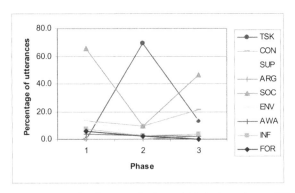

Figure C.23. Percentages of each communication variable in three phases of Workshop 7.

Figure C.24 and Figure C.25 illustrate the three most frequent variables and the six less frequent variables respectively and include data tables showing the percentage figures.

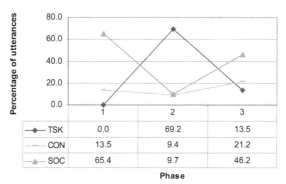

Phase	1	2	3
TSK	0.0	69.2	13.5
CON	13.5	9.4	21.2
SOC	65.4	9.7	46.2

Figure C.24. Percentages of the three most frequent communication variables (TSK, CON, SOC) in three phases of Workshop 7.

Figure C.24 shows that when the group was engaged in task-related communication, there was little conceptual or social communication. In Phase 1 and Phase 3, when task activity was low, there was a large increase in social communication and slightly more conceptual communication. Figure C.25 shows that each phase varies in the proportion of the six less frequent variables. After task, conceptual and social communication, the next most frequent type of communication concerns the environment. The group became more supportive over the period of this workshop. There was considerably more management of communication – both formal and informal – in the initial phase compared with the later phases.

There were a few instances in the first phase of this workshop in which participants disclosed more information about themselves, e.g.:

[Kirk]: I used to help at a home for the aged.. (u_{3125})
[Henry]: lucky i am a free thinker. (u_{3149})

The last phase was very supportive with participants expressing appreciation and support of the moderator's skill in leading the discussions, e.g.:

[Gail]: i enjoyed that louis, thanks a milliion (u_{3513})

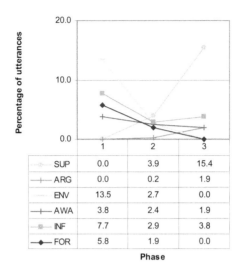

	1	2	3
SUP	0.0	3.9	15.4
ARG	0.0	0.2	1.9
ENV	13.5	2.7	0.0
AWA	3.8	2.4	1.9
INF	7.7	2.9	3.8
FOR	5.8	1.9	0.0

Figure C.25. Percentages of the six less frequent communication variables (SUP, ARG, ENV, AWA, INF, FOR) in three phases of Workshop 7.

C.2.12. Examination of Developmental Hypotheses for Workshop 7

The development hypotheses will be evaluated for short-term (within workshops) effects for Workshop 7.

Hypothesis $H_{1.1}$: *There are definable developmental phases in Workshop 7*
The timeline representations of the nine variables identify distinct turning points (Figure C.22), verified by specific utterances. These turning points indicate changes in the development of the group within the seventh workshop. Figure C.23 shows considerable variation between these three phases in the TSK, CON, SOC and AWA variables in particular. *Hypothesis $H_{1.1}$ is supported for Workshop 7.*

Hypothesis $H_{1.2}$: *In the early phase of the development of Workshop 7, the content of communication is more conceptual than task-oriented or social*
The timeline in Figure C.22 and the graph in Figure C.24 show that, in Phase 1, there is more conceptual than task communication. However, there is much more social communication than conceptual. Although the last phase has a similar (though much less pronounced) pattern of task, conceptual and social communication as in the first phase, it can be stated that, in the early phase of development, there is more conceptual communication than task communication but not social communication. *Hypothesis $H_{1.2}$ is partly supported for Workshop 7.*

Hypotheses $H_{1.3}$ and $H_{1.4}$: *In Workshop 7, during periods of low task activity, the content of communication is more social than task oriented; during periods of high task activity, the content is more task oriented than social*

The timeline in Figure C.22 and the graph in Figure C.24 show that in Phase 1 and 3 when there is very little task activity, the communication is more social. In Phase 2, when the communication is mostly concerned with the task activity, there is very little social communication. *Hypotheses $H_{1.3}$ and $H_{1.4}$ are supported for Workshop 7.*

Hypothesis $H_{1.5}$: *During later developmental stages of Workshop 7, participants engage in less disclosures about the physical and social attributes of themselves and others.*

The graph and figures in Figure C.25 show that there is a slight decrease of awareness communication from Phase 1 (3.8%) to Phase 3 (1.9%). *Hypothesis $H_{1.5}$ is weakly supported for Workshop 7.*

Hypothesis $H_{1.6}$: *Group cohesiveness increases over the period of Workshop 7.*

The graph and figures in Figure C.25 show that there is a significant increase in supportive communication from Phase 1 (0%) to Phase 3 (15.4%) with very little argumentative communication. *Hypothesis $H_{1.6}$ is supported for Workshop 7.*

C.2.13. Workshop 8

A total of 505 utterances were exchanged by participants throughout the one-hour topic discussions in the eighth workshop on 20 September 2000. Table C.7 shows the number and percentages of different types of communication in this eighth workshop. Compared with the previous workshop, there was more than a 50% increase in social communication (from 19.0% to 32.5%). Other notable variations was a slight decrease in task (from 56.7% to 52.5%), conceptual (from 11.0% to 8.1%) and environment (from 3.5% to 2.2%) communication.

Table C.7. Number and percentage of communication types in Workshop 8.

Code name	Code description	Number of utterances	Percentage of total W_8 utterance*
TSK	Task	265	52.5
CON	Conceptual	41	8.1
SUP	Supportive	28	5.5
ARG	Argumentative	3	1.0
SOC	Social	164	32.5
ENV	Environment	11	2.2
AWA	Awareness	5	1.0
INF	Informal	24	4.8
FOR	Formal	7	1.4

*Codes are not discrete categories, each utterance can be classified in a number of categories, hence percentages do not sum to 100.

Figure C.26 is a visualisation of Workshop 8 communication with transition regions identified.

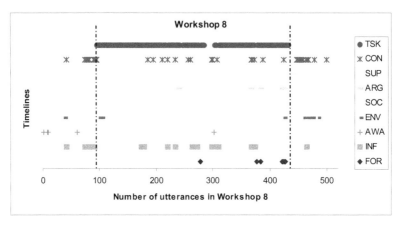

Figure C.26. Content-dependent timeline of Workshop 8 ($W_8 = [u_{3559}; u_{4063}]$)

Much of the social communication in the first phase was a series of concerned queries about the facilitator's health as she had been on sick leave:

[Henry]: HOW ARE YOU FAY? (u_{3614})
[Leah]: how r u fay (u_{3615})
[Joe]: fay u feeling better? (u_{3616})
[Gail]: are you back fay coz your back is better? (u_{3617})
[Monica]: feeling 100% again? (u_{3618})
[Adrian]: take care (u_{3624})

The discussions about the topic readings were initiated by one participant's reflection, which signaled the commencement of Phase 2:

[Gail]: i found the 2nd article much easier to read than the 1st, by the by (u_{3649})

Another participant's philosophical comment about the reading was the catalyst for a change in the workshop discussions and was the commencement of Phase 3.

[Louis]: I would like to point out that in life itself, everything changes. That is the one constant. As such, the skills the article mentions are applicable to everyone, not just IT. IT just changes faster (u_{3990})

The changes in the nine communication variables in the three development phases of Workshop 8 are shown in Figure C.27.

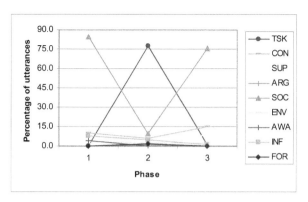

Figure C.27. Percentages of each communication variable in three phases of Workshop 8.

Figure C.28 and Figure C.29 illustrate the three most frequent variables and the six less frequent variables respectively and include data tables showing the percentage figures. Figure C.28 shows that when the group was engaged in task-related communication, there was little conceptual or social communication. In Phase 1 and Phase 3, when task activity was low, most of the communication was social.

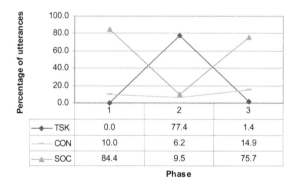

	1	2	3
TSK	0.0	77.4	1.4
CON	10.0	6.2	14.9
SOC	84.4	9.5	75.7

Phase

Figure C.28. Percentages of the three most frequent communication variables (TSK, CON, SOC) in three phases of Workshop 8.

Figure C.29 shows that each phase varies in the proportion of the six less frequent variables. The variables of interest in this workshop are supportive, environment and informal. The group became more supportive over the period of this workshop. The environment was discussed in Phase 3. The communication was managed formally, especially in the first phase.

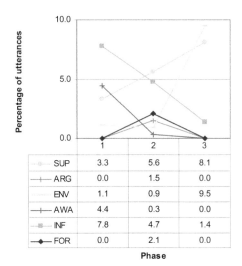

	1	2	3
SUP	3.3	5.6	8.1
ARG	0.0	1.5	0.0
ENV	1.1	0.9	9.5
AWA	4.4	0.3	0.0
INF	7.8	4.7	1.4
FOR	0.0	2.1	0.0

Phase

Figure C.29. Percentages of the six less frequent communication variables (SUP, ARG, ENV, AWA, INF, FOR) in three phases of Workshop 8.

The small number of awareness communication in this workshop were concerned with "stage directions"; that is, letting everyone know about their physical movements, e.g.:

> [Joe]: brb[9] (u_{3566})
> [Gail]: ok i am rb[10] (u_{3566})

The supportive tone increased throughout the session. In the last phase, participants again expressed appreciation and support of the moderator's efforts in leading the discussions:

> [Ruth]: good work Adrian (u_{4015})
> [Leah]: Adrian, your a legend, well done. (u_{4001})

C.2.14. Examination of Developmental Hypotheses for Workshop 8

The development hypotheses will be evaluated for short-term (within workshops) effects for Workshop 8.

Hypothesis $H_{1.1}$: *There are definable developmental phases in Workshop 8*

The timeline representations of the nine variables identify distinct turning points (Figure C.26), verified by specific utterances. These turning points indicate changes in the development of the group within the eighth workshop. Figure C.27 shows

---

[9] *brb* is used for "be right back"
[10] *rb* is used for "right back"

considerable variation between these three phases in the TSK, CON, SOC and AWA variables in particular. *Hypothesis $H_{1.1}$ is supported for Workshop 8.*

Hypothesis $H_{1.2}$: *In the early phase of the development of Workshop 8, the content of communication is more conceptual than task-oriented or social*
The timeline in Figure C.26 and the graph in Figure C.28 show that, in Phase 1, there was a little more conceptual than task communication, but almost all of the communication was social. Conceptual communication increased slightly over the period of the workshop. *Hypothesis $H_{1.2}$ is not supported for Workshop 8.*

Hypotheses $H_{1.3}$ and $H_{1.4}$: *In Workshop 8, during periods of low task activity, the content of communication is more social than task oriented; during periods of high task activity, the content is more task oriented than social*
The timeline in Figure C.26 and the graph in Figure C.28 show that in Phase 1 and 3 when there is very little task activity, the communication is social. In Phase 2, when the communication is mostly concerned with the task activity, there is very little social communication. *Hypotheses $H_{1.3}$ and $H_{1.4}$ are supported for Workshop 8.*

Hypothesis $H_{1.5}$: *During later developmental stages of Workshop 8, participants engage in less disclosures about the physical and social attributes of themselves and others.*
The graph and figures in Figure C.29 show that there is a decrease of awareness communication from Phase 1 (4.4%) to Phase 3 (0%). *Hypothesis $H_{1.5}$ is weakly supported for Workshop 8.*

Hypothesis $H_{1.6}$: *Group cohesiveness increases over the period of Workshop 8.*
The graph and figures in Figure C.29 show that, although there is a steady increase in supportive communication from Phase 1 (3.3%) to Phase 3 (8.1%) with very little argumentative communication. *Hypothesis $H_{1.6}$ is supported for Workshop 8.*

C.2.15. Workshop 9

A total of 484 utterances were exchanged by participants throughout the one-hour topic discussions in the ninth – and last – workshop on 11 October 2000. Table C.8 shows the number and percentages of different types of communication in this last workshop. Compared with the previous workshop, the most interesting variation was an almost twofold increase of supportive (from 5.5% to 9.7%) communication. Otherwise, there was an increase in task (from 52.% to 55.4%) communication, and a decrease in social (from 32.% to 25.2%) and environment (from 2.2% to 0.2%) communication.

Table C.8. Number and percentage of communication types in Workshop 9.

Code name	Code description	Number of utterances	Percentage of total W_9 utterance*
TSK	Task	274	55.4
CON	Conceptual	39	8.1
SUP	Supportive	39	9.7
ARG	Argumentative	7	1.7
SOC	Social	122	25.2
ENV	Environment	1	0.2
AWA	Awareness	9	1.9
INF	Informal	20	4.1
FOR	Formal	4	0.8

*Codes are not discrete categories, each utterance can be classified in a number of categories, hence percentages do not sum to 100.

Figure C.30 is a visualisation of Workshop 9 communication with transition regions identified.

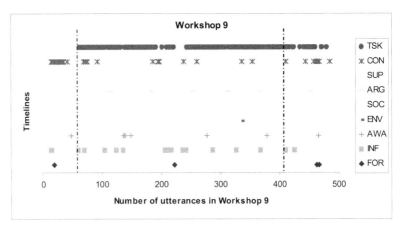

Figure C.30. Content-dependent timeline of Workshop 9 ($W_9 = [u_{4064}; u_{4547}]$)

Overall, this workshop was characterised by a general feeling of all participants being comfortable in the group and learning together. The article being discussed was about how metaphors can be used to define an information system. The cohesiveness of the group was demonstrated by the humorous and supportive nature of the discussions about this article. The commencement of Phase 2 was at utterance u_{4139} when the moderator posed the following question:

> [Donald]: So now group 3 i present you this question... (u_{4139})
> [Donald]: After reading this article do any of you guys fully understand the concept of a metaphor?? (u_{4140})

This question initiated the following conversation thread about metaphors:

[Donald]: well i looked it up and a metaphor is...metaphor n : a figure of speech in which an expression is used to refer to something that it does not literally denote in order to suggest a similarity (u_{4143})

[Donald]: Abbr. met., metaph. A figure of speech in which a word or phrase that ordinarily designates one thing is used to designate another, thus making an implicit comparison, as in 'a sea of troubles' or 'All the world's a stage' (Shakespeare). (u_{4145})

[Gail]: donald, i am impressed with your use of billy rattledagger (u_{4149})

[Donald]: rattledager? (u_{4151})

[Gail]: shake = rattle, dagger = spear, my little name for shakespeare (u_{4153})

[Donald]: oh... heheh (u_{4154})

[Donald]: to me this basically means to me that: you use a phrase to describe something i feel that the only way a metaphor can actually work effectively is only if the person you are describing the word to comprehends the phrase exactly how you intended it to be used... (u_{4156})

[Donald]: here is an example of what i mean, if u guys dont get what i am trying to say...imgaine person A lives in a society where houses are all mansions, and person B lives in a society where houses are all little huts. Now if person A tells person B "i want you to build me a boat as big as a house" the use of the metaphor would be pointless because person B will build the boat the size of what he thinks a house is (e.g. hut) while person A is expecting a boat as bit as a mansion. get it??? (u_{4161})

[Fay]: good example donald (u_{4166})

[Donald]: thanks... thought of it allll by myself (u_{4168})

[Gail]: you should do more thinking donald, your obviously good at it (u_{4170})

[Donald]: hehe thanks (u_{4171})

Other participants soon chimed in with examples of metaphors in the context of the workshop discussions:

[Doug]: we seem to be going around the mulberry bush (u_{4238})
[Lorna]: well we are trying to beat a dead horse (u_{4247})
[Fay]: however, now we understand metaphor, this tutorial is flying high (u_{4250})
[Monica]: or at least taking a stab in the dark (u_{4253})
[Duncan]: i think we are all now just clutching at straws (u_{4255})
[Fay]: ok, i think we all understand metaphors (u_{4270})
[Gail]: and metafives (u_{4271})
[Gail]: donald, you did a splendid job, "like a well honed spear" (u_{4287})

The humour was an aid for participants to learn about the concept of metaphors, but it also created a high degree of interactivity. One participant expressed his positive feeling about this workshop:

[Doug]: hahahahahahahahahahahah\ (u_{4258})
[Doug]: this is great (u_{4259})
[Doug]: best tute yet (u_{4260})

The final phase of the workshop was initiated when one of the key participants had to leave.

[Doug]: erm...i gotta go up to school...see my brother...bye all... (u_{4465})

The changes in the nine communication variables in the three development phases of Workshop 9 are shown in Figure C.31.

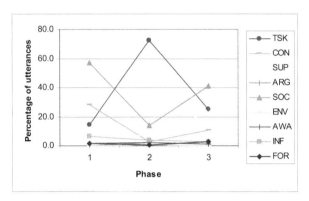

Figure C.31. Percentages of each communication variable in three phases of Workshop 9.

Figure C.32 and Figure C.33 illustrate the three most frequent variables and the six less frequent variables respectively and include data tables showing the percentage figures. Figure C.32 shows that when the group was engaged in task-related communication, there was little conceptual or social communication. In Phase 1, when task activity was low, there was more social and conceptual communication. In Phase 3, task activity was low and there was more social but less conceptual communication.

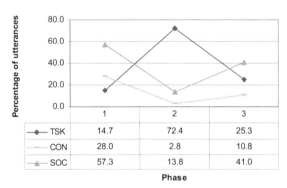

	1	2	3
TSK	14.7	72.4	25.3
CON	28.0	2.8	10.8
SOC	57.3	13.8	41.0

Phase

Figure C.32. Percentages of the three most frequent communication variables (TSK, CON, SOC) in three phases of Workshop 9.

Figure C.33 shows that each phase varies in the proportion of the six less frequent variables. The most significant trend in this workshop was the high proportion of supportive communication in the last phase; in fact, an increase from no support in the first phase to almost one in four utterances in the last phase. The only other variable of note indicated in Figure C.33 is the decrease in informal communication during the period of the workshop.

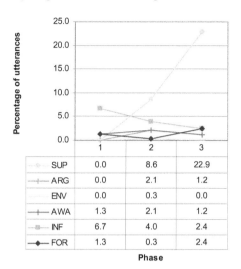

	1	2	3
SUP	0.0	8.6	22.9
ARG	0.0	2.1	1.2
ENV	0.0	0.3	0.0
AWA	1.3	2.1	1.2
INF	6.7	4.0	2.4
FOR	1.3	0.3	2.4

Phase

Figure C.33. Percentages of the six less frequent communication variables (SUP, ARG, ENV, AWA, INF, FOR) in three phases of Workshop 9.

There was almost no awareness communication in this last workshop, which is to be expected. By this time, participants had learned a lot about each other's personal lives and from which location they usually logged on to the chat room.

In the last phase, the supportive feeling was the strongest of any phase of any workshop. The following are some examples:

[Monica]: i agree with you Gail (u_{4486})
[Gail]: leah, what a great comment (u_{4488})
[Louis]: Good point leah (u_{4490})
[Donald]: applause (u_{4493})
[Gail]: dare i ask for an encore? (u_{4494})

C.2.16. Examination of Developmental Hypotheses for Workshop 9

The development hypotheses will be evaluated for short-term (within workshops) effects for Workshop 9.

Hypothesis $H_{1.1}$: *There are definable developmental phases in Workshop 9*
The timeline representations of the nine variables identify distinct turning points (Figure C.30), verified by specific utterances. These turning points indicate changes

in the development of the group within the last workshop. Figure C.31 shows considerable variation between these three phases in the TSK, CON, SOC and AWA variables in particular. *Hypothesis $H_{1.1}$ is supported for Workshop 9.*

Hypothesis $H_{1.2}$: *In the early phase of the development of Workshop 9, the content of communication is more conceptual than task-oriented or social*
The timeline in Figure C.30 and the graph in Figure C.32 show that, in Phase 1, there is almost twice as much conceptual as task communication; however, there is more than twice as much social as conceptual communication. Phases 2 and 3 have less conceptual than either task or social communication. It can be stated that, in the early phase of development, there is a higher percentage of conceptual communication than task communication but not social. *Hypothesis $H_{1.2}$ is partly supported for Workshop 9.*

Hypotheses $H_{1.3}$ and $H_{1.4}$: *In Workshop 9, during periods of low task activity, the content of communication is more social than task oriented; during periods of high task activity, the content is more task oriented than social*
The timeline in Figure C.30 and the graph in Figure C.32 show that in Phase 1 and 3 when there is very little task activity, the communication is more social. In Phase 2, when the communication is mostly concerned with the task activity, there is very little social communication. *Hypotheses $H_{1.3}$ and $H_{1.4}$ are supported for Workshop 9.*

Hypothesis $H_{1.5}$: *During later developmental stages of Workshop 9, participants engage in less disclosures about the physical and social attributes of themselves and others.*
The graph and figures in Figure C.33 show that there is very little difference in awareness communication between the three phases. *Hypothesis $H_{1.5}$ is not supported for Workshop 9.*

Hypothesis $H_{1.6}$: *Group cohesiveness increases over the period of Workshop 9.*
The graph and figures in Figure C.33 show that there is a significant increase in supportive communication from Phase 1 (0%) to Phase 3 (22.9%) with very little argumentative communication. *Hypothesis $H_{1.6}$ is supported for Workshop 9.*

C.3. Summary of Developmental Characteristics for Workshops 2-9

The analysis of Workshops 2-9 showed that the eight workshops exhibited three developmental phases within the one-hour period of each workshop. These three phases had similar patterns of task, conceptual and social communication, in that Phase 1 was mostly conceptual and social communication, Phase 2 was mostly task communication and Phase 3 was mostly conceptual and social communication again.

Among the other less frequent communication types, there was a general trend of awareness and environment communication occurring in the first phase and supportive communication occurring in the last phase. The communication tended to be managed more, both formally and informally, in the early phase.

Table C.9 is a summary of the percentages of each of the nine variables for each of the three phases of Workshops 2-9.

Table C.9. Summary of Workshops 2-9 with percentages of each variable in each development phase.

Variable	Workshop 2			Workshop 3			Workshop 4			Workshop 5		
	P1	P2	P3	P1	P2	P3	P1	P2	P3	P1	P2	P3
TSK	0.0	70.6	0.0	1.2	78.8	1.5	0.8	76.0	10.9	1.8	78.9	0.0
CON	31.2	7.0	37.1	45.3	4.7	35.4	45.9	6.1	27.3	19.6	1.3	4.8
SUP	0.0	2.4	12.1	3.5	3.8	20.0	1.6	4.5	9.1	5.4	6.3	9.5
ARG	0.8	1.5	0.0	1.2	0.0	0.0	0.8	3.5	1.8	3.6	0.3	0.0
SOC	44.0	13.0	46.2	30.2	3.8	43.1	41.8	9.9	38.2	48.2	11.0	76.2
ENV	7.2	3.3	0.8	14.0	8.0	1.5	0.0	1.3	1.8	14.3	1.0	0.0
AWA	17.6	4.1	6.1	10.5	0.9	6.2	7.4	1.6	1.8	7.1	2.5	4.0
INF	3.2	4.2	3.8	8.1	6.6	1.5	1.6	3.5	3.6	12.5	3.8	4.0
FOR	2.4	2.0	0.8	4.7	0.9	10.8	9.0	2.2	1.8	1.8	1.3	0.0
Variable	Workshop 6			Workshop 7			Workshop 8			Workshop 9		
	P1	P2	P3	P1	P2	P3	P1	P2	P3	P1	P2	P3
TSK	0.0	67.6	32.0	0.0	69.2	13.5	0.0	77.4	1.4	14.7	72.4	25.3
CON	30.8	10.5	10.7	13.5	9.4	21.2	10.0	6.2	14.9	28.0	2.8	10.8
SUP	0.0	7.6	6.7	0.0	3.9	15.4	3.3	5.6	8.1	0.0	8.6	22.9
ARG	1.5	1.5	18.7	0.0	0.2	1.9	0.0	1.5	0.0	0.0	2.1	1.2
SOC	50.8	13.8	29.3	65.4	9.7	46.2	84.4	9.5	75.7	57.3	13.8	41.0
ENV	3.1	2.2	0.0	13.5	2.7	0.0	1.1	0.9	75.7	0.0	0.3	0.0
AWA	12.3	2.2	0.0	3.8	2.4	1.9	4.4	0.3	0.0	1.3	2.1	1.2
INF	0.0	5.8	4.0	7.7	2.9	3.8	7.8	4.7	1.4	6.7	4.0	2.4
FOR	7.7	1.5	2.7	5.8	1.9	0.0	0.0	2.1	0.0	1.3	0.3	2.4

Table C.10 is a summary of the three most frequent variables (TSK, CON, SOC) in Workshops 2-9 showing percentages of utterances in each development phase with means and standard deviations.

Table C.10. Summary of three most frequent variables (%) in each development phase in Workshops 2-9.

	Task (TSK)			Conceptual (CON)			Social (SOC)		
	P1	P2	P3	P1	P2	P3	P1	P2	P3
W2	0.0	70.6	0.0	31.2	7.0	37.1	44.0	13.0	46.2
W3	1.2	78.8	1.5	45.3	4.7	35.4	30.2	3.8	43.1
W4	0.8	76.0	10.9	45.9	6.1	27.3	41.8	9.9	38.2
W5	1.8	78.9	0.0	19.6	1.3	4.8	48.2	11.0	76.2
W6	0.0	67.6	32.0	30.8	10.5	10.7	50.8	13.8	29.3
W7	0.0	69.2	13.5	13.5	9.4	21.2	65.4	9.7	46.2
W8	0.0	77.4	1.4	10.0	6.2	14.9	84.4	9.5	75.7
W9	14.7	72.4	25.3	28.0	2.8	10.8	57.3	13.8	41.0
Mean	2.3	73.9	10.6	28.0	6.0	20.3	52.8	10.6	49.5
SD	5.0	4.5	12.4	13.3	3.1	12.0	16.5	3.3	17.2

Table C.11 is a summary of the six less frequent variables (SUP, ARG, ENV, AWA, INF, FOR) in Workshops 2-9 showing percentages of utterances in each development phase with means and standard deviations.

Table C.11. Summary of six less frequent variables (%) in each development phase in Workshops 2-9.

	Supportive (SUP)			Argumentative (ARG)			Environment (ENV)			Awareness (AWA)			Informal (INF)			Formal (FOR)		
	P1	P2	P3	P1	P2	P3	P1	P2	P3	P1	P2	P3	P1	P2	P3	P1	P2	P3
W2	0.0	2.4	12.1	0.8	1.5	0.0	7.2	3.3	0.8	17.6	4.0	6.1	3.2	4.2	3.8	2.4	2.0	0.8
W3	3.5	3.8	20.0	1.2	0.0	0.0	14.0	8.0	1.5	10.5	0.9	6.2	8.1	6.6	1.5	4.7	0.9	10.8
W4	1.6	4.5	9.1	0.8	3.5	1.8	0.0	1.3	1.8	7.4	1.6	1.8	1.6	3.5	3.6	9.0	2.2	1.8
W5	5.4	6.3	9.5	3.6	0.3	0.0	14.3	1.0	0.0	7.1	2.5	4.0	12.5	3.8	4.0	1.8	1.3	0.0
W6	0.0	7.6	6.7	1.5	1.5	18.7	3.1	2.2	0.0	12.3	0.0	1.3	0.0	5.8	4.0	7.7	1.5	2.7
W7	0.0	3.9	15.4	0.0	0.2	1.9	13.5	2.7	0.0	3.8	2.4	1.9	7.7	2.9	3.8	5.8	1.9	0.0
W8	3.3	5.6	8.1	0.0	1.5	0.0	1.1	0.9	9.5	4.4	0.3	0.0	7.8	4.7	1.4	0.0	2.1	0.0
W9	0.0	8.6	22.9	0.0	2.1	1.2	0.0	0.3	0.0	1.3	2.1	1.2	6.7	4.0	2.4	1.3	0.3	2.4
Mean	1.7	5.3	13.0	1.0	1.3	3.0	6.6	2.5	1.7	8.1	1.7	2.8	6.0	4.4	3.1	4.1	1.5	2.3
SD	2.1	2.1	5.9	1.2	1.2	6.4	6.4	2.5	3.2	5.2	1.3	2.3	4.1	1.2	1.1	3.2	0.7	3.6

The means of the three most frequent and six less frequent variables are shown in graphic form in Figure C.34 and Figure C.35 respectively. These figures illustrate the average communication pattern in the developmental phases for Workshops 2-9 in Case Study 2.

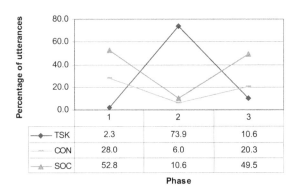

Figure C.34. Means of three most frequent variables (TSK, CON, SOC) for Workshops 2-9.

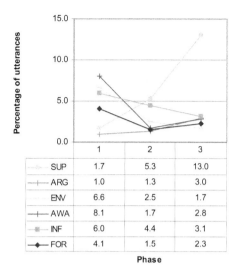

	1	2	3
SUP	1.7	5.3	13.0
ARG	1.0	1.3	3.0
ENV	6.6	2.5	1.7
AWA	8.1	1.7	2.8
INF	6.0	4.4	3.1
FOR	4.1	1.5	2.3

Phase

Figure C.35. Means of six less frequent variables (SUP, ARG, ENV, AWA, INF, FOR) for Workshops 2-9.

REFERENCES

Abraham, M. and Smith, J.: 1970, Norms, deviance and spatial location, *Journal of Social Psycholoty,* 80(1), 95-101.

ACA: 2003, Telecommunications reform adds billions to Australian economy, *ACA Media Release No. 60*, Melbourne, Australia, Accessed 22 April 2004, http://www.aca.gov.au/aca_home/media_releases/media_enquiries/2003/03-60.htm.

Aiken, L. R.: 1992, Some measures of interpersonal attraction and group cohesiveness, *Educational and Psychological Measurement,* 52, 63-67.

Andres, H.: 1996, The impact of communication medium on software development performance: A comparison of face-to-face and virtual teams, *Second Americas Conference on Information Systems*, Phoenix, Arizona. 16-18 August 1996, http://hsb.baylor.edu/ramsower/ais.ac.96/papers/VIRTTEAM.htm.

Anson, R., Bostrom, R. P. and Wynne, B. E.: 1995, An experiment assessing group support system and facilitator effects on meeting outcomes, *Management Science,* 41, 189-209.

Argyris, C. and Schön, D. A.: 1989, Participative action research and action science compared: a commentary, *American Behavioural Scientist,* 32, 612-623.

Austin, J. L.: 1962, *How To Do Things With Words*, Harvard University Press., Cambridge, MA.

Babbie, E.: 2002, *The Basics of Social Research*, Wadsworth, Belmont, CA.

Bailey, M. L. and Luetkehans, L.: 1998, Ten great tips for facilitating virtual learning teams, *Proceedings of the Annual Conference on Distance Teaching and Learning*, Madison, WI.

Bales, R. F.: 1950, An Interactive Process Analysis: A Method for the Study of Small Groups, Addison-Wesley, Reading, MA.

Bales, R. F.: 1980, *SYMLOG: A System for the Multiple Level Observation of Groups*, Free Press, New York.

Barge, J. K.: 1996, Leadership skills and the dialectics of leadership in group decision making, *in* R. Y. Hirokawa and M. S. Poole (ed.), *Communication and Group Decision Making*, Sage, Thousand Oaks, CA, pp. 301-342.

Barnes, S.: 2001, *Online Relationships*, Hampton Press.

Baron, N. S.: 1984, Computer-mediated communication as a force in language choice, *Visible Language,* 18, 118-141.

Bass, B. M.: 1990, *Bass and Stogdill's Handbook of Leadership,* 3rd edn, Free Press, New York, NY.

Baym, N. K.: 1995, The emergence of community in computer mediated communication, *in* S. G. Jones (ed.), *Cybersociety*, Sage, Newbury Park, CA, pp. 138-163.

BBC: 2004, Text record smashed for New Year, *BBC News*, UK, Accessed 22 April 2004, http://news.bbc.co.uk/1/hi/technology/3368815.stm.

Becker, B. and Mark, G.: 2002, Social conventions in computer-mediated communication: A comparison of three online shared virtual environments, *in* R. Schroder (ed.), *The Social Life of Avatars*, Springer, London, pp. 19-39.

Bennis, W. and Shepherd, H.: 1956, A theory of group development, *Human Relations,* 9, 418-419.

Berthold, M. and Sudweeks, F.: 1995, Typicality in computer mediated discussions - An analysis with neural networks, *International Conference on Neural Networks (ICNN'95)*, 2, IEEE Press, Piscataway, pp. 932-936.

Berthold, M., Sudweeks, F., Newton, S. and Coyne, R. D.: 1998, 'It makes sense': Using an autoassociative neural network to explore typicality in computer mediated communication, *in* F. Sudweeks, M. McLaughlin and S. Rafaeli (ed.), *Network and Netplay: Virtual Groups on the Interne*, MIT Press, Cambridge, MA, pp. 191-220.

Berthold, M. R., Sudweeks, F., Newton, S. and Coyne, R.: 1997, Clustering on the Net: Applying an autoassociative neural network to computer-mediated communication, *Journal of Computer Mediated Communication,* 2(4). http://www.ascusc.org/jcmc/vol2/issue4.

Bierstedt, R.: 1963, *The Social Order,* McGraw-Hill, New York.

Biocca, F., Harms, C. and Burgoon, J.: 2001, Criteria and scope conditions for a theory and measure of social presence, *Presence 2001, 4th Annual International Workshop,* Philadelphia.

Black, S., Levin, J., Mehan, H. and Quinn, C. N.: 1983, Real and non-real time interaction: Unraveling multiple threads of discourse, *Discourse Processes,* 6(1), 59-75.

Blackman, B. I. and Clevenger, T.: 1990, On-line computer messaging: Surrogates for non-verbal behavior, *International Communication Association Conference,* Dublin.

Blake, R. R. and McCanse, A. A.: 1991, *Leadership Dilemmas - Grid Solutions,* Gulf Publishing, Houston, TX.

Blake, R. R. and Mouton, J. S.: 1964, *The Managerial Grid,* Gulf Publishing, Houston, TX.

Blake, R. R. and Mouton, J. S.: 1969, *Building a Dyanmic Corporation through Grid Organization Development,* Addison-Wesley, Reading, MA.

Blake, R. R. and Mouton, J. S.: 1982, How to choose a leadership style, *Training and Development Journal,* 36, 39-46.

Blanchard, K. H., Zigarmi, D. and Nelson, R.: 1993, Situational leadership after 25 years: A retrospective, *The Journal of Leadership Studies,* 1(1), 22-36.

Blanchard, K. H., Zigarmi, P. and Zigarmi, D.: 1985, *Leadership and the One-Minute Manager: Increasing Effectiveness through Situational Leadership,* William Morrow, New York.

Bock, H.-H. and Diday, E.: 2000, *Analysis of Symbolic Data: Exploratory Methods for Extracting Statistical Information from Complex Data,* Springer, Heidelberg.

Borzo, J.: 1998, WorldCom completes CompuServe merger over weekend, IDG.net, Accessed 5 March 2001, http://www.idgnet.com/english/crd_worldcom_5735.html.

Breiman, L., Friedman, J. H., Olshen, R. A. and Stone, C. J.: 1984, *Classification and Regression Trees,* Wadsworth & Brooks, Monterey, CA.

Brown, J. D.: 1997, Skewness and Kurtosis, *Shiken: JALT Testing and Evaluation SIG Newsletter,* 1(1), 16-18. http://www.jalt.org/test/bro_1.htm.

Brown, P. and Levinson, S.: 1978, Universals in language usage: Politeness phenomena, *in* E. N. Goody (ed.), *Questions and Politeness: Strategies in Social Interaction,* Cambridge University Press, Cambridge, MA, pp. 256-289.

Brown, P. and Levinson, S.: 1987, *Politeness. Some Universals in Language Usage,* Cambridge University Press, Cambridge, MA.

Bryman, A.: 1988, *Quantity and Quality in Social Research,* Routledge, London.

Bryman, A.: 1992, *Charisma and Leadership in Organizations,* Sage, London.

Burke, K. and Chidambaram, L.: 1994, Development in electronically supported groups: A preliminary longitudinal study of distributed and face-to-face meeting, *Proceedings of the 28th Annual Hawaiin International Conference on System Science,* III, pp. 104-113.

Burns, J. M.: 1978, *Leadership,* Harper and Row, New York.

Burrell, G. and Morgan, G.: 1979, *Sociological Paradigms and Organisational Analysis: Elements of the Sociology of Corporate Life,* Heinemann, London.

Carey, J.: 1980, Paralanguage in computer mediated communication, *Proceedings of the 18th Annual Meeting of the Association for Computational Linguistics,* Philadelphia.

Chapanis, A.: 1975, Interactive human communication, *Scientific American,* 232, 36-42.

Chen, C.: 1999, *Information Visualisation and Virtual Environments,* Springer, London.

Chidambaram, L. and Jones, B.: 1993, Impact of Communication Medium and Computer Support on Group Perceptions and Performance: A Comparison of Face-to-Face and Dispersed Meetings, *MIS Quarterly,* 17(4), 465-491.

Chomsky, N.: 1980, *Rules and Representations,* Basil Blackwell, Oxford.

Chrislip, D. D. and Larson, C. E.: 1994, *Collaborative Leadership*, Jossey-Bass, San Francisco, CA.

Christiansen, N. and Maglaughlin, K.: 2003, Crossing from physical workspace to virtual workspace: Be AWARE!, *Proceedings of HCI International Conference on Human-Computer Interaction*, Lawrence Erlbaum Associates, pp. 1128-1132.

Ciba, D. and Rakestraw, T.: 1998, Student feedback on the use of Internet-based tools in traditional teaching situations, Proceedings of the North American Web Developers Conference (NAWeb98), Accessed September 2000, http://naweb.unb.ca/proceedings/1998/ciba/ciba.html.

Civin, M. A.: 1999, *Male Female E-mail: The Struggle for Relatedness in a Paranoid Society*, Other press.

Condon, C.: 1993, The computer won't let me: Cooperation, conflict and the ownership of information, *in* S. Easterbrook (ed.), *CSCW: Cooperation or Conflict*, Springer-Verlag, London, pp. 171-185.

Cota, A. A., Dion, K. L. and Evans, C. R.: 1993, A reexamination of the structure of the gross cohesiveness scale, *Educational and Psychological Measurement,* 53, 499-506.

Cragan, J. F. and Wright, D. W.: 1990, Small group communication research of the 1980s: A synthesis and critique, *Communication Studies,* 41, 212-236.

Culnan, M. J. and Markus, M. L.: 1987, Information technologies, *in* F. M. Jablin, L. L. Putnam, K. H. Roberts and L. W. Porter (ed.), *Handbook of Organizational Communication: An Interdisciplinary Perspective*, Sage, Newbury Park, pp. 420-443.

Curran, K. and Devin, B.: 2000, Helpmate: A multimedia web teaching framework, *First Monday,* 5(5). http://firstmonday.org/issues/issue5_5/curran/.

Daft, R. L. and Lengel, R. H.: 1986, Organizational information requirements, media richness and structural design, *Management Science,* 32, 554-571.

Damer, B.: 1998, *Avatars*, Peachpit Press.

Danet, B., Ruedenberg, L. and Rosenbaum-Tamari, Y.: 1998, "Hmmm ... Where's that smoke coming from?" Writing, play and performance on Internet Relay Chat, *in* F. Sudweeks, M. McLaughlin and S. Rafaeli (ed.), *Network and Netplay: Virtual Groups on the Internet*, AAAI/MIT Press, Menlo Park, CA, pp. 41-76.

Danowski, J. A. and Edison-Swift, P.: 1985, Crisis effects on intraorganizational computer-based communication, *Communication Research,* 12(2), 251-270.

Dansereau, F., Graen, G. B. and Haga, W.: 1975, A vertical dyad linkage approach to leadership in formal organizations, *Organizational Behavior and Human Performance,* 13, 46-78.

Deci, E. L. and Ryan, R. M.: 1985, *Intrinsic Motivation and Self Determination in Human Behavior*, Plenum, New York.

Dennis, A. R. and Valacich, J. S.: 1993, Computer brainstorms: more heads are better than one, *Journal of Applied Psychology,* 78(4), 531-537.

Doolin, B. (ed.): 1995, *Alternative views of case research in information systems*, Curtin University of Technology, Perth.

Dourish, P. and Bly, S.: 1992, Portholes: Supporting awareness in a distributed work group, *Proceedings of ACM CHI 1992*, pp. 541-547.

Downton, J. V.: 1973, *Rebel Leadership: Commitment and Charisma in a Revolutionary Process*, Free Press, New York.

D'Souza, J. and Bunt, S. (eds): 2000, *A comparison between the use of the Internet and conventional lectures in education*, Curtin University of Technology, Perth.

Duarte, D. L. and Snyder, N. T.: 1999, *Mastering Virtual Teams: Strategies, Tools and Techniques that Succeed*, Jossey-Bass, San Francisco.

Dubrovsky, V. J., Kiesler, S. and Sethna, B. N.: 1991, The equalization phenomenon: status effects in computer-mediated and face-to-face decision-making groups, *Human-Computer Interaction,* 6, 119-146.

Duncan, W. J. and Fieisal, J. P.: 1989, No laughing matter: Patterns of humor in the workplace, *Organizational Dynamics,* 17, 18-30.

Durkheim, E. and Mauss, M.: 1963, *Primitive Classification*, Cohen and West, London.

Erickson, T.: 1999, Persistent Conversation: An introduction, *Journal of Computer Mediated Communication,* 4(4). Accessed 9 May 2004 http://www.ascusc.org/jcmc/vol4/issue4/ericksonintro.html.

Ess, C. (ed.): 1996, *Philosophical Perspectives on Computer-Mediated Communication*, SUNY Press, New York.

Evans, M. G.: 1970, The effects of supervisory behavior on the path-goal relationship, *Organizational Behavior and Human Performance,* 5, 277-298.

Eveland, J. D. and Bikon, T. K.: 1989, Work group structures and computer support: A field experiment, *ACM Transactions on Office Information Systems,* 6, 354-379.

Fairhurst, G. T. and Chandler, T. A.: 1989, Social structure in leader-member interaction, *Communication Monographs,* 56(Sept).

Farris, G. F. and Lim, J. F. G.: 1969, Effects of performance on leadership, cohesiveness, influence, satisfaction and subsequent performance, *Journal of Applied Psychology,* 53(6), 490-497.

Feelders, A. J.: 2003, Statistical concepts, *in* M. Berthold and D. J. Hand (ed.), *Intelligent Data Analysis*, Springer, Berlin, pp. 17-68.

Fiedler, F. E.: 1964, A contingency model of leadership effectiveness, *in* L. Berkowitz (ed.), *Advances in Experimental Social Psychology, I*, Academic Press, New York, pp. 149-190.

Fiedler, F. E. and Garcia, J. E.: 1987, *New Approaches to Leadership: Cognitive Resources and Organizational Performance*, John Wiley, New York.

Finholt, T. and Sproull, L. S.: 1990, Electronic groups at work, *Organization Science,* 1(1), 41-64.

Finnegan, R. H.: 1988, *Literacy and Orality: Studies in the Technology of Communication*, Blackwell, Oxford, UK.

Fisher, B. A.: 1970, Decision emergence: Phases in group decision making, *Speech Monographs,* 37, 53-66.

Fisher, B. A.: 1974, *Small Group Decision Making: Communication and the Group Process*, McGraw-Hill, New York.

Fisher, B. A.: 1986, Leadership: When does the difference make a difference?, *in* R. Y. Hirokawa and M. S. Poole (ed.), *Communication and Group Decision Making*, Sage, Thousand Oaks, CA, pp. 197-215.

Fleishman, E. A.: 1973, Twenty years of consideration and structure, *in* E. A. Fleishman and J. G. Hunt (ed.), *Current Developments in the Study of Leadership*, Southern Illinois University Press, Carbondale, IL.

Fleishman, E. A., Mumford, M. D., Zaccaro, S. J., Levin, K. Y., Korotkin, A. L. and Hein, M. B.: 1991, Taxonomic efforts in the description of leader behavior: A synthesis and functional interpretation, *Leadership Quarterly,* 2(4), 245-287.

Foley, K.: 2001, Email: The wonder tool, Nua Internet Surveys Weekly Editorial, Accessed 13 March 2001, http://www.nua.ie/surveys/analysis/weekly_editorial.html.

Forsyth, D.: 1990, *Group Dynamics*, Brooks/Cole, Pacific Grove, CA.

French, R. P. J. and Raven, B.: 1959, The bases of social power, *in* D. Cartwright (ed.), *Studies in Social Power*, Institute for Social Research, Ann Arbor, MI.

Frey, L. R.: 1994, Introduction - the call of the field: Studying communication in natural groups, *in* L. R. Frey (ed.), *Group Communication in Context*, Lawrence Erlbaum, Hillsdale, NJ, pp. ix-xiv.

Fulk, J.: 1993, Social construction of communication technology, *The Academy of Management Journal,* 36(5), 921-950.

Fulk, J. and Steinfield, C. W.: 1989, *Organizations and Communication Theory*, Sage, Newbury Park, CA.

Galante, S.: 1998, AOL taps exec for CompuServe, *CNnet News.com.* http://news.cnet.com/news/0-1004-200-328998.html.

Gardner, J.: 1990, *On Leadership*, The Free Press, New York, NY.

Garfinkel, H.: 1967, *Studies in Ethnomethodology*, Prentice-Hall, Englewood Cliffs, NJ.

Garrison, D. R., Anderson, T. and Archer, W.: 2000, Critical inquiry in a text-based environment: Computer conferencing in higher education, *The Internet and Higher Education,* 2(2-3), 87-105.

Garton, L., Haythornthwaite, C. and Wellman, B.: 1997, Studying online social networks. Journal of Computer-Mediated Communication, *Journal of Computer Mediated Communication,* 3(1). Retrieved 28 February 2004 http://www.ascusc.org/jcmc/vol3/issue1/garton.html.

Gersick, C. J. K.: 1988, Time and transition in work teams: Towards a new model of group development, *Academy of Management Journal,* 31(1), 9-41.

Gersick, C. J. K.: 1989, Making time: Predictable transitions in task groups, *Academy of Management Journal,* 32(2), 274-309.

Gersick, C. J. K.: 1991, Revolutionary Change Theories: A Multilevel Exploration of the Punctuated Equilibrium Paradigm, *Academy of Management Review,* 16(1), 10-36.

Glaser, B. G.: 1978, *Theoretical Sensitivity: Advances in the Methodology of Grounded Theory*, Sociology Press, Mill Valley, CA.

Glaser, B. G.: 1992, *Basics of Grounded Theory Analysis: Emergence vs Forcing*, Sociology Press, Mill Valley, CA.

Glaser, B. G.: 1998, *Doing Grounded Theory: Issues and Discussions*, Sociology Press, Mill Valley, CA.

Glaser, B. G. and Strauss, A. L.: 1967, *The Discovery of Grounded Theory: Strategies for Qualitative Research*, Aldine de Gruyter, New York.

GlobalReach: 2004, Global Internet Statistics (by Language), Global Reach, Accessed 23 April 2004, http://www.glreach.com/globstats/index.php3.

Gower, J. C. and Legendre, P.: 1986, Metric and Euclidean properties of dissimilarity coefficients, *Journal of Classification,* 3, 5-48.

Graen, G. B.: 1976, Role-making processes within complex organizations, *in* M. D. Dunnette (ed.), *Handbook of Industrial and Organizational Psychology*, Rand McNally, Chicago, pp. 1202-1245.

Graen, G. B. and Scandura, T.: 1987, Toward a psychology of dyadic organizing, *in* L. L. Cummings and B. M. Shaw (ed.), *Research in Organizational Behavior, 9*, JAI Press, Greenwich, Connecticut, pp. 175-208.

Graen, G. B. and Uhl-Bien, M.: 1995, Relationship-based approach to leadership: Development of leader-member exchange (LMX) theory of leadership over 25 years: Applying a multi-level multi-domain perspective, *Leadership Quarterly,* 6(2), 219-247.

Greenspan, R.: 2002, Widespread use despite abuse, CyberAtlas, Accessed 26 January 2004, http://cyberatlas.internet.com/big_picture/applications/article/ 0,,1301_1462941,00.html.

Gunawardena, C. N. and Zittle, F. J.: 1997, Social presence as a predictor of satisfaction within a computer-mediated conferencing environment, *The American Journal of Distance Education,* 11(3), 8-26.

Hackman, M. Z. and Johnson, C. E.: 2000, *Leadership: A Communication Perspective*, Waveland Press, Inc, Prospect Heights, Illinois.

Hahm, W. and Bikson, T.: 1989, Retirees using email and networked computers, *International Journal of Technology and Aging,* 2(2), 113-123.

Hall, E. T.: 1981, *Beyond Culture*, Anchor Books, New York.

Hammersley, N. and Atkinson, P.: 1983, *Ethnography: Principles in Practice*, Tavistock, New York.

Handy, C.: 1995, Trust and the virtual organization, *Harvard Business Review,* May-June, 40-50.

Harasim, L.: 1999, A framework for online learning: The Virtual-U, *IEEE Computer Society*. http://www.telelearn.ca/g_access/news/r9044.pdf.

Harasim, L. M.: 1990, Online education: An environment for collaborations and intellectual application, *in* L. M. Harasim (ed.), *Online Education: Perspectives on a New Environment*, Praeger, New York.

Harasim, L. M.: 1993, Networlds: Networks as social space, *in* L. M. Harsim (ed.), *Global Networks: Computers and International Communication*, MIT Press, Cambridge, MA, pp. 15-34.

Hare, A. P.: 1976, *Handbook of Small Group Research,* 2nd edn, Free Press, NY.

Hare, P. and Naveh, D.: 1984, Group development at the Camp David Summit, *Small Group Behavior,* 15(3), 299-318.

Hartley, P.: 1997, *Group Communication*, Routledge, London.

Hartman, K., Neuwirth, C., Kiesler, S., Palmquist, M. and Zubrow, D.: 1995, Patterns of social interaction and learning to write: Some effects of network technologies, *in* Z. Berge and M. Collins (ed.), *Computer Mediated Communication and the Online Classroom, II*, Hampton Press, Cresskill, NJ, pp. 47-78.

Haythornthwaite, C.: 2003, Social network ties and Internet connectivity effects, *Information, Communication and Society/Oxford Internet Institute Symposium*, Oxford Internet Institute, Oxford, UK. Accessed 28 February 2004, http://alexia.lis.uiuc.edu/~haythorn/Hay_OII_paper.html.

Hellerstein, L.: 1989, *Creating social reality with computer-mediated communication*, PhD Dissertation, University of Massachusetts, Massachusetts.

Herring, S.: 1999, Interactional coherence in CMC, *Journal of Computer Mediated Communication,* 4(4). Accessed 9 May 2004 http://www.ascusc.org/jcmc/vol4/issue4/herring.html.

Hershey, P. and Blanchard, K. H.: 1969, Life-cycle theory of leadership, *Training and Development Journal,* 23, 26-34.

Hershey, P. and Blanchard, K. H.: 1975, A situational framework for determining appropriate leader behavior, *in* R. N. Cassel and R. L. Heichberger (ed.), *Leadership Development: Theory and Practice*, Christopher Publishing, North Quincy, MA, pp. 126-155.

Hershey, P. and Blanchard, K. H.: 1977, *Management of Organizational Behavior: Utilizing Human Resources,* 3rd edn, Prentice Hall, Englewood Cliffs, NJ.

Heylighen, F.: 1999, Change and information overload: Negative effects, *in* F. Heylighen, C. Joslyn and V. Turchin (ed.), *Principia Cybernetica Web*, Principia Cybernetica, Brussels.

Hill, G. W.: 1982, Group versus individual performance: Are N+1 heads better than one, *Psychological Bulletin,* 91(3), 517-539.

Hiltz, S. R. and Johnson, K.: 1989, Experiments in group decision making, 3: Disinhibition, deindividuation, and group process in pen name and real name computer conferences, *Decision Support Systems,* 5, 217-232.

Hiltz, S. R., Johnson, K. and Turoff, M.: 1986, Experiments in group decision making: Communication process and outcome in face-to-face versus computerized conferences, *Human Communication Research,* 13, 225-252.

Hiltz, S. R. and Turoff, M.: 2002, What makes learning networks effective?, *Communications of the ACM,* 45(4), 56-59.

Hofstede, G.: 1980, *Culture's Consequences: International Differences in Work-Related Values*, Sage, Beverly Hills, CA.

Hofstede, G.: 1991, *Cultures and Organizations: Software of the Mind*, McGraw-Hill, New York

Hopper, T. and Powell, A.: 1985, Making sense of research into the organizational and social aspects of management accounting: A review of its underlying assumptions, *Journal of Management Studies,* 22(5), 429-465.

Horvath, L. and Tobin, T. J.: 1999, Twenty-first century teamwork: Defining competencies for virtual teams, A. o. M. Conference (ed.), Chicago, IL.

House, R. J. and Mitchell, R. R.: 1974, Path-goal theory of leadership, *Journal of Contemporary Business,* 3, 81-97.

IEP: 1997, George Berkeley, Internet Encyclopedia of Philosophy, Accessed 31 March 2001, http://www.utm.edu/research/iep/b/berkeley.htm.

Jackson, P. (ed.): 1999, *Virtual Working: Social and Organisational Dynamics*, Routledge, London.

Janis, I.: 1972, *Victims of Groupthink: A psychological study of foreign policy decisions and fiascos*, Houghton Mifflin, Boston, MA.

Jarvenpaa, S. L. and Leidner, D. E.: 1998, Communication and trust in global virtual teams, *Journal of Computer Mediated Communication*, 3(4). 31 August 2001 http://www.ascusc.org/jcmc/vol3/issue4/jarvenpaa.html.

Jin, Z. and Mason, R. M.: 1998, Bridging US-China cross-cultural differences using Internet and groupware technologies, *7th International Association for Management of Technology Annual Conference (IAMOT'98)*, Orlando, Florida.

Johnson, C.: 1998, Public relations, collaborative leadership and community, *National Communication Association Convention*, Paper presentation, New York, NY.

Johnson, D. W. and Johnson, R. T.: 1989, *Cooperation and Competition: Theory and Research*, Interaction Book Co., Edina, MN.

Johnson, S. D., Berrett, J. V., Suriya, C., Yoon, S. W. and La Fleur, J.: n.d., Team development and group processes of virtual learning teams, College of Education, University of Illinois at Urbana-Champaign, Accessed 7 February 2002, http://www.hre.uiuc.edu/online/virtual_teams.pdf.

Jones, N.: 2001, Cellphone signals can monitor the state of your health, New Scientist, Accessed 22 February 2001, http://www.newscientist.com/dailynews/news.jsp?id=ns9999398.

Jones, S. (ed.): 1999, *Doing Internet Research: Critical Issues and Methods for Examining the Net*, Sage, Thousand Oaks, CA.

Jones, S. G. (ed.): 1995, *CyberSociety: Computer-Mediated Communication and Community*, Sage Publications, Newbury Park, CA.

Jones, S. G. (ed.): 1997, *Virtual Culture*, Sage Publications, London.

Jones, S. G. (ed.): 1998, *CyberSociety 2.0: Revisiting CMC and Community*, Sage Publications, Newbury Park, CA.

Jupiter: 2001, Delays on mobile services in US, Nua Internet Surveys, Accessed 13 March 2001, http://www.nua.ie/surveys/?f=VS&art_id=905356530&rel=true.

Kaplan, F., McIntyre, A., Numaoka, C. and Tajan, S.: 1998, Growing virtual communities in 3D meeting spaces, *in* J.-C. Heudin (ed.), *Virtual Worlds*, Springer, Heidelberg, pp. 286-297.

Katz, D. and Kahn, R. L.: 1978, *The social Psychology of Organizations,* 2nd edn, John Wiley, New York, NY.

Kaufman, D. B., Felder, R. M. and Fuller, H.: 1999, Peer ratings in cooperative learning teams, *Proceedings of the 1999 Annual ASEE Meeting*, ASEE.

Kayworth, T. and Leidner, D. E.: 2000, The global virtual manager: A prescription for success, *European Management Journal,* 18, 183-194.

Keim, D. and Ward, M.: 2003, Visualization, *in* M. Bertold and D. J. Hand (ed.), *Intelligent Data Analysis,* 2nd, Springer, Heidelberg, pp. 403-427.

Keyton, J. and Stallworth, V.: 2003, On the verge of collaboration: Interaction processes versus group outcomes, *in* L. R. Frey (ed.), *Group Communication in Context: Studies of Bona Fide Groups,* 2nd edn, Lawrence Erlbaum, Mahwah, NJ, pp. 235-260.

Kiechel, W.: 1998, The case against leaders, *Fortune*, 217-218.

Kiesler, S. and Sproull, L.: 1986, Response effects in the electronic survey, *Public Opinion Quarterly,* 50, 402-413.

Kirkpatrick, S. A. and Locke, E. A.: 1991, Leadership: Do traits matter?, *The Executive,* 5, 48-60.

Knafl, K. A. and Breitmayer, B. J.: 1989, Triangulation in qualitative research: issues of conceptual clarity and purpose, *in* J. M. Morse (ed.), *Qualitative Nursing Research*, Aspen, Rockville, MD, pp. 209-220.

Kolb, D. A.: 1984, *Experimental Learning*, Prentice-Hall.

Kostner, J.: 1994, *Virtual Leadership: Secrets from the Round Table for the Multi-Site Manager*, Warner Books, New York, NY.

Kraut, R. E., Egido, C. and Galegher, J.: 1990, Patterns of contact and communication in scientific research collaboration, *in* J. Galegher, R. E. Kraut and C. Egido (ed.), *Intellectual Teamwork: Social and Technological Foundations of Cooperative Work*, Lawrence Erlbaum, Hillsdale, NJ, pp. 149-171.

Kraut, R. E., Kiesler, S., Boneva, B., Cummings, J., Helgeson, V. and Crawford, A.: 2002, Internet paradox revisited, *Journal of Social Issues*, 58(1), 49-75. Accessed 10 January 2003 http://homenet.hcii.cs.cmu.edu/progress/jsiparadox-revisited.pdf.

Kraut, R. E., Patterson, M., Lundmark, V., Kiesler, S., Mukophadhyay, T. and Scherlis, W.: 1998, Internet paradox: A social technology that reduces social involvement and psychological well-being?, *American Psychologist*, 53(9), 1017-1031. Accessed 10 January 2002 http://www.apa.org/journals/amp/amp5391017.html.

Krippendorff, K.: 1980, *Content analysis*, Sage, Beverly Hills, CA.

Kuckartz, U.: 1995, Case-oriented quantification, *in* U. Kelle (ed.), *Computer-Aided Qualitative Data Analysis: Theory, Methods and Practice*, Sage Publications, Newbury Park, CA.

Kuypers, B. C., Davies, D. and Hazewinkel, A.: 1986, Developmental patterns in self-analytic groups, *Human Relations*, 39(9), 793-815.

Lacoursiere, R. B.: 1974, A group method to facilitate learning during the stages of a psychiatric affiliation, *International Journal of Group Psychotherapy*, 24, 342-351.

Lacoursiere, R. B.: 1980, *The Life Cycle of Groups: Group Development Stage Theory*, Human Service Press, New York, NY.

Lakoff, R. T.: 1982, Some of my favorite writers are literate: The mingling of oral and literate strategies in written communication, *in* D. Tannen (ed.), *Spoken and Written Language: Exploring Orality and Literacy: Advances in Discourse Process, 239-260*, Ablex, Norwood, NJ.

Landrum, N. and Paris, L.: 2000, Virtual Teams in the Classroom: A Case Study, *Mountain Plains Journal of Business and Economics*, 63-79. http://cbae.nmsu.edu/mgt/handout/nl/teams/.

Larson, C. F. and LaFasto, F.: 1989, *Teamwork: What Must Go Right/What Can Go Wrong*, Sage, Newbury Park, CA.

Lave, J. and Wenger, E.: 1991, *Situated Learning: Legitimate peripheral participation*, Cambridge University Press, New York.

Lea, M. and Spears, R.: 1991, Computer-mediated communication, de-individuation and group decision-making, *International Journal of Man-Machine Studies*, 34, 283-301.

Lea, M. and Spears, R.: 1992, Paralanguage and social perception in computer-mediated communication, *Journal of Organizational Computing*, 2, 321-341.

Lebow, D.: 1993, Constructivist values for instructional systems design: Five principles toward a new mindset, *Educational Technology Research and Development*, 41(3), 4-16.

Levine, D.: 1992, Bad posters drive out good, CMC-L, Accessed 26 May 1992, Posted 25 May, cmc%rpiecs.bitnet@pucc.Princeton.EDU.

Levine, J. and Moreland, R.: 1990, Progress in small group research, *Annual Review of Psychology*, 41, 585-634.

Levinson, P.: 1990, Computer conferencing in the context of the evolution of media, *in* L. M. Harasim (ed.), *Online Education: Perspectives on a New Environment*, Praeger, New York, pp. 3-14.

Lewin, K., Lippitt, R. and White, R. K.: 1939, Patterns of aggressive behavior in experimentally created "social climates", *Journal of Social Psychology*, 10, 271-99.

Lewis, R. J.: 2000, An Introduction to Classification and Regression Tree (CART) Analysis, *Annual Meeting of the Society for Academic Emergency Medicine*, San Francisco, CA. Retrieved 29 February 2004, http://www.saem.org/download/lewis1.pdf.

Lincoln, Y. and Guba, E.: 1985, *Naturalistic Inquiry*, Sage, Beverly Hills, CA.

Lindlof, T. R.: 1995, *Qualitative Communication Research Methods, Volume 3*, Sage, Thousand Oaks, CA.

Lipnack, J. and Stamps, J.: 1997, *Virtual Teams: Working Across Space, Time and Organizations*, John Wiley, New York.

Lord, R. G., DeVader, C. L. and Alliger, G. M.: 1986, A meta-analysis of the relation between personality traits and leadership perceptions: an application of validity generalization procedures, *Journal of Applied Psychology*, 71, 402-410.

Lukacs, G.: 1967, *History and Class Consciousness*, Merlin Press.

Lurey, J. S.: 1998, *A study of best practices in designing and supporting effective virtual teams*, Unpublished doctoral dissertation, California School of Professional Psychology, Los Angeles, CA.

Mabry, E.: 1998, Frames and flames: The structure of argumentative messages on the 'net', *in* F. Sudweeks, M. McLaughlin and S. Rafaeli (ed.), *Network and Netplay: Virtual Groups on the Internet*, MIT Press, Cambridge, MA, pp. 13-26.

Mabry, E. A.: 1993, Proliferation of E-publications, Interpersonal Computing and Technology, Accessed 18 November 1993, ipct-l@guvm.ccf.georgetown.edu.

Mabry, E. A.: 2002, Group communication and technology: Rethinking the role of communication modality in group work and performance, *in* L. R. Frey (ed.), *New Directions in Group Communication*, Sage, Thousand Oaks, CA, pp. 285-298.

Mabry, E. A. and Sudweeks, F.: 2003, Group-based mediational leadership in an online project team context, *International Communication Association Conference (ICA'03)*, San Diego, CA.

Mabry, E. A. and Sudweeks, F.: 2004, Oracles and other digital dieties: Using expert teams as "leaders" in an online, collaborative research project, *in* L. R. Frey (ed.), pp. to appear.

Macaluso, N.: 2001, New fees expected for online marketing, NewsFactor Network, Accessed 2 April 2001, http://www.newsfactor.com/perl/story/6955.html.

Macaulay, L.: 1995, *Human-Computer Interaction for Software Designers*, International Thomson Computer Press, London.

Mann, R. D.: 1959, A review of the relationship between personality and performance in small groups, *Psychological Bulletin*, 56, 241-270.

Mantovani, G. and Riva, G.: 1999, "Real" presence: How different ontologies generate different criteria for presence, telepresence, and virtual presence, *Presence: Teleoperators and Virtual Environments*, 8(5), 538-548.

Markus, M. L. and Robey, D.: 1988, Information technology and organizational change: Causal structure in theory and research, *Management Science*, 34(5), 583-598.

Marshall, C. and Rossman, G. B.: 1995, *Designing Qualitative Research*, 2nd, Sage, Thousand Oaks, CA.

Marx, K.: 1964, The German Ideology, *in* T. B. Bottomore and M. Rubel (ed.), *Karl Marx: Selected Writings in Sociology and Social Philosophy*, McGraw-Hill, New York.

Massey, A.: 1999, Methodological triangulation, or how to get lost without being found out, *in* A. Massey and G. Walford (ed.), *Explorations in methodology, Studies in Educational Ethnography, Vol. 2*, JAI Press, Stamford, pp. 183-197.

Matheson, K. and Zanna, M. P.: 1990, Computer-mediated communications: The focus is on me, *Social Science Computer Review*, 8(1), 1-12.

Mayes, T., Kibby, M. and Anderson, T.: 1990, Learning about learning from hypertext, *in* D. H. Jonassen and H. Mandl (ed.), *Designing Hypertext/Hypermedia for Learning*, Springer-Verlag, Heidelburg.

McCaulay, L.: 1995, Designing user interfaces to CSCW systems, *in* D. Howe and M. Campbell-Kelly (ed.), *Human-Computer Interaction for Software Designers*, International Thomson Computer Press, London.

McCauley, C. and Segal, M.: 1987, Social psychology of terrorist groups, *in* C. Hendrick (ed.), *Review of Personality and Social Psychology: Group Process and Intergroup Relations*, Sage, Beverly Hills, CA, pp. 231-256.

McCreary, E. and Brochet, M.: 1992, Collaboration in international online teams, *in* A. R. Kaye (ed.), *Collaborative Learning through Computer Conferencing*, Springer-Verlag, Berlin, pp. 69-85.

McCroskey, J. C. and Richmond, V. P.: 1998, Willingness to communicate, *in* J. C. McCroskey, J. A. Daly, M. M. Martin and M. J. Beatty (ed.), *Communication and Personality: Trait Perspectives*, Hampton Press, Cresswell, New Jersey, pp. 119-131.

McDavid, J. W. and Harari, H.: 1968, *Social Psychology*, Harper and Row, New York.

McGrath, J. E. and Hollingshead, A. B.: 1994, *Groups Interacting with Technology*, Sage, Thousand Oaks, CA.

McGregor, D.: 1960, *The Human Side of Enterprise*, McGraw-Hill, New York, NY.

McGuire, T. W., Kiesler, S. and Siegel, J.: 1987, Group and computer-mediated discussion effects in risk decision making, *Journal of Personality and Social Psychology,* 52, 917-930.

McInerney, C.: 1995, CMC and distance education at the College of St Catherine: A case study, *in* Z. Berge and M. Collins (ed.), *Computer Mediated Communications and the Online Classroom. Vol. III: Distance Learning*, Hampton Press, Cresskill, NJ, pp. 149-163.

McLoughlin, C.: 1999, The implications of the research literature on learning styles for the design of instructional material, *Australian Journal of Educational Technology,* 15(3), 222-241. http://cleo.murdoch.edu.au/ajet/ajet15/mcloughlin.html.

McLuhan, M. and Powers, B. R.: 1986, *The Global Village:Transformations in World Life and Media in the 21st Century*, Oxford University Press, New York.

McShane, S. L. and Von Glinow, M. A.: 2000, *Organizational Behavior*, McGraw-Hill, Boston, MA.

Mehrabian, A.: 1969, Some referents and measures of nonverbal behavior, *Behavior Research Methods and Instrumentation,* 1(16), 205-207.

Meindl, J. R., Ehrlich, S. B. and Dukerich, J. M.: 1985, The romance of leadership, *Administrative Science Quarterly,* 30, 78-102.

Milligan, C.: 1999, The role of VLEs in on-line delivery of staff development, JTAP Report 573, Accessed September 2000, http://www.icbl.hw.ac.uk/jtap-573.

Morss, D. A. and Fleming, P. A.: 1998, WebCT in the classroom: A student view, Proceedings of the North American Web Developers Conference (NAWeb99), Accessed September 2000, http://naweb.unb.ca/proceedings/1998/morss/morss.html.

Moscovici, S. and Zavalloni, M.: 1969, The group as a polariser of attitudes, *Journal of Personality and Social Psychology,* 12, 125-35.

Mullen, B., Salas, E. and Driskell, J. E.: 1989, Salience, motivation and artifact as contributions to the relation between participation rate and leadership, *Journal of Experimental Social Psychology,* 25, 545-559.

Mudrack, P. E.: 1989, Defining group cohesiveness: A legacy of confusion?, *Small Group Behavior,* 20, 37-49.

Myers, M. R., Slavin, M. J. and Southern, W. T.: 1990, Emergence and maintenance of leadership among gifted students in group problem solving, *Roeper Review,* 12(4), 256-260.

Nagel, K.: 1994, The natural life cycle of mailing lists, EarlyM-L, Accessed 7 February 2002, Posted 3 December 1994, http://afs.wu-wien.ac.at/earlym-l/logfiles/earlym-l.log9412a.

Napier, R. W. and Gershenfeld, M. K.: 1999, *Groups: Theory and Experience,* 6th edn, Houghton Mifflin, Boston.

Nemiro, J. E.: 1968, *Creativity in virtual teams*, Unpublished doctoral dissertation, Claremont Graduate University, Claremont, CA.

Niederman, F., Beise, C. M. and Beranek, P. M.: 1996, Issues and concerns about computer-supported meetings: The facilitator's perspective, *MIS Quarterly,* 20, 1-22.

Northouse, P. G.: 1997, *Leadership: Theory and Practice*, Sage, Thousand Oaks, CA.

Nunnally, J. C.: 1975, The study of change in evaluation research: Principles concerning measurement, experimental design, and analysis, *in* E. L. Struening and M. Guttentag (ed.), *Handbook of Evaluation Research, 1*, Sage, Beverly Hills, CA, pp. 101-137.

Ochs: 1989, *Language, Affect and Culture*, Cambridge University Press, Cambridge.

Olaniran, B. A.: 1994, Group performance and computer-mediated communication, *Management Communication Quarterly, 7*, 256.

Oliver, R.: 2001, Developing e-learning environments that support knowledge construction in higher education., *in* S. Stoney and J. Burn (ed.), *Working for Excellence in the E-conomy*, We-B Centre, Edith Cowan University, Perth, Australia, pp. 407-416.

Ong, W. J.: 1982, *Orality and Literacy: The technologizing of the word*, Methuen, London.

Osborn, A. F.: 1941, *Applied Imagination: Principles and Procedures of Creative Thinking*, Scribner, New York.

Palmquist, M. E., Carley, K. M. and Dale, T. A.: 1997, Two applications of automated text analysis: Analyzing literary and non-literary texts, *in* C. Roberts (ed.), *Text Analysis for the Social Sciences: Methods for Drawing Statistical Inferences from Texts and Transcripts*, Lawrence Erlbaum Associates, Hillsdale, NJ, pp. 171-190.

Pargman, D.: 2000, *Code begets community: On social and technical aspects of managing a virtual community*, Department of Communication Studies, Linkopings Universitet, Linkoping.

Parsons, T.: 1961, An outline of the social system, *in* T. Parsons, E. Shils, K. D. Naegele and J. R. Pitts (ed.), *Theories of Society*, Free Press, New York, pp. 30-79.

Pavitt, C.: 1999, Theorizing about the group communication-leadership relationship: Input-process-output and functional models, *in* L. R. Frey, D. S. Gouran and M. S. Poole (ed.), *The Handbook of Group Communication Theory and Research*, Sage, Thousand Oaks, CA, pp. 432-472.

Penuel, W. and Wertsch, J. V.: 1995, Vygotsky and Identity Formation: A socialcultural approach, *Educational Psychologist, 30*(2), 83-92.

Pliskin, N. and Romm, C.: 1997, The impact of e-mail on the evolution of a virtual community during a strike, *Information and Management, 32*, 245-254.

Polly, J. A.: 1992, Surfing the Internet, *Wilson Library Bulletin,* June, www.netmom.com/about/surfing.shtml.

Poole, M. S.: 1990, Do we have any theories of group communication?, *Communication Studies, 41*, 237-248.

Poole, M. S., Holmes, M., Watson, R. and De Sanctis, G.: 1993, Group decision support systems and group communication, *Communication Research, 20*(2), 176-213.

Poole, M. S. and Holmes, M. E.: 1995, Decision development in computer-assisted group decision making, *Human Communication Research, 22*, 90-127.

Poole, M. S. and Roth, J.: 1989, Decision development in small groups, V: Test of a contingency model, *Human Communication Research, 15*, 549-589.

Preece, J.: 2000, *Online Communities: Designing usability, supporting sociability*, John Wiley, Chichester.

Putnam, L. L. and Stohl, C.: 1990, Bona fide groups: A reconceptualization of groups in context, *Communication Studies, 41*, 248-265.

Rafaeli, S.: 1988, Interactivity: From new media to communication, *Sage Annual Review of Communication Research: Advancing Communication Science, 16*, 110-134.

Rafaeli, S., McLaughlin, M. and Sudweeks, F.: 1998a, Introduction, *in* M. M. a. S. R. F. Sudweeks (ed.), *Network and Netplay: Virtual Groups on the Internet*, MIT Press, Cambridge, MA, pp. xv-xx.

Rafaeli, S. and Sudweeks, F.: 1997, Net Interactivity, *Journal of Computer Mediated Communication, 2*(4). http://www.ascusc.org/jcmc/vol2/issue4.

Rafaeli, S. and Sudweeks, F.: 1998, Interactivity on the nets, *in* F. Sudweeks, M. McLaughlin and S. Rafaeli (ed.), *Network and Netplay: Virtual Groups on the Internet*, MIT Press, Cambridge, MA, pp. 173-190.

Rafaeli, S., Sudweeks, F., Konstan, J. and Mabry, E.: 1998b, ProjectH: A collaborative quantitative study of computer-mediated communication, *in* F. Sudweeks, M. McLaughlin and S. Rafaeli (ed.), *Network and Netplay: Virtual Groups on the Internet*, MIT Press, Cambridge, MA, pp. 265-281.

Ragin, C. C.: 1987, *The Comparative Method: Moving Beyond Qualitative and Quantitative Strategies*, University of California Press, Berkeley, CA.

Ramsden, P.: 1992, *Learning to Teach in Higher Education*, Routledge, London.

Reddin, W.: 1970, *Managerial Effectiveness*, McGraw-Hill, New York.

Regula, C. R. and Julian, J. W.: 1973, The impact of quality and frequency of task contributions on perceived ability, *The Journal of Social Psychology*, 89, 115-122.

Reid, E.: 1991, *Electropolis: Communication and community on Internet Relay Chat*, Honours Thesis, University of Melbourne, Melbourne, Australia.

Rettie, R.: 2003, Connectedness, awareness and social presence, *6th Annual Workshop on Presence (Presence 2003)*, Aalborg University, Denmark. Accessed 10 February 2004, http://www.presence-research.org/papers/Rettie.pdf.

Rice, R. E.: 1987, Computer-mediated communication and organizational innovation, *Journal of Communication*, 37(4), 65-94.

Rice, R. E. and Associates: 1984, *The New Media: Communication, Research, and Technology*, Sage, Newbury Park.

Rice, R. E. and Love, G.: 1987, Electronic emotion: Socioemotional content in a computer-mediated communication network, *Communication Research*, 14(1), 85-108.

Robbins, S. P.: 1994, *Organizational Behavior: Concepts, Controversies and Applications: Australia and New Zealand*, Prentice Hall, Sydney.

Rogers, E. M. and Rafaeli, S.: 1985, Computers and communication, *Information and Behavior*, 1, 95-112.

Romm, C. T. and Pliskin, N.: 1995, Group development of a computer-mediated community, *Working Paper*, University of Wollongong, Wollongong, Australia, Accessed

Rosch, E.: 1973, Natural categories, *Cognitive Psychology*, 4, 328-50.

Rosenman, M. A. and Sudweeks, F.: 1995, Categorization and prototypes in design, *in* P. Slezak, T. Caelli and R. Clark (ed.), *Perspectives on Cognitive Science: Theories, experiments and foundations*, Ablex, Norwood, NJ, pp. 189-212.

Rost, J. C.: 1991, *Leadership for the Twenty-First Century*, Praeger, New York, NY.

Rost, J. C.: 1993, Leadership in the new millennium, *The Journal of Leadership Studies*, 99.

Rothwell, J. D.: 1998, *In Mixed Company: Small Group Communication*, Holt, Rinehart and Winston, Orlando, FL.

Rouche, J. E., Baker, G. A. and Rose, R. R.: 1989, *Shared Vision (Transformational Leadership in American Community Colleges)*, Community College Press, Washington, DC.

Rourke, L., Anderson, T., Garrison, D. R. and Archer, W.: 1999, Assessing social presence in asynchronous text-based computer conferencing, *Journal of Distance Education*, 14(2), 50-71. Accessed 14 January 2004 http://cade.icaap.org/vol14.2/rourke_et_al.html.

Russell, B.: 1945, *A History of Western Philosophy*, Simon and Schuster, New York.

Sacks, H.: 1972, An initial investigation of the usability of conversational data for doing sociology, *in* D. Sudnow (ed.), *Studies in Social Interation*, The Free Press, New York, pp. 31-74.

Sacks, H., Schegloff, E. A. and Jefferson, G.: 1978, A simplest systematics for the organization of turn-taking in conversation, *in* J. Schenkein (ed.), *Studies in the Organization of Conversational Interaction*, Academic Press, New York, pp. 7-55.

Sanderson, D.: 1996, Cooperative and collaborative mediated research, *in* T. M. Harrison and T. D. Stephens (ed.), *Computer Networking and Scholarship in the 21st Century*, SUNY Press, Albany, NY.

Sarbaugh-Thompson, M. and Feldman, M. S.: 1998, Electronic mail and organizational communication: Does saying "hi" really matter?, *Organization Science*, 9(6), 685-698.

Sarker, S., Lau, F. and Sahay, S.: 2001, Using an Adapted Grounded Theory Approach for Inductive Theory Building About Virtual Team Development, *Journal of the ACM Special Interest Group on Management Information Systems,* 32(1).

Sarros, J. C., Densten, I. L. and Santora, J. C.: 1999, *Leadership and Values: Australian Executives and the Balance of Power, Profits and People,* Harper Business Publishers, Sydney.

Schein, E.: 1992, *Organizational Culture and Leadership,* 2nd, Jossey-Bass.

Schmidt, C.: 2001, Beyond the bar code, Technology Review, Accessed 22 February 2001, http://www.technologyreview.com/magazine/mar01/schmidt.asp.

Schmitz, J. and Fulk, J.: 1991, Organizational colleagues, media richness and electronic mail: a test of the social influence model of technology use, *Communication Research,* 18(4), 487-523.

Schön, D.: 1983, *The Reflective Practitioner,* Basic Books, New York.

Schön, D.: 1991, *Educating the Reflective Practitioner,* Jossey Bass, San Francisco.

Schreoder, R. (ed.): 2002, *The Social Life of Avatars: Presence and Interaction in Shared Virtual Environments,* Springer, London.

Schudson, M.: 1978, The ideal of conversation in the study of mass media, *Communication Research,* 5(3), 320-329.

Schultz, T.: 1999, Interactive options in online journalism: A content analysis of 100 US Newspapers, *Journal of Computer Mediated Communication,* 5(1). Retrieved 28 February 2004 http://www.ascusc.org/jcmc/vol5/issue1/schultz.html.

Schütz, A.: 1962, *Collected Papers I. The Problem of Social Reality,* Martinus Nijhoff, The Hague.

Schutz, W.: 1966, *The Interpersonal Underworld,* Science and Behavior Books, Palo Alto.

Scogin, F. and Pollio, H.: 1980, Targeting and the humorous episode in group process, *Human Relations,* 33, 831-852.

Scott, C. R.: 1999, Communication technology and group communication, *in* L. R. Frey, D. S. Gouran and M. S. Poole (ed.), *The Handbook of Group Communication Theory and Research,* Sage, Thousand Oaks, CA, pp. 313-334.

searchNetworking.com: 2003, ADSL, SearchNetworking.com, Accessed 25/1/04, http://searchnetworking.techtarget.com/sDefinition/0,,sid7_gci213764,00.html.

Searle, J.: 1969, *Speech Acts: An Essay in the Philosophy of Language,* Cambridge University Press, Cambridge.

Shea, G. P. and Guzzo, R. A.: 1987, Groups as human resources, *in* K. M. Rowland and G. R. Ferris (ed.), *Research in Personnel and Human Resource Management,* JAI, Greenwich, CT.

Shimanoff, S.: 1992, Group interaction via communication rules, *in* R. Cathcart and L. Samovar (ed.), *Small Group Communication: A Reader,* W. C. Brown, Dubuque, IA.

Shockley-Zalabak, P.: 2002, Protean places: Teams across time and space, *Journal of Applied Communication Research,* 30, 231-250.

Short, J., Williams, E. and Christie, B.: 1976, *The Social Psychology of Telecommunication,* John Wiley, London.

Siegel, J., Dubrovsky, V., Kiesler, S. and McGuire, T. W.: 1986, Group processes in computer-mediated communication, *Organizational Behavior and Human Decision Processes,* 37, 157-187.

Silverman, D.: 1993, *Interpreting Qualitative Data,* Sage, Thousand Oaks, CA.

Silverman, D. (ed.): 1997, *Qualitative Research: Theory, Method and Practice,* Sage, London, UK.

Simoff, S. J.: 1996, *Timeline visualisations for analysis of computer-mediated collaborative design,* Working Paper, Key Centre of Design Computing, University of Sydney, Sydney, Australia.

Simoff, S. J. and Maher, M. L.: 2000, Analysing participation in collaborative design environments, *Design Studies,* 21, 119-144.

Smircich, L.: 1983, Organizations as shared meanings, *in* L. R. Pondy and T. C. Dandridge (ed.), *Organizational Symbolism*, JAI Press, Greenwich, CT, pp. 55-67.

Smith, C. B., McLaughlin, M. L. and Osborne, K. K.: 1998, From terminal ineptitude to virtual sociopathy: How conduct is regulated on Usenet, *in* F. Sudweeks, M. McLaughlin and S. Rafaeli (ed.), *Network and Netplay: Virtual Groups on the Internet*, AAAI/MIT Press, Menlo Park, CA, pp. 95-112.

Smith, L.: 1979, An evolving logic of participant observation, educational ethnography, and other case studies, *in* L. Shulman (ed.), *Review of Research in Education*, Peacock, Itasca, IL, pp. 316-377.

Snow, C. C., Snell, S. A., Davison, S. C. and Hambrick, D. C.: 1996, Use transnational teams to globalize your company, *Organizational Dynamics,* Spring, 50-67.

Salomon, G. and Perkins, D. N.: 1998, Individual and social aspects of learning, *Review of Research in Education (eds. D. Pearson, A. Iran-Nejad)*, 23, 1-24. Accessed 30 March 2004 http://construct.haifa.ac.il/~gsalomon/indsoc.htm.

Sorrentino, R. M.: 1973, An extension of achievement motivation theory to the study of emergent leadership, *Journal of Personality and Social Psychology,* 26(June), 356-368.

Sorrentino, R. M. and Boutillier, R. G.: 1975, The effect of quantity and quality of verbal interaction on ratings of leadership ability, *Journal of Experimental Social Psychology,* 11, 403-411.

Sosik, J. J., Avolio, B. and Kahai, S. S.: 1997, Effects of leadership style and anonymity on group potency and effectiveness in a group decision support system environment, *Journal of Applied Psychology,* 82(1), 89-103.

Spears, R. and Lea, M.: 1992, Social influence and the influence of the "social" in computer-mediated communication, *in* M. Lea (ed.), *Contexts of Computer-Mediated Communication*, Harvester-Wheatsheaf, London.

Sproull, L. and Kiesler, S.: 1986, Reducing social context cues: electronic mail in organizational communication, *Management Science,* 32(11), 1492-1512.

Sproull, L. and Kiesler, S.: 1991, *Connections: New ways of working in the networked organization*, MIT Press, Cambridge.

Sproull, L. S., Kiesler, S. and Zubrow, D.: 1984, Encountering an alien culture, *Journal of Social Issues,* 40(3), 31-48.

Stake, R. E.: 1995, *The Art of Case Study Research*, Sage, Thousand Oaks, CA.

Steele, G.: 1984, *Common LISP, the Language*, Digital Press, Bedford, MA.

Steinfield, C. W.: 1986a, Computer mediated communication in an organizational setting: Explaining task related and socioemotional uses, *in* M. McLaughlin (ed.), *Communication Yearbook 9*, Sage, Newbury Park, CA, pp. 777-804.

Steinfield, C. W.: 1986b, Computer mediated communication systems, *Annual Review of Information Science and Technology,* 21, 167-202.

Steinfield, C. W.: 1987, Computer mediated communication systems, *Annual Review of Information Science and Technology,* 21, 167-202.

Stevenson, K., Sander, P. and Naylor, P.: 1996, Student perceptions of the tutor's role in distance learning, *Open Learning,* 20, 41-49.

Stogdill, R. M.: 1948, Personal factors associated with leadership: A survey of the literature, *Journal of Psychology,* 25, 35-71.

Stogdill, R. M.: 1963, *Manual for the Leader Behavior Description Questionnaire - Form XII*, Bureau of Business Research, Ohio State University, Columbus, OH.

Stogdill, R. M.: 1974, *Handbook of Leadership: A survey of Theory and Research*, Free Press, New York.

Stohl, C. and Walker, K.: 2002, A bona fide perspective for the future of groups: Understanding collaborating groups, *in* L. R. Frey (ed.), *New Directions in Group Communication*, Sage, Thousand Oaks, CA, pp. 237-252.

Stoner, J. A. F.: 1961, *A Comparison of Individual and Group Decisions Involving Risk*, MIT Press, Cambridge, MA.

Strauss, A. and Corbin, J.: 1994, Grounded theory methodology: an overview, *in* N. K. Denzin and Y. S. Lincoln (ed.), *Handbook of Qualitative Research*, Sage, Thousand Oaks, CA, pp. 273-285.

Strauss, A. L. and Corbin, J.: 1990, *Basics of Qualitative Research: Grounded Theory Procedures and Techniques*, Sage, Thousand Oaks, CA.

Strickland, L., Guild, P. D., Barefoot, J. C. and Paterson, S. A.: 1978, Teleconferencing and leadership emergence, *Human Relations,* 31, 583-596.

Sudweeks, F.: 2000, To mediate or not to mediate: The role of the mediator in the online classroom, *WebNet2000 - World Conference on the WWW and Internet*, Invited Talk, San Antonio, Texas, Association for the Advancement of Computing in Education.

Sudweeks, F.: 2003a, Connecting students with group work, *Computer-Based Learning in Science*, C. P. Constantinou and Z. C. Zacharia (eds), Nicosia, Cyprus, University of Cyprus, pp. 173-183.

Sudweeks, F.: 2003b, Promoting cooperation and collaboration in a web-based learning environment, *Proceedings of the 2003 Informing Science and Information Technology Education Conference*, Santa Rosa, CA, Pori, Finland, Informing Science Institute, pp. 1439-1446.

Sudweeks, F.: 2003c, The reflective learner: A framework for an integrated approach to e-learning, *Proceedings International Conference on Informatics Education and Research*, Seattle, WA, International Academy for Information Management, pp. 238-241.

Sudweeks, F. and Allbritton, M.: 1996, Working together apart: Communication and collaboration in a networked group, *in* C. D. Keen, C. Urquhart and J. Lamp (ed.), *Proceedings of the 7th Australasian Conference of Information Systems (ACIS96)*, 2, University of Tasmania, Hobart, Tasmania, pp. 701-712.

Sudweeks, F. and Berthold, M. R.: 1996, Net conversations: Applying a neural network analysis to computer-mediated communication, *International Association of Science and Technology for Development International Conference on Modelling, Simulation and Optimization (IASTED'96)*, Compact Disk Digital Data.

Sudweeks, F., Lambert, S., Beaumont, A., Bonney, J., Lee, S. and Nicholas, G.: 1993, Computer mediated collaboration and design: A pilot project, *in* S. Hayman (ed.), *Architectural Science: Past, Present and Future*, ANZAScA, University of Sydney, Sydney, pp. 299-309.

Sudweeks, F., McLaughlin, M. and Rafaeli, S.: 1997, Guest Editors of Special Issue on Network and Netplay, *Journal of Computer Mediated Communication*, 2(4). www.ascusc.org/jcmc/vol2/issue4.

Sudweeks, F., McLaughlin, M. and Rafaeli, S. (eds): 1998, *Network and Netplay: Virtual Groups on the Internet*, MIT Press, Cambridge, MA.

Sudweeks, F. and Rafaeli, S.: 1996, How do you get a hundred strangers to agree: Computer mediated communication and collaboration, *in* T. M. Harrison and T. D. Stephens (ed.), *Computer Networking and Scholarship in the 21st Century*, SUNY Press, Albany, NY, pp. 115-136.

Sudweeks, F. and Simoff, S.: 1999, Complementary explorative data analysis: The reconciliation of quantitative and qualitative principles, *in* S. Jones (ed.), *Doing Internet Research*, Sage, Thousand Oaks, CA, pp. 29-55.

Sudweeks, F. and Simoff, S.: 2000, Participation and reflection in virtual workshops, *Proceedings Western Australian Workshop on Information Systems Research,* J. Burns (ed.), Edith Cown University.

Sudweeks, F.: 2003, Connecting students with group work, in C. P. Constantinou and Z. C. Zacharia (eds), Computer-Based Learning in Science Vol.1, University of Cyprus, Nicosia, Cyprus, pp. 173-183.

Sudweeks, F. and Simoff, S. J.: 2005, Leading conversations: Communication behaviours of emergent leaders in virtual teams, *38th Hawaii International Conference on System Sciences (HICSS05)*, (accepted), Hawaii, USA.

Tajfel, H. and Fraser, C. (eds): 1978, *Introducing Social Psychology*, Penguin, Harmondsworth.

Tajfel, H. and Turner, J. C.: 1986, The social identity theory of intergroup relations, *in* S. Worchel and W. G. Austin (ed.), *Psychology of Intergroup Relations*, Brooks/Cole, Monterey, CA, pp. 7-24.

Tashakkori, A. and Teddlie, C. (eds): 2003, *Handbook of Mixed Methods in Social and Behavioral Research*, Sage, Thousand Oaks, CA.

Tiffin, J. and Rajasingham, L.: 1995, *In Search of the Virtual Class: Education in an Information Society*, Routledge, London.

Townsend, A. M., DeMarie, S. M. and Hendrickson, A. R.: 1996, Are you ready for virtual teams?, *HR Magazine*, 41, 122-126.

Townsend, A. M., DeMarie, S. M. and Hendrickson, A. R.: 1998, Virtual Teams: Technology and the Workplace of the Future, *The Academy of Management Executive*, 12(3), 17-30.

Trevino, L. K., Daft, R. L. and Lengel, R. H.: 1990, Understanding managers' media choices: A symbolic interactionist perspective, *in* J. Fulk and C. W. Steinfield (ed.), *Organizations and Communication Technology*, Sage, Newbury Park, CA, pp. 71-94.

Trevino, L. K., Lengel, R. H. and Daft, R. D.: 1987, Media symbolism, media richness and media choice in organizations: A symbolic interactionist perspective, *Communication Research*, 14, 553-574.

Tschudi, F.: 1989, Do qualitative and quantitative methods require different approaches to validity?, *in* S. Kvale (ed.), *Issues of Validity in Qualitative Research*, Studentlitteratur, Lund.

Tu, C.-H.: 2002, The measurement of social presence in an online learning environment, *International Journal on E-Learning*, 1(2), 34-45.

Tuckman, B. W.: 1965, Developmental sequence in small groups, *Psychological Bulletin*, 384-399.

Tuckman, B. W. and Jensen, M. A. C.: 1977, Stages of small-group development revisited, *Group and Organizational Studies*, 2(4), 419-427.

Turoff, M.: 1991, Computer-mediated communication requirements for group support, *Journal of Organizational Computing*, 1, 85-113.

Uhl-Bien, M. and Graen, G. B.: 1992, Self-management and team-making in cross-functional work teams: Discovering the keys to becoming an integrated team, *Journal of High Technology Management Research*, 3(2), 225-241.

Valacich, J. S., Dennis, A. R. and Connolly, T.: 1994, Idea generation in computer-based groups: A new ending to an old story, *Organizational Behavior and Human Decision Processes*, 57, 448-467.

Valacich, J. S., Paranka, D., George, J. F. and Nunamaker, J. R.: 1993, Communication concurrency and the new media: A new dimension for media richness, *Communication Research*, 20(2), 249-276.

Vecchio, R. P.: 1987, Situational leadership theory: An examination of a prescriptive theory, *Journal of Applied Psychology*, 72, 444-451.

Verdi, A. F. and Wheelan, S. A.: 1992, Developmental patterns in same-sex and mixed-sex groups, *Small Group Research*, 23, 356-378.

Voiskounsky, A. E.: 1998, Telelogue Speech, *in* F. Sudweeks, M. McLaughlin and S. Rafaeli (ed.), *Network and Netplay: Virtual Groups on the Internet*, AAAI/MIT Press, Menlo Park, CA, pp. 27-40.

Vonder Haar, S.: 1997, CompuServe bets the forum on web, Inter@ctive Week, Accessed 5 March 2001, http://www.zdnet.com/intweek/daily/970804a.html.

Vroom, V. H. and Jago, A. G.: 1978, On the validity of the Vroom/Yetton model, *Journal of Applied Psychology*, 63, 151-162.

Vroom, V. H. and Yetton, P. W.: 1973, *Leadership and Decision Making*, University of Pittsburgh Press, Pittsburgh, PA.

Vygotsky, L. S.: 1934/1987, Thinking and speech, *in* R. W. Rieber and A. S. Carton (ed.), *The collected works of L. S. Vygotsky, Volume 1: Problems of general psychology* . Plenum, New York.

Vygotsky, L. S.: 1978, *Mind in Society: The Development of the Higher Psychological Processes*, Harvard University Press, Cambridge, MA.

Vygotsky, L. S.: 1981, The genesis of higher mental functions, *in* J. V. Wertsch (ed.), *The concept of activity in Soviet Psychology*, Sharpe, Armonk, NY.

Walther, J. B.: 1992, Interpersonal effects in computer-mediated interaction: A relational perspective, *Communication Research,* 19, 52-90.

Walther, J. B.: 1994, Anticipated ongoing interaction versus channel effects on relational communication in computer-mediated interaction, *Human Communication Research,* 20, 473-501.

Walther, J. B.: 1997, Group and interpersonal effects in international computer-mediated collaboration, *Human Communication Research,* 23(342-369).

Walther, J. B., Slovacek, C. and Tidwell, L. C.: 2001, Is a picture worth a thousand words? Photographic images in long term and short term virtual teams, *Communication Research,* 28, 105-134.

Warkentin, M., Sayeed, L. and Hightower, R. T.: 1997a, An exploration of a world wide web-based conference system for supporting virtual teams engaged in asynchronous collaborative tasks, *Decision Sciences,* 28(4), 975-996.

Warkentin, M. F., Sayeed, L. and Hightower, R.: 1997b, Virtual teams versus face-to-face teams: An exploratory study of a web-based conference system, *Decision Science,* 28, 975-996.

Wartofsky, M.: 1979, *Models, representation and scientific understanding*, Reidel, Boston.

Wasserman, S. and Faust, K.: 1994, *Social Network Analysis*, Cambridge University Press, Cambridge, MA.

Watson, R. T., De Sanctis, G. and Poole, M. S.: 1988, Using a GDSS to facilitate group consensus: Some intended and unintended consequences, *MIS Quarterly,* 12(3), 463-480.

Weber, M.: 1947, *The Theory of Social and Economic Organization*, Oxford University Press, New York.

Weber, M.: 1964, *Wirtschaft und Gesellschaft. Grundriss der verstehenden Soziologie.*, Kiepenheuer and Witsch, Köln/Berlin.

Weiser, M.: 1996, Open house, *ITP Review,* 2. http://www.itp.tsoa.nyu.edu/~review.

Wellman, B. and Berkowitz, S. D. (eds): 1997, *Social Structures: A Network Approach*, JAI Press, Greenwich, CT.

Wells, G.: 1999, Dialogic inquiry in education: Building on Vygotsky's legacy., *in* C. D. Lee and P. Smagorinsky (ed.), *Vygotskian Perspectives on Literacy Research*, Cambridge University Press, Cambridge.

Wheelan, S. A.: 1994, *Group Processes. A Developmental Perspective*, Allyn and Bacon, Boston.

Wheelan, S. A. and Hochberger, J. M.: 1996, Validation studies of the group development questionnaire, *Small Group Research,* 27(1), 143-170.

Wheelan, S. A., McKeage, R. L., Verdi, A. F., Abraham, M., Krasick, C. and Johnston, F.: 1994, Communication and developmental patterns in a system of interacting groups, *in* L. R. Frey (ed.), *Group Communication in Context: Studies of Natural Groups*, Lawrence Erlbaum, Hillsdale, NJ, pp. 153-178.

White, R. K. and Lippitt, R.: 1968, Leader behavior and member reaction in three "social climates", *in* D. Cartwright and A. Zander (ed.), *Group Dynamics*, Harper & Row, New York, NY, pp. 318-335.

Williams, B. K., Sawyer, S. C. and Hutchinson, S. E.: 1995, *Using Information Technology: A Practical Introduction to Computers and Communications*, Irwin, Chicago.

Wilson, B. G.: 1995, Metaphors for instruction: Why we talk about learning environments, *Educational Technology,* 35(5), 25-30. http://www.cudenver.edu/~bwilson/metaphor.html.

Witmer, D.: 1998, Smile when you say that: Graphic accents as gender markers in computer-mediated communication, *in* F. Sudweeks, M. McLaughlin and S. Rafaeli (ed.), *Network and Netplay: Virtual Groups on the Internet*, MIT Press, Cambridge, MA.

Witmer, D. F.: 1997, Communication and recovery: Structuration as an ontological approach to organizational culture, *Communication Monographs,* 64, 324-349.

Witten, I. H. and Frank, E.: 2000, *Data Mining: Practical Machine Learning Tools and Techniques with Java Implementations*, Morgan Kaufmann, San Francisco, CA.

Worchel, S.: 1994, You can go home again: Returning group research to the group context with an eye on developmental issues, *Small Group Research,* 25(2), 205-223.

Worchel, S., Countant-Sassic, C. and Grossman, M.: 1992, A developmental approach to group dynamics: A model and illustrative research, *in* S. Worchel, W. Wood and J. Simpson (ed.), *Group Process and Productivity*, Sage, Newbury Park, CA.

Yalom, I. D.: 1975, *The Theory and Practice of Group Psychotherapy,* 2nd edn, Basic Books, New York.

Yin, R. K.: 1989, *Case Study Research: Design and Methods*, Sage, Newbury Park, CA.

Yoo, Y. and Alavi, M.: 1996, Emergence of leadership and its impact on group performance in virtual team environments: A longitudinal field study, *Proceedings of the 17th Annual International Conference on Information Systems.*

Yoo, Y. and Alavi, M.: 2001, Media and group cohesion: Relative influences on social presence, task participation and group consensus, *MIS Quarterly,* 25(3).

Yoo, Y. and Alavi, M.: 2002, Electronic mail usage pattern of emergent leaders in distributed teams, *Sprouts: Working Papers on Information Environments. Systems and Organizations,* 2(Summer). Accessed 6 February 2004. http://weatherhead.cwru.edu/sprouts/2002/020309.pdf.

Zigon, F. J. and Cannon, J. R.: 1974, Process end outcomes of group discussions as related to leader behaviors, *Journal of Educational Research,* 67, 199-201.

Zimbardo, P.: 1992, *Psychology and Life*, Scott, Foresman, Glenview, IL.

Zuboff, S.: 1988, *In the Age of the Smart Machines*, Basic Books, New York.

www.ingramcontent.com/pod-product-compliance
Lightning Source LLC
LaVergne TN
LVHW022300060326
832902LV00020B/3177